Modern
Catholic
Concerns

Modern Catholic Concerns

PETER MAZUREK

Library of Congress Control Number: 2019914717
ISBN: Hardcover   978-1-7960-0578-3
                Softcover   978-1-7960-0576-9
                eBook   978-1-7960-0577-6

Print information available on the last page.

Rev. date: 09/24/2019

To order additional copies of this book, contact:
Xlibris
1-800-455-039
www.Xlibris.com.au
Orders@Xlibris.com.au
801446

To my mother with Thanks for everything!

CONTENTS

Acknowledgements...xv
Introduction xvii

PART 1 PARAMETERS 1
1.1 The Reasoning Process.. 3
    1.1.1 The Proposition.. 3
    1.1.2 The Need for Truth.. 6
    1.1.3 Logic and Reason.. 6
    1.1.4 The Nature of Proof... 9
    1.1.5 The Nature of Evidence 18
    1.1.6 The Role of Faith and Knowledge 35
    1.1.7 The Primary Assumption.................................. 40
    1.1.8 Overview 45
1.2 Background Issues 51
    1.2.1 The Nature of God.. 51
    1.2.2 The Function of Science 55
    1.2.3 Scientific Evidence versus Faith....................... 62
    1.2.4 The Mechanism of Creation.............................. 67
            1.2.4.1 The Origin of the Universe 68
            1.2.4.2 The Formation of Our Planet........... 73
            1.2.4.3 The Development of Life on Earth.................. 76
            1.2.4.4 The Source of Intelligent Life on Earth 79
    1.2.5 The Necessity of Doubt..................................... 84
    1.2.6 Belief Status 90
    1.2.7 Realms...102

PART 2 THE EXISTENCE OF GOD............................119
2.1 The Major Arguments for the Existence of God 121
    2.1.1 Catholic Dogma 121

2.1.2 The Five Ways of Aquinas 126
2.1.3 The Ontological Argument 136
2.1.4 The Cosmological Argument 138
2.1.5 The Teleological Argument 147
2.2 The Minor Arguments for the Existence of God 160
 2.2.1 The Argument from the Existence of Human
   Consciousness 160
 2.2.2 The Argument from the Existence of Morality 163
 2.2.3 The Argument from the Existence of Miracles..........166
 2.2.4 The Argument from the Existence of Religious
   Experience 179
 2.2.5 Pascal's Wager 186
2.3 The Arguments against the Existence of God......................194
 2.3.1 The Cosmological Arguments 194
 2.3.2 The Teleological Arguments 196
 2.3.3 The Argument from Non-Belief in God 199
 2.3.4 The Anthropic Principle 201
 2.3.5 The Argument from the Existence of Evil.................217
2.4 Conclusion... 239

PART 3 THE DIVINITY OF JESUS CHRIST......................... 245
3.1 Overview... 247
 3.1.1 Significance.. 247
 3.1.2 Belief Justification 249
 3.1.3 Biblical Validity Issues 252
 3.1.4 The Nature of the Bible 252
 3.1.5 Evidentiary Value of Written Words......................... 253
 3.1.6 Translation Issues 255
 3.1.7 Modern Usage Issues 256
 3.1.8 Translation Differences 257
 3.1.9 Translator Issues 257
 3.1.10 The Importance of Truth... 259
 3.1.11 Relevant Evidence... 260
 3.1.12 The Historical Jesus and the Jesus of Testimony.......261
 3.1.13 The Gospels as Testimony 262
 3.1.14 The Gospels as Evidence 263

3.1.15 Current Views on Gospel Origins 264

3.1.16 A Balanced View 267

3.2 Man or Myth 276

3.3 Evidence of the Gospels 279

   3.3.1 Old Testament Biblical Prophecies 279

      3.3.1.1 The Virgin Birth of Jesus 284

      3.3.1.2 The Birth of Jesus 285

      3.3.1.3 Conclusion 289

   3.3.2 The Miracles of Jesus 290

      3.3.2.1 Water into Wine 293

      3.3.2.2 Healings: The Leper 295

      3.3.2.3 Healings: The Withered Hand 296

      3.3.2.4 Healings: Blindness 297

      3.3.2.5 Demons Cast Out: The Capernaum Synagogue 299

      3.3.2.6 Demons Cast Out: The Pig Demoniacs 301

      3.3.2.7 Feeding the Multitudes: The 5,000 303

      3.3.2.8 The Tempest Stilled 304

      3.3.2.9 Jesus Walks on Water 306

      3.3.2.10 Raising the Dead: The Widow's Son 308

      3.3.2.11 Raising the Dead: Jairus's Daughter 309

      3.3.2.12 Raising the Dead: Lazarus 311

      3.3.2.13 Raising the Dead: The Resurrection of Jesus ... 314

   3.3.3 His Teachings 317

      3.3.3.1 Overview 317

      3.3.3.2 Conclusion 319

   3.3.4 His Testimony 319

      3.3.4.1 Overview 319

      3.3.4.2 John's Question 320

      3.3.4.3 At the Baptism of Jesus 322

      3.3.4.4 Cure of the Paraplegic 324

      3.3.4.5 Peter's Confession of Faith 326

      3.3.4.6 Institution of the Eucharist 328

      3.3.4.7 Jesus before the Sanhedrin 329

      3.3.4.8 Jesus before Pilate 332

      3.3.4.9 Jesus on the Cross 334

3.3.5 The Legacy of Jesus 336
3.3.6 The Search for Truth.. 337
    3.3.6.1 The Meaning of 'Truth'............................ 337
    3.3.6.2 The Likelihood of Error........................... 340
    3.3.6.3 Thiering's Interpretation........................ 341
    3.3.6.4 The Dead Sea Scrolls.............................. 343
    3.3.6.5 The Controversy 344
    3.3.6.6 Obstacles to Thiering's Interpretation 347
    3.3.6.7 Conclusion... 351

PART 4 THE CATHOLIC CHURCH.................................. 355
4.1 The Nature of the Church.. 357
4.2 The Authenticity of the Catholic Church......................361
  4.2.1 Overview 361
  4.2.2 Foundation..361
  4.2.3 Church Identity..................................... 362
  4.2.4 Succession 365
    4.2.4.1 The First Clerics 365
    4.2.4.2 The Pre-Eminence of Rome.................... 368
    4.2.4.3 The Great Schism.................................. 370
    4.2.4.4 The Reformation 372
      4.2.4.4.1 The Lutheran Church 372
      4.2.4.4.2 The Anabaptists 375
      4.2.4.4.3 Calvinism...................................... 378
      4.2.4.4.4 Anglicanism 380
  4.2.5 The Argument from Property.................... 383
4.3 The Mission of the Church 387
  4.3.1 Foundation.. 387
  4.3.2 The Authority of Jesus 388
  4.3.3 Commissioning Imperatives 389
  4.3.4 How to Evangelise.................................. 394
  4.3.5 How to Provide Pastoral Care................... 397
  4.3.6 Evolution of the Mission 399
  4.3.7 Fidelity Issues....................................... 403
  4.3.8 Conclusion 405
4.4 Authority of the Church.. 406

4.4.1 The Nature of Authority 406
4.4.2 Mission Authority 407
4.4.3 Authority to Bind and Loose 412
4.4.4 Authority to Forgive Sins 419
4.5 The Church and Money 423
4.5.1 The Cost of Evangelisation 423
4.5.2 The Cost of Pastoral Care 424
4.5.3 The Role of Canon Law in Money-Raising 424
4.5.4 Church Ways of Money-Raising 425
4.5.5 Inappropriate Aspects of Money-Raising 426
4.5.6 The Church's Need for Wealth 428
4.6 The Teachings of the Church 431
4.6.1 The Current Content of Church Teachings 431
4.6.1.1 Overview 431
4.6.1.2 Ask a Priest 432
4.6.1.3 Private Research 433
4.6.1.4 The Catechism of the Catholic Church 434
4.6.1.5 The Dogmas of the Catholic Church 435
4.6.2 Challenges of Current Teachings 452
4.6.2.1 Magisterium 452
4.6.2.1.1 The Ten Commandments 455
4.6.2.1.2 The Four Gospels 455
4.6.2.1.3 The Acts of the Apostles 456
4.6.2.1.4 Papal Encyclicals and Church
Council Decrees 457
4.6.2.1.5 The Catechism of the Catholic
Church 459
4.6.2.1.6 The Compendium of the
Catechism of the Catholic Church 460
4.6.3 Natural Moral Law 461
4.6.3.1 Divine Law 461
4.6.3.2 Natural Law 462
4.6.3.3 Human Law 466
4.6.4 Conclusions 468

PART 5 CONTEMPORARY ISSUES 471

5.1 Modern Views on Killing... 473

   5.1.1 Overview 473

   5.1.2 Divine Law and Human Law 476

   5.1.3 Homicide... 478

       5.1.3.1 Defences.. 479

   5.1.4 Suicide 480

   5.1.5 Euthanasia 480

   5.1.6 Abortion.. 482

   5.1.7 Cloning.. 483

   5.1.8 Stem Cells 486

   5.1.9 Summary 490

   5.1.10 Perspectives 491

5.2 Anti-Catholicism.. 494

   5.2.1 The Issue 494

   5.2.2 Historical Insights... 495

   5.2.3 Modern Manifestations................................. 499

       5.2.3.1 Governments..................................... 499

       5.2.3.2 Other Religions 501

       5.2.3.3 Cults 502

       5.2.3.4 Individuals 504

       5.2.3.5 Perspective.. 505

       5.2.3.6 Holier than Thou 506

5.3 Terrorism 508

   5.3.1 Definition.. 508

       5.3.1.1 What Constitutes an Act of Terror?.............. 508

       5.3.1.2 Who Are Terrorists? 509

       5.3.1.3 Terrorist Motives and Objectives.................. 509

       5.3.1.4 Terrorist Methods..............................511

   5.3.2 The Islamic Diaspora 513

       5.3.2.1 Demographic.....................................513

       5.3.2.2 Church and State 514

       5.3.2.3 Jihad 514

   5.3.3 Catholic Terrorist Targets 515

   5.3.4 Catholic Attitudes to Terrorism 516

5.4 Catholic Cults..519
   5.4.1 The Issue 519
   5.4.2 Definition..519
   5.4.3 Cult Formation 520
   5.4.4 Membership 521
   5.4.5 Illustrative Examples....................................... 522
        5.4.5.1 The Society of St Vincent de Paul.................. 522
        5.4.5.2 Opus Dei.. 523
        5.4.5.3 The Order of St Charbel.............................. 526
   5.4.6 Conclusion 528
5.5 Modern Church–State Relationship 530
   5.5.1 The Issue 530
   5.5.2 The Function of the State.................................... 530
   5.5.3 The Function of the Church 531
   5.5.4 Some Historical Insights.................................... 532
   5.5.5 The Democratic Process..................................... 533
   5.5.6 Democratic Dissent.. 535
   5.5.7 The Church's Current Political Status 536
5.6 Child Sexual Abuse 538
   5.6.1 The Issue 538
   5.6.2 Nature of the Offence... 538
   5.6.3 Who Are the Offenders? 538
   5.6.4 Who Are the Victims?... 539
   5.6.5 Consequences.. 540
   5.6.6 Morality... 541
   5.6.7 Motives.. 542
   5.6.8 Church Responses 543
   5.6.9 Compensation 544
   5.6.10 Celibacy... 546
   5.6.11 Further Action... 547
   5.6.12 Confession 549
   5.6.13 Conclusion 552
5.7 The Tyranny of Numbers.. 553
   5.7.1 World Population Growth 553
   5.7.2 The Decline of Catholicism 554
   5.7.3 Church Renewal and Vitality Initiatives.................. 557

5.8 Our Church in the Future.. 563

    5.8.1 The Promise of Jesus 563

    5.8.2 The Evolution of Catholicism...................................... 563

    5.8.3 The Role of Theology 564

    5.8.4 The Future of Evangelisation 566

    5.8.5 The Future of Pastoral Care.. 567

    5.8.6 The End of the World 569

Sources... 571

Index... 583

ACKNOWLEDGEMENTS

Communications carry information which can lead to knowledge. All the knowledge about religion that I have, much of which is in this book, comes from books, teachers, family, friends and acquaintances. I acknowledge and thank all those who have communicated with me on relevant issues because it is what they have said that is the substance of this book, even where we did not agree. On the practical side I specifically wish to thank my friend Ronald McCall who first proofread this book and the staff of my publisher, Xlibris, who designed the cover, professionally edited and presented this book in its present form.

INTRODUCTION

Religion is a significant aspect of our lives and has been throughout recorded history. Our knowledge and opinions on this subject are formed by our education, upbringing, dialogue with others, and life experience. There are many different religions, each with a documented theology which forms the basis of its teachings. Each has adherents who generally bring up their children according to their beliefs.

In our lives, we encounter many people who have different religious beliefs from our own. These people may be relatives, friends, associates, acquaintances, or even strangers. At times, these people will tell us of their religious beliefs, and if we respect the knowledge, intelligence, and integrity of that person, then their beliefs could cause us some concern in relation to our own religious beliefs, especially if their religious belief is significantly different from ours and sounds reasonable.

The same concerns can arise through our modern media. Books, interviews with celebrities on television or radio, social media on the Internet, documentaries, and even fiction can present religious views. And in our lives, we sometimes encounter situations or circumstances which can cause us to question our own religious beliefs.

This book is written by me, a catholic layperson in the hope that it may assist other catholic laypersons confronted by some issues that cause concern. The people that I had in mind in writing this work are adult catholics who may have experienced or are experiencing a crisis of faith, other catholic adults who are interested in the present cultural position of our faith and who share the concerns raised in this work, and young Catholics who are in their last year of school, to prepare them for the arguments and ideas that they will encounter in their adult lives.

As such, I bring to these issues the experience of a non-clerical life, which includes friends and acquaintances saying things and saying them in a way that they would probably not say to a member of the Catholic clergy. Also, as a layperson, I do not need to be defensive or apologetic for the misdemeanours of some of the clergy in recent times and throughout history. This book is not intended to proselytise or to preach to the converted. Its aim is to explore issues of general concern and to provide some answers that affirm the validity and reasonableness of the Catholic faith. Because it assumes some knowledge of the Catholic faith, this is not a book for non-Catholics.

As Catholics, we believe that our faith underlies the purpose of our lives, and accordingly, we have a responsibility to ourselves to carefully consider any apparently reasonable view on important religious issues that come to our notice which disagree with our theology in any substantial way. Left unanswered, such views can diminish our faith by creating a nagging doubt. This, in turn, can lead to our participation in our Catholic liturgy coming to be perceived by us as mere meaningless ritual which is boring and futile. This will inevitably lead to a significant loss of faith.

To carefully consider such views and arguments, we need information and clear thinking. Our first resource is usually our Catholic education. But much of our education is about how to be Catholics and the meaning of the doctrines of our faith. The types of issues raised by friends or acquaintances that can cause us concern mostly go to our fundamental beliefs, which, if accepted, would undermine the whole structure of our faith.

Such issues are principally questions as to the existence of God, the divinity of Jesus Christ, the authenticity of the Bible, and the authority of the church. These issues are the foundation of our faith, and the theology underlying them is mostly assumed in bringing up children in the Catholic faith or in educating an adult who has indicated a desire to become a Catholic. Hence, our education in the Catholic faith and ongoing participation in our faith are not the appropriate resources to provide information on such issues.

There have been many books written about the existence of God, the divinity of Jesus Christ, the authenticity of the Bible, and the authority of the church. Some of these books were written long ago, and some are contemporary. There have not been any new arguments for many years. Accordingly, to carefully consider any conflicting views or arguments about any of these issues, it is not necessary for us to reinvent the wheel. It is almost certain that any argument that we are likely to hear from friends or acquaintances has been raised in theological literature and has also been dealt with in the books and other writing of educated and intelligent Catholic theologians, many of whom are priests. Consequently, the best resource to enable a careful consideration of questions that may cause us some concern is the work of such Catholic theologians.

It is not suggested that the works of Catholic theologians should take priority over documents presenting official church teachings, such as the *Catechism of the Catholic Church* or encyclicals. It is simply that the *Catechism* and these other documents do not address some of the issues that we may encounter which concern us.

There is a vast amount of theological literature on each of these topics. The answer to a specific question that has caused some concern may well be buried in some massive tome, shrouded in technical language and jargon, and cross-referenced with other unfamiliar and sometimes unobtainable works. It is therefore likely that to carefully consider an issue that has caused us some concern will require a considerable expenditure of time, effort, and resources.

Most people who have become concerned about some theological issue have no need or desire to acquire the depth of theological knowledge necessary to formally answer the question raised. They simply want to satisfy themselves or the person who raised the issue, that the Catholic view that they hold is also based on sound reasoning. What they want and need is the right answer, together with a succinct version of the essential reasoning supporting that answer.

The raising of such an issue is not a frequent occurrence in our lives, but neither is it all that rare. The majority of theological books are concerned with single topics like the existence of God or the divinity of Jesus Christ. What is missing from the bookshelves of Catholic libraries is a single volume that deals with these fundamental issues in a language and style appropriate to address the need of the broad spectrum of Catholics who wish to consider such an issue. That is the primary function that this book is intended to serve. The objective is to provide sufficient information in an objective format, both for and against any issue, enabling the reader to think it through and come to his or her own conclusions.

I have written this work in an objective third-person style. I have conscientiously avoided the use of such phrases as 'I think this' or 'I believe that', because for the purpose of providing information to any reader, what I think or believe is irrelevant. We are all responsible for our own decisions, and I consider it to be a failure to honour our responsibility to ourselves to accept something as fact or agree with some reason simply because some other person believes it to be so. I acknowledge that I do believe in the existence of God, I do believe in the divinity of Jesus, and I believe in the authenticity and authority of our church. Accordingly, it is inevitable that some of my beliefs have permeated into the intended objectivity of this work, but as already indicated, I have attempted to fairly present arguments both for and against the various issues considered. In short, I want my readers to consider the issues on their merits, without reference to who has raised the issue or how it has been raised.

This book is divided into five parts. The first part deals with the parameters of thought on which this work is based and some background issues. The second part deals with the existence of God. Part 3 deals with the divinity of Jesus Christ. Part 4 deals with the authority and authenticity of our church. Part 5 considers a number of contemporary issues. These, and some other issues, are not mentioned in the Gospels because they were not issues in the time of Jesus Christ, as the technology underlying these issues did not then exist or because the cultural norms of Judaism, in which Christ lived and taught, had not developed in a way which raised such issues.

For example, abortion. Jewish culture highly valued children. There were high infant mortality rates in those days. There were no social services, so the children had to look after their parents in their old age. Ordinary people did not have the culture of acquisition because there was not as much to acquire as there is today, nor was there such a thing as self-funded retirees, except amongst the very wealthy. Consequently, children were regarded as a valuable long-term investment. And because of the infant mortality rate and the vagaries of life which might eventuate in a child dying before its parents, the more children the better. Hence, an infant death was regarded as a misfortune, and abortion was unthinkable.

In our time, we have different cultural norms. Our Catholic faith is practised in most countries in the world, with different cultural norms in many countries. Furthermore, the norms of most countries have changed over the centuries since Jesus Christ taught. It has been one of the functions of the church, in teaching the gospel, to apply those teachings to the specific conduct countenanced by the norms of these various cultures over the years and in many different places. Essentially, the church has had to extrapolate from the Gospels and theology what Jesus Christ would have said if he had been confronted with the issues raised by those norms which differ from the norms in his culture.

The example of abortion illustrates this point. In our culture, one of the norms is that a woman has the right (subject to some limitations that are irrelevant to this issue) to do whatever she wishes with her own body. Another current norm is that people should not bring a child into this world if they cannot financially afford to bring the child up decently or if that child's financial needs will seriously and detrimentally affect the proper upbringing of other existing children. Yet another norm is that bearing a child will 'ruin the life' of a very young unmarried woman.

The church's teaching on this issue is clear. Abortion is the killing of a life in being, regardless of whether that life can survive independently of its mother, and as such, it is against the fifth commandment of God, given to the Jews in the Ten Commandments. Jesus Christ was a Jew, and he taught diligent observance of the laws of God. There can be no doubt that Jesus Christ fully endorses the church's teaching on abortion and that the church's teaching is fully justified and correct.

Similarly, the church has teachings about many other issues that arise from differences between the current cultural norms and those in Jesus Christ's time. Such teachings have been documented in papal decrees, council determinations, and many other official church documents. In recent years, the church has codified and simplified many such teachings and presented them to Catholics in the *Catechism of the Catholic Church*.

The *Catechism of the Catholic Church* is a wonderful book. It warrants close study but should at least be read from cover to cover by every Catholic. The *Catechism* is composed of four main parts.

The first part deals with what we, as Catholics, believe. It covers in detail what is in our profession of faith, supported by reasons or explanations for each of our beliefs, but it does not deal with arguments that challenge our beliefs. Accordingly, it does not provide any answer or rebuttal of such arguments. Nor should it, for that is not its function. It is such arguments and rebuttals that are explored in this book.

The second part deals with the how-to of leading a life as a Catholic. It covers in detail the Mass, the sacraments, and some other liturgical procedures, with explanations of how these procedures work, what they achieve, and their validity. Obviously, this part follows and assumes the beliefs specified in the first part of the *Catechism* and functionally has no persuasive value in relation to those arguments that challenge our fundamental beliefs, although there are some theological issues such as transubstantiation that are covered in this part, and this is something that most non-Catholics do not believe.

The third part is in two sections. The first section covers socio-religious norms and contains essentially the church's teachings on the issues, drawn from the church's understanding of the theologies and teachings of Jesus Christ. The second part covers in detail the Ten Commandments and gives the church's teachings as to their meaning and applications to the relevant issues of conduct in our time.

It is the type of issue covered in this second part that is the subject of the fifth part of this work. The church's teachings on issues that are covered in the *Catechism* are more than adequate, and it is not intended to canvas its teachings on such issues. However, there are other issues not considered in the *Catechism* which may concern modern Catholics. These issues are not in the *Catechism* because they emerged as issues after the publication of the *Catechism* in 1994. Examples of such issues are human cloning and stem cell research.

There are also issues arising from the changing global situation, especially since 1994. Examples of such issues are terrorism and ecumenism. Also, in recent times, some Catholic cults, such as Opus Dei, have become more widely known amongst Catholics, and some of the practices of these cults are surprising to most Catholics and consequently worth exploring. Further issues, such as anti-Catholicism, feature prominently in recent literature, especially some scandals which tend to diminish the clergy's reputation for integrity. Accordingly, these are also issues worth exploring.

The modern Catholic clergy and theologians have not been slow to respond to these issues, but their works are sometimes hard to find, are expressed in complex and technical language, and are dealt with comprehensively rather than succinctly. In these circumstances, it appears that a review by a Catholic layperson of a number of these issues, expressed succinctly in plain language, may be of assistance to modern Catholics who are concerned by such issues.

Obviously, such a review is not official and therefore cannot be authoritative. However, it is an honest view expressed in the belief that it is in accord with official church teachings, with sources of important facts and arguments provided.

The fourth part of the *Catechism* deals with Christian prayer and covers in detail our attitudes in our various communications with God. Again, this part does not cover challenging arguments and accordingly contains nothing helpful in considering those arguments which challenge our faith, although the practice of prayer is obviously helpful and necessary in the maintenance of our faith.

Inevitably, there will be some arguments and conclusions expressed herein with which not everyone will agree. That is as it should be if the reader thinks for himself or herself, which is necessary because of our responsibility for our own actions. If anything in this book causes our church leaders to review or amend any official church teaching on an issue, then the raising of that issue has served a worthwhile function. There is criticism of our church in parts of this work. However, as a non-cleric, I have no apprehension of any adverse repercussions of such criticism, because I expect our church to recognise that the criticism is intended to be constructive while being an honest opinion, diligently researched and considerately expressed, clearly intended to be helpful and in a work that is clearly based on fidelity to our faith.

There is a fair amount of repetition in this work, which I considered appropriate, so that each argument or point being made could stand alone, without tedious cross-references to previous sections. I apologise in advance if any reader finds this irritating.

PM

PART 1

PARAMETERS

1.1 The Reasoning Process

1.1.1 The Proposition

'We should carefully consider all arguments and views relating to our religious beliefs, both supportive and contradictory, that we encounter in our lives.'

To some people, this proposition is axiomatic and needs no further explanation or justification. To others, it raises a number of questions that require answers. Communication is fraught with difficulties that readily lead to misunderstandings. Inevitably, some readers will misunderstand the above proposition or its implications, even those who regard the proposition as axiomatic. Accordingly, to clarify the intended meaning, it appears appropriate to analyse the proposition in some detail.

'We'. This work is written by a Catholic, for Catholics, although persons of any religion or denomination and even atheists may find parts of this work informative. Certainly, in relation to the proposition under consideration, any reader who has not yet irrevocably committed to the belief that we do not have an immortal soul qualifies as a person who may find this proposition relevant. More explicitly, anyone who believes that they have or may have an immortal soul and have some responsibility for what happens to that soul after the death of our bodies would be well advised to consider the matters that may affect the future of that soul and accordingly is properly included in the 'we' of this proposition. Most people believe that we do have a soul, but not everyone accepts that it is immortal. However, the parameters of thought outlined in this section of this work may assist in an assessment of the available evidence on this issue as well.

'Should'. Whenever it is suggested that we *should* do something, it is legitimate to ask why. The answer to this question will be further considered under the heading of the primary assumption. Briefly,

if we have an immortal soul, it is clearly in our best interests to form a view as to whether how we live our lives can affect our happiness in our existence after the end of our physical lives.

'Carefully consider'. People who are highly educated in the various professions or sciences know how to carefully consider issues in their field of expertise. Philosophers and theologians are trained to carefully consider religious issues and can recognise most of the arguments and views on religious issues as variations or non-technical expressions of issues that they have studied. They have considered the strengths and weaknesses of such views or arguments. Most Catholics have only basic religious education in comparison. But Catholics lacking extensive theological education are not incapable of carefully considering religious issues, and accordingly, an outline of the mental tools necessary to make a careful consideration of such issues may be helpful. It may also be helpful to provide an outline of the most common and major issues so that Catholics can recognise different expressions of these arguments and have a competent grasp of the strengths and weaknesses of these arguments. To this end, it is essential that our religious beliefs are based on confidence in the reasoning process that led to our acceptance of such beliefs and that we are able to recognise the usual counterarguments and have some insight into the merits of such counterarguments so that our faith is not undermined by apparently reasonable arguments or views.

'All arguments and views relating to religious issues'. The 'all' in this phrase is not intended to imply that we should make diligent enquiry of all other religions in the world and atheists regarding their views and arguments in support of their views in order to carefully consider them. Nor do we need to consider arguments or views that are patently flawed. The 'all' is linked to the following phrase, limiting consideration to arguments and views that we encounter in our religious education and then in our ordinary lives, even or especially those that come from unreliable sources.

Giving careful consideration to patently flawed arguments and views enables us to summarily dismiss those arguments when we hear and recognise a different articulation of the same argument. Arguments and views from unreliable sources warrant careful consideration, because it is not the source that is important but the substance of the view or argument. The good credentials of a person proposing a view or argument do not make it valid, just as a lack of credentials of a proponent does not make their argument invalid.

'Both supportive and contradictory'. Our objective in considering religious issues is to find the truth. From experience, we know that there are no absolutes in this area. We also know that it is, in practical terms, impossible to consider every view and argument on religious issues. The usual course is that we are educated in our faith and accept the teachings of our faith, based on the evidence and arguments in support that we were taught. We then encounter views and arguments that contradict our beliefs. If we do not carefully consider such views and arguments, we are clearly not interested in the truth. Every argument that we carefully consider and reject strengthens our faith.

'That we encounter in our lives'. This phrase is intended to include all the forms in which arguments and views on religious issues appear in the lives of ordinary Catholics. Such arguments can be found in books, radio, television, music, or conversations with friends and acquaintances. The argument or view may be directly stated or embedded in fiction, documentary works, news, a story, or a joke, or it could even be implied in conduct. Furthermore, the expression of an argument or view on a religious issue is often difficult to recognise as one of the standard arguments or views dealt with in the philosophical or theological texts. This is particularly so in discussions with friends or acquaintances where such views or arguments are presented in layman's terms, imprecisely and somewhat more colourfully than in the standard texts.

1.1.2 The Need for Truth

What is truth? Philosophically, it is difficult to establish absolutes or a universally acceptable definition of truth. Fortunately, for our purposes, we are concerned only with the plain meaning of plain words. In ordinary usage, we all understand that the truth means 'that which really is'! That definition is sufficient, provided we accept that something cannot both be and not be at the same time. There are other philosophical wrinkles in the concept of truth, but in ordinary usage, it means things like if a person says that they did something, believing that they did do the thing, and they did actually do that thing, then the person is telling the truth.

The role of truth in the careful consideration of a religious issue is that it is the objective of the careful consideration. In other words, we think about such issues in order to discover that which actually is about the issue. If the careful consideration is not aimed at discovering the truth, then it is either a waste of time or the construction of an argument for the purpose of deception.

The problem with truth is that it is rarely possible, especially in relation to religious issues, to conclude that the facts sought to be established by an argument are absolutely true. Usually, the truth of some alleged fact is accepted or rejected according to the persuasive value of the argument supporting or opposing the existence of the alleged fact. The danger in this is that we may accept something as true when it is not actually true, or we may refuse to accept as true something that is actually true. It is this dilemma that has enabled the current plethora of inconsistent religious beliefs, which in turn suggests that we should be very careful about what we accept or reject as truth.

1.1.3 Logic and Reason

There are two main aspects in the process of reasoning. The first aspect of the process is called *a priori*. This part of reasoning is independent of the truth or falsity of the fact or conclusion being argued or considered, and it is concerned solely with the logical validity of the reasoning process. A good example of this is the syllogism in the rules of logic. Consider the following:

Major premise: All apples are green.
Minor premise: The man ate an apple.
Conclusion: What the man ate was green.

This argument is logically valid, but it is plainly untrue because we know from experience that the major premise is false. Apples can be red, green, yellow, or any shade in between. It may, in fact, be true that the apple that the man in this example ate was green, but one cannot draw that conclusion from this argument, because of the falsity of the major premise.

For a logical argument to be true, both the major premise and the minor premise must be true, and they must relate to each other. Most arguments are substantially more complex than the simple example above. Many arguments involve a number of propositions or premises that are interdependent. Logically, such arguments may be valid but fail to deliver truth because of uncertainty about the truth of one of the premises. Fortunately, most people have an intuitive ability to perceive the logical validity of an argument, but this ability is not infallible. Accordingly, there is the need for great care in considering important views or arguments. Some arguments are convoluted and may contain irrelevant premises. Such arguments can only be properly considered by the tedious process of careful examination of each premise within the argument, and we have the ability to do this.

The second aspect of the reasoning process is called *a posteriori*. This part of reasoning draws conclusions as to the truth or falsity of an argument from evidence, experience, or observation of the world by human senses.

Consider the following conclusion: 'Most birds can fly'. We are aware that there are many species of birds and that a few of them are flightless. Anyone who is old enough to read this and who is not disabled in a relevant capacity has almost certainly seen birds in flight many times. There is also a vast amount of literature that refers to the power of flight of birds. This conclusion is so abundantly supported by empirical evidence that it requires no further proof.

Unfortunately, not every conclusion sought to be supported by empirical evidence is as readily acceptable.

Consider the following scenario:

A man is found standing beside the body of another man. The deceased has a knife plunged into his chest, and this clearly caused his death. Only the fingerprints of the man found standing over the body were found on the knife. The standing man was charged with murder. The accused says that he is a special forces soldier and that he was practising hand-to-hand combat in a dark room to simulate the night-time when he accidentally stabbed the deceased, who he did not know was there. The prosecution argues that the accused's explanation is implausible, and the prosecution further supports its case with the evidence of a witness who says that he heard the accused and the deceased exchange angry words some hours before the stabbing.

On that evidence, a jury may justifiably draw the conclusion that the accused is guilty of murder. But what if the defence calls a witness who says that the accused and the deceased were good friends, that their disagreement some hours earlier was minor, and that the deceased had told him that, as a joke, he intended to sneak up on his friend in the dark room to scare the daylights out of him? On that evidence, a jury may justifiably acquit the accused of murder.

But what if the accused is unaware of the evidence that the witness for the defence can give? Or what if the witness is unable to give this evidence, for some good reason? If we assume that the evidence of the witness for the defence is true, then a jury may well convict an innocent man.

From this scenario, it is apparent that in real life, the process of empirical argument is fraught with difficulties. Much of human experience is parochial or of limited application. There are very few absolutes. Science supports many inferences that can be drawn from circumstantial evidence, but history has shown that science itself is subject to growth and change; accordingly, it cannot be relied on as an absolute.

Most reasoning is a combination of the a priori and a posteriori aspects of reasoning. In the area of religious issues, the process becomes even more complex, because issues concern spiritual things which cannot be accessed a priori and which are not accessible to the human senses and therefore cannot be supported a posteriori either.

1.1.4 The Nature of Proof

What we want to be able to prove is the truth of some fact, theory, or proposition. For our purposes, the following definition may suffice: *Proof is the conclusion that can be drawn by the application of reason to the evidence relevant to the truth of that fact or proposition that satisfies us to the appropriate degree of the truth of that fact or proposition.*

There are essentially two types of proof. The first type is called analytic. This type of proof does not involve the consideration of evidence beyond what is axiomatic from our experience of the world. For example, the proof of a mathematical theorem is the application of reason using the fundamental rules of mathematics to derive the theorem. Such a proof can be described as conclusive because such a proof *must* be accepted by every normal person, unless it can be shown that there was some error in the reasoning used or that there is some invalidity in the application of the fundamental rules of mathematics applied. Such a proof can also be described as an objective proof because it does not depend on the evidence or observations of some individual, who could possibly be mistaken. The views of anyone who rejects such a proof for any other reason may cheerfully be disregarded.

The second type of proof is evidentiary proof. This type of proof is subjective in that it does depend on the observations or evidence of persons. Because of the possibility that persons can be mistaken, there are various degrees to which such proofs will satisfy us. These degrees are as follows:

(i)   compelling proof
(ii) proof beyond reasonable doubt
(iii) proof to comfortable satisfaction
(iv) proof to the balance of probabilities
(v)   insufficient proof
(vi) The Burden of Proof.

(i)   <u>Compelling Proof</u>

There is a philosophical proposition, credited to Bertrand Russell, that suggests that the world was created ten minutes ago and that all our memories going back more than ten minutes are false memories implanted by the Creator. Naturally, such an argument cannot be disproved. There are also propositions derived from quantum physics and science fiction suggesting the existence of multiple dimensions and parallel universes. Unless and until such things can be proved, the assumption underlying this work is that the world is as we actually see it and as we remember it.

There are many things that have been proved conclusively from empirical evidence. For example, the fact that our world is approximately spherical in shape, air is a physical substance, airplanes can fly, etc. Most of our laws of physics are based on observation of the real world. These observations led to a hypothesis of a law, and subsequent testing of the hypothesis found no exceptions. Accordingly, these laws can be regarded as having been proved conclusively. This is axiomatic, and we all have a clear understanding of the compelling persuasive value of such proofs.

The only cautionary note here is that sometimes scientists discover something and proclaim it to be a truth before the hypothesis is exhaustively tested, and subsequently, their hypothesis fails. Perhaps the wise option is to regard as truths or laws those scientific discoveries that have stood the test of time.

(ii) <u>Proof beyond Reasonable Doubt</u>

This is the standard used in our legal system to establish the guilt of a person accused of committing a criminal offence. This proof, as with all proofs, is derived from the totality of the available evidence. That means that it is not necessary for each individual piece of evidence to be proved to this standard or for all the evidence that exists in the world to be considered.

An example of what this means can be seen in the trial of a person accused of a crime. In a jury of twelve persons, some may conclude, from the evidence presented in the trial, that the accused is guilty, while others may conclude, from the same evidence, that the accused is not guilty. Both views may be honestly held, and neither can be shown to be wrong. The members of the jury, like all of us, are individuals with different life experience and reasoning skills, and unless the proof is conclusive, it is legitimate and ethically incumbent on each individual to come to the conclusion that he or she honestly believes to be correct.

Subject to the above, what this standard of proof requires is that the individual considering the fact or proposition is certain that the fact or proposition is true. Naturally, if a fact or proposition cannot be proved to the compelling degree, there must necessarily be some doubt about the truth of the conclusion. This standard of proof requires that any such doubt is properly regarded as fanciful or far-fetched. For example, if the guilt or innocence of an accused depended on fingerprint evidence. Theoretically, there is no known reason two persons cannot have the same fingerprint. However, experience has never found identical fingerprints from separate individuals, including identical twins. Of course, not everyone in the world has had their fingerprints recorded and compared with the fingerprints of all other persons; however, there have been millions of comparisons of the fingerprints of different persons, and no identical fingerprints have been found, using only about fifteen points of similarity. Accordingly, if an accused person argued that the fingerprints found at the scene of the crime were not his but the forensic evidence showed that they were identical with the accused's fingerprints, a jury should be strongly persuaded that the fingerprints found were those of the accused and reach whatever conclusion may follow from that persuasion. The doubt raised by the accused's denial that they were his fingerprints would properly be regarded as fanciful.

(iii) Proof to Comfortable Satisfaction

This standard is also derived from our legal system, which requires that standard of proof in cases where a person is accused of some conduct that is reprehensible but not criminal. Usually, such cases come before the disciplinary tribunals of various professional organisations, for them to consider whether or not someone acted unprofessionally. Commonly, there are several tribunal members that hear such a case, and no juries.

As with proof beyond reasonable doubt, this standard is subjective in that the individual members of the tribunal must each form a view as to the guilt or innocence of the person accused of unprofessional conduct from the totality of the evidence presented in the hearing. It is not unusual for there to be disagreement between the members of the tribunal hearing a matter.

This standard of proof requires that the person considering the evidence is comfortably satisfied that the fact or proposition at issue is true. This standard permits the existence of reasonable doubt as to the truth of the fact or proposition, but it does require that the conclusion that the issue has been proved to this standard is very much more likely than the opposite conclusion.

For example, suppose a doctor is accused of having an affair with a patient in circumstances that make this conduct unethical. The doctor denies it. The evidence is that the doctor was seen going into a motel room with a patient by a person who knows the doctor very well. The doctor says that he was not there and that it is a case of mistaken identity, but he cannot provide any evidence as to his whereabouts at the relevant time. The witness is a highly respected member of the community, with unimpaired vision and no conceivable or suggested motive for lying. The witness saw the doctor from about three metres away in good daylight, although the doctor was wearing a hat and sunglasses and the witness did not hear the doctor's voice at that time. The witness is firmly convinced that it was the doctor that he saw.

We all know that mistaken identity can occur, especially if the person identified is of average height and weight for that age group. Some people look remarkably similar to other persons. Greeting someone that we think we know, only to find that it is not the person that we thought, has probably happened to most of us, but not very often.

On the evidence outlined above, the members of the tribunal considering such a matter may and should have reasonable doubt as to the guilt of the doctor. The circumstances of the identification allow for the possibility that the witness was mistaken, and this is not a fanciful or far-fetched possibility. However, the tribunal members may be comfortably satisfied that the doctor is guilty for the following reasons: the doctor has no alibi; the witness has no motive to lie, whereas the doctor has; the witness is a highly respected member of the community, implying that he would not engage in serious mischievous conduct; the witness is competent enough to make a visual identification; the doctor is well known to the witness; the identification was made at close range and in good daylight; and the witness is firm in his evidence.

As with proof beyond reasonable doubt, this standard *enables* a finding of guilt, whereas the standard of conclusive proof *compels* acceptance of the fact or proposition at issue.

(iv) Proof to the Balance of Probabilities

This standard is also used and illustrated by our legal systems. It is primarily used in civil cases, which usually do not have a jury. Civil cases are those in which the criminality or ethics of the conduct at issue is not relevant. Essentially, the effect of civil law is to compensate people if other people cause them some damage or injury through negligence, failure to honour a contract, or some unfair commercial conduct. To some degree, civil law does enforce this morality, but this is incidental to its primary function, which is preserving peace and harmony in the community and fostering prosperity.

Every day there are many persons accidentally injured and many, many commercial transactions which encounter problems that can only be solved by litigation. These matters are important, but not as important as criminal matters. Bearing in mind the vast amount of civil litigation that happens and the heavy demand on the resources of the individuals involved in the litigation and on the community providing the litigation facilities, the only practical standard of proof which will keep the expenditure of resources in perspective is the balance of probabilities.

Again, this standard is subjective. The matters are usually heard by a single judge or arbitrator, and the outcome may be different if it is heard by another individual. The court's appeal systems do not generally interfere with a judge or arbitrator's findings of fact, but they will correct errors of law.

Within these parameters, the level of proof required to achieve this standard is that on the totality of the evidence, the fact or proposition sought to be established is more likely than not. It is not helpful to attempt to quantify likelihood, because likelihood is not amenable to precise quantification. However, if a proposition or fact is proved to be even just a little more likely than not, the standard of proof has been reached. To illustrate this point, it has been suggested that the test is like a beam balance and that a slight tilt to one side enables a decision. No tilt in either direction means that the fact or proposition sought to be established has not been established.

Typically, in a civil case, there will be conflicting evidence. One side says that the fact at issue is true, and the other says that it is false. There is no logical reason to prefer the evidence of one side over the other, and the mere number of witnesses called by each side is not of itself determinative. But a decision *must* be made. The courts cannot simply say that they do not know the answer and send the parties away without a result, because the parties expended considerable resources to obtain a result. The courts would be failing the community if they declined to come to a conclusion. Consequently, a decision is often made on the basis of intangible factors, such as the demeanour of witnesses, apparent or suspected motives, or even the life experience of the judge.

This point need not be further laboured, because this standard of proof is well known to most people and also because this standard has only comparative relevance to the subject of this work.

(v) Insufficient Proof

In each of the standards of proof considered above, the proof may not reach the standard aimed at, but this does not mean that the evidence for the truth of the fact or proposition supported fails entirely. For example, if it was sought to prove something conclusively but failed to reach this standard, the evidence may well satisfy someone to the standard of beyond reasonable doubt. Similarly, an argument intended to prove something beyond reasonable doubt that fails to reach this standard may well reach the standard of proof to comfortable satisfaction or proof to the balance of probabilities.

This category of insufficient proof is intended to cover proofs which fall short of the intended or required level of proof but which still satisfy one of the lower levels of proof. Of course, if a proof fails to reach even the standard of balance of probabilities, then it cannot support any degree of satisfaction in the truth of the fact or proposition at issue. But that does not mean that the fact or proposition at issue is false. It means only that the fact or proposition was not proved to be true to any standard because the evidence and reason in support were insufficient. The same standards of proof apply to proving the falsity of some fact or proposition as apply to proving its truth. However, the arguments to disprove some fact or proposition which do not necessarily establish the falsity of the fact or proposition to the required degree may be considered successful if they prevent the proof of the truth of the fact or proposition reaching the required standard.

(vi) <u>The Burden of Proof</u>

The mere assertion that some fact or proposition is true cannot be regarded as proof to any standard. The purpose of proof is to convince oneself or other people that the fact or proposition is true. The appropriate method to achieve this is to examine or present all the evidence and reasoning in support of the truth and falsity of the fact or proposition, and to then judge the level of satisfaction that the evidence and reasoning supports. In an adversarial legal system, it is only necessary to present one side of the argument, but in relation to religious issues, it is appropriate to consider both the arguments for and against. Accordingly, any proof of a religious issue which deals with only one side or which is summarily dismissive of opposing arguments should be viewed with caution.

1.1.5 The Nature of Evidence

In considering a posteriori arguments and issues, we must necessarily rely on evidence. But what is evidence, and to what degree should it persuade us of the truth of the argument or issue to which the evidence relates? Is our own experience of the world evidence? How much evidence is enough? Must evidence allow only one conclusion to be drawn from it? These and other questions need to be considered to enable us to assess the weight or persuasiveness of evidence.

The first consideration is the form in which evidence appears. The major forms of evidence are as follows:

(i)   common knowledge
(ii) what people say about:
    (i)   their own words or actions
    (ii) their observations of the words or actions of others
    (iii) their observations of events
    (iv) their observations of things
(iii) circumstantial evidence
(iv) documentary evidence
(v)   statistics.

Each of these forms warrant some consideration of their reliability.

(i)   <u>Common Knowledge</u>

We all know some things that require no further proof. For example, the fact that the sun rises in the east and sets in the west. By convention, we have named certain directions as north, south, west, and east. From our own observations, we are aware that the sun always rises from approximately the same direction and sets in approximately the opposite direction. If a man were to say that he was travelling in the direction from which the sun rose, we can safely assume that he was travelling in an easterly direction. This is an assumption. There are many assumptions that can be drawn from what is common knowledge. Assumptions regularly appear in the arguments for or against the truth of various propositions or facts, without the underlying common knowledge being identified. There is nothing wrong with this, because it would be tedious and cumbersome to have to identify the common knowledge underlying every assumption. However, some arguments make assumptions that are not based on true common knowledge but rather are based on hypotheses or the view of the world of the proponent of the argument. These may or may not be valid.

Accordingly, in relation to important issues, it is necessary to identify all the assumptions in the arguments about the issue and to relate such assumptions to the item of common knowledge from which it arises. If the source of the assumption cannot be regarded as true common knowledge, then the assumption must be regarded as unsupported, unless it is otherwise supported. Unsupported assumptions in an argument make the entire argument unacceptable.

(ii) <u>What People Say About . . .</u>

(i) . . . Their Own Words or Actions

As a general rule, what people say about their own words or actions is the best available evidence as to the truth of what that person said or did. But it is common knowledge that some people sometimes tell lies. The purpose of a lie is to deceive, and consequently, it is not always easy to discern when someone is lying. However, lies are often inconsistent with other known facts, and an exploration of the surrounding facts may enable the conclusion that the person giving evidence about his or her words or actions is lying, despite that person's vehement adherence to their evidence. But not finding any inconsistencies does not necessarily mean that the person is telling the truth.

Accordingly, we should not draw the conclusion that when a person gives evidence about his or her own words or actions, what they are saying is true and correct, without some exploration of the surrounding circumstances. They could be telling what they believe to be the truth, but their memory may be flawed or they may be lying. If inconsistencies are found, then their evidence should only be accepted with caution.

(ii) ... Their Observations of The Words or Actions of Others

This category of evidence is essentially the same as what persons say about their own words or actions if their evidence about the words or actions of others is based on what the witness heard or saw. Again, the best evidence is what persons say about their own words or actions, so what a person says about the words or actions of others is only second best. But sometimes a person has an obvious strong motivation to lie about the words or actions of others, or they may be mistaken. In such circumstances, the evidence should be weighed in the light of other known facts, and again, some exploration of the evidence is warranted.

Often this type of evidence is given in circumstances where the person who could give evidence about his or her own words or actions is not available to give evidence. In such circumstances, what people say about the words or actions of others is the best evidence available.

This type of evidence becomes less reliable if the person giving the evidence says that the words or actions of others about which he testifies are not based on his own observations or hearing but are based on what some third person has told him were the words or actions at issue. This third person may not have personally seen or heard what he or she has reported to the witness, or he or she may be mistaken or lying. In our courts, such evidence is called hearsay, and it is not normally accepted as part of the evidence in the case. Our considerations are no less important than the considerations of judges and juries, because the results of our consideration can lead to life-changing decisions. Accordingly, for our purposes, such third-person evidence must also be regarded with great caution. Unfortunately, it is only this type of evidence that is available to support the truth of facts alleged to have occurred further in the past than any living person can testify to from personal observations or hearing. Nor does such evidence become any weightier merely because the third-party report is in written form. This is one of the main difficulties that we encounter in considering the probative value of the entirety of the Bible!

(iii). . . Their Observations of Events

Events can be the words or actions of others, in which case this category overlaps the previous category. But often people see things happen without seeing or recognising the person or thing that caused the event to happen. For example, a person may hear a sound like a gunshot without seeing anyone firing a gun. A person may see two cars collide without being able to identify the driver of either vehicle. The range of events about which a person can give evidence is a broad as the range of events known to human experience.

Again, the evidence of the witness may be a deliberate lie, but the most common problem with such evidence is the accuracy of the evidence. In the gunshot example, the witness may say that he or she heard a specific number of gunshot sounds. But the witness may be mistaken about the number, especially if the witness did not immediately anticipate that there would be more gunshot sounds and start counting as soon as he or she heard the first shot. Or the witness may have been apprehensive about where the shots were coming from and at whom they were aimed, perhaps being more concerned with his or her personal safety, and did not really count at all. The specific number testified to could then only be regarded as an estimate.

There are many reasons a person's observations of events may be inaccurate, so much so that our courts often become suspicious of collusion if the evidence about an event from two different persons is identical.

And then there is the problem of the extent of the conclusions that can properly be drawn from the evidence. For example, the gunshot sounds may not have been gunshots at all but the sounds of a car backfiring. If the evidence extended to seeing a person firing a gun, then the conclusion that the sounds were gunshots would be acceptable. In the two-car collision example, the evidence of the witness would enable only the conclusion that the collision occurred as the witness described. It would require further evidence to establish the ownership of the vehicles and who was driving them at the time. It is the totality of the acceptable evidence that may prove, to some standard, what actually happened.

A further complication is that the totality of the evidence must have sufficient probative value to support the conclusion to the required standard of proof. Individual items of evidence may not be necessary to the proof but may be supportive of it. In the collision example, if the witness gave evidence of the colour and make of one of the vehicles and if there was other evidence that one of the persons found in the vehicles owned a vehicle of that make and colour, it may be concluded to the degree of the balance of probabilities that the person found in the car owned that car. If there was further evidence of the registration number of the car and that the person found in the car was the registered owner of a vehicle having that registration number, it may be concluded to the degree of comfortable satisfaction that the person found in the car owned the car. So the evidence of the make and colour of the car is not necessary to this proof, but it is supportive of it.

The most difficult aspect of this issue is whether the whole is greater than the sum of its parts. In other words, can one be satisfied to a certain standard if some of the essential items of evidence have probative value to a lower standard? The answer will depend in each case on the number of items of the lower probative value and the probability of these items occurring in the circumstances. If the probability is significantly increased by the aggregation of the supporting items of evidence, then it is possible to be satisfied to a higher degree than the individual items of evidence can support. But caution must be exercised in drawing such a conclusion, because it is not merely the number of items of evidence that increases the likelihood that the conclusion they support is true; rather, it is the likelihood of all these different things or events, which all separately support the conclusion, occurring in the same matter that can increase the probative value of the totality of the evidence.

(iv) . . . Their Observations of Things

This category is very similar to the previous category but warrants separate consideration because this type of evidence is essentially descriptive, in contrast to the chronicle-like evidence of the previous category. The main issue with this type of evidence is that descriptive evidence comes from the powers of observation and recollection of the witness, and it is common knowledge that we humans have a wide range of ability in this regard.

A humorous illustration of the difficulties of this type of evidence that most of us will have encountered is the situation where a friend is telling us about something that he saw while he was on holiday with his wife. Often the wife interrupts the narrative to correct some of the details related by her husband. The husband usually disputes the correction, and a short argument ensues. The husband will then resume the narrative when he remembers correctly or asserts that he is correct or that the difference is irrelevant. Usually, the wife is right, because generally women have a better eye for detail than men, especially if the subject matter is more important to them. It is also common knowledge that more men are colour-blind than women.

Another illustration of differences between individuals can be seen in the description of a motor vehicle that may have been involved in an accident. If the witness was a car enthusiast, he may be able to provide the make and model of the vehicle and possibly some further information about the performance characteristics of the vehicle. If he was not an enthusiast, then he may only be able to say that it was a sedan of a particular colour.

Even evidence from the same person will differ on different days, depending on how alert and generally well the person feels. In addition, a person will not always see what is available to them to be seen because the person might be distracted or preoccupied.

Clearly, there are numerous reasons a person might not give an accurate or complete description of something that he or she saw. For two persons to give identical evidence, it must be assumed that they have identical powers of observation, that they were equally alert and undistracted at the time of the observation, and that their ability to recollect is equally accurate. So even if we accept that two witnesses are both honestly giving their best recollection of what they saw, it is most likely that there will be differences, and those differences may be critical. The problem is how to discern which witness is accurate and reliable and which is not, and to do this, we usually have to rely on our knowledge and experience of the world.

If two of us hear divergent evidence from two witnesses, each of us might legitimately prefer a different version of the evidence, depending on our view of the reliability of the two witnesses. Neither of us could claim to be right. We simply make a choice based on our view of how the world works. Much of our assessment of evidence results in such a choice.

(iii) Circumstantial Evidence

Circumstantial evidence is the description given to a number of items of evidence which do not contain any items of direct evidence about the issue. An alternative description might be 'indirect evidence'. For example, if the issue was whether a man had stolen some money, the man himself may give direct evidence that he did not steal the money. The prosecution may then present evidence which shows that he had a motive to steal the money, say, gambling debts to violent people; that he had an opportunity to steal the money without being observed; that the money was known to be not stolen before he had his opportunity; that the money was missing after he had his opportunity; that he had paid his gambling debts after the money had been stolen; and that such payment was beyond his normal income. The totality of this circumstantial evidence may well enable the conclusion that the man did steal the money, in the absence of any acceptable explanation from him of the circumstantial evidence.

The problem with this type of evidence is that each individual item of circumstantial evidence is not strongly persuasive, because there are usually reasonable explanations or alternative views of what conclusions the evidence supports. In this example, suppose the man explains the circumstantial evidence as follows: he admits that he had a motive to steal the money (his gambling debts), but he says that so did many other people and that financial difficulty is not the only motive for theft. Many thefts occur out of greed or for other reasons. He admits that he had an opportunity to steal the money, but he says that so did several other persons. He admits that he paid his gambling debts after the money was known to be stolen, but he says that he paid this with other gambling winnings. These explanations would be plausible, especially if he can show that he did, in fact, have a gambling win big enough to pay his gambling debt. Thus, if he can provide some support for his explanations of the circumstantial evidence, then the proof of his guilt will not reach the standard of proof necessary to warrant a conviction of this crime.

Circumstantial evidence is often dependent on common knowledge or common human experience, and it is rarely conclusive. Even a person's fingerprints on a murder weapon do not prove that the person was holding the weapon at the time that it caused the death of the deceased, even if there were no other fingerprints on the murder weapon, because another person wearing gloves could have been the actual murderer.

Accordingly, it is appropriate to take into account alternative explanations of circumstantial evidence, with the proviso that the totality of some circumstantial evidence can be highly persuasive, especially in the absence of acceptable explanations.

(iv) <u>Documentary Evidence</u>

Documents are, by definition, things that were created to provide evidence of some fact. Documents can range in nature from contracts to wills and many other types in between.

The key aspect of a document is its authenticity. Most people are aware that if they sign a document, they are providing evidence that they affirm that the contents of the document are true and correct. That assumes that the person who signed a document read it in its entirety and fully understood every aspect of the document. That assumption is the law, and our society could not function if it were not (although in some legal communities, there is a requirement for additional evidence to support the assumption). But the assumption is not a practical reality. Many contracts, for example, are lengthy and complex, and they are expressed in complex terminology. It is probably fair to say that most people who sign a legally binding contract have not read it but rather relied on their lawyer to explain it to them in lay terms. However, lay terms are not always adequate to give a full understanding of all the implications of a contract. Accordingly, the first caution about documentary evidence is that a person's signature on a document does not necessarily mean that the person has fully read and understood the document before he or she signed it.

Another problem with signed documents is that signatures can be forged. This is common knowledge, and because it is common knowledge, persons who did actually sign a document are able to allege that their signature is a forgery, if they wish to avoid the consequences of having signed the document. Fortunately, scientific evidence as to the authenticity of a signature is very reliable in modern times, but it is not absolutely certain.

Another category of document that does not require any signature is the certificate type. This usually bears some sort of seal of authenticity and a stamped signature rather than an actual signature. These can also be forged. An example is the number of forged passports that were created during the war years.

The largest category of documents in existence is the normal business and administrative record. These can range in type from government census records to file notes of a telephone conversation or a carbon copy of a letter sent. Receipts, invoices, and all sorts of forms and papers kept on ordinary business files can be documentary evidence. Most of the documents in this category are not usually signed and are easily forged, but their authenticity is not usually challenged if they are shown to be the normal type of business record of the person who created the record.

Such documents can have substantial evidentiary value, especially financial records such as ledgers, journals, and accounts. Keeping such records is often required by law for taxation and other purposes. Mostly people keep such records for their own management purposes, because of the unreliability of human memory. Memory alone will not enable modern businesses to function efficiently. Indeed, business records were kept even in our earliest civilisations. Strangely enough, even criminals keep records of their criminal activities in relevant types of crimes, although such records are usually secret.

The main problem with this type of evidence is the accuracy of the document. For example, a file note of a telephone conversation contains only one side of the conversation, even if it purports to record all that was said. The file note may not have been made contemporaneously. It may omit things thought to be unimportant by the maker of the file note, or things may have been omitted because the conversation proceeded too rapidly to record fully. If recorded in handwriting, such writing may be illegible or ambiguous to someone else subsequently trying to determine what was said.

It is common knowledge that we humans do make mistakes, such as clerical and administrative errors. Then there are typographical errors and errors due to language or educational differences. Suffice it to say that there are many errors made in this type of document, and there always have been! In modern times, many records are created and maintained electronically on computers. But this has not completely solved the error problem, because computers still need input from human operators who can and do make errors. Computers themselves have been known to do some strange and unexpected things!

The type of document that is most relevant for our present purposes can be described as a historical document. This is not really a separate category, but rather, it is any of the above types of documents used to determine something that happened in history. Usually, this involves letters, government records, business records, legal documents, inscriptions on tombstones, and many other types of documents.

There are several problems with historical documents. Often such documents are old and therefore fragmentary and incomplete. That begs the question of the significance of what is missing and why it is missing. The answer to this is usually unknown. Secondly, it is often not known who created the document or what the reason is for its creation. Thirdly, it is difficult, if not impossible, to independently verify the accuracy of the document. Fourthly, the meaning of the contents of the document is often uncertain, because the meaning of words changes over the years because of cultural changes and developments. Fifthly, many historical documents are written in other languages and even ancient languages, and there is often disagreement as to the accuracy of a translation. Some historical documents have been translated through several different languages.

Historical documents are usually the only evidence available of what happened in the past. The forgoing observations make it clear that the reliability of such documents is subject to numerous difficulties and should only be accepted with caution, if at all. But this does not mean that we should abandon the effort to learn the lessons that history can teach us, or to reject as untrue those historical facts currently accepted to be most likely to be true by reputable authorities. In other words, the scholars who present what they believe to be the true meaning of historical documents are well aware of the abovementioned difficulties, and we should start by accepting their intelligence, diligence, and integrity.

(v) <u>Statistics</u>

Many people regard statistics as powerful and persuasive evidence. In fact, statistics are not usually evidence at all but rather are an a priori argument intended to indicate the probability of a conclusion to which those statistics relate. Statistics thus presented are usually in the form of a statistical analysis, which postulates a number of facts, applies some mathematical operators to those facts, and from the quotient of these operators, suggests the likelihood of some conclusion.

There are three major problems with statistical arguments. Firstly, the facts that are postulated are usually themselves conclusions based on unverified or dubious evidence. Secondly, even if the postulated facts are acceptable, the reality of our world is that the occurrence of phenomena is almost never as is suggested by statistics, except in processes involving very large numbers. Thirdly, statistics generally rely on the acceptability of 'similar fact' type of evidence. This type of evidence is generally unacceptable in our courts, and there is no good reason for us to incautiously accept such evidence in our consideration of religious issues.

Perhaps an example will assist in perceiving the benefit of statistics in relation to religious issues.

Simcha Jacobovici has written a book and made a DVD in which he argues that he has found the lost tomb of Jesus. There are a number of flaws in his argument, but it is not the present purpose to rebut the argument. However, in his argument, he does use statistics, and this usage is a good example. He states that a number of ossuaries (small coffins containing only the bones of a deceased person) were found in a tomb at Talpiot in Jerusalem. These ossuaries were made of stone and had names roughly carved on them. They were placed in family vaults, and the names were placed so that the relatives who later added ossuaries to the vault might know who was where in the vault. The names that were found on the ossuaries in the Talpiot tomb were Jesus, son of Joseph; Mariamne; Matia; Jose; and Maria. Simcha Jacobovici argues that these were the names of members of the family of Jesus and that one would expect to find these names in the tomb of Jesus. He then lists the frequency of these names occurring in that society at the time Jesus lived, which are as follows:

Jesus, son of Joseph	Frequency	1 in 190
Mariamne	Frequency	1 in 160
Matia	Frequency	1 in 40
Jose	Frequency	1 in 20
Maria	Frequency	1 in 4

He then argues (through a mathematician) that to calculate the probability that this is the tomb of Jesus, you must multiply all these frequencies together. This gives a probability of 1 in 97,280,000. He then eliminates Matia from the equation, reducing the frequency of the remaining names occurring in the same tomb to 1 in 2,400,000. He then divides this frequency by 4 to eliminate bias, reducing the frequency to 1 in 600,000, and then divides by 1,000 to allow for all first-century tombs. This reduces the frequency to 1 in 600. He then concludes that the probability that the Telpiot tomb is *not* the tomb of Jesus to be 1 in 600 *if* the name Mariamne can be linked to Mary Magdalene.

These statistics do not, in fact, *prove* anything. Their function is to suggest that the probability that the Telpiot tomb is the tomb of Jesus is high enough to persuade people that the conclusion is true. This is a legitimate function of statistics, but it is essential to examine the facts on which the statistics are based and to be satisfied that they are true and correct before the conclusion proposed by the statistics can be accepted. The questions raised by the statistics presented in this example are as follows:

(a) It is postulated that the names Jesus and Joseph were common names during the time of Jesus. Is the frequency of 1 in 190 of men named Joseph having a son named Jesus based on the actual number of men with these names, or is it based on an extrapolation from some sample that may or may not be random?

(b) It is postulated that the name Mariamne was uncommon at that time. Again, is the frequency of 1 in 160 of women called Mariamne based on the actual number of women with this name, or is it based on an extrapolation from some sample that may or may not be random? Her name was actually Mary, and she was from Magdala. The evidence that she was called Mariamne is unconvincing. There is no evidence that she was related to Jesus, so the reason for her being buried in the family tomb is dubious. The evidence that she died in or near Jerusalem is uncorroborated and therefore tenuous.

(c) Matia was suggested as being the brother of Jesus, and accordingly, it is reasonable to find his ossuary in this tomb. However, there is still doubt as to whether Jesus had any brothers or sisters, even though many scholars think that Jesus did have brothers and sisters. If Matia has been expelled from the equation because of doubt about his relationship to Jesus, then the presence of his ossuary in this tomb must be explained. It cannot simply be ignored because of the doubt about his status. And if he is expelled from the formula, why was he included in the first place, as it makes no difference to the quotient to include him and then to exclude him?

Again, is the frequency of 1 in 40 of men named Matia based on the actual number of men with this name, or is it based on an extrapolation from some sample that may or may not be random?

(d) Jose was a nickname for another of the alleged brothers of Jesus. Why is he included as such when Matia has been excluded as such? Why are the alleged other brothers and sisters not included? The bones of the other brothers and sisters were not found in the ossuaries found in this tomb. Since it was a family tomb, why were they not here? Again, is the frequency of 1 in 20 of men nicknamed Jose based on the actual number of men with this nickname, or is it based on an extrapolation from some sample that may or may not be random?

(e) The ossuary marked 'Mary' is believed to contain the bones of the mother of Jesus, and clearly, her presence in this tomb is most likely. Is the frequency of 1 in 4 of women named Mary based on the actual number of women with this name, or is it based on an extrapolation from some sample that may or may not be random?

There are several other questions that are raised by these statistics, and in fairness, it should be stated that some of these are addressed in other parts of the DVD. However, the point is that to be acceptable as persuasive, statistics must be based on provable facts, and such facts must be disclosed and proved in a proper presentation of the statistics.

There is also need to consider the accuracy of the calculations of statistics and the appropriateness of the mathematical approach and methodology. In this example, the calculations were substantially correct, although they were rounded. The actual final probability based on the frequencies given was 1 in 608. The methodology employed in this example leaves something to be desired, because it results in a negative conclusion, i.e. it is postulated that the Telpiot tomb is the tomb of Jesus and that with the names found on the ossuaries, the probability that it is *not* the tomb of Jesus is 1 in 600. A more persuasive approach would have been to postulate what one would reasonably expect to find in the tomb of Jesus, calculate the probability of other tombs containing the same things, and then state what has been found, pointing to those things that support the conclusion and explaining the absence of things that were expected to be found and how this affects the probability. This would lead to a positive conclusion rather than to a negative one.

The above example has made it clear that statistics do not actually prove anything and that they have merely suggestive or persuasive value. They can be helpful in the consideration of issues, but the factual basis of the statistics must be carefully examined, along with the mathematical processes applied and the accuracy of the calculations.

1.1.6 The Role of Faith and Knowledge

The word *faith* has many meanings, most of which we comprehend from the context in which the word is used. The word can be a noun, as in *Catholic faith* or *Islamic faith*. It can be used in a non-religious context, such as having faith in the fidelity of a spouse. The word is sometimes used as a synonym for the words *hope* or *confidence*, where for example, someone says 'Have some faith in me' to indicate that he or she intends to do something and has a reasonable expectation of being able to do the thing.

However, the principal use of the word is in the religious context. Fundamentally, it means believing in the truth of some fact or proposition without having *compelling* reasons to support that belief, coupled with a rejection of all arguments, known to the believer, contradicting the truth of the subject belief. That, subject to contextually obvious exceptions, is the sense in which the word is used herein.

As human beings on this planet for only a short time, our main concern is in the quest for truth about all things, as anything else is a waste of time. The issue here is the quest for truth about religious issues. Unfortunately, as is almost universally agreed, the quest for truth about religious issues is not discernible from compelling evidence, although there is plenty of persuasive evidence both for and against on such issues. Accordingly, we must resort to looking to a priori arguments as well.

Over the years, philosophers and theologians have produced a vast number of arguments and propositions about religious issues, the reasoning process, the nature of knowledge, and many other topics. Some of these arguments or propositions are simply implausible conjecture. It is beyond the scope of this work to review and evaluate all arguments and propositions related to religion, and consequently, it is necessary to set the parameters of what will be considered.

The fundamental parameter in a quest for truth is to consider only those arguments and propositions that have some basis in our reality. An example of an implausible conjecture is as follows: the world was created ten minutes ago, and everything that we remember from more than ten minutes ago is a false memory implanted by the Creator, who also gave all persons created consistent memories and created a world in which those memories appear to be of actual events.

Obviously, such an argument cannot be either proved or disproved. It may be entertaining to consider such an argument, but we cannot derive any truth from such consideration. The reality that is presupposed for the purposes of our consideration is the reality of the known world. To define this reality, we must firstly understand the nature of knowledge.

Philosophers tell us that there are three essential ingredients to knowledge, which are as follows:

1. The person claiming knowledge of something must genuinely believe that what he or she claims knowledge of is true.
2. The person claiming knowledge of something must have valid reasons for his or her belief.
3. The thing claimed knowledge of must actually be true.

The first of these essentials is entirely subjective. The genuineness of someone's belief in something cannot be known by another person, because only the person claiming the knowledge truly knows the genuineness of his or her belief, no matter how vehemently he or she may profess the belief. Of course, we have lie detectors, but these are only an indication and cannot give us knowledge. In other words, we cannot know the truth of another's belief, although we can know that about which the other person claims knowledge.

The second essential ingredient attempts to link the basis of belief with valid reasons for holding the belief. This means that if a person claims knowledge of something and then gives his or her reasons for holding the belief and those reasons can be shown to be invalid, that person's belief is reduced to something less than knowledge, even if there are other valid reasons supporting the belief which are unknown to the believer and even if the thing believed is actually true. In other words, one cannot *know* something for the wrong reasons, even if it is true.

The third essential ingredient is entirely objective and requires that the truth of the thing claimed to be known be demonstrably and absolutely true. Unfortunately, there are very few absolutes in our world; therefore, if we accept this requirement in the strictest sense, very little could actually be known, and our reality would be very limited indeed.

For anything useful to come from the concept of knowledge, we must apply common sense to the concept. We can know things through the perception of our senses, although most of us have had the experience of having our senses deceived or confused. For example, we know that yesterday the sun rose in the east and set in the west, because we saw it do so, assuming we did see it rising and setting and had a clear view. We do not know that the sun will rise tomorrow, although we have a reasonable expectation that it will do so. We know that our world is roughly spherical in shape. We have not been in space and seen this shape with our own eyes, but we have seen some of the vast amount of compelling evidence that supports this fact. It is not necessary for us to be aware of all the evidence that our world is spherical in shape to satisfy the second essential for knowledge, so long as what we do know is valid and sufficient to support the belief.

On the other hand, most of us have seen stage magicians do apparently impossible things. We believe that they are an illusion, but we cannot identify the means by which our senses were deceived. Illusions and deception of our senses also occur in ordinary life, sometimes just as a phenomenon, but it can also be a deliberate deception implemented by other persons for a variety of reasons.

With these considerations in mind, we may consider our reality as that which we genuinely believe to be real based on our perceptions with our senses and demonstrably sound a priori reasoning, with the proviso that there are few absolutes and that our senses could be misleading.

Of course, our reality is broader than the knowledge of any individual, and no human individual knows everything. Indeed, no two individuals possess exactly the same knowledge. But much of what we know is common to most people, so for the purposes of our consideration, our reality is that which is common knowledge to most people.

Faith, then, is not something that we can know. While the subject of our faith is something about which we can hold genuine beliefs and our reasons for those beliefs may be compelling and valid to us, those reasons are not universally regarded as valid or compelling. Consequently, those who do not find our reasons compelling or valid can and do assert that we do not know that what we believe is true. Of course, the subject of our beliefs can only be actually true or not true. But we see our faith as knowledge because we genuinely believe it to be true, because we have valid reasons to support the belief, and because it is actually true, although we cannot prove this. Because of the difficulty of proving this third essential, we cannot claim that our faith is knowledge. The farthest we can go is to claim that our faith is based on valid reasons.

A further complication is that our faith is proportional to the degree to which we are persuaded of the truth of our faith by our reasons, both evidentiary and a priori. Most of us have heard the phrase 'Ye men of little faith' in relation to Christ's description of the apostles at various times. This description clearly indicates that the strength or size of a person's faith depends on the degree to which the believer is satisfied that the subject of his beliefs is true. The apostles saw Christ work miracles, yet the degree of their belief that Christ was divine was apparently only to the degree of the balance of probabilities. Only Peter was game to try to walk on water; however, he began to sink, so obviously he retained some doubt, which indicates that his belief was, at most, to the degree of comfortable satisfaction.

In our time, we cannot base our faith on direct personal observation of the works of Jesus. Very few miracles have occurred in our time; even those that have occurred are dismissed as unexplained phenomena, and their attribution to God is challenged. But our faith is not therefore necessarily weaker than that of the apostles. We have the benefit of the testimony of the Gospels and the refinement of Christian theology over the past 2,000 years by some very great minds indeed.

Accordingly, it may well be easier for us to have a strong faith, based on a belief to the degree of beyond reasonable doubt, than it was for the apostles. But faith to this degree must countenance and dismiss all substantial counterarguments; otherwise, it may well fail when confronted by such counterarguments. The major counterarguments are considered later herein, but greater strength of belief may be obtainable from an examination of the positive reasons for faith in various issues, which are also considered later herein.

In the Gospels, there is reference to 'having no doubt'. This degree is necessary to enable miracles. We must believe that this degree of faith is possible, because Jesus said so, but for most of us, this degree of faith is as unreachable as believing that we can walk on water. It is not the purpose of this work to encourage miraculous faith; rather, it is to preserve and strengthen the faith that we already have in the face of reasonably arguable doubts.

1.1.7 The Primary Assumption

The primary assumption that underlies our consideration is that we all have an immortal soul. We do not know the precise nature of our souls, but from evidence, research, and the thinking of many great minds, we can glimpse its nature. The basic insight comes from a consideration of how our bodies work.

Our bodies are organic matter, specifically flesh, blood, bones, and organs. Our brains are organs of our bodies, which have two principal aspects: conscious and subconscious. The subconscious part of our brain keeps our bodies alive and functioning. It does this by sending electric signals along our nervous system to the heart to keep pumping, our lungs to keep breathing, and all the other organs to perform their respective functions. It also stimulates the movement of our bodies in response to instructions from the conscious aspect of our brains, which our conscious aspect perceives as the exercise of our will to move. Our bodies also have sensory organs, which respond to stimuli. Some of these stimuli are external, and some are internal. These organs, when stimulated, transmit a signal to our brains about the nature and extent of the stimulation registered, and the subconscious part of the brain then processes this information and responds in some way.

The conscious aspect of the brain is difficult to explain. An easy explanation is that if you are reading this, then you are conscious, and you know what that is. More informatively, our consciousness appears to be the functioning of a dedicated part of our brain. Part of the function of this part of the brain is to receive signals from the subconscious part of the brain as to the nature and extent of the stimulation of our sensory organs. Thus, our brains can make sense of external stimuli, like sights and sounds, and registers internal stimuli, such as pain from our various nerves. Our consciousness also contains what we call our intelligence, with which we determine how to respond to the signals from our subconscious, although our subconscious brain clearly functions in an intelligent and organised way.

It appears that the subconscious part of the brain records every sensory stimulation and response and also the thoughts of the conscious part of the brain. These are stored in some sort of archive in the subconscious part of the brain. It is not clear whether the subconscious has a process which cleans out the trivia from this archive or whether our brains have the capacity to store a lifetime of sensory data and thoughts. What we do know is that there are some things that we do not remember, even if reminded of them. This archive we call memory, and we know that the conscious aspect of the brain can recall some of the data stored in its memory if it has been flagged by the conscious part in some way. Things that have been forgotten may have been deleted or cleaned out of the brain by the removal of the cells holding this data in the body's process of metabolism. Regression hypnosis suggests that the primary memory remains intact for life. Sleep appears to be a reduction of the activity of the conscious part of the brain to a standby mode, which is apparently periodically necessary for the continued healthy functioning of the entire body.

There is much more to it than this, but for our purposes, this functional outline is sufficient.

Some philosophers have proposed that we are the sum of our memories. No doubt the sum of our memories is a substantial part of what we are, but memory alone lacks the completeness to be called a soul. In addition to memory, we have intelligence in the conscious aspect of our brains. This enables us to respond to the life situations that we encounter daily. In dealing with these situations, we often refer to our memory, which can indicate whether we should respond similarly to our response on the previous occasion that we encountered such a situation or whether we should respond differently, to avoid making the same mistake. In situations that we have not encountered previously, where memory cannot assist us, we use our ability to reason to determine our response. And if reason cannot assist us in making a decision, then we have the ability to choose at random or in accordance with some emotional preference or intuition.

Perhaps the word *personality* is a near synonym for *soul*. We attribute a broad range of attributes to a person's personality, such as courage, frugality, cheerfulness, humorousness, dourness, etc. We often describe other persons by reference to a dominant or notable aspect of their personality, such as good-natured, generous, volatile, etc. All these characteristics and many others may be displayed. Having consistently displayed a particular characteristic, a person is then attributed with having this type of personality and may even be described as having a soul of that type. No doubt many of us have heard a person described as 'a cheerful soul' or suchlike.

So far, what has been described is common to most animals as well as to humans. Those of us who have owned a pet can confirm that animals sleep and dream, that they have consciousness and memory, that they have sufficient cognitive ability to consistently recognise us and things familiar to them, and that they have sufficient intelligence to remember and correctly respond to their training and conditioning. Animals also have personality attributes, such as courage, as is exhibited by animals defending their young against stronger predators. But the level of intelligence of animals appears to be an order of magnitude lower than that of humans, in that they lack the ability to reason logically in situations where there are several options for a response. They appear to respond in accordance with their conditioning or instinct. In any event, it is clear that animals do have individual personalities.

It is almost universally agreed that we humans do each have a soul, as do most animals. Most people accept that the soul of an animal is mortal—that when the animal dies, its soul ceases to exist in any form. What is not universally agreed on is that the human soul is immortal—that is, that it survives the death of the host body and continues to exist in a spiritual and conscious form.

The primary assumption for our purposes is that the human soul is immortal. If our souls were merely mortal, then the existence of God and the Divinity of Christ would be irrelevant and the consideration of the issues herein a waste of time. Accordingly, the primary assumption necessarily underlies these considerations.

It is called an assumption because there is neither compelling evidence nor any a priori reason to compel the conclusion of fact that our souls are immortal. But that does not mean that there is no evidence or reason to support this proposition.

The evidence for the existence of spiritual beings, including human souls, has been extensively documented in the literature of the occult. Much of this can be dismissed as the work of charlatans or deluded persons, but there remain some testimonies which are unexplained or not adequately refuted. Personal encounters with spiritual beings are outside the experience of most of us, so we must necessarily assess the truthfulness and reliability of those who claim to have had such encounters.

One witness who we may consider reliable is Jesus himself. It is implied in the life, teachings, and death of Jesus that our souls are immortal. The objection to this view is that it is flawed. Those who do not already believe in the divinity of Jesus must necessarily believe that he was a charlatan or that he was deluded, because Jesus himself clearly asserted that he was divine. Thus, those who do not accept the divinity of Jesus say that nothing Jesus said is trustworthy or reliable, and accordingly, they dismiss his testimony as to the immortality of the human soul. They argue that an assumption based on another assumption does not avail acceptable evidence and that you must first prove the divinity of Jesus before his testimony can be acceptable. The divinity of Jesus is dealt with elsewhere in this work, and as with such issues, there is no compelling evidence to support it. But as will be seen, there is ample evidence to support a very strong belief in the divinity of Jesus, and if this view is accepted, then the view that the human soul is immortal can be held with equal conviction.

Logically, there is no valid reason or argument to support the view that our souls are immortal. But logic can assist us with the following set of premises:

If our souls are not immortal, then we should live our lives accordingly. If our souls are immortal, then we should live our lives accordingly.

If our souls are not immortal, then we have no reason to live our lives in accordance with God's commandments in the hope of eternal salvation. If our souls are immortal, then we have a reason to live our lives in accordance with God's commandments in the hope of eternal salvation, because that salvation is conditional on obedience to God's commandments.

Living our lives as if our souls are not immortal gains very little, if anything, over living our lives as if our souls are immortal, and risks eternal damnation.

Living our lives as if our souls are immortal loses little, if anything, over living our lives as if our souls are not immortal, and potentially offers the chance of eternal happiness.

Because the evidence is not compelling, what we believe on this issue must be our choice, based on the degree to which we are satisfied either way. What appears to be most persuasive is the risk factor. Why gamble with something that may be more important than life itself for no significant gain?

1.1.8 Overview

It is important to carefully consider religious issues, because the conclusions that we reach after such considerations will be significant factors in many, if not most, of the moral decisions that we make in our lives. It is also important because if we have immortal souls—i.e. there is some form of existence for us after death—then how we live our lives must impact the nature of our post-death existence, and to be aware of this impact, we must form a view about the fundamental religious issues.

Each of us is responsible for our own decisions. We cannot excuse a wrong or poor decision by saying that we acted on the advice or opinion of someone whose intelligence and integrity we respect. This principle is analogously illustrated when we drive a motor vehicle. The driver must know the relevant laws and must drive in accordance with these laws. The driver must disregard any urging from any passenger to drive otherwise than in accordance with these laws, including instructions to travel in some direction if going in that direction involves some dangerous or unsafe manoeuver. But a driver may heed a warning from a passenger of some danger or fact relevant to safe driving that assists the driver, especially if the driver was unaware of it. Ignorance of the law is no excuse. In the same way, ignorance of the fundamentals of religious issues is no excuse, as it makes no sense to prefer the advice or opinion of another in relation to decisions about our own souls, for which we alone are responsible.

To make decisions which do involve our view on religious issues, it is not necessary that we become expert theologians, just as it is not necessary to become an expert in motor vehicle law in order to drive a car. All that the law requires to drive a car is that we have a fundamental grasp of the rules, combined with an attitude that gives priority to the safety of all road users, including ourselves and our passengers. Similarly, with religious issues, all we need is a fundamental grasp of the main issues, combined with an attitude that gives priority to implementing our beliefs accordingly.

The mental tools outlined in this chapter are far from comprehensive, but a comprehensive knowledge of these tools is not necessary to carefully consider religious issues. We all have natural intelligence to an average or competent degree and, at least in our modern Western society, a very high degree of literacy and education, which is expanding almost exponentially with technological advances. The tools outlined herein come from the disciplines of theology, philosophy, and law, and they may not be familiar to laymen to these disciplines. Nor is it necessary to give close study and learning to acquire skill with these tools. All that is necessary is that we be generally aware of them when considering religious issues and that we ask ourselves some key questions in our considerations. These key questions will then remind us of the tools appropriate to properly consider the issues.

Most of the religious issues that we encounter are supported by evidence. There are some issues that are essentially analytic or a priori arguments, but even these have a fundamental evidentiary base, generally some axiom. An example is the argument that nothing can happen without a cause. This axiom is based on the whole experience where nothing has ever been observed to happen without a cause, although sometimes the cause is unknown.

In arguments and issues based principally on evidence, careful consideration requires that we assess the evidence. The key questions in such an assessment are as follows:

- What fact does the evidence primarily suggest?
- Is the evidence compelling, or does it allow for alternative explanations or facts?
- Is the evidence truthfully given?
- Is the evidence reliable?
- What is the probative value of the evidence as against alternative explanations or facts and contradictory evidence?

An example may assist to illustrate how these questions may function. This example comes from the story of a gunfight in the old American West. Suppose that there is a witness to the gunfight who gives the following evidence:

> RS was a peaceful man who came to town to settle and open a business. He had negligible gunfighting skills. LV was a gunfighter who lived near the town, and he had a high level of gunfighting skills. LV provoked RS into having a gunfight, which RS accepted in circumstances indicating great courage on the part of RS. They faced each other at night outside the town saloon. RS came carrying his gun in his right hand. LV drew his gun and shot RS

in the right arm, causing RS to drop the gun. RS picked up his gun with his left hand, and when the men were about forty feet apart, both fired at each other. LV fell down and died from a bullet to the heart. RS was not further injured.

The issue is whether RS shot and killed LV. Let us now apply the key questions to our assessment of this evidence.

- What fact does the evidence primarily suggest?
  The primary conclusion that can be drawn from this evidence is that RS shot and killed LV.

- Is the evidence compelling, or does it allow for alternative explanations or facts?
  Here we have an eyewitness account. The evidence is strongly persuasive if the evidence is truthful and reliable. However, it is possible that there was another person in the shadows that night, unseen by the witness, who shot and killed LV. There is no evidence that this did happen, as there was no autopsy or ballistic evidence in those days. Thus, this evidence cannot be regarded as compelling or conclusive, although it is certainly most likely.

- Is the evidence truthfully given?
  This witness was not a friend of RS or LV. He was simply a bystander who witnessed the gunfight. He has no apparent motive to lie about what he saw, and what he says he saw is not contentious. In these circumstances, we can accept this evidence as truthfully given.

- Is the evidence reliable?
  The gunfight occurred at night, but there was enough light coming from the saloon to identify both RS and LV. The fact that RS was uninjured after LV fired at him the second time suggests that RS fired fractionally before LV; otherwise, RS would also have been shot a second time, having regard

to LV's superior gunfighting skills. So the evidence that they both fired at the same time is not completely reliable, but in the circumstances, it is acceptable. The witness does not say that there was no one in the shadows and cannot reliably say that. The evidence does not become unreliable merely because it is not comprehensive. This evidence may be accepted as reliable.

- What is the probative value of the evidence as against alternative explanations or facts and contradictory evidence?

  The relative gunfighting skills of RS and LV make the outcome that occurred most surprising. There is the possibility that someone other than RS shot and killed LV by firing from the shadows at about the same time that RS fired at LV, but there is no evidence to suggest that this is what occurred. Since there is neither reasonable alternative explanation of what happened nor any evidence to contradict the account of the witness, the probative value of this evidence can be regarded as highly persuasive.

  On the evidence, it appears that RS shot and killed LV in a gunfight in circumstances that would not suggest that the action by RS was criminal. This example comes from the story 'The Man Who Shot Liberty Valance'. The movie of this name starred James Stewart and John Wayne. If you want to know what really happened, you should watch the movie if you have not already seen it.

As seen from the above example, the ultimate issue is what the evidence proves. This is not an objective criterion, because 'what the evidence proves' really means the degree to which it satisfies any individual considering the evidence. In the example, if RS were being tried for the wrongful killing of LV, most of us would be satisfied beyond reasonable doubt that RS did, in fact, shoot and kill LV. There may well be some doubt as to whether the killing was wrongful, but there would be little doubt about the facts.

The point is that the important thing in assessing evidence is to identify the limits of what the evidence is capable of proving. In our example, the evidence was not capable of proving that there was no one in the shadows and that such person may have shot LV, even though we are satisfied beyond reasonable doubt that RS shot LV. Unexplained occurrences, coincidences, or substantial gaps in the evidence should arouse our suspicions and accordingly stimulate caution in assessing evidence, even if these things appear to be unimportant or irrelevant.

1.2 Background Issues

1.2.1 The Nature of God

Over the years, much has been written and said about the nature of God. The principal issues have been to identify God's attributes from known human attributes and to perceive the extent of those attributes. The first difficulty with these objectives is that God may have attributes not found in or known to human nature or attributes that are inconceivable to human intelligence. A second difficulty is that at least some of God's attributes are thought to be infinite, while others are thought to be perfect. It is logically impossible for a finite being like a human being to completely perceive something infinite. The best we can do is have a fuzzy concept of what the word *infinite* means. Nor can we fully perceive God's perfect attributes like perfect justice without applying that justice to every possible relevant situation, especially if the number of relevant situations is infinite.

Needless to say that it is impossible to define God, as to define means to specify the limits of the thing defined. It is not surprising, therefore, that despite the vast amount that has been said and written about the nature of God, there has been little consensus or agreement as to the nature and extent of God's attributes. This may lead some to the view that a consideration of the nature and extent of God's attributes is futile and not worthwhile. However, if one wishes to consider the threshold question of existence of God, one must have some clear, albeit limited, concept of the attributes of God that are fundamental to his existence. Of course, if one already believes in the existence of God, then a consideration of his attributes is still worthwhile as a devotional exercise.

Every person may well have a different concept of God's attributes, and in private meditation or consideration, this is acceptable. However, if this issue is to be discussed with others, then there must be some consensus about the concept being discussed and considered; otherwise, the entire discussion is at cross purposes and therefore meaningless.

It is well beyond the scope of this work to identify even the limited version of God's attributes. One of the big questions that most of us ask ourselves at some time during our lives is 'What is the purpose or meaning of life?' To answer this question, we need to know how we came to be on this planet. This leads to the question of 'Who created us, and why?' As Catholics, our answer to this question is *'God created all that is, both seen and unseen'*. The existence of God necessarily underlies this belief. Accordingly, we can use this attribute of God as the Creator of all that is, both seen and unseen, to consider the issue of the existence of God. Our consideration can focus on the issues of whether God has the ability to create all that is, that God was motivated to create all that is, and that God did actually create all that is. This consideration may also assist in illuminating our answer to the big question referred to above.

This very minimalist formulation of God's nature is all that is necessary to consider the question of God's existence. To avoid confusion and cross purposes, it is necessary to limit our consideration to these parameters and to be careful not to allow the parameters to include other attributes about which there is no conceptual consensus. However, even the specified parameters have implications that should be identified before proceeding.

God's ability to create all that is implies that God has the intelligence to create all that is. We human beings have intelligence, which has led to a vast body of rules and information that is our science. But we have never been able to create life from lifeless materials. If God exists and he created life, then God's intelligence and science is vastly superior to ours. This raises the question of whether any of our science is valid, because some would argue that if God can create all that is, then God can do anything, including things contrary to our known scientific principles.

This is obviously a paradox, and while it may be entertaining to consider questions such as whether God can create a rock that is so heavy that even he cannot lift it, it is not productive in our serious consideration. For the purposes of our consideration, we must accept that some of our intelligence and science is equally valid in God's intelligence and science, since God created our science, with the proviso that some of our intelligence and science may be invalid in God's intelligence and science because the development of our science in these areas is incomplete. For example, we have our rules of logic. No doubt our basic syllogism is as valid to God as it is to us. But we cannot, and do not, always use the rules of logic to test the validity of lengthy and complex arguments. For this, we rely on an intuitive logic, which has often proven to be erroneous. But there may well be more advanced rules of logic known to God which we have not yet discovered. In other words, we accept that God can do all that is possible to do, even though we do not know all that is possible to do, and we reject the proposition that God can do self-contradictory things, which are just mind games.

In addition to having the intelligence to create all that is, God must also have the power to create all that is. Science tells us that matter can be converted into energy, so presumably, energy can be converted into matter. One of the aspects of God's nature that is almost universally agreed on is that God is a spiritual being. We do not really understand what this means. The nearest example that we have is our conscious minds. Each of us know that we have a mind and that this mind is not a physical part of our brain. We do not know what happens to our mind when we sleep or when we die. In science fiction and the occult, there is the concept of mind over matter, although how this is supposed to work is a mystery to us.

Our concept then is that God is a being like our own minds but vastly more intelligent and having complete control over matter and energy. We do not know where the matter or energy comes from, nor do we understand how God's power of mind over matter/energy works. Our ignorance of these things may be due to the limitations of human intellect or due to the possibility that our science has not yet discovered the answers to these questions. If either of these explanations is correct, then we cannot reject the existence of God just because we cannot understand how God's power of creation works. This is in accord with the fundamental concept that God is above human nature and understanding. Accordingly, we can accept that God, to be God, must have the ability to create all that is, even though this power seems like magic to us now. Most of us find it hard to believe in magic, but it may help to remember that our present technology would undoubtedly seem like magic to early mankind; we can only speculate as to where our technology will lead us.

The second parameter of this issue is that God was motivated to create all that is, including mankind. We see ourselves as the pinnacle of life on this planet and believe that we alone on this planet have the ability to worship God. Some people argue that if God exists, he needs worshippers, and that God created us because he needs us to serve this function. If God is truly God, then he is infinite in self-sufficiency and therefore does not need us. Accordingly, God's need cannot be God's motivation for creating us.

Another argument is that God wanted companionship, so he created us. The response to this is that God may have created the angels for companionship. Our mythology of angels is that they are spiritual beings, extremely powerful but not infinite. Some of the angels refused to worship God and were banished from his presence. One might expect that this was a disappointment to God. If it was, why would he then create creatures less intelligent than angels and far more wilful and contrary?

The question is, why did God create us on this relatively insignificant planet in this vast universe? In fact, our science does not yet know whether there is intelligent life in the universe other than ourselves. Nor has God, if he exists, revealed this to us. Perhaps this is none of our concern. God has not revealed to us why he created us, so we can only speculate as to his reasons. But he has revealed, by word and action, that he loves us.

One speculation as to God's reason for creating us flows from this. It may be that God created us because he wanted someone to love. God knew that love is naturally reciprocated but that love that is not freely given is not true love and is therefore worthless. In his wisdom then, he created us with insufficient intelligence to be able to prove his existence, but in a situation and environment where we could freely accept or reject it. If we accept his existence, then we love him. Love of God by a lower order of being necessarily entails worship of God. So if we love God, then we are acceptable companions for God, although that acceptability is a function of God's love for us, since we, as a lower order of being, can never be worthy companions for God in our own right.

This may not be God's reason, but it appears to be reasonable to us. It does not answer our big question with any degree of proof, but it is an answer that is capable of acceptance by us.

The third parameter of this issue is that God did actually create all that is. Obviously, we are here, and we exist. The question is whether God caused us to exist or whether there is some other cause of our existence. This is the question that this section of this work will seek to explore, but before we can consider the arguments for and against the existence of God, there are a couple of additional parameters that require identification.

1.2.2 The Function of Science

Some people say that they will not believe anything unless they are given scientific proof that the proposition is true. This attitude has a lot to commend it, because what they are really saying is that they will only believe that which can be shown to be true.

Making truth a prerequisite for belief is what we are seeking in considering religious issues, and naturally, we accept scientific proof in our considerations.

However, there are a number of qualifications that we should take into account when considering scientific proofs.

The first qualification is the very nature of science. Essentially, science is knowledge about our world and how things work. It is defined as *'the systematic study of nature and the behaviour of the material and physical universe, based on observation, experiment and measurement'*. From this definition, it is clear that science is not concerned with the study of the spiritual universe. That does not mean that the spiritual universe does not exist; it merely means that science does not address spiritual issues. Yet some people reject belief in the spiritual universe simply because there is no scientific proof of its existence.

In most of our arguments and reasoning on religious issues, our observations of the material world are essential to the validity of our argument, and in this way, we use and rely on science. Even our purely analytic or a priori arguments rely on real-world phenomena, such as cause and effect. But our arguments and reasoning go beyond the physical universe, and accordingly, the qualification is that we should not limit our considerations to the physical universe.

The second qualification is that many of the so-called scientific proofs are not compelling. A scientific method starts with the formulation of a hypothesis or theory based on observations, followed by the design of experiments to test the hypothesis, and then the implementation of the experiments. The results of the experiments are then analysed, and from this, an argument is formulated to prove or disprove the hypothesis. One of the essentials of a valid scientific method is that the experiments conducted are repeatable and will produce similar or supporting results. If the hypothesis is sufficiently supported by the experimental results and these results provide a rational explanation of what actually happens and all possible alternative explanations are disproved, then the hypothesis becomes a scientific principle or fact.

There are many scientific principles and facts, and we should recognise the contribution of those who discovered them. Unfortunately, there are some areas of the physical universe that are not amenable to scientific proofs, and in these areas, the best that science can do is formulate a hypothesis or theory supported by limited experimental data and the absence of disproof of all alternative explanations of the phenomenon. For example, the Big Bang theory is accepted as probably correct by many scientists, but it can never be more than a theory, because it occurred (if it occurred) 13.7 billion years ago and there is no direct evidence available to prove that this is how it happened. The same applies to scientific theories about the origin of our planet, the formation of life on our planet, and the theory of evolution. The qualification then is that if a proposition or argument can rely, at best, on what is only a scientific theory, it cannot be regarded as necessarily true and correct.

The third qualification is referred to as undiscovered scientific knowledge. A hundred years ago, some people said that there was nothing left to be discovered by science. We all know how wrong they were, to the point where some people now say that nothing is impossible and that someday we will discover how to do anything that we can imagine. The truth lies somewhere in between. No doubt there is much left to be discovered by science, but we do know enough from what we accept as scientific truths that some things, such as wormholes in space, are impossible, despite some theories of the contrary. Currently, such concepts and theories are literary devices intended to suspend disbelief to support the storyline, and we can safely regard them as such until there is a reputable theory or hypothesis to support the existence of such phenomena.

The experience over the last hundred years has shown that many scientific proofs and principles have been overturned. Many things that were previously thought to be impossible are now commonplace—for example, mobile telephones. Logically, that should instil some apprehension about the reliability and stability of scientific knowledge. But the opposite appears to be the more common attitude. Many people accept current scientific knowledge as the apex of knowledge about our physical universe, subject to ongoing technological development but with more significant scientific discoveries relegated to the distant irrelevant future. However, science is not limited to nuclear physics and cosmology. There is science in archaeology, geology, biology, and many other areas of human existence. Imminent discoveries in any of these fields may well substantially change our present knowledge in these areas, and some of these changes may be relevant to the consideration of religious issues.

The qualification then is that if something relevant to a religious issue is regarded as merely a theory, then it should not be unquestioningly accepted, and that even if that something is regarded as a scientific fact or principle, we should remain mindful of the possibility that science itself may change or disprove that principle or fact through further research and discovery.

The fourth qualification relates to the human nature of scientists. We are all fallible human beings, and scientists are no exception. We should assume that scientists are intelligent persons, highly educated in their field of expertise and having intellectual honesty and integrity. Given these attributes, they should be highly respected and regarded as an asset to their community. But being human, they can and do make mistakes. Of course, they do check their work thoroughly, but like the rest of us, they can have blind spots because of their investment of time and effort to prove something that they already believe. And scientists also have their own agendas. Sometimes funding tempts them to overstate their case, and media reports of such overstatements can mislead us. Sometimes professional kudos tempts them to go public with an incomplete study, and again, this can be misleading.

Of more concern is the highly respected scientist who publicly pronounces on religious issues and purports to use his or her scientific knowledge to support their religious views. Of course, everyone is entitled to express their views on religious issues, but eminent scientists should be careful to make it clear that they are expressing personal views and not the views of the scientific community in their respective field. They should also state their qualifications, if any, to speak or write on religious issues. Provided the scientist has attended to these requirements, we should consider the substance of what he or she says, along with a consideration of the scientist's reputation and personal agenda, if that is necessary, to assess the validity of the scientist's views.

The qualification then is that we should not accept what any scientist says as true and correct merely because it comes from a reputable scientist. Rather, we should carefully consider the issue in question in the light of the scientist's views, which we may expect to be lucidly expressed.

The fifth qualification is the use of mathematics. Many scientific theories and hypotheses are expressed and supported by university-level mathematics, as are most of our scientific principles and our computer and electronic technology. We know that our scientific principles are true and correct and also that our electronic technology works, so we can safely assume that the mathematics underlying these areas of knowledge is correct, even if we do not understand the mathematics.

Mathematics is nothing more or less than a priori quantitative analysis. The symbols used in mathematics are simply shorthand for ordinary language. There are basically two types of symbols used. The first type represents quantities, and these are our numbers. Numbers can be known quantities, such as any number that we can imagine. Numbers can also be expressed in complex form, such as a power or other expression that is the simplest form of expressing a very large or complex number. The quantities that numbers represent can also be unknown quantities, which are represented by non-numerical symbols that have been defined to represent such quantities as in, for example, algebraic notation.

The second type of symbol is the function or process symbol. These symbols indicate some manipulation of numeric quantities which produces some further numeric quantity that is either an answer or a quantity that may be further processed to ultimately lead to the answer being sought.

In modern times, we use the Arabic system of numbering (i.e. the symbols *1, 2, 3,* etc.) to express quantities, and we generally use alphabetic symbols to represent unknown quantities, such as *x, y, z,* etc. Our function or process symbols are basically non-alphabetic graphics, such as + (plus), – (minus), × (multiply), and ÷ (divide). More complex functions use uniquely designed symbols which are specifically defined and are often symbols from the Greek alphabet or symbols in common use in the respective field of science.

Most scientific theories and hypotheses are about finding some quantity (the measurement component of the scientific method). Over the years, our brilliant mathematicians have developed the concept of the formula, which is usually reduced to an equation in which the sought quantity is on one side of the equation and the other side is the process of known and unknown quantities as defined. The simplest example of this development is $e = mc^2$. Citing this example is not intended to suggest that this formula is correct or valid, as it is still only the distillation of a theory.

With this concept of mathematics, we can assess the role and value of mathematics as persuasive elements in a theory or hypothesis. The first aspect of this is that mathematics is an appropriate means of presenting any argument involving quantitative analysis. The second aspect is that the use of symbols representing quantities and processes is also appropriate because using the full verbal definition of quantities and processes in each instance would be extremely cumbersome and confusing, to the point of being unintelligible and potentially misleading.

With these two points in support of the way that mathematics is currently used in arguments, we can reconsider the main objection to the use of mathematics in arguments. The axiomatic proposition is that if we do not understand an argument, then either we lack the intelligence to understand the argument or the argument is defective in form and substance. In either case, we cannot accept the validity of the theory or hypothesis that the argument proposes, because we cannot, in logic and good conscience, accept as true and correct any argument that we do not fully understand.

We must acknowledge that scientists and mathematicians are intelligent persons who are highly educated in their respective fields. Some of them even have genius in their respective fields. But we should not concede that we as laypersons to a particular field of science lack the intelligence to understand scientific argument if it is presented in a form that is comprehensible to an intelligent layperson. Nor is it proper for a scientist to present his or her arguments to a layperson in technical terms with the expectation that his or her argument is acceptable in that form. That is tantamount to the scientist saying 'Trust me, I'm a scientist'. That is no more acceptable than the generally unaccepted aphorism 'Trust me, I'm a lawyer!'

Scientists must and do present their arguments in technical terms in their respective fields, in the various specialist journals of their field and at conventions and other meetings of scientists in the same discipline. Such presentations are intended for persons who have the education to understand the arguments and are familiar with the jargon and commonly used symbols in that discipline. Such presentations are often used as a sounding board to test and further develop some theory or hypothesis, and this is an appropriate format. But it is not an appropriate format to obtain general support or acceptance of a theory or hypothesis from the general population. The general population requires a comprehensible presentation in lay terms, without the use of higher mathematics or jargon. This may require considerable linguistic skill on the part of the scientist, which may be beyond some scientists, but arcane theories are simply not otherwise generally acceptable.

Our conclusion then is that while mathematics is a useful, valuable, and in certain situations, appropriate component of arguments, we must be mindful that there is potential for error in mathematics, that quantitative analysis may not always be an appropriate or valid aspect of proof, that scientists do have their own agendas, and that incomprehensible arguments cannot be accepted.

1.2.3 Scientific Evidence versus Faith

As has already been considered, there are a number of qualifications to be borne in mind in assessing the validity of scientific evidence or proofs. However, even persons who claim to abide strictly by the philosophy of non-belief in the absence of scientific proof do not apply their philosophy consistently. For example, most people believe that modern technology such as motor vehicles and computers work, without knowing the scientific principles underlying this technology. Instead, they rely on their own observations of the validity of this technology, which falls far short of proper scientific proof. In answer to this apparent inconsistency, these people say that the evidence of their own senses is acceptable scientific proof, sufficient to sustain a personal belief. But as has also been considered, human senses are capable of being deceived or in error.

In relation to the subject of this work, the attitude becomes a refusal to believe in the spiritual universe because there is no proper scientific proof or sensory evidence of the existence of the spiritual universe. The holders of this attitude are also unmoved by the observation that neither is there any proper scientific evidence or sensory evidence that the spiritual universe does not exist.

When we encounter this attitude or are tempted to adopt it, we must consider its validity. This consideration raises two main questions. Firstly, can scientific knowledge of the physical universe prove the existence of any part or aspect of the spiritual universe? Secondly, can the tenets of religious belief or faith prove or explain some otherwise inexplicable manifestations in the physical universe, thereby proving their own existence?

In relation to the first question, we can recall that scientific knowledge, as we have defined it, comes from observation, experimentation, and measurement of parts of the physical universe. Science is a search for truth about the physical universe, with much science being incapable of ever being more than theoretical or hypothetical. Furthermore, the spiritual universe does not respond to physical stimuli; consequently, the scientific method of observation, experimentation, and measurement is an inappropriate means of seeking knowledge about the spiritual universe. Indeed, one of the tenets of our faith is that experimentation is proscribed in that we are forbidden to put the Lord our God to the test!

Accordingly, we can form the view that the truths of science and the scientific method cannot assist us in discovering religious truths. That appears to be correct, at least in relation to a posteriori considerations. However, there are also a priori considerations.

In a priori considerations we deal with the very existence of the physical universe, its complexity, its origin, and its size. Obviously, this involves observations of the physical universe and how it works. Through the process of reason, we draw certain conclusions. Many of the arguments considered in this work come from this process, although, as will be seen, they do not provide compelling proof of the existence of the spiritual universe, nor can they be regarded as proper scientific proofs.

The second question is more readily answered. Put another way, this question is whether miracles or paranormal manifestations are real. Obviously, the Catholic Church believes in miracles and is prepared to canonise persons on evidence that they somehow caused the miracles to happen. Of course, it deals with the evidence of miracles with great caution and scepticism, but there are nevertheless many saints. The problem with evidence of miracles is that it is vulnerable to the argument that the miraculous occurrence is explainable by natural phenomena of the physical universe, the evidence of which was not available to the investigators or the science of which has simply not been discovered yet. On occasion, some sceptical persons have proposed completely preposterous explanations of miracles, and these only support the spiritual explanation.

As to other paranormal manifestations, such as ghosts, demons, angels, demonic possession, levitation, telepathy, telekinesis, etc., most of the evidence to date is unreliable. Even where the evidence is reliable, the objection of undiscovered science cannot be dismissed.

Perhaps the most common argument against the existence of the spiritual universe is the assertion that science has already disproved many of the tenets of the various religions, particularly Catholicism.

It is true that modern science provides compelling proof that some of the assertions in the Bible, particularly in the book of Genesis, are incorrect. A later section of this work deals at some length with the question of the authenticity of the Bible; however, in relation to the present issue, it is sufficient to concede that God did not make the world as set out in the book of Genesis, nor is the universe as described in that book. But this does not concede that God did not make the physical universe, including our world. In other words, we can still believe the fundamental proposition that God did create all that is seen and unseen (although we do not know how God did this) even though the account in Genesis is unacceptable.

Much of the Old Testament is the history of the Jewish people. Some parts are laws and ordinances said to be imposed by God on the Jewish people; other parts are genealogies, parables and fables, devotional prose and verse, and general teachings. In fact, very little of the Old Testament is open to disproof by modern science, because of the nature of the subject matter. However, the Old Testament does contain many accounts of paranormal events, particularly manifestations of God, the longevity of some of the persons mentioned, the crossing of the sea mentioned in the book of Exodus, etc. These events are still regarded as miraculous and beyond acceptance as natural occurrences, and although some scientists have proposed natural explanations of these events, these explanations fall short of satisfying us to any degree of proof. Thus, in relation to the Old Testament, it is simply not correct to assert that science has disproved much of it, although it is correct to say that science has disproved the account of Creation as set out in the book of Genesis.

In relation to the New Testament, the discovery of the Dead Sea scrolls, the Hammadi texts, and the gnostic gospels has produced evidence of facts different from the facts set out in the New Testament. Again, this issue is more fully considered later herein, but for the present consideration, we must remember that the Gospels in the New Testament are also evidence. The factual account of the life of Jesus is set out in the three Synoptic Gospels, so called because they are reasonably consistent with one another. An objective assessment of the weight of the evidence of the recent archaeological discoveries would give them less weight than the evidence from the Synoptic Gospels in the New Testament; hence, the recent discoveries do not prove anything, although they do warrant consideration.

Another example of modern science claiming to disprove the Gospels is in the work called *The Lost Tomb of Jesus*, considered above. This work starts with the supposition that Jesus did not rise from the dead as stated in the Gospels, but that his disciples stole the body and later buried the remains in the family tomb. That the remains of Jesus were contained in this tomb and that this was the family tomb of Jesus was deduced from the names scrawled on the ossuaries, supported by a statistical analysis of the frequency of this combination of names. The conclusion that the archaeologist proposes is that he has discovered the tomb of Jesus and that, therefore, Christ did not rise from the dead and the New Testament is false in relation to these facts.

A close analysis of the evidence shows that it is largely based on uncertain translations of unofficial marks on the ossuaries; that there is an assumption that Jesus had brothers and sisters, which is still disputed by many reputable authorities; and that the statistical analysis leaves much to be desired, even though the computational component of the statistics appears to be correct. In short, this work has very little persuasive value. There are other works, such as *The Holy Blood and the Holy Grail*, which also propose unconventional views of history, and again, a careful consideration of such works reveals that the evidence presented is uncertain or ambiguous, and consequently has little persuasive value. That is not necessarily a criticism of the authors but rather an example of the limitations of science to prove such things, although some authors write such books primarily for monetary considerations.

Works such as *The Da Vinci Code* are works of fiction and do not pretend to be anything more. Most reasonably informed people know that authors must research their stories, especially if they are connected to real history. Some people assume that the research underlying the plot is true and correct. Such an assumption is not warranted, because the author's research is not necessarily accurate, is not subject to scrutiny, is not disclosed, and even if it is correct, is legitimately variable by the author if necessary to make the plot work. In short, fiction should not be given any weight as regards historical truth but should merely be enjoyed as fiction.

The overall conclusion is that the assertion that science has disproved much of religious belief is simply not correct, and accordingly, this assertion should be challenged by requiring the person making the assertion to prove it.

1.2.4 The Mechanism of Creation

The issue we wish to consider is whether it was God who created all that is seen and unseen. To consider how God created all that is seen and unseen appears to be a totally different issue. And God being God, with powers and abilities we cannot imagine or understand, the mechanism he employed for Creation is probably also beyond our understanding. But the arguments and objections of those who do not accept that God exists and therefore believe that he did not create all that is necessarily depend on some comprehensible or scientific explanation of the mechanism of Creation. Consequently, to understand their arguments and views, we should be aware of the current scientific theories as to the mechanism of Creation.

A consideration of the scientific theories of the mechanism of Creation does not necessarily require a consideration of the nature of Creation, which is an issue so vast as to be well beyond the scope of any one book. But we should recognise, as has been indicated, that the mechanism of Creation portrayed in the book of Genesis is untrue. If we assert the belief that God created all that is, the onus is on us to prove that or to justify our belief. We do that in the arguments that will follow, but we must concede that those arguments do not include an explanation of the mechanism of Creation. Our position is that we simply do not know how God did it, while accepting that he did actually create all that is.

The position of the non-believers is that if they can show that all that is came about through a mechanism independent of the existence of God, then God, if he exists at all, did not create us and is accordingly irrelevant to us. However, none of these natural theories of Creation, as distinct from our theory of divine Creation, exclude the possibility that a creator set these mechanisms in motion in the first place. The writings of many scientists and cosmologists who accept the natural explanation of Creation indicate that they still believe that God exists and that he set the mechanism of Creation in motion.

At this stage, it seems appropriate to consider the scientific explanations of Creation in order to understand what the non-believers are saying. The areas of Creation generally raised in such considerations are as follows:

- the origin of the universe
- the formation of our planet
- the development of life on Earth
- the source of intelligent life on Earth.

1.2.4.1 The Origin of the Universe

Throughout human history, we have asked the question 'Why are we here?' in a variety of forms in which this question can be asked, such as 'What is the meaning of life?' To answer this question, we have explored theories of how we came to be here, because if we can discover that, then we may learn whether we were created or just a random permutation of the collision of particles of matter. If we were created, we may discover why we were created and thus have an answer to our question.

The first recorded theory of Creation is that set out in the book of Genesis in the Bible. But that is not really a theory about the creation of the universe, even though it mentions the creation of the firmament, because at the time that it was written, the science of astronomy and cosmology was limited to what was visible to the naked human eye, and that was very misleading. At that time, they were not aware of our solar system or the existence of galaxies, let alone the universe. It is not surprising then that the Genesis account is now generally regarded as the Creation myth.

It is not the function of this work to review the history of Creation theories but to identify the theories that have popular support in modern times. An appropriate starting point is 1927, when a Belgian astronomer named Georges Lemaître, who was also a Jesuit priest, produced a theory of the creation of the universe. According to this theory, all the matter in the universe was packed into a sphere about thirty times larger than our sun, which he called the 'primaeval atom'. For reasons unknown, the primaeval atom exploded to become the universe, which developed in accordance with physical laws to become what we see today.

The word *exploded* is not adequate to describe the concept of what happened. According to the theory, all space and time was also inside the primaeval atom, so the explosion was not simply the flying off in all directions of the particles of matter but also the expansion of space inside the primaeval atom which carried the substance of the universe with it. An analogy that illustrates this concept is the baking of a loaf of raisin bread. Before baking, it is a small lump of dough with raisins scattered throughout it.

On being baked, it expands in all directions, carrying the raisins with it, although the raisins are not moving in relation to the dough immediately around each raisin respectively. The dough is analogous to space, and the raisins are the galaxies. Applied to the universe, this means that the galaxies are not flying through space under a force of propulsion from the explosion away from where the primaeval atom was initially, but rather, they are relatively stationary; it is the expansion or 'inflation' of space that is carrying them still. The galaxies are moving away from one another just as the raisins in the loaf of bread are moving away from one another.

Lemaître's theory was not universally accepted. In 1948, another theory called the steady-state theory was introduced. According to this theory, attributed to Thomas Gold, the universe has always been the same as it is today and will remain so forever. It is postulated that while suns do extinguish, new suns are formed to replace them.

The notable British astronomer, Fred Hoyle, supported the steady-state theory and disparagingly referred to Lemaître's theory as 'the Big Bang theory'. The primaeval atom was also irreverently referred to as 'the cosmic egg'. Subsequent astronomical observations and discoveries have supported the Big Bang theory and contradicted the steady-state theory to the extent that, at present, the steady-state theory has very few supporters, although the name 'Big Bang' has survived!

Currently, there is a third theory called the plasma theory, proposed by a Swedish astrophysicist, Hannes Olof Gösta Alfvén. According to this theory, the universe was formed out of magnetic and electrical phenomena acting on plasma, which is electrically charged atoms and electrons at very high temperatures. The primary assumption of this theory is that 99 per cent of all matter in the universe is plasma and that the interaction of the electrical fields at the molecular level produces swirling strands of matter when they clump together in a self-sustaining process which eventually forms the stars, planets, and other celestial bodies.

One of the main pieces of evidence that weighed against the steady-state theory was the discovery of quasars, which only occur at the far reaches of our universe. If the universe were homogenous, as the steady-state theory postulates, then quasars should be spread evenly throughout the universe, which is not the case.

The existence of cosmic background radiation was postulated by George Gamow in 1948, when he also estimated that such radiation would be only a few degrees above absolute zero in temperature. Arno Penzias and Robert Wilson discovered such background radiation in 1963 by accident and measured its temperature to be three degrees above absolute zero. One of the main pieces of evidence supporting the Big Bang theory was found in 1992 by NASA's Cosmic Background Explorer (COBE), which detected tiny temperature changes in this cosmic radiation, which is consistent with gravitational disturbances that could have eventually come together to form the celestial bodies of our universe.

In 1929, Edwin Powell Hubble discovered that all matter in space is moving away from all other matter, which shows the universe to be expanding in a way similar to the expansion of the baking of the loaf of raisin bread in our example.

An expanding universe, quasars, and the background radiation are together persuasive evidence that the steady-state theory is incorrect, whilst supporting the Big Bang theory. The supporters of the plasma theory argue that this evidence is also consistent with their theory.

The Big Bang theory is currently the most popular theory, although it has been considerably modified from Lemaître's initial description. Most of the modifications relate to the various ways that the particles of matter and energy interact, and it has been calculated that this Big Bang occurred about 13.7 billion years ago. But the most startling conceptual variation is that the source of all matter was not some cosmic egg but a singularity. A singularity is a space so small that it cannot be seen with the naked eye. It is difficult, if not impossible, to imagine all matter, space, and time compressed into such a small space. Furthermore, the singularity concept implies that there was no space or time outside the singularity and that the 'inflation' of the singularity created the space and time into which it expanded.

More recently, Paul J. Steinhardt and Neil Turok have proposed that the Big Bang is cyclic, in that after completing its expansion to the limit, the universe contracts back to the volume of the singularity and then explodes again with another Big Bang. This, they say, has been going on forever and will continue to go on forever. There are some eminent cosmologists who support this view.

There are still many problems and unanswered questions about the Big Bang theory. Many of the concepts, like space being manufactured by the expansion of the singularity, are completely incomprehensible and unprovable gibberish to the layman. Of course, a person should not accept or support a theory that he or she does not understand. Perhaps language is inadequate to express the concepts in the undoubtedly brilliant minds of our cosmologists. On the other hand, perhaps because our cosmologists know that they cannot prove the mechanism of the origin of our universe to any highly persuasive degree, they feel free to speculate with fanciful concepts and possibly to indulge their own sense of humour.

In any event, none of the current theories of the origin of the universe deal with the issue of a creator of the universe. The focus of these theories is 'How and when?' rather than 'Who, if anyone?' Accordingly, these cosmological theories do not prove or disprove the existence of God, because they do not address this issue. Consequently, any argument that modern cosmology proves anything about God must be regarded as unsustainable.

Since modern cosmology does not deal with the existence of God, we are free to accept or reject any such theory, according to our fancy. Bearing in mind that they are only theories involving fanciful concepts and expressed in terms such as 'may have' and 'could have', we are also free to say that because cosmologists do not know and cannot prove how the universe was formed or made, we can reject all their theories, even if we understand what they are saying.

1.2.4.2 The Formation of Our Planet

The Creation myth in Genesis is essentially about the creation of our planet Earth and the life on it. The author of Genesis did not know that the Earth was a roughly spherical celestial object orbiting the sun in a solar system in a galaxy we call the Milky Way. In a later chapter, the implications of this will be considered in more detail, but for the present, we can assume that the process described in Genesis is not accurate, although we cannot go so far as to conclude that the Creator had no part in the formation of Earth.

Nor is it necessary to adopt one or other of the theories about the creation of the universe to obtain a scientifically rational explanation of how the Earth was formed. We can obtain such a rational explanation by looking at the evidence that is within reach of scientific experimentation and measurement, such as radiocarbon dating, bearing in mind that this explanation is still a theory, because no one was there to witness it, which makes the evidence entirely inferential and thus cannot be regarded as compelling proof, although it is persuasive.

The scientific story of Earth's creation begins about 4.6 billion years ago. At that time, the gases left over from a star that had previously occupied 'our space' but that had gone supernova coalesced to form some gigantic spheres of gas and other heavier debris. The largest of these clumps of gas ignited to become our sun. The other clumps of gas and heavier matter had been orbiting the sun due to the presence of gravity. After the sun ignited, the clumps of gas closest to the sun were eventually vaporised, but the clumps further away survived, as did the clumps of heavier matter. Thus, our solar system was formed, with the heavier planets closer to the sun and the gaseous planets further away.

During these early times, Earth was quite inhospitable. It had no atmosphere, and there was no solid ground, the entire surface of the Earth being a viscous crust of molten rock and other heavier elements. There was no water and obviously no oceans or any kind of life, and the days were only four hours long. But then about 30 million years after the sun ignited, an extraordinary event occurred. Another planet, which has been called Theia, was travelling in the same orbit as Earth but at a different speed. Eventually, Earth and Theia collided.

The force of this impact shattered the surface of Theia into billions of fragments, which flew into high orbit around Earth and, after about one year, coalesced to form our moon. The core of Theia, which was mostly iron, sank to the centre of the fluid Earth to become Earth's core. On the surface of the Earth, the impact caused a huge splash which was like the eruption of thousands of volcanoes, releasing gases held under the crust and thus forming Earth's rudimentary atmosphere.

One of the key effects of this collision was that the iron core of Theia gave Earth a magnetic field, which repelled and deflected the intense and highly lethal radiation emitted by the sun, which is now known as the solar wind. This solar wind is entirely inimical to any form of life, and it also has the effect of breaking down water into its component elements of hydrogen and oxygen.

Of course, the Earth had no life or water at that time, so this benefit of the magnetic field was not immediately relevant.

The next extraordinary event in Earth's history happened about 3.7 billion years ago. The formation of the planets also led to the formation of a vast number of smaller rocks, many of which were locked into orbit around the sun, near Jupiter. It is believed by scientists that it was not uncommon for the planets to have minor digressions from their orbit around the sun. In one of these digressions, the gravity of Jupiter caused these smaller rocks, which we now call comets and asteroids, to fly out of their orbits towards the sun. Some of these comets and asteroids were attracted by Earth's gravity and collided with the Earth and its moon. Many of these comets and asteroids were composed largely of ice, so when millions of them struck Earth's atmosphere, the ice vaporised to form Earth's water supply and also had a cooling effect on the planet.

At this point, the Earth had all the elements that we have today, although there was considerable development before it reached our present conditions. One such development was the mutation of our atmosphere to what it is today, and this involves the development of life on our planet, which is considered in the next section.

It is also worth repeating that the forgoing account is still only theory and not proven fact. Also, this theory does not address the issue of a creator, again focusing on how rather than who. However, the extraordinary events of the collision with Theia and the bombardment of Earth by comets and asteroids, which together enabled the development of life on this planet, are so unlikely that their randomness is questionable, and the intervention of some design becomes more likely.

1.2.4.3 The Development of Life on Earth

The issue of the source of life on Earth is probably the most important issue underlying the question of the existence of God. If it can be shown that life developed naturally, then the formation of Earth is more likely to have been simply a random combination of circumstances and the formation of the universe also simply a natural phenomenon. These likelihoods do not overcome the arguments that the laws of physics controlling the behaviour of matter and energy appear to have an intelligent cohesion, and that even the matter of the universe had to come from somewhere. But they do distance God from one of the main dogmas of Catholic theology, which is that we can be satisfied as to the existence of God from our observations of the world around us, which shows an intelligent design cohesion and complexity strongly persuasive of the action of a creator.

Before the collision of Earth and Theia, the Earth had been completely sterilised by the solar wind. There was no life on Earth whatsoever. One of the effects of the collision was the formation of Earth's magnetic field, which deflects the solar wind. The absence of the solar wind enabled life to form and develop without being instantly killed by the solar radiation. But the environment of Earth was still, at that time, very inhospitable to any form of life. In fact, life needs an environment of amino acids to develop.

In 1951, Professor Harold Urey and his student, Stanley Miller, experimentally demonstrated that amino acids could have been formed from the elements present on Earth, in the environment and conditions on Earth after the bombardment by the comets and asteroids, which occurred about 3.7 billion years ago. This is not a surprising discovery in hindsight because we know conclusively that there is life on Earth and that the Creation myth in the book of Genesis is incorrect.

But it must be stressed that the amino acids are necessary for the *development* of life. They have not been shown to be the cause or source of life. To this day, no one has been able to produce or create even one simple living cell from any lifeless cocktail of chemicals and conditions in a laboratory. That does not mean that it can never be done, but our technology is fairly advanced in this area. Consequently, it is appropriate to confine our considerations, which are relevant to our real-life decisions, to the state-of-the-art knowledge. Accordingly, we can conclude that, for the present, the evidence is that life cannot originate from any known natural process.

A secondary issue for consideration under this heading is whether the theory of evolution is valid. According to this theory, all life developed from a single cell which had the ability to divide itself into two cells, both identical to the parent and retaining the ability to duplicate themselves. Evolution holds that the subsequent duplicates mutated to adapt and survive in a changing environment, to the degree of forming life as we know it today.

After the comet and asteroid bombardment, the Earth changed. Early oceans formed, and the crust of the Earth cooled. Volcanoes formed in the hardened crust to relieve the subsurface fluid pressures, and the volcanoes erupted, releasing gases and lava. There were also volcanic eruptions under the oceans. The atmosphere became composed of nitrogen, ammonia, methane, oxygen, hydrogen, and carbon dioxide. The hydrogen and oxygen mixed, and the mixture was ignited by lightning in massive electrical storms, which were almost constant at that time. This chemical reaction formed even more water, until about 70 per cent of the surface of the Earth was covered with water.

Some scientists hold the view that the first living organisms that appeared on Earth, called methanogens, developed deep in the oceans, near volcanic vents. From there, an adaptive mutation was able to use sunlight to split carbon dioxide and water for food. This process is called photosynthesis, and these cells are called cyanobacteria. Over the next few billion years, these cyanobacteria released the oxygen produced by their feeding into the atmosphere while reducing its carbon dioxide component to create the atmosphere we breathe today. These cyanobacteria developed and lived in rocks called stromatolites, which are the oldest rocks known.

What happened next is the beginning of a long and complex history of biological development, which is beyond the scope of this work. In short, single-cell organisms combined with other organisms—sometimes symbiotically, sometimes predatorily—to form more complex cells, which eventually became complex enough to store the information necessary for the duplication of identical cells. This information was stored in a chemical called deoxyribonucleic acid, which is generally abbreviated to DNA. There were later several extraordinary geological and environmental occurrences that significantly influenced the development of life. These can all be regarded as natural phenomena, but they also support the argument of design by some creator.

There is no theory or argument as to the origin of the methanogens or any of the other simple cells that appeared at about that time. The view that they sprang up spontaneously from their chemical environment is unsustainable in the absence of any proof or evidence that such a thing is even possible. We know that living organisms do not always breed true and that mutations do occur to adapt to a changed environment. Often such mutations occur incrementally over a number of generations. To this extent, the theory of evolution appears to be valid and acceptable, but this still does not explain the source of the original cells or even the number of different types of single cells that appeared initially. It is also worth noting that in modern times, there are a number of reputable biologists who have documented the view that in some areas, the differences between some species previously thought to have been linked in the evolutionary system are too great to be explainable by any known evolutionary process.

The conclusion then is that the theory of evolution is certainly correct and valid in part, but it does not disprove Creation at the fundamental level and cannot account for the existence of some modern complex species.

1.2.4.4 The Source of Intelligent Life on Earth

To consider this issue, we must first define what we mean by 'intelligent life'. Obviously, computers and other machines that simulate intelligence even to the extent of appearing to have the ability to 'learn' things are not alive and therefore need not concern us. Animals such as chimpanzees, dogs, dolphins, etc. do display some attributes indicating intelligence, but even the most sophisticated display of animal intelligence is an order of magnitude less than that of an ordinary human adult. Human intelligence has the ability to consider its own origin. Human intelligence has built cities, fed millions through agriculture, enabled travel around our planet in aircraft, enabled man to walk on the moon, and produced art, music, literature, mathematics, philosophy, etc. So what we are considering is human intelligence.

The issue then is, what is the source of human intelligence? The Creation story in the book of Genesis asserts direct creation of human beings by God with the same level of intelligence that we have today. Science has provided ample persuasive evidence of the existence of intelligent human beings long before the events described in Genesis, which according to genealogical calculations, occurred only about six thousand years ago. But the fact that Genesis is incorrect does not prove that God did not directly or indirectly infuse intelligence into human beings. The problem with God acting indirectly is that evolutionists argue that the development of intelligence is a natural part of the evolutionary process and that, therefore, God did not create human intelligence. To consider this argument, we need a general understanding of how the evolutionary process is alleged to work.

The theory of evolution is still just that—a theory. There is still much disagreement and debate amongst evolutionary scientists as to how it happened and when, although as indicated above, the evolutionary process is generally regarded as at least partially valid.

For our purposes, the human evolutionary process began about 3.2 million years ago. It has been shown that human genes are about 96 per cent similar to those of a chimpanzee, which suggests that we evolved from the chimpanzee genus. According to the molecular clock theory, the split from the chimpanzee genus cannot have occurred more than 5 or 6 million years ago, so any discoveries going back further than this must account for the molecular clock theory, although there have been no such discoveries to date.

In November 1974, near the Awash River in Ethiopia, Donald Johanson found about 40 per cent of the remains of a creature he called Lucy. When alive, this creature was about 1.1 metres tall and weighed about 29 kilograms. This creature appeared to be a female chimpanzee, but from the shape of her pelvis, it appeared that she walked on two feet. In 1978, another team of scientists discovered footprints in Tanzania clearly made by bipedal creatures, dating back 3.7 million years.

Evolution appears to favour practical improvement. Walking upright frees the hands to carry and use weapons, and it thereby increases the chance of survival. The scientists suppose that these early bipeds must have thought that it was a good idea to walk on two feet only. Also, a recent study found that walking on two feet uses only 25 per cent of the energy used by walking on all four. This means that it was appreciably less tiring and that a species walking on two limbs could move for longer and had two limbs free to carry food and weapons and could even feed on the move.

Since the discovery of Lucy, there have been a number of discoveries of similar creatures. But Lucy's brain was the size of a chimpanzee's brain, about 350 cc, whereas the modern human brain is about 1,350 cc. The next stage in this evolutionary sequence occurred about 2.4 million years ago with the appearance of *Homo habilis*, who had a brain capacity of about 650 cc. This species is the first recognisable human being, although not much is known about where this species came from. This species used tools such as stone axes. Their appearance marks the beginning of the Old Stone Age.

Studies have shown that relative to the other animals living in that age that were about the same size, the brain of *Homo habilis* was four times larger. It is also known that our brains need about 20 per cent of our average daily calorie intake to function. So developing a bigger brain started a self-sustaining growth pattern that works as follows: bigger brains need more energy, which can be obtained by hunting and eating meat. The more efficient the hunt, the more food the brain gets, the more it grows, and the better it is able to design and use tools and weapons for more efficient hunting. This appears to be the process of evolution commenced by *Homo habilis*.

About 2 million years ago, the human species called *Homo erectus* appeared. It is thought that they evolved from *Homo habilis*, who then died out. All this occurred in Africa. In 1984, Richard Leakey discovered the remains of a *Homo erectus* in Africa and called his finding the Turkana Boy. This species had lost their body hair, had sweat glands, and had hair on the top of the head. The specimen found also had a protruding nose and a brain capacity of about 1,100 cc. It is thought that this species was the first to make spears, which made them the supreme hunters of their time. This species is also believed to have discovered how to make and control fire, which gave them protection from other predators and led to the discovery of the caloric advantages of cooked food. Campfires dating back 1.5 million years have been discovered. They also made bigger and better stone axes than *Homo habilis*. However, skeletal analysis suggests that this species could not communicate by talking, but they could make a variety of grunts.

About 1.7 million years ago, *Homo erectus* expanded by emigrating from Africa to Europe and Asia. About 350,000 years ago, the human species called Neanderthals appeared in Asia, and they spread to the same environments occupied by *Homo erectus*. The species of *Homo erectus* appears to have died out about 70,000 years ago. The Neanderthals were much like us in many ways, with a brain capacity equal to or possibly slightly larger than our own. They were adept at using tools and were the first to build houses and to bury their dead, which suggests some spiritual beliefs. They were able to speak as we do, and a Neanderthal flute has been discovered.

But we did not descend from the Neanderthals. *Homo sapiens* first appeared in Africa, with the oldest remains of specimens of this species being dated at about 160,000 years old. Evolutionists say that genetic research findings support the proposition that all of today's humans evolved from this species. Indeed, modern human genetic code is so similar in all modern humans that geneticists believe that at some time, the entire human population was reduced to a single community of between 1,000 and 10,000 individuals in number. This reduction in numbers could have been caused by the eruption of a supervolcano at Toba about 75,000 years ago. A disaster on this scale and at this time could also account for the extinction of *Homo erectus*, although the Neanderthal species survived until about 24,000 years ago.

Homo sapiens expanded from Africa into Europe and Asia about 50,000 years ago. About 40,000 years ago, they reached Australia, and about 14,000 years ago, they came to North and South

America. In Europe and Asia, they lived in the same areas as the Neanderthals, and while there was some interbreeding, it was not widespread. It is believed that red hair, freckles, and pale skin are the Neanderthal contribution to the human gene pool.

Thereafter, the history of humankind makes no significant contribution to the theory of evolution, save that the achievements of humankind flow from human intelligence and that many discoveries have come in times of conflict when there was a threat to survival. The history of discovery and invention shows steady progress. We know that the early Greek philosophers were as intelligent as modern humans from the sophistication of their science and literature, although they did not have the modern knowledge base. What is startling is the technological development of human knowledge since the Industrial Revolution, which was less than 200 years ago. What this means may well raise some concerns amongst the evolutionists.

The weakness in the evolutionists' argument is that there is no explanation of where *Homo habilis*, *Homo erectus*, the Neanderthals, and *Homo sapiens* came from. We are to assume that their distant ancestors were chimpanzees who thought it was a good idea to walk on two limbs rather than the usual four. Furthermore, the process of evolution selects mutations that are logically correct and viable, from species that clearly did not have any concept of evolution and certainly did not deliberately control their breeding mutations. Of course, non-viable mutations would not have survived, and the species were intelligent enough to recognise the advantages of superior mutations; however, this does not satisfactorily explain the apparent inherent design in the entire process, unless it can be shown that we could have evolved into something greater than we already are.

The conclusion is that the theory of evolution helps explain the origins of the physical bodies of our human species. We had to come from somewhere, and direct creation by God is implausible on the evidence. But to argue that our intelligence flows from a chimpanzee who decided to walk upright is equally improbable. The spark of human intelligence, which we have been unable to transmit to animals no matter how long they associate with us or how much we train them, must come from somewhere. Since it is not a physiological thing but rather an aspect of human consciousness, the proposition that this intelligence was somehow infused by a creator cannot be dismissed in the face of this very inconclusive evidence.

1.2.5 The Necessity of Doubt

One of the main questions asked by atheists and agnostics is 'If God exists, why does he not manifest himself so that the evidence of his existence is compelling?' They argue that if God exists, he certainly has the power to manifest himself in an unambiguous way. They further argue that if God did manifest himself and everyone believed in the existence of the one true God, the world would be a much more peaceful and better place, and if God is the loving god that believers portray him to be, who loves and wants the best for all his children, then he would manifest himself for this purpose. Accordingly, since he does not manifest himself, he is either not a loving god or he does not exist.

The logic of this argument appears to be reasonable, but it is, in fact, flawed in several ways. Firstly, for God to manifest himself in a way that leaves no doubt, he would have to make his manifestation immortal, because this proof would be required by every generation, since many people will not accept evidence that they have not personally perceived. Secondly, the manifestation would need to be clearly divine by exhibiting superhuman powers such as omnipotence and omniscience, because without these attributes, many would not believe that the manifestation was God. Thirdly, the manifestation would have to rule the world by punishing any disobedience to his laws, of which he is aware through his omniscience; otherwise, many would regard

God as impotent. Thus, if God did manifest himself with these necessary attributes, it is plain that while the world would be more peaceful and there would be little, if any, crime or other sin, such a manifestation would displace human freedom forever. Many would see this as oppressive and as proof that God is not a loving god.

We, as Catholics, believe that God did manifest himself in the person of Jesus Christ. Jesus claimed divinity and exhibited superhuman powers by performing many miracles. He proved his immortality by raising himself to life after he had been killed. He demonstrated his omniscience by stating in his teachings what others were thinking without them having revealed this to him beforehand. His teachings were entirely aimed at producing peace and love between all humans, but he never undertook any function of human rule or coercion of his audience to believe his teachings or punishment for rejection of his teachings. He made it clear that his kingdom was not of this world. Jesus's divinity will be considered more fully in a later section of this work, but for the purposes of this issue, the above summary shows that any manifestation by God of himself that does not demonstrate and use the attributes set out above will not be regarded by all, in his own time or by subsequent generations, as proof of God's existence, because today many people do not believe that Jesus is divine.

Even we Catholics occasionally have doubts about the divinity of Jesus. Who amongst us, faced with a difficult decision or crisis in our lives, has not prayed to God to give us some unambiguous sign as to what we should do? And when no such sign was forthcoming, did we not wonder whether God really exists or whether all our religious teachings are there merely to provide motivation for children to behave? Of course, sometimes things do occur which we interpret as signs, and we act accordingly. But a sceptic would say that the sign was a dream or hallucination or mere coincidence, and we would have to concede that our 'sign' does not amount to compelling objective evidence proving the existence of God. This phenomenon is called 'faith based on personal religious experience' and is also further considered later herein.

From the forgoing, it appears that God does not manifest himself because to do so would extinguish our freedom. However, some philosophers hold the view that freedom does not really exist, and consequently, this cannot be the reason for the absence of some manifestation of God in our world. To consider this argument, we need to understand the philosophical concepts of free will and determinism.

Essentially, free will is our ability to choose which action to take in a situation where there are two or more available courses of action and where there is no compulsion to choose or not choose any one of the available options. This concept is the foundation of moral responsibility, for we cannot be held morally responsible for any action or for the consequences of any action if we were compelled to take that action.

We believe that we have free will, because we remember making decisions involving similar or identical considerations previously, when sometimes we made one decision and sometimes another. We remember not being under any compulsion to make the decision one way or the other, but the philosopher John Stuart Mill (1806–1873) argued that we always act in accordance with our strongest motivation. This is plausible, because we do experiment and learn from experience. But people have also been known to act contrary to our strongest motivation—i.e. our survival instinct—for relatively weak motivations, such as avoiding being considered a coward by persons who do not matter to the individual concerned.

Causal determinism is the proposition that the state of the physical universe at any given time is necessitated or caused by its earlier states in addition to the laws of nature. In relation to human conduct, this is extended to include Mill's view that we always act in accordance with our strongest motivation in that our motives are not part of the physical universe but are part of human nature. From this comes the argument that everything is predetermined. In other words, everything that has ever happened in this world and everything that will ever happen, including the decisions that we will make, is causally related to the initial structure and motion of the universe, subject to the laws of nature.

From this, it follows that we cannot be morally responsible for any of our actions because we have no control or input into what we are and what we do. Determinism does not necessarily reject the existence of God, but it clearly rejects any concept of sin or accountability to God for our actions, because determinism implies that he made us the way we are and made us do what we do right from the beginning of creation.

There is some support for determinism in the Bible, in particular the references to the Book of Life, in which it was postulated that everything that would ever happen in the world was written down from the beginning. This is shown in Psalm 139:16, which goes as follows:

> *You had scrutinized my every action, all were recorded*
> *in your book, my days listed and determined, even before*
> *the first of them occurred.*

But much greater support is given to the concept of free will by those same verses, which suggest that God might strike someone's name from the Book of Life. If everything was predetermined, then God would not have written in the Book of Life the names of persons who are to be struck off the Book of Life in the first place. The only reason for striking someone's name from the Book of Life is that they offended God, and this can only happen if there is some accountability or responsibility for our actions. This, in turn, can only occur if we have free will.

The essential aspect of determinism is predictability. If we could predict what everyone would do until the end of time, then determinism would be true. We mere mortals are not very good at predicting. Our weather forecasters have a poor record for accuracy, and the fiscal predictions of our economists make the weather forecasters look good. To predict things with 100 per cent accuracy requires a vast amount of information. God can do it because he is omniscient and certainly has the brainpower. But what is the point of creation if nothing can happen that was not planned by and known to God? In any event, we humans cannot predict our own future with any certainty. Accordingly, since the evidence to support determinism depends on predictability, our inability to make 100 per cent accurate predictions about every future event is a sound reason to reject determinism as true, until such time when we can make 100 per cent accurate predictions about future events. That leaves us with free will, which feels right to most of us and is necessary for meaningful existence, and the concept of moral responsibility and accountability to God as set out in the Bible.

Returning to the main issue, we can now draw some conclusions. If God exists, he does not manifest himself in our world so as to provide compelling ongoing proof of his existence, because to do so would extinguish our free will. So why does God want us to have free will?

The central characteristic of God in our religion is that he loves all humankind as we love our children. Those of us who have children love them and want them to love us in return. We can forgive them almost anything if they love us. It appears that God feels the same way about us. God has revealed his love for us and his wish that our love for him be the most important concern in our lives. The Bible is full of stories showing God's love for us and his desire that we love him in return. The first of the Ten Commandments is that we love God. Jesus confirmed that the first and greatest commandment is that we love God with all our hearts and with all our minds and with all our strength.

But a love that is not given freely is worthless. If we try to compel someone to love us, the result will most likely be that they will end up hating us, even if it is secretly. No doubt the same applies to God. If he tried to compel us to love him, many would end up hating him, and we cannot keep secrets from God.

Our love for God is much like a child's love for his or her parents. It comprises gratitude for all that the parents have provided, such as food, clothing, shelter, education, etc. It also contains an aspect of affection and concern for the welfare of the parent. Another aspect is the companionship and support in difficult times. A further aspect is trust that the parent is always on their side and a willingness to confide and reveal the inner self, based on this trust. A child does not usually express this love in words (although the words often come after the child has reached maturity) but in simple obedience to what the parent tells the child to do.

Our love for God contains most of these aspects. The expression of our love is primarily in obedience to his words. If God manifested himself and ruled the world and punished every act of disobedience, he would be depriving us of the choice to obey him of our own free will and thereby express our love for him, because we would have to be insane to disobey him, knowing that he will certainly know of every act of disobedience and will certainly punish such disobedience.

Clearly, if God exists, he wants us to love him; therefore, it is necessary that we have some doubt about his existence so that if we recognise that our lives and all that we have personally comes from him, we can freely love him in return.

1.2.6 Belief Status

Our objective in being Catholics is to have our immortal soul spend eternity with God. We have been told that we can achieve this objective by living our present physical lives in a manner that is pleasing or acceptable to God. Living our lives is all about our conduct or behaviour, our acts and omissions in word and deed. What we believe is not of itself part of our behaviour. But all our behaviour is motivated. Our primary motivators are our reason, emotions, instinct, and intuition. Sometimes a combination of these drivers is our motivation. Reason reveals the benefits or detriments of a particular course of conduct, and certainly in relation to conduct having religious implications, what we believe is essential to the reasoning process because truth is necessary to the reasoning process, although we do sometimes deceive ourselves or our emotions override our reason.

From this, it is clear that our beliefs underlie our behaviour, and accordingly, to achieve our objective of being Catholics, we must have a set of beliefs that support or require the kind of behaviour necessary to achieve our objective.

But that is not the whole story. We have also been told that the first and greatest requirement of God is that we love him with all our hearts and with all our souls and with all our strength and with all our minds and that we love our neighbour as ourselves. Love is an emotion and, to an extent, is independent of any beliefs. But reason shows us how to love, and thus, our beliefs function to determine the quality of love we can give.

Instinct also motivates us but operates at a subconscious level. It appears to be survival-related conduct, and it manifests in reflex action or knowledge of how to do something that we have not been taught to do. The source of such knowledge remains a mystery. For example, we instinctively recognise danger and are then motivated to fight or fly. Our conscious mind can and at times does override our instinct.

Intuition is like instinct in that it processes sensory information subconsciously. It appears to use both reason and emotion to arrive at a conclusion in accordance with our relevant objective and presents this conclusion to the conscious mind. An intuition is often mistakenly evaluated as an unreasoned emotion and accorded little weight. However, recent studies have suggested that intuition is formed from the rational processing of information at a speed beyond the capacity of the conscious mind to observe, and accordingly, it goes unnoticed by the conscious mind.

Our objective as Catholics, referred to above, makes three major assumptions which should be identified for clarity. Firstly, there is the assumption that we have an immortal soul. This assumption has been considered previously, and belief in this proposition is tenable. The second assumption is that God exists. The evidence and arguments to support that belief are considered in the next chapter, but for now it remains an assumption. The third assumption is that it is true that it is possible that our souls can spend eternity with God. This assumption is based on the teachings of Jesus and is acceptable to the same degree that we accept the divinity of Jesus, which is also an issue dealt with in a later chapter.

<u>Necessary Beliefs</u>

So what is this set of beliefs that supports or requires the type of behaviour necessary to achieve our objective? An appropriate starting point is the Nicene Creed, which we hear at Mass every Sunday. That creed is as follows:

> *We believe in one God the Father, the Almighty, maker of*
> *heaven and earth, of all that is seen and unseen.*
> *We believe in one Lord, Jesus Christ, the only son of God.*
> *Eternally begotten of the Father, God from God, Light*

from Light, true God from true God, begotten, not made, one in being with the Father. Through Him all things were made. For us men and for our salvation He came down from heaven: by the power of the Holy Spirit He was born of the Virgin Mary, and became man. For our sake He was crucified under Pontius Pilate; He suffered, died, and was buried. On the third day He rose again in fulfilment of the Scriptures; He ascended into heaven and is seated at the right hand of the Father. He will come again in glory to judge the living and the dead. And His kingdom will have no end.

We believe in the Holy Spirit, the Lord, the giver of life. Who proceeds from the Father and the Son. With the Father and the Son, He is worshipped and glorified. He has spoken through the prophets.

We believe in one catholic and apostolic church.

We acknowledge one baptism for the forgiveness of sins.

We look for the resurrection of the dead, and the life of the world to come.

Amen.

This is said as a continuous prayer but has here been set out in paragraphs to separate the principal concepts, although the sequence of words remains unchanged.

The first paragraph essentially declares belief in the existence of God as our creator. This is so fundamental that without it, all other aspects of religion become irrelevant and meaningless. But its fundamental nature is not proof of the existence of God, and even though we recite it every week, we can still have doubts about its truth. The arguments and reasons for believing this proposition are considered in the next chapter in order to enable us to put our doubts into a rational perspective and renew our acceptance of this belief.

The second paragraph is perhaps disproportionately long and is all about Jesus. It begins by stating that Jesus Christ is the only Son of God. That is a clear statement of the divinity of Jesus Christ and is probably all that is necessary for a creed, since much necessarily follows if the divinity of Jesus Christ is accepted. Anyhow, this paragraph goes on to state some mystical theological propositions and also recounts some of the facts relating to the birth and death of Jesus Christ. There is, of course, no doubt that Jesus Christ existed. His birth and death are widely accepted as historical fact. What is not accepted by non-Christian religions is that he was divine. The proposition that he rose from the dead and is alive today at God's right hand is rejected by most non-Christian religions. These assertions in the creed are sometimes presented as proof of the divinity of Jesus, but such arguments assume acceptance of the fact that Jesus rose from the dead. This proposition is simply not accepted by non-Christians. The converse, of course, is readily acceptable. That is, if you accept the divinity of Jesus, then his resurrection is well within the power of the divine, and the evidence supports such an event.

Accordingly, the essential belief in this paragraph of the creed is that Jesus Christ was divine. If we accept that, then all that he said and did becomes important and integral to our faith and easily acceptable, subject to the accuracy and reliability of the modern versions of the Gospels, which are a record of all that he said and did. It also enables acceptance of the theological propositions that necessarily flow from the concept of the divinity of Jesus Christ.

The evidence supporting the belief in the divinity of Christ is considered later in this work to enable us to assess the credibility of the arguments that deny his divinity and to possibly expand the reasons for our belief in this proposition. The arguments against the divinity of Jesus simply aver that he did nothing that proved his divinity; they tend to explain his miracles as natural occurrences or misreporting, and the evidence we present is dismissed as having little probative value. However, there is some value in the volume of evidence that supports the divinity of Jesus Christ, and it is not our objective to persuade non-believers but rather to satisfy ourselves of the truth of this proposition, subject to the necessary doubt.

The next paragraph declares our belief in the existence of the Holy Spirit. This declaration makes it clear that the Holy Spirit is also divine. But we believe that there is only one God, which necessarily leads to the concept of the triune nature of our God. This concept is incomprehensible to the human mind because we have no experience with any living being that has a triune nature. We can say that God is a spiritual being with three separate coexisting personas that are equal in power, that love one another equally, and that have a single will and divine nature. But these words do not enable us to understand the true nature of the trinity of God, because we simply cannot imagine how this can be.

The proof of the existence of the Holy Spirit is implicit in the proofs of the existence of God, if we accept that there is only one god. The triune nature of God is an aspect of the nature of God, and as such, it is beyond the scope of this work. However, Jesus Christ referred to the Holy Spirit in terms implying his divinity, and accordingly, if we accept the divinity of Jesus, then the existence and divinity of the Holy Spirit necessarily follow. In considering the existence of God as the Creator of all that is seen and unseen, we can include the Holy Spirit in our considerations, on the basis that it was the will of the Holy Spirit, jointly with God the Father and God the Son, that the world be created, and that it was God the Father who implemented this will through his power of creation.

The Holy Spirit has clearly been the most low-profile persona of God in the history of mankind. God the Father was the Creator and appears to have been the persona manifested in the Old Testament accounts of human interaction with God, although if we accept that the Holy Spirit has 'spoken through the prophets', then clearly the Holy Spirit took an active part in the early management of mankind. The New Testament concerns the manifestation of God the Son, save for the manifestation of the Holy Spirit in the Pentecost account. Since the ascension of Jesus, it seems that the Holy Spirit is solely conducting the management of the world through his gifts to all mankind and his guidance of our church. But the Holy Spirit has remained low-profile, without any specific manifestations since Pentecost, and consequently, there is little evidence of the existence of the Holy Spirit.

We cannot—nor is it appropriate for us to—question why the Holy Spirit has not manifested himself over the last 2,000 years. Bearing in mind the necessity of doubt, it is reasonable to conclude that the Holy Spirit has not needed to manifest himself over this period because what God wants from us was made known to mankind through the evangelical action of the Catholic Church established by Jesus, together with substantial development in human literacy, theology, and philosophy. In other words, we today stand on the shoulders of giants who perceived the true will of God, and therefore, it was unnecessary for the Holy Spirit to direct human knowledge of God's will through direct intervention.

In any event, for the purpose of identifying necessary Catholic beliefs, we must believe that the Holy Spirit exists. From that belief, it follows that the Holy Spirit has been guiding the Catholic Church towards true knowledge of God's will, although history shows that, perhaps because of the necessity of doubt, the Catholic Church has not always followed the direction inspired by the Holy Spirit.

The next paragraph affirms the existence of the Catholic Church as apostolic. There is no doubt that the Catholic Church exists and that it is Catholic in nature. And if we accept the divinity of Jesus Christ, then it is also clear from the Gospels that Jesus established this church and gave authority to his apostles and their successors to act as his agents. Accordingly, there is no difficulty in accepting this belief if we accept the divinity of Jesus.

However, history shows that this authority of the church has sometimes been abused and applied in incorrect ways, despite the guidance of the Holy Spirit. This issue warrants further careful consideration, which is attempted in a later chapter.

The next paragraph acknowledges the sacrament of baptism as being for the forgiveness of sins. This is a theological proposition, but again, if we accept the divinity of Jesus, there is no difficulty in accepting this proposition, because Jesus himself was baptised.

Theologically, it appears that by being baptised, Jesus Christ became part of the body of persons who were and would be baptised. As God, he naturally became the head of this body. He became incarnate to reconcile God with man by seeking God's forgiveness for the sins of mankind. God forgave Jesus through his passion and death, and thus, all who were part of his body of the baptised were forgiven.

This theological concept of the mystical body of Jesus Christ is not very relevant to what motivates our day-to-day behaviour and is more an explanation of how God can forgive the sins of mankind. This enables us to have confidence and hope in the possibility of reconciliation with God, especially when we recognise our personal insignificance compared to the pre-eminence of God. Accordingly, it is a necessary belief, and what flows from it is hope in the approachability of God for the forgiveness of sins. Without this hope, having sinned once and with no hope of forgiveness, we would have no reason to further behave in the way that God wishes us to behave.

The last paragraph is an averment of the existence of the immortality of our souls and the fact that there is a hereafter in which our souls will exist. Again, belief in the divinity of Jesus compels belief in the truth of all that he said and did, to the extent that we believe in his divinity. Jesus taught, in terms and concepts familiar to his audience, that there was a Kingdom of God and that it was at hand and that people could be saved to exist in this kingdom. This is one of the fundamental messages of the Gospels, and it is readily acceptable. Without this belief, there would be no point in living in a way to save our souls, and because of this, this belief is fundamental to motivating us in relation to every choice or decision that we make that relates to the future of our souls; therefore, it is a necessary belief. However, because it relates to something that will be after our death, we sometimes lose sight of the future benefits of a particular course of action and are decisively motivated by more immediate concerns.

Ancillary Beliefs

In addition to the core beliefs of our faith, there is a large number of additional beliefs that follow from our necessary beliefs. Such beliefs arise out of the theological considerations by leading church theologians and generally comprise the Catholic Church teachings. Most of these teachings have been promulgated in various papal decrees, bulls, encyclicals, catechisms, and documents of the several Catholic Church councils, including the recent Vatican Councils. The recent *Catechism of the Catholic Church*, which contains all our core beliefs, is a fairly comprehensive compendium of these ancillary teachings and beliefs which is aimed at ordinary Catholics who are not members of the clergy or formally educated theologians. For the clergy, there is also the canon law, and for theologians, there are many documents and other religious publications which are generally beyond the interests of ordinary Catholics.

All our necessary beliefs and some of our ancillary beliefs have been proclaimed by the church authorities to be dogma. The status of dogma is that the particular belief proclaimed to be dogma is true and correct. No Catholic may teach anything contrary to dogma, and every Catholic must profess belief in dogma. That is what we do when we say the Nicene Creed, although that creed does not contain all the Catholic dogma. Denial of a belief or even private rejection of a belief declared to be dogma raises the question of the genuineness of that Catholic's membership of the Catholic Church. Obviously, anyone who denies belief in the existence of God or the divinity of Jesus is being hypocritical in claiming to be a Catholic. But the issue is more difficult with beliefs such as the resurrection of our human bodies in the hereafter.

Most of our ancillary beliefs are not dogma, and the church acknowledges our entitlement to at least privately reject acceptance of any non-dogmatic belief. However, they are still taught by the church, and any public teaching contrary to the church's teachings challenges the teaching authority of the church and should not be undertaken lightly or without first giving church authorities the opportunity to review or amend its teaching on the contentious issue.

Church authorities carefully consider every issue that reaches the status of a church teaching, and no doubt the individuals involved in granting a belief the status of a church teaching genuinely believe that the subject teaching is true and correct. But these church authorities are human and do make mistakes in non-dogmatic teachings. Our church is mature enough to recognise this and, from time to time, changes or abandons teachings that have become obsolete or that are, for some other reason, no longer tenable. Dogma, however, cannot be changed, which raises the teaching and necessary belief that the Holy Spirit is guiding the Catholic Church in identifying correct dogma and intervenes indirectly to prevent incorrect beliefs becoming dogma, and that this is so because dogma is divine truth, which is as immutable as God himself.

An example of ancillary dogma and teaching is in relation to Mary, the mother of Jesus Christ. It is dogma that Mary was conceived free from the stain of original sin. This dogma is theologically necessary because it would be degrading Jesus to believe him to have been conceived in a human who had the stain of original sin on her soul at the time of conception. Perhaps it would have been different if Mary had been baptised before the conception of Jesus Christ, but baptism did not exist at that time and cannot have the effect of retrospectively changing past events. Thus, we should not find it difficult to accept the dogma of the Immaculate Conception.

It is also a dogmatic church teaching that Mary remained a virgin during the birth of Jesus Christ and for the rest of her life after the birth. There is no theological necessity for this belief. It arises out of respect and devotion to Mary and from the corollary view that Mary was free from all human inclination to sin. We can easily accept that Mary never committed any sin, and there is no evidence whatsoever that she did ever commit any sin. But it is harder to accept that she remained a virgin after the birth of Jesus Christ. Such a belief would suggest that the modern translations of the Gospels are inaccurate where they refer to Jesus Christ as having brothers and sisters but are accurate in other instances of the use of the word *brother*. It also implies that her marriage to Joseph was never consummated, which in turn raises questions about the validity of the marriage. This teaching has been part of church teaching for many years. In early times, it was based on an assumption that Mary may have taken a vow of perpetual virginity. If that were so, would it not have been dishonest and dishonourable for Mary to marry anyone? It is not the purpose here to argue against this belief but rather to identify some of the reasons this belief is hard to accept, even though it seems that the theologians who formulated this teaching were not unaware of the difficulties identified above. It is surprising that even a devotional dogma of the Catholic Church is open to such serious questions.

The point of considering this example is to show that some teachings of the church need not be accepted. Even the dogma of the Immaculate Conception is only an ancillary belief; it is most unlikely to be a factor in motivating our behaviour to act in accordance with our belief as to how God wants us to behave. Devotion to Mary justifies praying to her, because she obviously has the 'ear of God'. But unjustified flattery is likely to be seen for what it is. Just being the mother of Jesus and the Immaculate Conception gives ample scope for praise and devotion.

Devotional Beliefs

The Catholic Church is a vast and diverse church. In spreading the Word of God throughout the world, it has sometimes been necessary to accommodate long-held beliefs within the structure of the Catholic faith, so long as these did not conflict with necessary beliefs or dogmatic theology. Also, perhaps because of the tyranny of distance, some areas of the Catholic Church have become parochial and have developed some eccentric beliefs. Such beliefs are countenanced by our church authorities, again, so long as they do not conflict with necessary beliefs or dogmatic theology. In some cases, there was such conflict, resulting in a schism and the formation of another Christian church.

The present situation is that the Catholic Church tolerates a significant number of eccentric beliefs. Such beliefs are held by various cults, such as the charismatics. Most of these cults are essentially devotional, with the source or focus of their devotion being some miracle or saint. The church is very careful in declaring some event to be miraculous and in canonising persons, and to some extent, it encourages additional devotion relevant to such an event. However, while adhering to the validity of such pronouncements, the church does not give such pronouncements the status of necessary beliefs or dogmatic theology, and it accordingly regards beliefs arising from such pronouncements as optional.

There are also many charitable works-oriented organisations within the church. Some of these are comprised of clerics and others of laypersons. Most of these have mainstream beliefs, plus a belief in the laudability or necessity of the charitable work they perform. Mostly, such organisations are endorsed and supported by church authorities, but again, their supplementary beliefs are not regarded as necessary beliefs.

Another group that is commended by the church is Opus Dei. The members of this group are staunchly mainstream in their beliefs, to the point where they are somewhat intolerant of eccentric beliefs and practices, although they themselves practise some severe archaic forms of devotion. Again, their devotional beliefs are not considered to be necessary beliefs.

Conclusion

Catholicism is a monotheistic religion. Membership of any monotheistic religion requires the belief that there is only one true god. What distinguishes Catholicism from the two other major monotheistic religions is our belief in the divinity of Jesus. From that belief flows belief in the existence of the Holy Spirit and, accordingly, the triune nature of God.

The necessary beliefs of Catholicism are headed in the Nicene Creed, which declares belief in the divinity of Jesus Christ. From this then flows the necessary belief in the truth and correctness of all that he said and did, as recorded in the Gospels, subject to their historical accuracy and the accuracy of modern translations. In those Gospels, Jesus Christ frequently referred to and endorsed sacred scriptures. Accordingly, belief in Jesus requires belief in the relevant parts of the Old Testament.

The other parts of the Nicene Creed all depend on belief in the divinity of Jesus Christ, as they flow from what he said and did. In particular, belief that our church is apostolic leads to recognition and acceptance of the church's authority to teach the gospel, to identify the proper application of Jesus Christ's teachings in changing times, and to compile and teach theology, some of which may be dogmatic.

Over the past 2,000 years, the Catholic Church has grown and become diverse. The teachings of Jesus Christ were essentially about our behaviour towards God and one another, which can be encapsulated in his command that we love one another as he loved us. The only thing that Jesus Christ exhorted us to believe in was himself, i.e. in his divinity. But many additional beliefs flow from belief in his divinity.

The church founded by Jesus Christ has, over the years, considered and developed a substantial body of beliefs, referred to herein as ancillary beliefs. Some of these beliefs are fundamental and necessary, and those have been proclaimed as dogma. Others are not necessary beliefs but are nevertheless important and taught by the church as true and correct. Such beliefs need not be accepted, but they should not be rejected lightly and should not be attacked in any form, although there are means of stimulating reconsideration of such issues by the church. A third category of beliefs are those countenanced by the church but not actually taught by the church as mainstream Catholicism. Acceptance of such beliefs is optional, and criticism of them permitted, provided it is made in a Christian manner.

1.2.7 Realms

In considering issues such as the existence of God, it is essential that we remain constantly mindful that what we are considering has no physical substance. Our brains process concepts, and we mostly communicate with words. If someone says the word *elephant*, assuming that we have seen a real elephant or a picture of one, some image of an elephant comes to our minds. If several people hear the word *elephant*, it is almost certain that each person's mental image of the elephant will be different, but each will be an accurate picture of a real elephant. Our brains can also process abstract concepts, and words referring to things that have no physical existence, such as the word *fear*, also cause an image to come to mind. But with such words, the images of several persons who hear that word are almost certainly vastly different. One person may be afraid of spiders, and an image of a spider nearby may be what he imagines when he hears the word *fear*. Another may be afraid of heights and may see himself or herself precariously perched at the top of a precipice. The range of images that such a word can produce is vast, and it is clear from the two examples given that each kind of fear imagined is different, although generally both fears relate to potential personal injury or death. Of course, there are many other adverse consequences that people can fear.

It is immediately apparent that our individual concepts of things that have no physical existence are substantially different from other persons' concepts of the same thing. A more profound problem with abstract concepts is proving that they were real or present at a particular time and place. In our fear examples, we could look at behaviour. In these situations, we must normally choose between flight or fight. So killing the spider is an indication that fear was present, but such killing could also indicate other things. Carefully stepping away from the precipice is also such an indicator. If we had some equipment connected to a person who is feeling fear, we could measure such things as heart rate, perspiration, and adrenaline secretion. And, of course, the person could tell us that he or she felt fear. But fear is not a physical thing. There is no molecule, element of matter, or subatomic particle that can be called fear, although fear causes a chemical change in our bodies which is precipitated by some perception in our brains. But we all know that it is real.

To enable us to avoid confusion between what is real that has physical substance and what is real that has abstract reality, it may be helpful to describe the physically real as belonging to the material realm and what has abstract reality as belonging to the spiritual realm.

Our concept of the material realm is fairly easy to describe and is generally well understood, because it is the realm in which we live. It is our universe. It contains galaxies of suns, planets, moons, gas clouds, comets, meteors, and some other celestial bodies. Our planet is in the galaxy we call the Milky Way. Our planet is composed of elements listed on our periodic table of elements, together with other subatomic particles. This we call matter. There are certain intangible forces that act on matter, such as gravity, magnetism, and electricity. We do not know what these forces really are, but we know a lot about how they work. At this stage, we do not know why they work, but that may not be a meaningful question. The various different types of matter also have different properties. Our sciences have revealed most of these properties, and our technology has used this knowledge to produce our present living conditions. We also have life on this planet, ranging from microscopic bacteria to us human beings. All the animal, vegetable, and mineral things on our planet are composed of matter, and the intangible forces, such as gravity, are part of the physical realm as properties of individual elements or the larger conglomerate of the entire universe.

We do not know everything that there is to know about our own material realm, and perhaps there is much left to discover. We have used scientific method and observation to reach our present level of knowledge, but some knowledge may well remain forever undiscovered by these means.

Conceptualising the spiritual realm is more difficult. We can be certain that the spiritual realm exists because we know that such things as love, courage, justice, fear, anger, hatred, and malice are real. But the question can fairly be asked whether these things have any reality beyond the function of our brain or whether they are merely a property of chemicals reacting in our brains. Let us consider the spiritual thing we call love.

It is clear from studies in natural science that not only humans but also animals can love. This is illustrated by the apparent affection that most species have for their offspring and the ferocity with which they defend their young from predators. No doubt evolutionists would argue that love is an evolutionary requisite for the survival of a species, but that does not make it any less a spiritual thing.

In human history, we can only imagine how many persons have said 'I love you' to another. We can accept that most of them said it because they felt the love and believed their statement to be true. Of course, some would have said this in pursuance of some hidden agenda. Our emotions and feelings come from chemical reactions in our brains. Our senses provide electrical impulses to our brains which are processed for understanding and recognition. Once recognised, our brains then compare the data with data in our memory, and from that comparison, the brain stimulates the release of certain chemicals in the brain which we feel as our emotions.

As far as we know, love can only be found or detected in the actions of conscious life, which can cause love to grow or diminish. Inanimate objects are incapable of love, and love cannot be seen in places devoid of conscious life, such as space or on our moon. Again, there is no particle of matter that can be identified as love, but few, if any, would dispute that love is real.

For the purposes of our consideration, we can regard love as something that exists in the spiritual realm, and we can assume that it, along with other spiritual things like courage, justice, etc., only manifests where there is conscious life and that with some of these spiritual things, the conscious life must necessarily have human intelligence.

It does not serve our consideration to catalogue all these things that belong to the spiritual realm. It is sufficient to acknowledge that such spiritual things are real. But before proceeding further, we may note that there is a difference between spiritual things and abstract things such as mathematics, the rules of logic, human laws, etc. These things are also real, and although they are only perceived by intelligent life, they are independent of life. For example, the numerical ratio of the diameter of the circle to its circumference is a universal constant that we call pi. It existed before our planet was formed and is certainly independent of conscious life, although only intelligent life can be aware of it. Such things need not be considered as belonging to the spiritual realm, as they are independent of conscious life.

In relation to the issues considered herein, we need some concept of what is in the spiritual realm and how these things interact with us as conscious human beings. It has already been shown that there is a spiritual realm and that it contains such things as love, courage, justice, etc. These things are not living things, but we can accept their reality. The more difficult question that we need to explore is whether there are any living beings in the spiritual realm.

There are several major difficulties in considering this question. Firstly, we, as living human beings in the material realm, can only conceptualise life as something that is composed of organic matter. The things of the spiritual realm have no physical substance whatsoever, so we have no knowledge or experience as to how a spiritual life can be created and sustained. Arguably, spiritual life needs no sustenance, and accordingly, if it exists, it is necessarily immortal, unless there are some ways, unknown to us, for spiritual life to end.

The second major difficulty lies in the persuasive value of the proofs that spiritual beings exist. Since we cannot imagine how spiritual life comes to exist and is sustained, we need highly persuasive proof that such beings do exist. But spiritual beings are not composed of any matter. They occupy no space and are not affected by or subject to any of the laws of nature that govern beings in the material realm. As non-material beings, they are unaffected by gravity, electricity, and light. Since they have no physical substance, they cannot reflect light and therefore cannot be seen by human eyes or detected by any equipment or devices of the material realm, such as cameras. Therein lies the problem. We need persuasive proof, but the nature of the subject makes it inaccessible to observation, scientific method, and any physical equipment.

The third problem, which compounds the second problem, is that we do not know the rules or laws, if any, that govern the spiritual realm; how the spiritual realm works; or the powers and abilities of the beings of the spiritual realm.

These difficulties do not compel the conclusion that spiritual beings do not exist. Nor can it be said that there is no evidence of the existence of spiritual beings. There is a vast amount of evidence that spiritual beings do exist, although this evidence is essentially anecdotal, without the persuasive value of evidence produced by the scientific method, and therefore necessarily vulnerable to substantial unanswerable questions.

Our concern is to consider the evidence for the existence of spiritual beings and to form a view as to whether a belief in the existence of the spiritual realm is reasonable.

As Catholics, we believe that we have an immortal soul, which is a spiritual thing, and that on our physical death, our soul leaves our body. During our lives, our soul is somehow connected to our body, but on our physical death, that connection is somehow broken. Where the soul goes is unknown. But the question may be meaningless, as non-material beings do not occupy any space and therefore cannot be in any particular place in the material realm, although the soul presumably has some form of existence in the spiritual realm which itself somehow overlaps or intersects the material realm. On this basis, we can consider ghosts, i.e. the souls or spirits of humans who have died, as being one of the types of beings that inhabit the spiritual realm.

Throughout history, there have been a vast number of ghost stories, many of which have been claimed to be true. In more recent times, the study of paranormal phenomena along scientific lines has achieved a level of respectability, and there has been much well-documented research, experimentation, and investigation. At the same time, our knowledge of the powers and capacities of the human mind has also increased substantially, to the point where we now accept that there is still much to learn.

The fundamental approach to the study of the paranormal is scepticism. Perhaps this is because scientists recognise that the absence of any natural explanation for some paranormal phenomena or event does not compel the conclusion that the explanation must be supernatural. It could be that the explanation is natural but that the science underlying the explanation has not yet been discovered or that the evidence of the phenomena or event is insufficient to enable any conclusion and may remain so. However, there have been very many well-documented investigations containing testimony from apparently reliable witnesses about paranormal events that remain unexplained by natural sciences. No doubt some of these were pranks or hoaxes, and others are scams by charlatans; however, without evidence of this, we cannot simply dismiss them. There is an onus of proof in an objective search for truth.

For our purpose of trying to conceptualise the spiritual realm, it may be helpful to raise a number of the sceptical questions.

Many, if not most, claimed experiences of ghosts report sightings of ghosts as misty or transparent objects of roughly human form, mostly white in colour. Sometimes these shapes can pass through walls, and sometimes they have clearly recognisable human faces and clothing. The problem with these descriptions is that if the ghost is a spiritual being, it has no substance and therefore cannot reflect light of any frequency on the electromagnetic spectrum. This means that there is no reflected light from the ghostly apparition entering the eyes of any observers. From this, it follows that the apparition is entirely in the mind of the observers. Certainly, real physical matter cannot simply pass through walls. But that does not mean that the ghost is not real, because we do not know whether or not ghosts have the power to physically affect the human mind so that it believes it is perceiving an apparition as a real object.

Nor do we know whether or not ghosts have the power to manifest themselves as real physical objects that do reflect light. There is a large number of photographs of what may be ghosts. Indeed, entire books of such photographs have been published. Of course, photographs can easily be faked, and the photographic process can produce inexplicable anomalies that may be misinterpreted as ghosts. Again, we cannot simply dismiss them all without some evidence. If any of the photographs are genuine, then it appears that some ghosts are able to manifest themselves as real physical objects in a particular place at a particular time.

There are also numerous reports and physical evidence of what we call poltergeists. Again, simply hearing a sound like chains being dragged across the stone floor may simply be an illusion created in the mind of the observer, if that sound had not been recorded on sound-recording equipment. But there are other reports of normal objects moving without any human or natural cause, of people being levitated, and of a variety of sounds. There is the testimony of apparently reliable witnesses, some photographic evidence, and also some sound-recording evidence. Again, such evidence is not compelling and must be regarded with caution, but here too we cannot simply dismiss these incidents without some evidence of trickery or error. And again, if any of them are genuine, then it appears that some ghosts have the power of mind over matter, i.e. they can cause events in the physical realm with the power of their spiritual minds. How this is possible, we simply do not know.

The next type of beings that may inhabit the spiritual realm are angels and demons. As Catholics, we believe in angels and demons. Objectively, however, there is very little evidence of the existence of angels. Demons, of course, are the devil and his angels. In relation to demons, there is a substantial amount of evidence. Demons probably have all the powers of all types of ghosts, and therefore, we cannot be sure that what appears to be the action of a ghost is not actually the action of a demon. The most recognisable power of a demon is the power to possess some human beings. There are a number of recorded cases of demonic possession recorded in the Bible, but as evidenced, it is uncorroborated and must be regarded with caution.

However, in the history of our church, there have been a number of cases of demonic possession. The church has investigated these and usually assigned specially trained priests, called exorcists, to deal with them. In addition, there have been cases outside the church which are well-documented in popular literature. Such possession by demons often involves physical harm to the person possessed, a bad smell in the vicinity of the possessed person, cold air in the vicinity of the possessed person, the possessed person speaking in a strange voice and sometimes other languages, and physical levitation of the person possessed. Often, what the demon says through the possessed person is blasphemous and obscene.

Such possessions have been reasonably well-documented. Again, there is the testimony of apparently reliable witnesses and photographic, video, and sound-recorded evidence. Of course, this type of evidence has all the weaknesses already identified. As before, we cannot dismiss these cases just because the evidence is not compelling. The power to possess a human being is extraordinary. It seems to override the free will of the person possessed, and there is a real question as to why God would allow this, even rarely. Presumably, angels have the same power. However angelic possession is not considered to be undesirable, and thus, there are no instances of them being exorcised. And since angels would not do anything wrong, like overriding the free will of a human being, angelic possession has probably never happened.

Modern psychiatrists also have natural explanations for conditions that appear to be demonic possession, but such explanations are not satisfactory in all reported cases and cannot explain paranormal events external to the possessed person, unless we accept that the human mind also has the power of mind over matter.

The final type of spiritual being of the spiritual realm is God. Naturally, God has all the powers and abilities of angels and demons, and then some. God has rarely manifested himself, except in the person of Jesus Christ, which will be considered shortly. His main manifestations are recorded in the Bible. In these, he manifested as a disembodied voice, as a burning bush, and as a column of smoke. Whether these were real physical manifestations or altered perceptions of the observers is unknown and cannot be known, because there is no objective evidence of these manifestations, such as photographic evidence. Not that it matters. In any event, there is no claim or report of any manifestation of God in modern times, and there has never been any claim of possession of a human being by God.

The manifestations of God that are recorded do not tell us much about the nature of God, which can assist us in conceptualising him. As has been mentioned, a consideration of the nature of God is beyond the scope of this work. Our concern here is with a concept of God as a spiritual being having the power to create all that is, both seen and unseen. That means that God created both the spiritual realm and the material realm. In relation to the material realm, that means that God not only has the power of mind over matter, but he can also transmute matter and even cause it to come into existence out of nothing. Human intelligence is simply not capable of understanding how this is possible, because it is contrary to logic and to the sum of human experience. But our inability to understand this does not mean that it is not true or real.

In order to conceptualise something, we usually form a mental image of what that something looks like. A spiritual being has no physical substance and therefore cannot look like anything that we can imagine, as we can only form mental images of material things. Over the centuries, many persons have attempted to conceptualise God, and many artists have attempted to depict God and other spiritual beings. Obviously, it is impossible to draw or paint something that has no physical substance. Artists have done the best they can from suspected attributes of the spiritual beings. Ghosts are usually portrayed as transparent humans or misty humanlike shapes. Angels are portrayed as beautiful humans with birdlike wings. Demons are depicted as ugly deformed humans with horns, a tail, and bat-like wings. Sometimes they are huge and sometimes tiny. The classic portrayal of God is in the Creation mural in the Sistine Chapel of the Vatican. It shows God as a powerful old man with a long white beard.

With our best artists giving us such mental images of spiritual beings, it is easy to see how our thought processes tend to consider spiritual beings as part of the material realm and accordingly expect evidence of their existence to be found in the material realm. This is a common error which does not warrant criticism, because we need to conceptualise spiritual beings in order to consider issues that involve them. There is no easy solution to the dilemma of misconceptualisation of spiritual beings. The best that we can do is use our misconceptualisations, being mindful that they are misconceptualisations and frequently testing whether our reasoning and conclusions assume that the spiritual being under consideration is part of the material realm. An example is a drawing or graphic of a heart to represent love. We all know that love is in the mind and not the heart, but we all recognise the heart icon and know what it means.

The manifestation of God in the person of Jesus Christ warrants special consideration. In our faith, we believe that Jesus was conceived of the Virgin Mary through the power and action of the Holy Spirit. There was then the normal gestation period, and Jesus was born as a normal human being who matured to adulthood in the normal way.

We do not know when the spiritual being that is Jesus bound himself to the physical being that was Jesus, but we can assume that it was at conception. For our purposes of conceptualisation of the spiritual realm, we can assume that Jesus is a part of our triune God, and therefore, his physical human body was a real physical manifestation of God.

Our church teaches that the term *hypostatic union* describes how God the Son took on a human nature in the person of Jesus yet remained fully God at the same time as being fully human. The church concedes that our finite minds cannot fully comprehend the nature of our infinite God, and accordingly, we cannot conceptualise the nature of the Son of God. We do not know how it can be possible for a spiritual being to become a material being, although we can see that this is different from a spiritual being possessing or controlling the actions of an already existing person. But we can conceptualise the fully human being that is Jesus, even though we do not have any pictures of him, without in any way diluting either his divine nature or his human nature.

Concise Collins Dictionary defines the word *avatar* as 'the manifestation of a deity in human or animal form'; it is derived from Hinduism. This word is inadequate to encompass the two natures of Jesus Christ, but since the concept exists for the human mind, it can be used to provide a working concept of Jesus, because it reminds us of his divine nature while conveying some mental image of the human man as part of our material realm.

Modern science has no idea of how an embryo can be created in a female virgin without the participation of a male. Our scientists have developed In Vitro Fertilization, but this still involves matter from a human male. What the conception of Jesus involves is the spontaneous creation of male matter inside the womb of the Virgin Mary or perhaps the transmutation of some matter already there to provide the necessary male matter which contained the unique DNA of Jesus. Human science has not been able to achieve such a thing. However, if we assume for the purposes of this conceptualisation that God exists and that he created a universe containing about 7 trillion galaxies, the spontaneous creation or transmutation of a small amount of matter, even with a unique DNA, is well within his power. Accordingly, the proposition that Jesus Christ was born of the Virgin Mary should not be an impediment to our concept of Jesus.

Our sacred writings suggest that Jesus transferred his spirit into the body that had been created for him, but he did not transfer that part of his spirit that was his mind, with all its memory and powers, until later in his life. For his own reasons, which we can guess were to avoid providing compelling proof of his divinity, he grew as a normal human, and it was not till he matured and his ministry commenced that he exhibited his divine nature. This is evidenced by the fact that Jesus did not exhibit divine powers from birth, he transferred his spirit into the bread and wine at the Last Supper while his physical person remained whole, and his spirit is transferred into each host at every mass while his material body remains whole, since his ascension.

From this analysis, we can conceptualise Jesus as an avatar of the second person of our triune God, whose divine spirit remains as God but also fully human.

In addition to the things of the spiritual realm, such as love and hate, and the beings that are of the spiritual realm, it may be useful to consider whether there are locations, such as heaven and hell, in the spiritual realm.

Historically, heaven and hell have been thought of as places in our material realm. Heaven was thought to be above us, perhaps amongst the stars but at least above the clouds, which was then unreachable by mankind. As recently as the time of Jesus, it was written that Christ 'came down' from heaven and that after his death and resurrection, he 'ascended' into heaven. Our church teaches that Our Lady also ascended into heaven.

Hell, on the other hand, has been regarded as being a place somewhere below the crust of our Earth. The ancient mythologies of various cultures portray it as an inner world full of torments, and there are references to the 'netherworld' in the Old Testament. Even Jesus described hell as the 'everlasting fire that was prepared for the devil and his angels'.

We do not know whether heaven and hell are real places in our material realm or whether they are the spiritual existential environment of the beings of the spiritual realm. The modern view is that they are the states of mind of spiritual beings.

To the mind of a person who believes in the existence of God or some other deity, it is a bad thing to do something that angers or displeases God, because God's wrath will undoubtedly be unpleasant. The worst thing that can happen to us is that we permanently alienate God. Accordingly, the consequences of permanently alienating God are the worst thing that the human mind can imagine, and since human imagination of pain and suffering is most clearly expressed in terms of our suffering experienced in the material realm, it was natural that hell was described as a place in which the greatest human pain imaginable is eternally suffered. Death by fire has long been believed to be the most painful of deaths. Dante, in his *Inferno*, portrayed different kinds of suffering on a layered scale of painfulness, in accordance with his view of the seriousness of various sins. This concept has survived to the modern concept, in which some people think that some types of sin are punished in 'the deepest depths of hell'.

However, most modern theologians consider that Jesus was speaking metaphorically when describing heaven as paradise and hell as a fiery pit. It is now believed that the anguish that a person or soul feels at having permanently alienated God is worse than any physical pain imaginable. Furthermore, if souls are spiritual beings, then they cannot be affected by anything that causes pain in the material realm, nor can they be confined to any place in the material realm, since they occupy no space and apparently have the ability to pass through matter. With these factors in mind, it is reasonable to consider heaven and hell as the spiritual existential environment of spiritual beings, heaven being more like permanent happiness and euphoria, and hell being more like permanent sadness and depression than actual places in our material realm.

A complication to this view arises from our dogma of the resurrection of our bodies at the end of time. It is generally believed that after this resurrection, those who are saved will reside with God in paradise or heaven forever, and therefore, heaven must be a material place.

Certainly, when our material bodies are resurrected, they will need to exist in a material environment. The New Jerusalem described in the book of Revelation is clearly a description of a place in the material realm, where our resurrected bodies can reside eternally in a state of happiness in the light of God. Granted that Revelation is essentially allegorical and was intended for Israelites, it may also indicate what God has in mind for the resurrected, and this is consistent with the modern view that heaven and hell are more a state of mind than places in our material realm. Revelation also refers to the pit of 'fire and sulphur' as the destination of the resurrected who are not saved, but we have no idea of where this is located, although it too is clearly of the material realm.

For the sake of clarity in conceptualisation, only heaven and hell have been mentioned in this context, but we believe that limbo and purgatory are also aspects of the spiritual realm and can be considered in the same way. There could also be other such aspects, but we do not know what these are called or who they are for. There remain many unanswered (and probably unanswerable) questions about the spiritual realm, but for the purposes of considering religious issues, we probably know enough to enable a reliable, if not completely accurate, working conceptualisation.

Conclusion

It is not the purpose of the forgoing outline to offer any proof of the existence of beings of the spiritual realm. As Catholics, we believe in the existence of the souls of deceased humans, angels and demons, and God. We are free to accept or reject a persuasion of the truth of any particular alleged supernatural event (except as recorded in the Gospels) from the evidence available in support of the alleged event.

The point of this outline was to clarify that spiritual beings (except Jesus Christ) are and always remain entirely non-material and that they have a range of abilities or powers with which they can interact with objects and persons of our material realm, although we do not understand how this can be.

The importance and value of this point lies in us being mindful of the non-material nature of spiritual beings in every consideration of spiritual beings. Graphic representations of spiritual beings in art, literature, and other forms of communications are necessarily false and misleading, but they are legitimate because they are the best we can do to communicate the concept of beings that have no material substance. However, we need to be alert to the tendency to draw conclusions from arguments about spiritual beings which conceptualise them as having some material substance and the idea that, therefore, there ought to be some material evidence of their existence or presence. This is a particularly common error amongst persons who believe or argue that the spiritual realm does not exist.

As was suggested above, we can, by analogy, conceptualise Jesus as an avatar, because he was a real material human being. It is not suggested that this is theologically correct, because we do not know the full and true nature of God, but it may help our conceptualisation of Jesus in order to avoid confusion and error.

PART 2

THE EXISTENCE OF GOD

2.1 The Major Arguments for the Existence of God

2.1.1 Catholic Dogma

For us, as Catholics, the logical starting point for our consideration of the question of the existence of God is the teaching of our church. Our church has teachings on virtually every religious issue that has arisen in the past and on contemporary issues. Of course, the church is not hasty in formulating and promulgating teachings on any issue, so teachings on the very latest issues require sufficient time for proper consideration before they can be formulated.

Also, the teachings of the church have differential status, depending on the source of the teaching, the theological necessity of the teaching, the authority of the church entity formulating the teaching, and the relevance of the teaching to motivating the behaviour of the Catholic community, both generally and in accordance with the practicalities of cultural diversity. In other words, some teachings must be accepted as true and correct by all persons as a condition of membership of the Catholic Church, some teachings should be accepted by all Catholics as true and correct but may be privately doubted on reasonable grounds, and other teachings which are not inconsistent with either of the above categories are optional.

That category of teaching which must be accepted and professed by all Catholics is called dogma. The Vatican Council identified this category as follows:

All those things are to be believed by divine and Catholic faith which are contained in the Word of God written or handed down and which are proposed for our belief by the Church either in a solemn definition or in its ordinary and universal authoritative teaching.

The status of dogma itself is an issue, but for the present, we are only concerned with identifying what it is that the church teaches about the existence of God at its highest authoritative level. Of course, if a person does not or no longer believes in the existence of God, then any dogma of the church has no authority or weight, but our concern is to identify the dogma which the church says is a necessary belief for all Catholics.

So what is the Catholic dogma in relation to this issue? There appear to be two dogmas relevant to this issue. The first is as follows:

God, our creator and Lord, can be known with certainty by the natural light of reason from created things.

The most significant aspect of this dogma is that it is not of itself proof of the existence of God, nor is it evidence of the existence of God. What it says is that the evidence of the existence of God can be found in created things. In practical terms, what this means is that if we study created things with reference to how they came to be and draw the proper inferences from our studies, we will see beauty, love, and an intelligent design that has not been adequately explained by any secular theory of Creation, leaving only the conclusion that these created things were indeed created and their creator we conceive to be God.

This teaching does not require a study of all created things; in our belief, God created all that is, so his involvement in the creation of any particular thing can be apparent from a study of that thing. However, if we study a natural thing, like an animal or tree or rock, we must logically regress our consideration to the formation of our planet or the development of life on our planet, so some knowledge of this history is necessary so that we do not base our conclusion that God exists on our admitted ignorance of such history.

The troublesome word in this dogma is the word *certainty*. Unfortunately, it has not been defined for this context. The normal rule of interpretation is 'Plain words, plain meaning'. But the exact meaning of some words change over time, and there are often no exact synonyms in other languages. This dogma was formulated by the Vatican Council and promulgated in Latin. We must also take into account that it was not decreed that a study of created things with the natural light of reason will produce objective and *compelling* proof of the existence of God. This dogma is subjective in its use of the word *certainty*. It must therefore mean that an individual who studies created things in relation to the question of the existence of God can be satisfied that God does exist to the degree that enables that individual to honestly acknowledge his or her belief that God does exist. That such a belief is subjective and not compellingly objective is demonstrated by people who change their belief in this regard for various reasons. Also, it cannot be denied that some very intelligent and well-educated persons have studied created things and have not been able to conclude the existence of God from their studies.

Another difficulty arising from this formulation of the dogma is that it can be seen as a circuitous proposition. In other words, it can be perceived as meaning that if one believes that God exists and created all things, then when one studies any created thing, one can see that God created these things; therefore, that perception proves that God exists. This dogma was framed by clerics who obviously believed that God exists and who refer to him with reverence and devotion, as is appropriate. However, as an immutable dogma, it could have been more objectively phrased. In particular, the phrase 'created things' assumes that the things were created, and that, in turn, implies a creator. Perhaps a less assuming phrase in lieu of 'created things' would have been 'things that exist'.

The answer to this criticism is that the dogma was clearly intended to apply to individuals studying created things with no fixed view about the existence of God one way or the other. Some individuals who undoubtedly possess the natural light of reason have studied created things and failed to perceive that what they studied was, in fact, created. This may be explained by the proposition that these individuals had a fixed belief that God does not exist when they undertook their studies.

From our point of view, this dogma is necessarily valid and can stand alone, but few of the specific arguments to prove the existence of God are based on a study of things that exist. Also, early last century, there was substantial contention by philosophers and theologians, identified as modernists, as to the validity of this dogma. In response to this, Pope Pius X in 1910 extended the Vatican definition in this regard as follows:

The existence of God can be formally proved through reason by means of the principle of causality.

As will be seen, there are difficulties with the principle of causality, and while this supplement to this dogma enables the application of this dogma to some modern arguments about the existence of God, it is not itself dogma, although it is clearly a Catholic Church teaching from the highest authority and cannot be lightly disregarded.

The second dogma on this issue is as follows:

God's existence is not merely an object of natural rational knowledge, but also an object of supernatural faith.

This type of belief cannot be explained by the application of reason, and accordingly, it is usually referred to as the gift of faith, the gift coming from God. Critics of this type of faith say that it is not valid because it has no reasonable basis. Of course, that is correct, because a supernaturally granted faith cannot have a basis amenable to human reason or proof. But that does not make it any less real or valid. This is an impasse which cannot be resolved through the use of reason. These critics also argue that what we call the gift of faith is merely a belief arising out of the accident of birth into a Catholic family, sociocultural conditioning, the influence of our parents, the Catholic education system, and other similar influences.

We cannot deny that our beliefs can be shaped or influenced by such factors, and the criticism may well be correct in identifying the mechanism God uses to deliver this gift to the souls of his choice. We simply do not know what mechanism God uses to deliver his gifts, but his use of apparently natural means does not disprove the supernatural nature of this type of faith. Nor does this criticism explain the conversion of mature adults who have been brought up and have lived their lives without a belief in the existence of God, where such conversion arose from factors other than exposure to the rational arguments about the existence of God.

We do know that this gift is fragile, because it is known that many lose this type of faith after separation from the influences that gave rise to such faith, particularly if respected associates of the person who had such faith have undermined it with their views or if some events have occurred that the person cannot reconcile with his or her concept of God. The loss of this type of faith may not be easily regained. It is hoped that exposure to the rational arguments supporting the existence of God set out in this work may enable a person who has lost the gift of faith to recognise the weaknesses in the arguments or events that have led to his or her loss of faith, and may perhaps restore it or provide a rational alternative basis for faith. The rational arguments referred to have been devised and formulated by some of the greatest minds in both ancient and modern times, and it is highly unlikely that anything new or unprecedented has caused anyone a loss of faith. The challenge is to know the arguments and then identify the modern event or formulation causing a loss of faith within the classical structure of relevant arguments.

2.1.2 The Five Ways of Aquinas

Mankind's earliest records indicate that people have been thinking about the question of the existence of God throughout recorded history. Their conclusion has mostly been that there is a god, and in some cases, that there are many gods. Polytheism was eventually replaced by monotheism, on the logic that there can be only one supreme being, although even today Hinduism is a polytheistic religion. For our consideration of the question of whether or not God exists, we do not need to reinvent the wheel— i.e. we do not have to follow the development of the theological and philosophical ideas from first principles, but it may help to have an overview of the concepts.

Our considerations can start with Plato, who postulated the existence of forms which had divine attributes. Aristotle refined this to a single divine form-like being, which is the basis of the Christian concept of God. He also attempted to prove the existence of such a being with the unmoved mover argument, which Aquinas later used as the basis of the first of his five arguments to prove the existence of God. Aquinas was also aware of and built on the arguments of other theologians and philosophers, such as St Augustine and St Gregory, and Jewish and Islamic scholars, such as Averroes and Moses Maimonides, the latter being the source basis for Aquinas's second way. St Anselm argued for the existence of God with a priori arguments, later described as ontological arguments, which have little support in modern times. Aquinas did not pursue this style of argument, preferring the a posteriori style of argument, although he gave a lot of thought to necessary attributes of God, which is largely a priori and based on divine revelation.

St Thomas Aquinas was born in about 1224 and died in 1274. He was a Dominican priest who worked as a professor of theology in the University of Paris. He was a prolific writer, his best-known work being the *Summa Theologiae*. This work contains his

Five Ways, which are for proving the existence of God. Modern theologians and philosophers have refined and developed the arguments presented by Aquinas, but they still have sufficient influence to be dealt with in most modern texts dealing with this issue. Aquinas was a 'giant standing on the shoulders of giants'. Modern theologians are standing on the shoulders of Aquinas, and accordingly, it is appropriate to have some awareness of the concepts underlying modern thinking on this question. Aquinas's Five Ways, with comments, are as follows:

The First Way

The first and most obvious way is based on change. It is certain and clear to our senses that some things in the world undergo change. But anything in the process of change is changed by something else. For nothing can be undergoing change unless it is potentially whatever it ends up being after its process of change, while something causes change insofar as it is actual in some way. After all, to change something is simply to bring it from potentiality to actuality, and this can only be done by something that is somehow actual; thus, fire (actually hot) causes wood (able to be hot) to become actually hot, and it changes and modifies it. But something cannot be simultaneously actually x and potentially x, though it can be actually x and potentially y (something actually hot, for instance, cannot also be potentially hot, though it can be potentially cold). So something in the process of change cannot itself cause that same change. It cannot change itself. Necessarily, therefore, anything in the process of change is changed by something else. This something else, if in the process of change, is itself changed by yet another thing, and this last by another. But there has to be an end to this regress of causes; otherwise, there will be no first cause of change and, as a result, no subsequent causes of change. For it is only when acted on by a first cause that intermediate causes produce change (if a hand does not move the stick, the stick will not move anything else). So we are bound to arrive at some first cause of change that is not itself changed by anything, which is what everybody takes God to be.

Comment

We must bear in mind that this argument is a translation from something that was written in the thirteenth century and based on a concept formulated by Aristotle. The language and philosophical style are not contemporary English, but the concept is clear enough. Essentially, the argument is that nothing changes unless it is changed by something else that already exists. If we then trace the imparting of change back, we must come to a first changer, which was not itself changed by anything, and this is God.

This argument cannot be supported under modern scrutiny. There are several substantial impediments to a general perception of the validity of the argument. Firstly, the argument assumes that there is an unbroken chain of contact between everything that exists and the first changer. The argument is a posteriori in that it relies on common experience to support this assumption. Certainly, inanimate objects do not usually change anything unless something stimulates them to bring about a change in another thing, but there are exceptions, such as spontaneous combustion, which appears to change the nature of the thing burning without the action of some other thing. And people and animals mostly appear to initiate the action which brings about change in themselves. Secondly, the analogy of the fire making the wood hot and thereby changing it is flawed, because becoming hot is not change in the usual sense of the word. Usually the word *change* implies a change in the nature of the thing changed, whereas wood becoming hot is merely a change in the property of temperature of the wood, which is a property that all things have. Thirdly, Aquinas concludes that the logically necessary first and unchanged changer is understood by everyone to be God. That may be just a figure of speech to express the conclusion, because Aquinas uses a similar formula to conclude each of his arguments, but it is certainly not true as a general statement in modern times, because this argument is understood by theologians and philosophers who nevertheless adhere to their atheistic belief.

While the Big Bang theory is still only a theory, many people accept it. To these people, the concept of regression or tracing of the transference of motion can only go back to the Big Bang, some 13.7 billion years ago, and therefore, the concept of infinite regression is untenable. To this extent, they support this argument. For them, the question then becomes one of 'Who or what changed the contents of the singularity from compressed matter into our known expanding universe?' A chain of changes in which objects stimulate change in another object, which in turn stimulates change in still other objects, and so on raises the concept of a chain of causation, which is more fully considered under Aquinas's second way. But it may be noted that this first way is generally considered to be a causation-type argument.

The Second Way

The second way is based on the notion of the efficient cause. We find there is an order of efficient causes in the observable world. Yet we never observe, or ever could something efficiently causing itself, for this would mean that it preceded itself, which it cannot do. But an order of efficient causes cannot go back infinitely. An earlier member in it causes an intermediate, and the intermediate causes a last (whether the intermediate be one or many). If you eliminate a cause, however, you also eliminate its effect. So there cannot be a last cause or an intermediate one unless there is a first. If there is no end to the series of efficient causes, therefore, and if, as a consequence, there is no first cause, there would be no intermediate efficient causes either, and no last effect, which is clearly not the case. So we have to posit a first cause, which everyone calls God.

Comment

This argument is based on both logic and experience. Essentially, he argues that in all human experience, we have never found anything that does not have a cause which preceded it; therefore, everything that exists or happens has been caused to exist or happen. He then argues that there cannot be an infinite regression of causes, because that would mean that there is no first cause and that, therefore, there cannot be an effect which then becomes a second cause or any subsequent effect and so on. Therefore, there must be a first cause, and this cause was the action of God.

To understand this argument, we must understand how cause and effect works and what meaning Aquinas intended to convey. For something to produce an effect, there must be some connection between the cause and effect. Let us consider the example of a golfer striking a golf ball. The event to be considered is the motion of a previously stationary golf ball. A ball lies motionless on the ground or on a tee. The golfer takes a golf club in his or her hands by the grip part of the club, holding it in a way conducive to swinging the club. The golfer then takes up a position and posture in relation to the ball that is conducive to striking the ball and then turns his or her body and swings his or her arms in a motion known as a golf swing. The golf club, held in the golfer's hands, moves in an arc. At a point in the arc of the club's motion known as the bottom of the downswing, the face or head of the golf club comes into contact with the golf ball. The club head has a mass substantially greater than the mass of the golf ball, and the club head is moving at a relatively high speed. The contact between the club head and the golf ball results in the golf ball going into motion in roughly the direction that the club head was travelling and facing at the point of contact. In this example, we can say that the golfer's action in swinging his or her arms while holding a golf club in a certain way and in a certain position relative to the position of the golf ball *caused* the golf ball to go from a state of rest to a state of motion.

If the effect that we were considering was that the golf ball had moved from position A on a golf course to position B on the golf course, we might ask why it ended up in position B rather than some other position. We would know what caused the ball to move, i.e. the action of the golfer, but we would then find that a number of other factors affected the trajectory of the ball after the action of the golfer was complete, resulting in the ball coming to rest again in position B. Such factors may be things like the force and direction of the wind, the contour of the terrain, the air temperature, etc. These are all factors beyond the control of the golfer and are unconnected to the action of the golfer—i.e. they are non-human or inanimate factors. But because they do contribute to the final effect under consideration, they could be described as secondary causes, whereas the action of the golfer in this example is the primary cause. The causal connection in the primary cause in this example is the golfer holding the golf club in his or her hands and the contact between the club face and the golf ball. The causal connection in the secondary causes in this example is the contact between the golf ball and the surrounding air and then the contact between the ball and the ground.

That does not mean that inanimate factors cannot be primary causes. For example, a strong gust of wind could cause an avalanche in a snow-covered mountain range, which in turn could cause the destruction of a ski chalet (hopefully empty at the time). In this example, the causal connection is the contact of the wind with the snow and then the contact between the snow and the ski chalet. There may well be secondary causes in such an event.

Raising the concept of the regression of causes may lead to some confusion as to the continuity of causes, and it is therefore appropriate to define the difference between a causal connection and a causal link. In the example of the golfer, the cause was the golfer swinging the golf club. The golfer was motivated to swing the golf club, and he or she initiated the swing on his or her own volition. No physical factor caused the golfer to swing the golf club. Some people might argue that motives are causes. Presumably, our golfer made the decision to play golf on the day of our example because he or she likes to play golf. But that did not cause him or her to swing the golf club through any physical connection. From our perspective, motives cannot be causes, for if they were, then their effects would be predictable; this would lead to the conclusion that there is no such thing as free will. Conceptually then, the golfer's swing has no cause other than the volition of the golfer. The effect of the swing is to put the ball in motion. If, on landing, the ball struck a rock and bounced sharply away from its previous line of motion and landed in a lake, it is clear that the golfer did not cause the ball to end up in the lake, although there is a causal link.

A common example of a sequence of events having some causal link is the biblical genealogy following Abraham. Abraham begat Isaac, Isaac begat Jacob, etc. Abraham took some action which led to the birth of Isaac. Isaac took some action which led to the birth of Jacob. Obviously, nothing that Abraham did was a factor in the action that Isaac took which led to the birth of Jacob. But Isaac would not have been able to take this action if he had not been born, and he would not have been born but for the action of Abraham. Thus, we can validly say that there is a *causal link* between the birth of Jacob and the action taken by Abraham in fathering Isaac, but there is no *causal connection*. A series or sequence of events which have a causal connection is usually called a chain of events or causal chain. It seems that the type of regression that Aquinas had in mind in this argument involves tracing back all the linked events in a causal chain of events, although he clearly understood the nature of a causal connection, as is apparent from his phrase *'if a hand does not move the stick, the stick will not move anything else'*, which was in his first way.

A common misapprehension in tracing back a chain of causation is to conclude that some event is part of a causal chain on the basis that the event being considered always precedes some other event, and therefore, these two events are part of a causal chain. This is not necessarily true. For example, golf is always played in daylight, so a sunrise always precedes a game of golf. We could argue that but for the sunrise, the game of golf would not have taken place, but clearly, as a matter of common sense, the sunrise is in no sense causative of the game of golf. Perhaps the test question is whether the preceding event ever happens without the subsequent event ever occurring. But the real answer here is to rely on common sense to determine whether any two associated events are part of a causal chain.

This argument by Aquinas raises the proof for the existence of God on the basis of the principle of causality, and it is this principle that Pope Pius X had in mind when he extended the church's dogma on the proof of the existence of God. It is therefore very important to the theological concepts and arguments dealing with the question of the existence of God, and it is vital that the concept is clearly understood. This concept has been considered by modern theologians and will be considered later herein.

The Third Way

The third way is based on the possible and the necessary, and it runs as follows. Some of the things we encounter are able to be or not to be, for we find them generated and perished (and therefore able to be or not to be). But not everything can be like this. For something that is capable of not being at some time is not. So if everything is able not to be, at some time there was nothing in the world. But if that were true, there would be nothing even now, for something that does not exist is only brought into being by something that does exist. Therefore, if nothing existed, nothing could have begun to exist, and nothing would exist now, which is patently not the case. So not everything is the sort of thing that is able to be or not to be. There has got to be something that must be. Yet a thing that must be either does or does not have a cause of its necessity outside itself. And just as we must stop somewhere in a series of efficient causes, so we must also stop in the series of things which must be and owe this to something else. This means that we are forced to posit something which is intrinsically necessary, owing its necessity to nothing else, something which is the cause that other things must be.

Comment

This argument is essentially a variation or application of the principle of causality. What it says is that in our experience, all things come into existence and then pass away, and everything that comes into existence is brought into existence by something else that already exists. It then argues that you cannot have an infinite regression, as demonstrated in the previous causality argument, and that therefore, it must necessarily be that there was some being in existence who brought the first things into existence, that being having not been brought into existence by anything else, and that this being is God.

The logic of the argument that there cannot be an infinite regression is not demonstrably correct, because of the impossibility of demonstrating anything involving the concept of infinity. Aquinas argues a priori that there must be a first cause; otherwise, you could not have a second and subsequent causes. Thus, he sidesteps involvement with the concept of infinity. The modern Big Bang theory is some posthumous support for Aquinas's argument if we accept that God caused the Big Bang to happen. But some modern cosmologists hold the view that the universe is pulsating with Big Bang cycles—i.e. the universe explodes with a big bang, expands for a time, and then contracts back into a singularity, which then explodes again with a big bang—and that this cycle has been going on forever. This view clearly raises the concept of infinity, and this argument by Aquinas has no validity to persons who hold this view.

Nevertheless, the argument is still important, and it has some biblical support which predates Aquinas in the text of Exodus, where God identifies himself as 'I Am Who Am', which implies eternal existence. But that support is only meaningful when one has already accepted that God exists, as Aquinas clearly had done.

The Fourth Way

The fourth way is based on the gradation that we find in things. We find some things to be more or less good, more or less true, more or less noble, and so on. But we speak of things as being more or less F insofar as they approximate in various ways to what is most F. For example, things are hotter and hotter the closer they approach to what is hottest. So something is the truest and best and most noble of things and hence the most fully in being. For, as Aristotle says, the truest things are the things most fully in being. But when many things possess some property in common, the one most fully possessing it causes it in the others. To use Aristotle's example, fire, the hottest of all things, causes all other things to be hot. So there is something that causes in all other things their being, their goodness, and whatever other perfection they have, and we call this God.

Comment

This argument appears superficially to be an application of the causality principle in that it argues that the qualities of all things are caused by the thing that has the maximum possible of those qualities and that the being with the perfection of all qualities is God. This argument raises substantial theological difficulties and cannot survive close scrutiny in the light of modern science. It may have some appeal, but as an argument, it contains a number of unproven and unprovable assumptions; accordingly, it is not highly regarded by modern theologians.

The Fifth Way

The fifth way is based on the governance of things. For we see that some things that lack intelligence (i.e. material objects in nature) act for the sake of an end. This is clear from the fact that they always, or usually, act in the same way so as to achieve what is best (and therefore reach their goal by purpose, not by chance). But things lacking in intelligence tend to a goal only as directed by one with knowledge and understanding.

Arrows, for instance, need archers. So there is a being with intelligence who directs all natural things to ends, and we call this being God.

Comment

This argument may well be what the church had in mind in formulating the first dogma in relation to the existence of God. In the process of looking at the things of this world with a view to considering the purpose or meaning of life, we would ask questions as to how it is possible that unintelligent things can appear to have intelligent purposes and functions. This formulation of the argument by Aquinas is undeveloped, but the concept he raised has been subsequently developed and is probably the most potent modern argument in support of the existence of God. More will be considered on this issue in relation to the modern arguments, but in the present perspective, this argument can be regarded as a major milestone.

Conclusion

The arguments of Aquinas are expressed in thirteenth-century theological style, in texts intended for theology students who were familiar with this style and who had an underlying knowledge of the history and development of the issues up to their time. There has been substantial development of the arguments since Aquinas, and although the Five Ways are inferior in dealing with modern arguments against the existence of God, they do enable us to see where modern theologians are coming from and do help us understand the modern arguments.

2.1.3 The Ontological Argument

This is a purely a priori argument which has been rejected by most modern theologians and philosophers. It is included for the sake of completeness and to enable acceptance of any assertion that in modern times, this argument has little, if any, persuasive value.

The argument was first formulated by St Anselm but was rejected by Aquinas. The philosopher Descartes defended it, and there arose a movement called ontologism. However, since that time, the argument has been almost universally rejected by theologians and philosophers.

Essentially, the argument is as follows: God is defined as an all-perfect being—that is, a being containing all conceivable perfections. These perfections include such things as omnipotence, omniscience, and the like. These attributes must also include the attribute of existence, for if it did not, then the being containing it would be less than perfect in all respects. Therefore, God must exist.

The flaw in the argument is that existence is not an attribute. Attributes follow existence in that only something that actually exists can have actual attributes. We could define some fictional being as having all sorts of attributes, even perfection, but our imagination would not make the being any more real. Whether God exists or not is not dependent on our imagination.

Ontologism is a philosophy that arose in France in the nineteenth century that seems to have little, if any, relationship to the ontological argument. The philosophy asserts that human reason knows infinite being intuitively and that this knowledge is present in our human minds. It follows from this that we know what things really are and how they came to exist. Essentially, God himself is the guarantee of the correctness of human ideas. This view does not make any sense and is not supported by any evidence. Indeed, the frequency of error in human ideas powerfully contradicts the view. In any event, the Holy Office of the church condemned the view and proclaimed that it could not be taught or held.

2.1.4 The Cosmological Argument

Perhaps the most fundamental fact that we can conceive is the fact of our own existence. The philosopher Descartes put it in the following terms: 'I think therefore I am.' While it is possible to play some word games about the nature of our reality, it is now universally accepted that the physical things that we can perceive with our senses have real existence. From this fundamental fact, philosophers and theologians have contemplated and attempted to discover, with the assistance of human experience, how we came into existence.

Before scientists developed resources that enable our modern perception of the nature and extent of our existence, the considerations of philosophers and theologians were based on speculation and a priori thinking, as is exemplified in the Five Ways of Aquinas. Modern science has discovered much more about the nature of the universe, from the subatomic to the cosmic, and accordingly, the views of philosophers and theologians about the origins of our universe have become known as cosmological views. But that does not mean that there is no longer any speculation and a priori thinking underlying these modern views.

As has been considered, Aquinas searched for the origin of our existence in the application of the principle of cause and effect. From experience, he argued that nothing can come into existence uncaused. Applying a priori thinking, he notionally traced the cause of our present existence. He did not know about the theory of evolution or our modern theories about how the universe came into existence. He may well have believed some version of the Creation myth in Genesis. Consequently, his views turned on the a priori deduction that you cannot have an infinite regression of cause and effect. He argued that there must be a first cause of everything; otherwise, there would be no effect/second cause or any subsequent effect/cause, which would lead to the conclusion that nothing exists. This would contradict the fact of our existence and is therefore nonsense. His first cause was the act of God performing Creation.

In modern times, this argument has been reformulated in many different ways. The Big Bang theory is now widely accepted, so it is no longer necessary to rely on the a priori premise of the impossibility of an infinite regression, although that does not invalidate the argument. Under the Big Bang theory, the regression can only be traced back to the Big Bang about 13.7 billion years ago.

The essence of the modern theists' cosmological argument to support the existence of God is then briefly as follows:

The universe exists. That existence began about 13.7 billion years ago with the sudden, almost instantaneous explosion or inflation of a singularity which contained all the matter in our universe. There is no known natural law which could cause such an event; therefore, the cause of the Big Bang must, for the time being, be regarded as having a supernatural cause. This supernatural cause we can suppose was the act of God in creating the singularity and the matter inside it and causing it to explode or inflate.

Our consideration of these issues is pointless unless they lead to some genuine belief. But even genuine belief can be extinguished by arguments that raise doubts. Accordingly, more durable beliefs must countenance opposing arguments before being accepted as a true belief. To this end, we must consider counterarguments and objections in our assessment of the persuasive value of the cosmological argument for the existence of God. The first part of this process is to consider what theists acknowledge as weaknesses of the argument and then the counterarguments and objections of atheists.

Our initial task then is to identify what, if any, evidence supports this argument. It is axiomatic that our universe exists, so we need no further evidence of this. The principle of cause and effect accords with the entirety of human experience in relation to the proposition that nothing can come into existence spontaneously or uncaused and out of nothing. The only alleged exception to this is the phenomenon called vacuum fluctuations, which will be considered shortly. So again, we need no further evidence of the validity of this proposition. However, it must be acknowledged that our experience of the principle of cause and effect operates in a way in which the cause brings about change in the state of properties of the matter on which the cause operates, with the effect being that change in state of properties. For example, we might boil some potatoes to make them edible. The cause is the boiling of the potatoes, and the effect is the changed state of the potatoes, which makes them edible. The cause has not created potatoes out of nothing. So our principle of cause and effect must be regarded as a process of change and not as a process of creation. But this does not change the human experience of never having seen anything come into existence spontaneously.

Scientists have theoretically traced back the process of change in the state of our universe to a point about 13.7 billion years ago, when all that existed was compressed into a singularity which exploded or inflated with a big bang. Our consideration must assess the reliability of the scientific evidence to support this theory. Obviously, there were no witnesses to the Big Bang, so the scientific evidence can at best be regarded as 'expert opinion evidence', drawn from expertise in the fields of astronomy and cosmology. We can accept that these experts are intelligent and well educated in their fields and that their opinions are given honestly and seriously. Modern scientific instrumentation and resources applied with a state-of-the-art scientific method warrants serious consideration of such experts' opinions. In particular, using telescopes, scientists have observed many celestial objects in apparently different stages of change, so that the laws and processes of cosmic evolution are now well known and understood by such scientists.

Given the general acceptability of scientific expert opinion evidence in this area, we must nonetheless remain mindful that the Big Bang theory is still just a theory and not proven fact. The observations and calculations by Hubble in 1927 that our universe is expanding support the theory but do not prove it. This fact would be proof if the only possible explanation of an expanding universe was its origin in such a big bang. The discovery of cosmic background radiation by COBE, as predicted by Robert Dickie, also supports the theory, but again, it does not amount to proof in the absence of evidence or other reasons showing that the only possible cause of this radiation was the Big Bang.

Another essential ingredient of the modern Big Bang theory is that all the matter in the universe existed inside the singularity before it exploded or inflated, and when this occurred, the explosion or inflation also created time and space. The words *singularity, time,* and *space* refer to concepts which require some clarification in this context if the cosmological argument is to be understood by us laypersons, for without understanding, we cannot accept and believe the theory, although we cannot say that it is wrong either.

In this context, a singularity is the smallest volume of space imaginable which remains mathematically usable. The size of this volume is usually defined as a Planck sphere, which has a radius of 1.6×10^{-35} metres, which is called a Planck length. Other scientists have described the singularity as a volume smaller than a full stop on a printed page. Yet others have said that a singularity has zero magnitude. In all this, there is still debate amongst scientists as to whether there was a singularity before the Big Bang.

We can safely discard any view based on the concept of the singularity having zero magnitude, because anything having zero magnitude does not exist, and all the matter in the universe cannot be compressed into nothingness. The physical laws of the conservation of matter/energy support this view.

So how can all the matter in the universe be compressed into a singularity that does have some size, no matter how small? At this stage, scientists have not demonstrated that nuclear particles such as neutrons, protons, and electrons can be compressed. Nuclear fission and fusion shows that there are immense amounts of energy holding such particles together in their atomic structure, so it may not even be possible to eliminate the space between the nucleus of an atom and its surrounding electrons, which means that matter has very little, if any, compressibility. But even if this were possible and all neutrons, protons, electrons, and other subatomic particles could be placed side by side, the amount of matter in the universe would certainly occupy a volume greater than any concept of the size of a singularity. So how can such a volume of matter, not known to be compressible, be compressed into a volume the size of a singularity?

Some scientists have argued the speculation that gravity causes coalescence of matter and that as more and more matter coalesces, the gravity becomes greater and greater until it becomes infinite, so that nothing can exist outside the singularity. The singularity then acquires infinite density because of all the matter contained within it. For these purposes, the word *infinite* does not mean true infinity, but rather 'a very large number'. However, scientists do not know what gravity is. They know how it works but not why. The support for this speculation comes from the existence of black holes in our universe. These black holes apparently have vast and immensely powerful gravity fields, so that not even light can escape the gravity field. The size of such a gravity field is vast but finite, and there is no evidence that these fields are growing in size. Nor is there any evidence of the true size of the black holes. They may be as small as a singularity in size, but they could also be the size of our planet. Their existence does not prove that nuclear particles are compressible. Indeed, to most scientists, a black hole is something from which 'no further information can be extracted'.

The next concept for clarification is space. It is asserted by some scientists that before the Big Bang, there was no space as we know it, and the inflation of the singularity created its own space. Literally, this is inconceivable, but we can conceive that before the singularity inflated, wherever it was, it was surrounded by infinite omnidirectional nothingness. If the scientists, in referring to the space created by the Big Bang, mean space as we know it from within our universe, which is filled with light and other vibrations on the electromagnetic spectrum and particles of matter, then there is no difficulty in accepting this concept, although a clearer definition of *space* by these scientists is desirable. If they mean that there was not even nothingness surrounding the singularity initially, then their concept is incomprehensible and, accordingly, unacceptable.

The third concept requiring clarification is time. The theory is that the inflation of the universe created time. We measure time in relation to the motion of physical objects. For example, a year is the amount of time that elapses when our planet completes one orbit around our sun. A day is the amount of time that elapses when our planet completes one rotation on its own axis. People have then arbitrarily subdivided a day into twenty-four hours, with each hour having sixty minutes and each minute having sixty seconds. We can conceive that before the singularity exploded or inflated, there was nothing surrounding the singularity and that the singularity was not moving. Thus, there was nothing moving, and accordingly, there was no way that time could be measured. Therefore, we have no way of knowing how long the singularity existed before it exploded or inflated. In terms that mean something to us, the singularity may have existed for many billions of years or the smallest fraction of a second. Like nothingness surrounded the singularity, timelessness preceded the explosion of the singularity.

If this is what the scientists mean, then again, it is a matter for a clearer definition by the scientists. If they mean that time itself did not exist, regardless of its measurability, then this concept is incomprehensible and, accordingly, unacceptable.

Some scientists argue that the Big Bang is cyclic in that it is a continuing process of expansion followed by contraction into a singularity, which then explodes and expands, and that this process has been going on forever. They must necessarily hold the view that the Big Bang did not create time and that time is infinite, although there have been some weird speculations, such as time running backwards during the contraction phase of the cycle. For our purposes, such speculations are irrelevant because they are completely unsupported by any evidence; they add nothing to the Big Bang theory and have no practical implications for humanity in the foreseeable future.

In passing and for what it is worth, the Bible reports God as identifying himself as 'I Am Who Am'. This is not proof of God's existence, because it is self-serving. In other words, you have to believe in God and that he said this, in order to believe in God! But it does show that whoever wrote this part of the Bible had a concept of temporal infinity and believed that God existed and that God claimed such temporal infinity. This occurred long before the concept of infinity was developed as a mathematical concept.

Despite the evidentiary and conceptual difficulties, some theists have addressed the Big Bang theory on the assumption that it may be the means used by God to create our universe. They argue that it was God who created the singularity and all that it contained, and then he caused it to explode or inflate. They do not claim to know how God did this. They reject the cyclic universe theory on the grounds that there is absolutely no evidence to support this variation of the theory.

The atheists respond by arguing that there are no known physical laws or rules of logic that require that there be a creator of the universe and that our present existence can be explained by the operation of natural forces and processes acting on matter that has existed eternally. They further assert that there is absolutely no evidence that proves that God created our universe, and therefore, we must conclude that God does not exist.

Another marginal argument by the atheists is that even if it is incomprehensible that matter has existed eternally, scientific experiments have shown that matter can spring into existence from nothing, and thus, the matter of our universe could similarly have sprung into existence from nothing. These scientific experiments have shown that 'an electron, positron and photon occasionally emerge spontaneously in a perfect vacuum. When this happens, the three particles exist for a brief time, and then annihilate each other, leaving no trace behind.' This phenomenon is called a vacuum fluctuation and is alleged to be commonplace in quantum field theory.

The flaw in the conclusion drawn from observations of this phenomenon is that it assumes that there is such a thing as a perfect vacuum. To date, scientists have not succeeded in creating a perfect vacuum, which requires not only that there be no physical matter in the designated volume but also that there be no light or other vibrations on the electromagnetic spectrum. Nor can there be any other subatomic particles there or any stray electrons from the matter containing the designated volume! A far more likely explanation of this phenomenon lies in the possibility of some yet undiscovered law of physics in such an environment. For the present, we need not abandon the law of the conservation of matter/energy, as proof that matter can come into existence spontaneously out of nothing will require much more evidence than these unexplained vacuum fluctuations.

Conclusion

The essence of cosmology is human knowledge as to how our universe came to be what it is today. Both theists and atheists claim that cosmological knowledge supports their conflicting views as to the existence of God. Both claims have strengths and weaknesses.

The strength of the theists' view is that it relies on reason drawn from human experience. This reason is that anything that exists must necessarily have been created. The human experience is that it is completely unknown for anything to have come into existence spontaneously or through the operation of natural laws or processes.

The weakness of the theists' view is also the strength of the atheists' view. Essentially, it is that because human experience does not contain any instances of the creation of matter, there is no rational basis to believe that what exists was, in fact, created, rather than the proposition that matter has always existed in one form or another.

Theists do not rely on the Big Bang theory for support, but they address it and say that the mechanism that this theory describes leaves room for the possibility of the creation of the matter in the singularity by God and the explosion or inflation of the singularity as caused by God. This applies equally to any current theory of the origin of our universe. The matter must have come from somewhere, and the mechanism of change in the state of the matter was an act of God.

Atheists rely on the Big Bang theory while conceding that it is still only a theory and that the future may bring better theories, possibly from the science of quantum physics. They also concede that the Big Bang theory has conceptual and evidentiary difficulties, in addition to the difficulties outlined above. In the face of all these conceptual and evidentiary weaknesses in their argument, it may be concluded that their argument that matter has always existed has little persuasive value.

However, both the theists' argument and the atheists' argument lack supporting evidence. There is a difference between as yet undiscovered laws and facts and undiscoverable laws and facts. The cosmological argument on both sides falls into the category of undiscoverable laws and facts. What this means is that neither the theist view nor the atheist view about the existence of God based on cosmological knowledge will ever become capable of being *compelling*. Of course, both the theists and the atheists believe their respective arguments to be true. The difficulty for our consideration is that neither view is even strongly persuasive, let alone compelling.

However, neither of these views stands alone. The theists' view can be considered part of a larger body of arguments and evidence, including the teleological argument, while the atheists' view is supported by the argument against the existence of God from the existence of evil. These are considered in the following sections.

2.1.5 The Teleological Argument

This argument is essentially that from our observations of the things of this world, we may see design, purpose, and order. From the presence of these characteristics in the things of this world, it is logically valid to conclude that the things of this world were designed and caused to exist by an intelligent designer. The complexity of the observed design is beyond human capacity to create, and therefore, the designer must be superhuman. The short word for a superhuman being is *god*. Therefore, if we find design, purpose, and order in the things of this world, then God exists.

Obviously, if the intelligent designer did not cause the things of this world to exist, then the existence of the intelligent designer is irrelevant, and the argument is necessarily invalid and fails.

The argument is derived from Aristotle's distinction between the various types of causes and is foreshadowed in Aquinas's fifth way, where he says:

The fifth way is based on the guidedness of nature. An orderedness of actions to an end is observed. They tend towards a goal just as an arrow is directed to a target by an archer. The one who orders and directs nature we call God.

The modern formulation of this argument was presented by William Paley in 1802. He compared the inferences that can be drawn from finding a rock with those that can be drawn from finding a watch. In relation to the stone, he said:

A stone is simply 'there' and suggests no particular inference about its nature and origin.

In relation to the watch, he said:

When we come to inspect the watch we perceive . . . that its several parts are formed and put together for a purpose e.g. that they are so formed and adjusted as to produce motion, and the motion so regulated as to point out the hour of the day . . . [which] yields an inference [which] is inevitable, that the watch must have had a maker.

Paley's watchmaker illustration of how the teleological argument works is quite lucid, and he could have used any complex man-made machine in his example. Applying the argument to natural things, he identified the mechanism of the eye, which he believed was designed for the purpose of sight.

Philosophers and theologians both before and after Paley have regarded the teleological argument as having merit, even though some have identified weaknesses in the argument. The philosopher Hume (1711–1776) pointed out that while the logic may be basically valid, it does not require that the intelligent designer be a single infinite entity. But this observation focuses on the nature of God rather than his existence and, accordingly, does not weaken the point of the argument.

The persuasiveness of the argument lies in the absence of any alternative explanation for the apparent design or purpose in the thing examined. The science of cosmology did much to provide a theoretical alternative explanation for the origin of the universe. Equally, modern cosmology is also providing evidence and theories suggesting an order and design to the universe that was previously unsuspected.

In the same way, the theory of evolution, with its modern sophistications of genetic mutation and DNA modification, has provided an alternative explanation for the appearance of the vast number of different species, where previously there was no explanation other than direct creation. Of course, it is still only a theory, because it works too slowly to be observable in a human lifetime, but scientists have shown that genetic mutation and DNA therapy do work. Accordingly, evolution is now acceptable as an explanation of some of the apparent design found in nature. The core concept of evolution is the survival of a species through the process of adaptation to environmental variation by the individual members of that species and then passing that adaptation on to succeeding generations. It does not explain why living things have a survival instinct or how life sprang from non-living things in the first place. Nor does it preclude the possibility that an intelligent designer created life and gave it a survival instinct so as to use the mechanism of evolution to produce the life forms known to us today. In addition, modern thinking is to the effect that some things that are properties of living organisms are too complex to have come about through the process of evolution. In particular, the human eye appears to be too complex to have evolved naturally in the time since the first appearance of any life on this planet.

The theory of evolution and its sophistications have clearly provided an explanation for the apparent design found in the structure and function of many living things that is an acceptable alternative to the explanation of direct creation. But it has not completely refuted the teleological argument, although it has narrowed the scope of the perception of design in living things to those aspects of design that cannot be attributed to the process of evolution.

With this perspective, we can continue our consideration of the teleological argument with the observation that the teleological argument is not really an argument at all in the usual sense of a proposition supported by evidence or a priori reasoning, but it is rather a description of a process. That process is to examine some particular things amongst the vastness of the things of this world and to form a view as to whether or not the structure and/ or function of the thing examined exhibits an intelligent design either of itself or in the context of its environment that is not explained by the process of evolution.

Accordingly, to assess the persuasive value of the teleological argument, what we need to do is to examine some of the things of this world, looking at how they work, how they came to be what they are, and how they fit and relate to the broad functioning of our planet. If we conclude from such an examination that the function, existence, and role in our planet's ecology of the thing examined suggests a design that goes beyond evolution or any other theory, we may then draw the conclusion that God exists, and we may be persuaded of the correctness of this conclusion according to the degree of supernatural design observed.

Some people end such an examination with the proposition that any apparent design in the thing examined is simply 'the nature of things'. This has been said in relation to the functioning of both biological and non-biological things. Some have even personified nature, with clichés such as 'That is how Mother Nature works!'

Others conclude their analyses with axioms like 'Such apparent design is consistent with the laws of nature or the laws of physics, which govern the operation of our universe'. Such conclusions are unsatisfactory because they are incomplete. They do not countenance the ultimate question. In particular, who or what is Mother Nature if not God? Or who made the laws of nature or the laws of physics?

In relation to the laws of nature for biological things, we must consider the reasons underlying the patterns of behaviour of biological things. If evolution is essentially about survival of the species through the survival of the fittest individuals of that species, why do these biological creatures have a survival instinct, and where does it come from?

In relation to non-biological things, some people say that all matter has always existed and that the laws of physics are immutable and eternal. The Big Bang theorists say that before the Big Bang, there was nothing, not even the laws of physics, and that the laws of physics were created by the Big Bang. The unsatisfactoriness of this explanation becomes apparent when we recall that modern science cannot explain why gravity works, why magnetism works, or why electricity works. Scientists can tell us how these things work but not why.

Another unanswered question is the true nature of matter. The smallest particle of matter was said to be the photon, which is light. But what colour is it? What shape is it? Can it ever be stationary? Is it solid? What type of substance is it? The same questions can be asked about subatomic particles, such as neutrons, protons, positrons, and electrons, and also about various subatomic particles that have been discovered. Even today, scientists are still not sure whether photons are particles of matter or a wave form. If they are a wave form, what is the nature of the medium that is being vibrated at the light source? In passing, we can note that biological things are also composed by these fundamental building blocks of matter, so the same questions can be asked about biological things.

Then there is the more difficult question about the nature of life. Why does life cause the inanimate building blocks of matter to do such things as grow? And why do some biological beings possess such abstract qualities as emotions and intelligence? Where do they come from? What is their true nature? How do they fit into evolution, and how did evolution determine that some of these abstract things would enhance or augment the survival instinct, which is itself an abstract thing?

These as yet unanswered questions are a two-edged sword. Theists can answer such questions with the axiom that it is unknowable because it is part of God's plan for creation. Atheists argue, validly, that the fact that the answers to such questions have not yet been provided by science does not mean that they will never be provided; hence, it is not logically valid to say that God's plan for creation is the only possible answer. On the other hand, atheists cannot disprove the existence of God with purely theoretical answers to such questions, and some of these questions appear to be unanswerable because of the smallness of the fundamental particles of matter and the metaphysical aspects of life. So the debate on these issues is likely to remain unresolved.

Our concern is not to find these ultimate answers but rather to perceive the elements of design in the things examined with the aid of science and then to assess whether any such findings of design or purpose enable the conclusion that God exists and to assess the degree to which we are persuaded of the truth of such a conclusion. If we accept the necessity of doubt as essential for the existence of free will, then we must accept that we will never find a *compelling* argument to prove the existence of God and that the best we can achieve is to find an argument that is persuasive enough to confidently make our life's important decisions on the basis that God does exist.

Conclusion

The existence of God is the first fundamental issue in our personal theology and in the body of beliefs essential to our religion. It is unarguable that either God exists or he does not. There is no third possibility. Many of the important decisions in our lives will depend on or be influenced by our belief in the existence of God. Agnostics are persons who are not persuaded to any relevant degree that God exists, nor are they persuaded to any relevant degree that God does not exist. They acknowledge the possibility that God may exist, but they do not form a view, one way or the other. They sit on the fence, as it were. When faced with an important decision that would be strongly influenced by a belief in the existence of God, an agnostic does not have the benefit or motivation of a clear persuasion and will at best be inconsistent in such decisions. Wisdom suggests that it is better to have a clear view, one way or the other. Thus, if any argument for the existence of God does not persuade us one way or the other, then we should look further. We should have an understanding of all the major arguments for and against the existence of God so that our persuasion is more substantial and consistent than a reed in the wind.

It is beyond the scope of this work to consider all or even many of the things of this world in order to test the persuasiveness of the teleological argument. Furthermore, the degree of persuasion generated by a particular application of the teleological process is subjective—i.e. two persons looking at the same thing for evidence of purpose or design can come to different conclusions or levels of persuasion. Ideally, one should examine those things about which one has extensive knowledge or expertise. The more things that are examined in depth, the more apparent will be the conclusion as to whether there is a big picture. But few of us have expert knowledge on a sufficiently wide range of subjects. Accordingly, it seems that the appropriate way to apply and test the teleological process is to obtain information from the experts in the fields relevant to the things selected for examination. Such information is readily available in books and other media. A few suggestions are as follows:

The Ingenious Mind of Nature	by George M. Hall	Plenum Press 1997
Unsolved Mysteries of Science	by John Malone	John Wiley 2001
Why Us?	by James Le Fanu	Pantheon 2009

Reading such books may be interesting and informative, but the key to applying the teleological process is to look for purpose or design in the facts presented. Often this is done in the book itself, but sometimes such analysis is absent or obscure because the author wishes to avoid theological issues. In relation to such works, we must ask ourselves the right questions and have some personal knowledge about how evolution and/or the laws of nature and physics work. Hopefully, a brief example will illustrate this process.

Let us consider the life cycle of the Pacific salmon. They are born in the upper reaches of rivers in British Columbia, in fresh water. They immediately migrate to the Pacific Ocean, where they live for four years. Each year, about half a billion of them attempt to return to the lagoon in which they were born, where they will spawn and then die. The remarkable thing about this life cycle is their return journey to the lagoon of their birth. To make this journey, they must swim upriver against strong currents and jump up rapids. Of course, they were not all born in the same lagoon. For some of them, the lagoon of their birth is only a few kilometres upstream, but others have been known to travel over two thousand kilometres upstream. Along the way, there are predators, especially bears. Many are caught by bears as they attempt to jump up rapids and others by a variety of predators as they wait in shallow lagoons for the rains to bring sufficient water for them to swim upriver. As they enter the freshwater section of the river, their systems shut down, as they can no longer tolerate fresh water, so they no longer feed. They use their remaining strength to make the journey, and after spawning, they die, essentially from exhaustion and starvation. Many are not strong enough to make the journey and die along the way. Their carcases are mostly taken by predators and scavengers. Only the strongest and fittest are able to complete the journey, and this gives a clear example of evolution in action.

For the purpose of this example, we need not consider how they evolved from single-cell life forms to being Pacific salmon, but we can consider some of their genetic attributes.

Firstly, how do they find the very river in which they were born and then the very lagoon of their birth after swimming around in the Pacific Ocean for four years? Do they have some biological mechanism that instructs them where and when to go, or is it some intangible aspect of their instinct? Scientists have discovered a minute particle of metal in their brains, so the supposition is that they have some type of magnetic guidance system, with obviously incredible sensitivity. From an evolutionary point of view, it is logical for them to return to the lagoon of their birth, because it is obviously suitable for spawning, safe enough for this, and obviously reachable. We also know that they must spawn in fresh water, because we know that their roe cannot survive in salt water. It is this evolutionary restriction which forces the salmon to return to fresh water to spawn.

Secondly, soon after they spawn, they die. Their bodies decompose in the water, thereby providing nutrients to the water, which enables their offspring to survive. Many of their carcases are taken to land by predators and scavengers, where they are partially consumed. The remains then decompose on land and thereby provide nutrients to the surrounding forest. In short, no part of their bodies is wasted, and many species of both plants and animals benefit and even thrive because of the presence of the salmon.

Evolution, as we understand it, is a closed system within each individual species. It is a process whereby individual members of a species change their own genetic structure or DNA in response to environmental changes to enable those individuals and their progeny to survive in the changed environment. Members of the species that do not make those changes or do not make them adequately do not survive. It is sometimes suggested that evolution works to ensure the survival of the species as a whole. This is probably giving evolution too much credit. We can accept that the survival instinct of the individual members of a species drives the evolutionary process of genetic change, but it appears to be a genetic ability of most, if not all, species to be able to pass on genetic changes to their offspring. It is then the strong instinct to reproduce, in combination with the evolutionary process, which enables a species to survive. But many species have become extinct, so evolution is not always successful, apparently if there is insufficient time to mutate or the extent of mutation required is beyond the capability of the biological system. In our example of the salmon, it is clearly the instinct to reproduce that drives the salmon to undertake the arduous journey upriver to spawn and then die, as such a journey is contraindicated by the best interest for the survival of the individual members of this species of salmon. Indeed, the logic of survival would require that they turn back to sea as soon as they see the bears waiting for them at the rapids. Presumably, the instinct to reproduce is stronger than the individual's survival instinct.

Thirdly, they spawn a large number of eggs. This may not always have been so, but the large number of salmon lost to predators at sea and on the return journey requires that they spawn in large numbers to enable the species to survive. Initially, their land-based predators, mostly bears, may not have known about the salmon's life cycle, but when it was presumably serendipitously discovered by the bears, they opportunistically adapted their own life cycle to take advantage of the presence of the salmon at that time of the year, thereby enhancing their own prospects of survival. Accordingly, the salmon may have had to spawn in ever-increasing numbers. This appears to be the type of environmental change that individual members of a species recognise and their biological systems respond to through the evolutionary process.

The life cycle of the Pacific salmon does not appear to have much purpose beyond providing a simple existence for the members of this species for a few short years. But in a broader perspective, this species is a major food source. It enables many other species to survive and some even to thrive. Even forest growth around the salmon-bearing rivers is more prolific than elsewhere. It was suggested above that the bears and other predators may serendipitously have discovered the salmon, but perhaps such a discovery was inevitable by predators foraging in that area. If this is correct, then clearly the life cycle of the Pacific salmon is vital to the ecology of that region.

To date, the evolution of the salmon has been robust enough to enable this species to survive and even thrive. The large number of other species that benefit from this life cycle of the Pacific salmon suggests that the salmon are exactly what is needed to sustain the ecology of the region. And if the ecology of a region is complex enough to make it improbable that it could have happened by chance, then the conclusion that this ecology was created by design is open.

The conclusion of design in this example will not be accepted by every person who reads it, because the conclusion is not compelled by the evidence. The evidence is only persuasive on a subjective level. This example was used to indicate the kind of issues to consider in relation to an examination of biological things. If this example, which is necessarily short and superficial, does not persuade, then perhaps a more in-depth consideration, as is done in the books referred to above, may be the next step. A more in-depth consideration is nevertheless amenable to the same sort of questions that were asked here; however, it will also clarify the point that not only biological things can be considered, but also non-biological things and even abstract things, such as mathematics and the laws of physics.

If our consideration of any such thing persuades us that there is some supernatural design in something that we have examined, then we can ask where this design came from. The only answer to this question is that it must come from a creator. This answer does not identify the creator or tell us much about the nature of the creator other than what we can infer from the nature of his creation. But at least we can be persuaded to the necessary degree that a creator exists. Our word for and form of address to such supernatural creator is *God*.

The persuasiveness of the teleological argument depends on whether or not we are persuaded as to the existence of God from our personal considerations of the things of this world, even though such consideration may be drawn from expert knowledge about the things considered provided by other people. As already observed, the teleological argument is really the description of a process, and as such, it has no persuasive value in itself. It is our application of this process that may persuade us. In this regard, we can link the teleological argument to the Catholic dogma that it is possible to be persuaded to the necessary degree of certainty that God exists from an examination of the things of this world. It is immediately apparent that the teleological argument and the Catholic dogma are almost identical and that they complement each other. The teleological argument tells us what to look for when examining the things of this world, i.e. design, order, and purpose. The dogma tells us that the teleological process is capable of persuading us, to the degree of certainty, that God exists. The teleological process is subjective, and the dogma does not purport to be a compelling objective process and is as valid and applicable today as it was when Aquinas formulated his Five Ways.

To date, philosophers and theologians have been unable to produce any *compelling* argument or proof that God either exists or does not exist. But we need to acquire a persuasion one way or the other about this issue to enable us to make consistent decisions about important matters where the issue of the existence of God is relevant. The teleological process enables us to form a clear and firm view on this issue if we apply it properly in a diligent examination of a sufficient number of the things of this world. Bearing in mind that our persuasion is subjective, inasmuch as two persons could properly apply the process in an examination of the same things of this world and come to different conclusions, the process is nevertheless the best general resource available to consider this issue, although some persons may obtain deeper persuasions through some of the minor arguments considered hereunder.

2.2 The Minor Arguments for the Existence of God

2.2.1 The Argument from the Existence of Human Consciousness

The factual basis for this argument is that we, as human beings, know that we have thoughts and feelings, desires and aversions, the ability to set and achieve goals, and the ability to formulate and hold beliefs. Our recognition of these and other human attributes comes to us in our conscious state. We also know that while still alive, we can be in an unconscious state, such as sleep, after some traumatic head injury or under general anaesthetic. We sometimes remember a dream, which suggests that our brain activity continues during unconsciousness, but there is no evidence to suggest that we can formulate and hold beliefs or perform other higher brain functions during unconsciousness.

In an early formulation of this argument, John Locke asserted that it is axiomatic that matter itself cannot produce thought. We can take this to mean that inanimate objects have never been known to produce any thought. This appears to be correct at the level of fundamental particles of matter, such as atoms, neutrons, protons, electrons, etc. But complex constructs of matter, such as modern computers programmed with artificial intelligence, do produce a simulation of thought, although not of the higher creative functions of the human brain. These computers, just like the human brain, are constructed of the fundamental particles of matter. Of course, a computer is just a machine, and if its power supply is interrupted, it is just an inanimate object incapable of producing any thought. Equally, when a human being dies, the brain activity ceases, and what was once a person becomes an inanimate object incapable of producing thought.

From this, it becomes apparent that consciousness and its capacities are manifest only in living organisms that have a brain. There are, of course, living organisms that have no discernible brain, but such organisms have never been known to produce thought.

Many of us who have owned pets, such as dogs or cats, know that these animals have consciousness and that they also sleep. We may have observed some bodily movement of our pets during their sleep, which suggests that they also dream, which means that their brain activity also continues during unconscious states. However, there is an order of magnitude of difference between animal consciousness and human consciousness. The focus of this argument is on the highest level of consciousness known to exist, and that is human consciousness, because it contains a level of intelligence far beyond that found in any other species of animal.

The key fact underlying this argument is that science cannot explain the relationship between the physical activity of the brain and the related thoughts and feelings experienced by a conscious human being, or why these events are linked to each other, whereas how computers simulate thought is well known to science.

The modern form of this argument is attributed to John Swinburne, who argues that the abstract nature of thoughts and feelings shows that we are a combination of body and soul, that all creatures that have thoughts and feelings have a soul, and that the function of the soul is beyond scientific analysis. The existence of God, who created both body and soul for his purposes and who maintains the link between body and soul, is an explanation for the existence of human consciousness. This, Swinburne argues, makes it probable that God exists.

The first observation that we can make from Swinburne's argument is that it is not presented as having persuasive value beyond the level of the balance of probabilities. But even at this level, there are substantial factors that diminish the persuasive value of this argument.

Firstly, in recent years, there has been much research on how the human brain works, and such research is continuing. Currently, science cannot fully explain how the human brain works, but substantial knowledge has been gained. For example, certain chemicals in the brain, occurring naturally or artificially introduced, consistently produce feelings such as euphoria, and the precise area of the brain that causes such feelings has been identified. We cannot ascertain what further knowledge the continuing research will produce, and consequently, we cannot argue that science will never produce an acceptable alternative explanation for the link between brain activity and thought.

Secondly, although the argument is framed in terms of the existence of a phenomenon (human thought) which requires an explanation, it is, in effect, arguing that this phenomenon could not exist unless it was caused to exist. Since there is no scientific explanation of the cause of its existence, then there must be a supernatural cause of its existence, which is God. Framed in this way, it is easily seen that this argument is simply an application of the second way of the Five Ways formulated by Aquinas. As such, it is subject to all the weaknesses and objections applicable to the second way. In respect to this particular argument, evolutionists can argue that consciousness is a necessary attribute of any species that needs to move about to acquire food, because such a species needs to identify, capture, and consume its food; this can only be done with consciousness.

The argument that life developed spontaneously on our planet has already been considered and been found to be unconvincing in the absence of the ability of science to create life in any conditions. But even if we disregard this objection, there is still the issue of the development of human intelligence, which is manifested in human consciousness. Human intelligence, which may well have aided the survival of the human species, has also enabled humanity to destroy itself and has certainly caused the extinction of a number of other species. It is unreasonable to argue that evolution gave humans the ability to exterminate itself and many or all other species, unless it is argued that the ultimate purpose of evolution is the extermination of all life on this planet.

The conclusion that this leads to is that consciousness in animals may well be part of the evolutionary process, with the proviso that the spontaneous development of life is not yet proven. Human intelligence appears to be beyond the function or purpose of evolution, and in the absence of an acceptable scientific explanation of why it exists and how it works, the only available explanation is that it was caused to exist through direct creation. But this conclusion does not exclude the possibility that science may, in the future, provide an explanation of the source and function of human consciousness.

The bottom line is that the argument for the existence of God from the existence of human consciousness is certainly not compelling and that its persuasive value is confined to the time during which science is unable to provide an acceptable alternative explanation of the source and function of human consciousness, although science may never be able to provide such an explanation.

2.2.2 The Argument from the Existence of Morality

This argument has two premises. The first premise proposes that there objectively exists a universal code of moral conduct for all living creatures. This proposition may be argued by evolutionists who suggest that moral conduct intra- and interspecies is conducive to order and peaceful coexistence of species that do not prey on one another, and that this is, in turn, conducive to the survival of all existing species.

Against this argument, we know that animals do not behave morally. Some birds steal eggs from other birds' nests. Alpha males of many species fight to the death for dominance. Ants actually make war. Carnivores remorselessly kill members of species that they prey on, regardless of whether or not they make that species extinct. Some species prey on their own young. Clearly, such behaviour functions to enable the survival of the fittest individuals and has no moral component. Furthermore, the intelligence of animals is insufficient to enable awareness of moral choices. What they do is simply a behaviour pattern consistent with survival of the individual and survival of their species.

If the argument were confined to sentient species, we cannot find evidence of such morality outside our human species, because there is no evidence for the existence of non-human sentient species. Accordingly, this premise of this argument has little, if any, persuasive value.

The second premise is that humans have a conscious awareness of the moral nature of our interpersonal conduct. There does not appear to be an objective and identifiable code or body of precepts of what is moral in relation to specific conduct, although there is extensive literature in the field of ethics. Cultural and customary behaviour is often at odds with the ethics of other cultures, and even religious precepts of morality differ significantly between various religions. However, in support of this argument, it is said that some precepts of morality are universally regarded as valid and that the recognition and acceptance of these precepts comes to us through the operation of our individual conscience.

The argument then is that our awareness of the moral aspects of certain conduct is not something that has any reason to occur naturally. The best or simplest explanation of this phenomenon is that it was instilled in us by our Creator, whom we call God. Conscience is regarded by many as God letting us know what is right and what is wrong, and accordingly, the existence of conscience is the basis of this argument.

The persuasive value of this argument is, at best, an argument for the probability of the existence of God. This argument has the same weaknesses as any argument that considers a phenomenon. If a natural or rational explanation for the existence or cause of the phenomenon cannot be found, then the conclusion argued is that the phenomenon is supernatural. This form of argument is also used where there may be some unprovable natural or rational explanation of the phenomenon or where a possible natural or rational explanation has not yet been discovered but may in the future be discovered.

In this argument, it is asserted that there is no natural or rational explanation for the existence of human conscience. But this is not conceded by opponents of this argument. These opponents say that conscience may simply be consciously or subconsciously remembered sociocultural or religious conditioning imparted by our upbringing in the relevant culture or religion. Alternatively, it may be nothing more complex or inexplicable than a natural function of human intelligence. Common sense and reason enables us to perceive whether the consequences of some proposed or committed behaviour is harmful to other persons, and our ability to empathise with the person harmed determines the strength of our aversion to the proposed conduct or our feelings of guilt for the committed conduct.

At this stage, we do not know enough about how the human brain works to enable dismissal of the above explanations and make the leap to the supernatural explanation. Perhaps, in the future, science will enable us to make such a leap.

An issue related to this argument is the question of whether or not conscience influences people's behaviour. Unfortunately, the evidence relevant to this issue is anecdotal and subjective. If we suppose that the above explanation of how conscience works is plausible, then we should have regard to the operation of conscience in those persons who profess to have no religious belief or any sociocultural moral conditioning to determine whether conscience exists and has any effect. Unfortunately, the existence of such persons is virtually impossible. Furthermore, we know that even persons with strong religious beliefs or strong sociocultural conditioning behave immorally from time to time. It appears then that conscience enables us to perceive what is moral conduct but does not override our freedom of will to behave immorally.

It is almost universally accepted that every person has a conscience, even if it is only regarded as a function of human intelligence. The question then becomes 'Why would someone who genuinely does not believe in the existence of God ever act morally?' At this point, we could ask ourselves whether we know of anyone who professes a genuine belief in the non-existence of God. Common experience suggests that there are such people and that in many, if not most, instances, they behave morally in the culture in which they live. Indeed, sometimes they behave most unselfishly, generously, and helpfully. Of course, there may be a perfectly natural explanation for their behaviour, such as fear of the law, fear of rejection or ostracisation by the community in which they want to live, the desire to earn respect and kudos in their community, etc. The point is that they do know what is considered to be moral behaviour from their own human intelligence.

Accordingly, we can be satisfied that conscience does exist, but we may not be persuaded that its existence is strong proof of the existence of God.

2.2.3 The Argument from the Existence of Miracles

The essence of this argument is that the happening of miracles is strong evidence that God exists. On the assumptions that we know what a miracle is, that we are satisfied that the alleged event did actually happen, and that the event qualifies as a miracle, this argument has some persuasive value in support of the argument that God exists. But a belief based on assumptions cannot be sustained if the assumptions are invalid or dubious. Accordingly, it is necessary to examine our assumptions in order to carefully consider the persuasive value of this argument.

Before considering our assumptions, it may be helpful to identify the type of event that may be or has been regarded as being a miracle. There are several categories of such events. The essence of a miracle is that it is an event that cannot have occurred naturally or consequent to any causative action by any human being. Throughout history, there have been many events believed to be miraculous, and many of these have been generically similar—for example, spontaneous cures of incurable diseases or terminal illnesses. Of course, spontaneous cures are rare, so rarity is one of the indicators of a miracle, although it need not be unprecedented. The essence is that the event is not natural and that it cannot be duplicated by any human action.

There are many accounts of a variety of events that are considered to be miraculous set out in both the Old Testament and the New Testament of the Bible. Most New Testament miracles were caused to occur by Jesus, and in our faith, Jesus is the second person in the Trinity of God. His miracles warrant special consideration because acceptance of his miracles goes to prove his divinity, not his existence, since it is an accepted historical fact that Jesus did actually live. His miracles will therefore be considered in another section of this work.

A plentiful account of miracles can be found in the Old Testament book of Exodus. The first miracle we may consider here is Moses turning his staff into a snake, recorded in Chapter 6, verses 8 to 13. The interesting part of this account is that Pharaoh's sorcerers also turned their staffs into snakes, which suggests that the event was an illusion or that the sorcerers also had magical powers. The next set of miracles, recorded in chapters 7 to 11, are the ten plagues inflicted on Egypt. Some plagues do occur naturally, but what is striking is that the Israelites, who were then living in Egypt, were not affected by these plagues. Perhaps the best known of miracles is the parting of the Red Sea, which allowed the Israelites to cross the sea on dry land but which destroyed the Egyptian army when they attempted the crossing. This event is set out in Chapter 14. There have been attempts to explain this miracle through the action of natural phenomena, but such explanations are pure speculation and accordingly unconvincing. Even if natural phenomena were involved, the timing of these events is so extraordinary that it is arguable that God used these natural forces to achieve his will. Another miracle is set out in Chapter 16. This is the miracle of the quail and the manna, which appeared mysteriously on the ground six out of every seven days during the forty years that the Israelites roamed the desert, in sufficient quantity to feed 600,000 men, plus children. Even speculation has not provided the identity of any natural forces that could cause this.

There are many other miracles recorded in the Bible, and it does not serve our purpose to catalogue them and consider each in detail. But there are evidentiary difficulties obstructing the acceptance of these biblical accounts as literally true and correct, and accordingly, we may consider more recent alleged miracles that are better documented and that have more evidentiary support.

There are, of course, miracles claimed by other religions. Since these involve some deity that we, as Catholics, do not believe in, we need not consider them, because they do not take proof of the existence of God any further than our own miracles. It suffices to note that they have the same difficulties in proving the existence of their deity from the happening of the alleged miracles as we do, and that none of them have produced *compelling* proof that their deity exists. Another type of miracle that involves the occult rather than the religious is the miraculous cures performed by shamans and witch doctors. Typically, these practitioners are very secretive about the process and materials used in their activities, and accordingly, there is no evidentiary basis to consider such events as miraculous, although we must recognise that there have been inexplicable cures of illnesses attributed to such practitioners.

In our faith, we have canonised saints. Our church authorities require persuasive evidence that a person being considered for canonisation is responsible for several miracles before it will canonise that person. In many cases, these miracles are, in effect, spontaneous cures of illness or disease, but there have been cases of levitation during prayer, the stigmata, and other extraordinary events. Many instances of such events can be found in the literature about the lives of saints. However, usually these miracles are not sufficiently public or publicly documented to have strong persuasive value for us, although the church is obviously satisfied from its investigations in relation to anyone that is canonised. Theologically, it is not argued that the purpose and function of these miracles is to prove the existence of God, and accordingly, there is no reason for the church to publish its investigations in such matters.

There are several more recent miracles which we can consider in relation to this issue. One of these miracles is the events at Fátima, particularly the 'dancing sun' witnessed by about fifty thousand people. Another is the large number of cures that have occurred at Lourdes since the apparitions reported by St Bernadette. These miracles are well-documented, and detailed accounts are readily available. It is miracles such as these that can form the evidentiary basis for our consideration of this argument.

Returning now to a consideration of our assumptions, the first assumption is that we have a clear understanding of the nature of a miracle. Most dictionaries define a miracle as some wondrous event or phenomenon which cannot be explained by the laws of nature and which was therefore caused to occur or exist by a deity having power over the laws of nature. Such a definition is not appropriate for a consideration of the existence of the deity, as the definition assumes the existence of the deity as the explanation of the occurrence of the event. To assume the existence of the deity to prove the existence of the deity from the occurrence of some events is a circular argument having no persuasive value.

For our consideration, we must also take into account whether 'the occurrence of some event or phenomenon which cannot be explained by the laws of nature' is adequate. The problem here is that there may be events or phenomena which cannot be explained by contemporary state-of-the-art scientific knowledge of the laws of nature, but which may be scientifically explicable after future advancement of scientific knowledge of the laws of nature. Few people would argue that science has already discovered all that there is to know about the laws of nature. Also, many alleged miracles occurred in the past when science had not achieved the modern level of knowledge, and thus, it may be possible to explain some of these older miracles according to the current level of scientific knowledge. Furthermore, it is not always certain that the state-of-the-art knowledge at the time the older miracle occurred was correctly or fully applied to the event to determine whether it was miraculous or not, particularly if the alleged miracle occurred in a remote location.

To avoid these criticisms, it seems appropriate for our purposes to narrow the definition of a miracle to events or phenomena that have been or can be shown to be contrary to the laws of nature known to modern science, to the extent that any reasonably foreseeable future advance in knowledge of the laws of nature explaining the event or phenomena is fanciful. The word *fanciful* is intended to refer to explanations of phenomena that exist in the realm of science fiction. We must form our views on the basis of current knowledge of the laws of nature, such laws being well known, clearly and precisely formulated, and absolute in that there are no known exceptions. It must be conceded that advancement of human knowledge of the laws of nature is likely, and therefore, any unexplained phenomenon or event that is demonstrably repeatable should be excluded from our consideration as a miracle pending the advancement of knowledge of the relevant laws of nature.

The next assumption to be examined is that the event occurred as reported. If it did not occur as reported, then we do not know what really happened, and consequently, we cannot form a view or draw any relevant conclusions from the alleged facts. The appropriate criteria for considering whether the alleged facts actually occurred as reported have been outlined earlier in this work and need not be repeated here. However, miracles are inherently unbelievable allegations and, as such, warrant some additional evidentiary scrutiny.

The type of miracle that is relevant to this issue is generally limited to what are called public events. Such miracles are witnessed by members of the public in sufficient numbers to render any suggestion of conspiracy or collusion as highly improbable. Alleged miracles experienced and reported by only the person involved, their relatives or associates, or only a few strangers may still be considered under the heading of 'religious experience', which is the next section.

Next, we should consider the reliability of the records available of such public events. For an allegation that a miracle occurred to be acceptable as a miracle, whatever documents are relied on to evidence the miracle must themselves be reliable. The miracles reported in the Bible mostly have no corroborative evidence in addition to what is recorded in the Bible itself, and the authenticity of the Bible is a major issue warranting separate consideration. Non-biblical miracles are not generally recorded in public records. Rather, they are recorded in the organisational records of the religion concerned. That situation raises the question of whether such records may be skewed to retain consistency with the tenets of that religion. Consequently, official records of some miraculous event, which is generally in the nature of a statement of the event that occurred together with a statement of how or why it occurred, may be useful in providing an outline of the facts of the matter and identifying the evidence to support proof of the relevant facts.

As has already been indicated, the best evidence of any fact is usually the testimony of a number of independent witnesses. Ideally, such evidence should be recorded together with a thorough cross-examination of the witness, together with disclosure of their religious persuasion, connection with the event, and relevant personal information, such as quality of eyesight, state of sobriety, etc. as may be relevant to the evidence. It is not suggested that persons of unknown or dubious background are unacceptable witnesses, but rather that well-educated persons who are highly respected members of their communities are less likely to be parties to a deception or error in testimony regarding the occurrence of an incredible event than persons who do not have these attributes. Accordingly, their evidence has more persuasive value.

Unfortunately, the reality is that such evidence is rarely available to support the occurrence of a miracle. There are several reasons for this lack of the best evidence. Firstly, most of the events alleged to be miracles occurred long ago and are recorded only in ancient religious writings, some of which were collated into what we now know as the Old Testament of the Bible. In those times, literacy was limited to the elite of society, who were often also the religious leaders of their communities. Secondly, even after the invention of the printing press, when literacy became more common, many alleged miracles occurred in remote areas and involved poor people or children who were still illiterate, and consequently, any records of such events were usually created by clergy who were called in to deal with the event.

Thirdly, the modern concept of requiring rigorously tested evidence to support the occurrence of an extraordinary event is the product of the relatively recent development of the philosophical concept of the scientific method and the development in Western culture of those aspects of legal systems aimed at discovering the truth of evidence. Even today not all cultures have the same parameters to determine the persuasive value of evidence.

It was suggested above that witnesses' evidence is the best evidence available. In modern times, we have digital video and audio recording, from which we may see for ourselves the alleged facts. Unfortunately, this technology is also easily faked. The special effects in modern movies can make virtually anything imaginable appear to be absolutely real. And while video cameras are now commonplace in mobile telephones, they are not always present at the time and place of the occurrence of miracles. Furthermore, many miracles, such as cures from illness, occur internally and cannot be filmed, even if their occurrence is sensed at the time. Accordingly, modern video evidence is often not useful and must always be regarded with caution because of the ease with which it can be falsified.

The next consideration is the possibility of deliberate deception. No doubt many of us have seen stage magicians perform 'impossible' feats, either live or on television. The art of magic is principally illusion, which makes us believe that we have seen something which has not actually happened. We need not labour the point that our senses can be deceived to the degree that we believe that we have seen an impossible event and have no idea of how it happened. With regard to stage magic, we know that it was an illusion, and we applaud the magician for entertaining and amazing us. Relevant to our consideration of this issue is recognition of the possibility that the witnesses to some extraordinary event have been deliberately subjected to an illusion without their knowledge or consent.

The question that arises is, why would anyone want to fake a miracle? The motive to fake a miracle would obviously be kept secret, so we can only speculate as to possible motives. From our experience, we know that reports of miracles will bring many curious people to the scene of the event. This can result in substantial financial benefit through increased tourism, book sales, etc. In short, the motive can be financial gain. Another motive could be personal power over those who believe that a miracle has occurred and who accept the 'message' that the miracle carries, since virtually all miracles carry some message; otherwise, it would be pointless. There may well be other motives in the diverse range of human motivations, the point being that it is realistic to consider deception as a possibility in assessing the persuasiveness of evidence in support of an alleged miracle.

Our final assumption is that the event qualifies as a miracle. The test that justifies this assumption is that it is reasonable to conclude that the event could only have occurred through the action of a deity. For the purposes of defining a miracle, a deity is a supernatural being having the power to cause events to occur which are proscribed by the known laws of nature. In our faith, we have a variety of supernatural beings, namely our triune God, the choirs of angels, the choirs of demons, and the souls of humans who have died. The ancient Greek, Roman, and Norse cultures had pantheons of gods, as do the modern Hindus and some other minor religions. We do not know what powers the non-God supernatural beings have; consequently, we cannot say that they do or do not have the power to cause events which are proscribed by the known laws of nature.

There are people who believe in supernatural beings but do not believe that there is a god, in the sense of a creator of all that is, amongst those beings. Such people would argue that even if there were highly persuasive evidence that an event had occurred and that science categorically showed that the event was contrary to the laws of nature, the conclusion that the event was caused to happen by God is not justified unless you can also show that either the only supernatural being is God or that no other supernatural being has the power to cause the event under consideration to happen. Thus, the proponents of this argument (that the existence of miracles proves the existence of God) have the onus of linking the event to causative action by God and no other.

Mostly, the miracles of the Old Testament were caused to occur by a being who identified himself as God. Some were caused by angels of God, and in some cases, the causative being did not identify himself. There is no difficulty in linking these miracles to God. The same applies to the miracles of Jesus and other miracles of the New Testament performed by holy men in the name of Jesus. Many later and recent miracles involve Our Lady. We do not know the extent of her powers, but clearly, as the mother of Jesus, her powers come from God. In relation to miracles attributed to saints, these usually involve prayer by the saint directly to God or prayer to the saint for intercession to God, so if the prayer is answered by a miracle, then it comes from God.

Thus, in our faith, we have no difficulty in linking miracles to causative action by God. What is also clear from a study of these miracles is that the purpose or message of the miracle was to correct some situation in the church or to answer some private prayer. It did not occur to prove the existence of God, although this is a logical inference from the happening of the miracle.

In support of the argument that the existence of miracles proves the existence of God, it is also argued that God has reason to intervene in human affairs by performing miracles and that there is teleological harmony through divine intervention. Swinburne develops these issues in his book, *The Existence of God*. It may well be that the exercise of human free will can result in situations incompatible with God's overall plan for humanity and that there may arise from time to time a need to tweak the course of history through some miracle. However, it seems to be presumptuous to claim knowledge of the will of God, and accordingly, these generalisations must be regarded with caution. Since they are generalisations, they have little persuasive value in particular cases.

Another criticism of this type of argument and this argument in particular is that we humans are too quick to jump to a supernatural explanation for some mysterious event if science fails to explain it. It is suggested that we should reserve our judgment until science can reliably explain or declare inexplicable the mysterious event. There is some merit in this criticism, but practicalities must also be taken into account. Seemingly inexplicable events happen, and we want and need explanations within a relevant time frame. Those persons charged with the responsibility to explain such events cannot defer explanation indefinitely until science provides its answer, because science may never be able to explain the event or be able to declare that the event was scientifically impossible. Explanations have to be given based on the best available evidence and the state-of-the-art science. If such explanation involves the supernatural, then so be it, subject to the proviso that the explanation may change on the discovery of better evidence or scientific advancement enabling an acceptable scientific explanation.

As Catholics, who believe in the existence of God, the divinity of Jesus Christ, and the authenticity of the Bible, we have no difficulty in accepting the miraculous nature of miracles, accepted by our church as such. Indeed, since our God is omnipotent, no miracle is unbelievable. But caution must be used in accepting new events as miraculous, because of the possibility of deliberate deception or delusion. Most of us are unqualified to investigate miracles; however, the church has its experts in this area, so we can rely on the official findings of our church.

The situation is vastly different for someone who does not already believe in God or who has lost the faith. The argument that the existence of God is proved by the occurrence of miracles requires strict or highly persuasive, if not compelling, proof. The facts of the event need to be proved fully; state-of-the-art science should be able to categorically declare that what happened is contrary to the laws of nature and that the possibility of some future scientific advancement explaining the event is remote. Given this type of evidence, it is rational to conclude that a deity caused the event to occur.

It is, of course, obvious that this level of proof is virtually unobtainable in the vast majority of cases. Consequently, this argument is inappropriate to prove the existence of God.

Before leaving this argument, it is worth noting that this argument has significant logical validity in a negative way. Logically, atheists have to say that they do not believe in miracles, because they cannot countenance the inference that a deity caused the event to occur. There are two bases on which an atheist may justify his or her disbelief, both of which are logically flawed.

The first basis is that the atheist may say that the evidence that he or she has seen in support of the allegation that the event was a miracle does not persuade him or her to the degree necessary to accept the event as a miracle. This is legitimate so far as it goes, provided that the atheist is a qualified investigator and has personally investigated the event. If the event was not personally investigated by the atheist, then the atheist must have considered all the relevant evidence in the available documentation of the event. Having done that, the atheist can legitimately say that he or she is not persuaded by the evidence. That position falls short of being able to say that the event was a deception or that the honestly given evidence was demonstrably incorrect, because such an assertion requires proof, and the onus is on the atheist to provide such proof.

But that position does not go far enough, because it is not just one miracle which carries the inference of being caused by a deity, but all of them. It is highly unlikely that any atheist has studied all the available evidence relating to every event that has been declared miraculous by every religion and found himself or herself unpersuaded that any of these alleged miracles were, in fact, miraculous. Unless the atheist does this, the position that he or she is unpersuaded by the evidence is flawed, because even the acceptance of one event as miraculous carries the inference of being caused by a deity. Thus, the atheist who has not examined all the evidence of every alleged miracle is ignoring the evidence of an event that has the potential to persuade him or her that God exists.

The second basis is the a priori argument that because the atheist believes that God does not exist, the atheist must believe that there cannot be any events caused by God. That is logical, but it ignores the facts and evidence of the world in which we live. To ignore the facts that throughout the history of mankind there have been many reports of extraordinary events which have been accepted by many as miraculous is simply prejudice, and any atheist relying on this argument can have no credibility. Similarly, an atheist may say that he or she does not accept that an event is a miracle because the facts alleged are contrary to the known laws of nature. But this is the whole point. An event cannot be regarded as a miracle unless it is contrary to the known laws of nature, which leaves the only explanation for its occurrence as being caused by a deity.

If an atheist has not examined all the evidence of every recognised miracle, then his or her only intellectually honest answer to the argument that miracles, by implication, prove the existence of God is to say that he or she simply does not know about miracles that he or she has not studied. This begs the question of whether or not the atheist is sufficiently concerned about the possible welfare of his or her immortal soul to undertake an examination of all the evidence of all recognised miracles. We may reasonably expect that very few, if any, atheists would undertake to study the evidence of all recognised miracles, and from this, we can see the flaw in the atheists' position and the value of the argument that the existence of miracles carries the implication that the deity that caused the miracle to occur exists.

2.2.4 The Argument from the Existence of Religious Experience

A common formulation of this argument is as follows: if a person has an experience directly of God or of some supernatural being, thing, or event which necessarily implies the existence of God, then God exists. Experiences directly of God are almost exclusively limited to the events recorded in the Old Testament. Religious experiences recorded in the New Testament, such as the one experienced by St Paul on the road to Damascus, depend on acceptance of the divinity of Jesus and, accordingly, cannot be used to prove the divinity of Jesus.

Since the time of Jesus, many persons have reported having a religious experience. Indeed, it is believed that such experiences are so common that many persons who have had a religious experience have not reported it, for a variety of reasons. The number of unreported experiences is necessarily pure conjecture. To understand the issues in relation to this argument, it may be helpful to identify the various types of religious experiences under consideration.

The first type we can easily identify is the private miracle. This is probably the best documented of all types of religious experience, especially if the event has been investigated by our church. Again, we are not concerned with the religious experiences of members of other religions, for the same reasons that we are not concerned with the public miracles claimed by other religions.

Many religious experiences are recorded in published accounts of the lives of saints. If such experience has been accredited as a miracle, then we should consider it as such, having regard to the issues raised in relation to public miracles in our assessment of the persuasive value of the evidence supporting the alleged miracle. If a religious experience has not been accredited as a miracle but has been investigated by our church, then we are free to form our own view of it, although we cannot publicly contradict any official published view. If the event has not been investigated by our church, we are free to form our own view, but again, we cannot put our views as anything more than that.

The most common experience of this type involves private prayer to God or some saint for the cure of some illness or disease in the person praying or in someone else, which is subsequently cured either gradually or immediately.

The next type is the answered prayer for the occurrence of some natural event. If such natural event has a reasonable chance of occurring anyway, then it has little or no value as a religious experience, because the essence of a religious experience is that it is an extraordinary event. But if the natural event is unlikely to occur, then it may qualify as a religious experience. The more unlikely the event or outcome, the more properly we may regard it as a religious experience. But other factors may be relevant. For example, if a person prays to win the lottery and does win it, we should consider how many other persons prayed to win the same lottery and did not win it, because there can be only one winner. The winner might regard it as a religious experience, but objectively, such an event has little persuasive value as proof of the existence of God. Nevertheless, there are events of this type that can be seriously considered.

The next type is visions of God, angels, saints, or ghosts of deceased persons. These can occur in internal manifestations during dreams, trances, and hallucinations, or they can appear to be real phenomena external to the person experiencing it. In most cases, these apparitions also speak to the person experiencing it. One of the main problems with this type of religious experience is the manner in which such an experience is reported. Usually it is reported as a real phenomenon, but if it was not witnessed by others, then there is no way of knowing whether it was real or internal. Clearly, internal manifestations have little persuasive value as proof of the existence of God, because they are likely to be a personal mental aberration, which can have a variety of natural causes. If a vision is reported as a dream or otherwise internal, it is usually not credited as authentic, although there are numerous examples of dreams being accepted as coming from God in both the Old Testament and the New Testament.

The next type of religious experience is the hearing of voices. Again, this can be either internal or external. An example of this type of religious experience is set out in the Old Testament in Chapter 3 of 1 Samuel. Here Samuel, a boy having no prior knowledge or experience of God, heard his name called. He thought it was Eli calling him and presented himself to Eli. Eli denied that he had called him, and he sent him back to bed. This happened three times, and after the third time, Eli realised that it was God calling to Samuel. Eli instructed Samuel on how to respond. From this account, we can conclude that Eli did not hear the voice, so it was presumably internal to Samuel. A more modern and more fully documented occurrence of voices as a religious experience is the voices heard by Joan of Arc. Again, no other person heard the voices, and the voices were not claimed to be the voice of God. From documented accounts, we have no independent evidence of who they were or what they said, so we can conclude that this was an entirely internal experience. In the case of the experience of St Paul, recorded in the New Testament at Acts 9, there were witnesses who did not see what Paul claimed to see, but they had heard something. Unfortunately, their testimony is not recorded, except for what they told St Paul.

The next type of religious experience is even more internal. People sometimes claim to feel or to have felt some supernatural presence or to have experienced some transcendental state of consciousness, enabling perception of the supernatural realm. Such experiences are almost always experienced while the person is alone, so there is rarely any corroborating evidence. Such experiences include visions of ghosts, voices of ghosts, things moving by themselves, etc. Obviously, this is the least reported type of religious experience and also the most difficult to express in precise comprehensible language. In other words, what really happened cannot be clearly communicated, let alone proved to have actually happened. Even if they did happen, the nature of this type of religious experience does not point to God, as the Creator of all that is, as having caused this manifestation. Accordingly, this type of religious experience is not really amenable to an objective proof of the existence of God.

Although there are additional types of religious experience, the final type to be identified for our purposes is what is referred to as extrasensory perception (ESP). This includes such experiences as déjà vu, telepathy, clairvoyance, etc. Such experiences are fairly well-documented and occur so frequently that most of us have experienced them. They are extraordinary in that they cannot be explained by modern science. They are so common that relatively few of such experiences are fully investigated or even reported. Only a few such experiences involve any religious component sufficient to qualify the experience as a religious experience. Again, such experiences are essentially internal and, accordingly, have evidentiary difficulties which greatly diminish the objective persuasive value of the experience as proof of the existence of God. But because such experiences are so common, the reality of such experiences is widely accepted, and the persuasive value to the person who has the experience is legitimate.

This argument, to prove the existence of God from religious experience, makes the same assumptions as the argument from the existence of miracles. The weaknesses of these assumptions were dealt with in our consideration of that topic and need not be reconsidered here. However, this argument has a few additional nuances that are worth expressing.

The first point is that proof of fact of an entirely internal event is exceptionally difficult because the facts usually cannot be corroborated or even expressed in precise scientific terms. Professor Swinburne, in his book, argues that we should apply what he calls the principle of credulity to religious experience. Briefly, this principle proposes that, in the absence of positive grounds to suppose otherwise, we should accept that things really are as others perceive them to be. In essence, this principle accepts the competence of people to correctly identify their perceptions. He then extends this principle with a second principle that he calls the principle of testimony. This principle proposes that in the absence of positive grounds to suppose otherwise, we should accept that the experiences of persons are true and correct as they report them. He argues that in ordinary life, we believe 'that what others tell us that they perceived probably happened'. From this, he justifies applying the principle of credulity and the principle of testimony to reports of religious experience.

While Professor Swinburne may be correct in saying that we commonly accept as correct reported perceptions, this really applies to only the mundane or relatively unimportant things in our lives. In relation to important issues, we are far more demanding and discerning about the perception evidence in support of alleged facts. For example, in criminal law, where important issues such as the liberty of an accused person is at stake, we do not accept the guilt of the accused merely on some person's uncorroborated perception evidence. There are rules to enable the accused to present contrary evidence in defence, and witnesses are cross-examined to test their veracity and reliability. Some matters even require corroboration as a matter of law. Even in civil law, an allegation such as the existence of a contract is not acceptable merely on the allegation by one party that such a contract exists. That is why important contracts are required by law to be evidenced in writing, signed, and witnessed. Certainly, Professor Swinburne puts in the proviso 'in the absence of positive grounds to suppose otherwise'. Surely in relation to important issues, this proviso imposes the duty on us to make a thorough search for any positive reasons to not accept the evidence, and even if we do not find such grounds, we are still at liberty to refuse to accept the perceptive evidence if we suspect some deception or unreliability in the evidence, although mere suspicion does not justify declaring the evidence to be false or incorrect.

The question of whether or not God exists is fundamental to many of the important decisions that we make in our lives, even though this issue is not in the forefront of our minds when we make such decisions. Consequently, this issue is important enough to warrant very careful consideration of the evidence available in support or contradiction of this issue. Furthermore, miracles and religious experiences are extraordinary events implicitly involving the supernatural. The normal reaction is to doubt the truth or accuracy of an account of some extraordinary event, and such doubt will be greater the more unlikely or inexplicable the event, because such events are outside common experience. This means that the evidence in support of the alleged event must be highly persuasive to enable the conclusion that the event did actually happen as reported. Accordingly, the principle of credulity and the principle of testimony, while valid in some situations, are not appropriate guides in considering whether a miracle or religious experience actually happened as reported.

The second point to consider is the requirement that the experience be scientifically inexplicable as a natural event. As with miracles, if the experience is not merely inexplicable under the laws of nature but actually contrary to the known laws of nature, it is more readily acceptable as a genuine religious experience, although the proof of the fact will be more demanding. But because religious experiences are usually internal, they are vulnerable to the proposition that what happened was caused by some anomaly in the mind of the person claiming to have had the religious experience. We know that the placebo effect and psychosomatic illnesses are caused by the human mind, and we suspect that the mind has many more as yet undiscovered powers and functions. If this is considered to be plausible, then many religious experiences simply cannot be objectively accepted as coming directly from God. But equally, we cannot dismiss them as not coming from God, because future discoveries about the mind may show that the claimed religious experience is beyond the power of the mind. For the time being, we can accept such events as levitation during prayer as being beyond the known powers of the human mind, with the proviso that even such an event is not absolutely certain to be beyond the power of the human mind.

The third point to consider is linking the religious experience to God. As with miracles, it is difficult to identify God as the cause of the religious experience, and many religious experiences, being internal and difficult to articulate clearly, appear so nebulous that the involvement of God is, at best, merely an inference. The second part of this point is that not only does the religious experience need to be caused by God, it must be of such a nature that it can only have come from a supernatural being with the power of God and who has identified himself as the Creator of all that is. But as with miracles, there are substantial evidentiary difficulties impeding the acceptance of ancient biblical events as true and correct as reported.

From all the forgoing, we can draw some conclusions. Firstly, it is not appropriate to consider religious experience in support of an argument that God, as the Creator of all that is, exists. The subjective internal nature of religious experience has little, if any, persuasive value to prove a fact that requires strong objective evidence.

Secondly, our church does not usually investigate religious experience unless it is related to or in the nature of a miracle. Consequently, we have little guidance from our church in relation to claimed religious experience. We are therefore free to accept or reject reports of religious experience as true and correct, depending on the extent to which we are persuaded by the evidence in support of the report. The use that we can make of reports that we accept as being true and correct is essentially devotional and supportive of the faith that we already have.

Thirdly, while the evidence in support of this argument cannot objectively prove this argument, we can accept that the person who had the religious experience is fully persuaded by his or her experience or the inference from that experience, that God exists. There is nothing wrong or illogical in a belief based on personal religious experience, but it is simply not objectively persuasive to prove the existence of God, particularly if the purpose of the religious experience was something other than to prove the existence of God. Perhaps persons who have had a religious experience are lucky, but that luck may have cost them the ability to believe in God of their own free will.

2.2.5 Pascal's Wager

Blaise Pascal (1623–1662) formulated this argument, which was first published in 1670, after his death. The essence of his argument is that it is rational to believe in God, because the reward of a life lived in accordance with theistic requirements outweighs the rewards of a life lived with disregard to theistic requirements. The argument is relevant to persons who are not persuaded by the evidence that God exists, but it does not apply if the evidence for the existence of God is infinitesimally small.

Pascal postulates that if one leads a life in accordance with theistic requirements and it turns out that there is a God, then one gains the reward of eternal existence with God in paradise. If it turns out that there is no God, then one has lost little, if anything, by leading a life in accordance with theistic requirements. The corollary is that if one leads a life with disregard to theistic requirements and it turns out that there is a God, the consequence is eternal separation from God and the loss of paradise. And if it turns out that there is no God, then there is little, if any, benefit over having lived a life in accordance with theistic requirements.

Obviously, this is not an argument that offers any proof of the existence of God or any evidence to support this proposition, and therefore, it cannot have any persuasive value as proof. It is included here because it is nevertheless an argument to live our lives as if God does exist. This has value because as may be already clear, there is no compelling proof that God exists, and therefore, we must all have some doubts. If those doubts are strong enough to overcome faith, then this argument is a substantial and valid argument to retain the practice of our faith. Furthermore, while it is true that our beliefs guide our actions, it is also true that in relation to issues on which our beliefs are equivocal, we consider the outcome most favourable to our self-interest as having priority.

Another reason to consider this argument is that in the final analysis, it is what we do that matters more than what we believe. Proof of this fact is that even people with a strong faith in the existence of God sometimes choose to do things contrary to the requirements of their faith, i.e. sin. Such action is freely chosen to obtain what is perceived to be some benefit from it. Pascal's argument brings into consideration the long-term intangible benefits of a choice of action and may assist us to lead better lives.

To consider this argument, it is necessary to examine the premises of the argument to determine their validity. The first premise is that if God exists and we live our lives as he wants us to, then we will be rewarded with eternal existence with him in paradise. This assumes that we have immortal souls, because if we do not have immortal souls, then the existence of God is irrelevant, and we are no worse off than if God does not actually exist. That God will reward us with eternal existence with him in paradise if we live our lives as he wants us to assumes that God loves us, and this is the fundamental teaching of our religion and is axiomatic to this issue.

The next premise is that if we lead our lives in accordance with theistic requirements and it turns out that God does not actually exist, then we have lost little, if anything, by leading a life in accordance with theistic requirements, compared to leading a life with disregard to theistic requirements. As we have seen in the argument from the existence of morality, most people who believe that God exists live moral lives, at least partially, to comply with the requirements of their faith. People who do not believe in the existence of God live basically moral lives for a variety of other reasons. These reasons can include such things as the self-image of the non-believer as a good or worthwhile person; a desire to live in a community which requires living in accordance with moral standards acceptable to that community; fear of punishment under the laws of the entire society, which prohibit certain types of immoral conduct; etc. In many cases, non-believers do not just act in accordance with the minimum requirements of their chosen system. They are often respectable, generous, helpful, and considerate persons who are highly regarded in their communities.

The difference between the lives of believers and non-believers is that believers mostly belong to an organised religion and are guided in their action by the teachings of their religion, even if they are not liturgically active in their religion. Non-believers lead similarly moral lives guided by their own sense of morality and their knowledge of what their chosen system requires of them. The believer has some obligation to participate in the liturgical activities of his or her religion, whereas the non-believer has no such obligations. Before the advent of the modern anti-discrimination laws of our society, it was, in some situations, an impediment to career advancement to be a member of some religions, particularly our Catholic faith. Equally, there were career opportunities available to only members of a particular religion. For the most part, such discrimination is a thing of the past, although it is still prevalent in some cultures. Of course, some discrimination of this type is justified. For example, an atheist cannot become a priest, and many religions will not employ persons who are not at least nominally members of their faith as teachers in the schools of that denomination. Of course, there is still discrimination based on non-religious criteria.

As Catholics, our primary obligation is to live in accordance with the Ten Commandments and to love all people as Jesus loved us. Essentially, that requires us to love God and our neighbour. Non-believers live in accordance with a legal or moral code which is essentially the same as those of the Ten Commandments, dealing with our behaviour towards other people. Legal and moral codes do not require a love of God, and their purpose is to preserve peace and order in their respective societies. Essentially, the conduct required of non-believers is very similar to that required of believers by their faith, and non-believers certainly recognise the Golden Rule.

Our religion requires us to participate in some liturgical activities. This requires us to attend Mass on Sundays and a few other special days and to participate in the sacraments as appropriate, i.e. confession at least once a year, marriage in the church and compliance with the church's laws regarding marriage, some small financial support of our clergy, and some other minor requirements. There is much more that we can do, but all that is voluntary. Non-believers do not have any of these obligations.

The question is whether these obligations are so onerous that not having them is a substantial benefit which significantly improves the quality of life of the non-believer. Our obligations as Catholics are obviously not particularly onerous, and it is arguable that we obtain worldly as well as spiritual benefits from performing our obligations. In particular, attending Mass gives us the feeling of belonging to a supportive community, confession absolves us of feelings of guilt and enables us to feel at peace with the world after true contrition and appropriate reparation, and marriage in the church gives us social respectability. Knowing that we cannot divorce makes the initial commitment a more serious undertaking and therefore more sincere.

From these considerations, it appears correct to regard the proposition that there is little, if any, difference between a life lived according to theistic requirements and a life lived with disregard to such requirements, in relation to the quality and prosperity of our human lives.

The next proposition is the first part of the corollary, i.e. that if God exists, we risk the loss of eternal companionship with him in paradise if we live in a way that displeases him. This proposition raises two theological issues. Firstly, it is not for us to judge anyone else. We cannot say that we lead better lives than non-believers, so we cannot know what God has in mind for non-believers who lead basically good lives. However, our church teaches that Jesus said, 'No one comes to the Father, except through me' (John 14:6). This, the church teaches, means that only baptised followers of Jesus can obtain the reward of eternal existence with God in paradise.

Secondly, the primary function of the church is to spread the gospel, and the principal secondary function is pastoral care, which means helping us to lead lives pleasing to God. We all offend God (sin) from time to time. Our faith provides us with the means to be reconciled with God through confession. This reconciliation is more than merely sincerely apologising to God and making the appropriate reparation. The theology is that we humans are a lower order of being than God, and therefore, we do not have the status to apologise directly to God for the offence given. Through confession, Jesus apologises to God the Father on our behalf, and through the authority Jesus has given to his priests, we receive absolution, which enables us to feel at peace with God. The non-believer cannot apologise to a god that he or she does not believe in, and accordingly, they can never obtain forgiveness or absolution. Of course, a non-believer can obtain forgiveness from the human harmed by some offence, provided proper contrition and reparation is made, but society generally does not forgive; it merely punishes, and people often find it hardest to forgive themselves. Thus, if there is a God, the non-believer will have offended him and will not have been able to make an apology to obtain forgiveness and absolution, and that is clearly a parlous situation.

Arguments to prove the existence of God which rely on the assumption that God exists are circuitous or self-serving, and they have no logical validity. But this is not an argument to prove the existence of God. It is merely a reason to live our lives as if God does actually exist. The logical premise on which this theology rests is that either God exists or he does not. There is no other possibility. If we assume that God exists in order to consider the validity of Pascal's proposition, we can look to what he is alleged to have revealed to mankind and the relative status of divine nature over human nature. Accordingly, the theological issues raised are proper issues in our consideration of Pascal's wager, although the divinity of Jesus, which is assumed in the first theological issue raised above, is a factual matter which is yet to be considered in this work.

In this context then, we have reason to accept that if we do not lead our lives as God wants us to, then he will exclude us from eternal existence with him in paradise. Theologically, we have the concept of heaven, hell, purgatory, and limbo. God has not revealed any other supernatural environments, but that does not mean that there are none, because we do not know all that God knows, only what he has chosen to reveal to us. We believe God to be just and merciful, so it is difficult to conclude that God would inflict eternal punishment or torment on a non-believer who has led a basically good life. On the other hand, we do not know what is just for a person who has offended God and not apologised in any way acceptable to God, even if human apology has been made.

The second corollary proposition is that if God does not exist, then the non-believer has gained little, if anything, by leading a life with disregard to theistic requirements. This proposition is substantially identical to the proposition to which it is the corollary and need not be reconsidered, because the conclusion is the same—i.e. this proposition and its corollary appear to be valid.

Pascal's wager is worth consideration by persons who are not already persuaded by the evidence that God exists or by the arguments and evidence that God does not exist—i.e. agnostics. It may also be worthy of consideration by atheists who concede that there is more than insignificant evidence in support of the existence of God, and also by believers who have developed some real doubts about the existence of God. The merit of this argument arises from the axiom that either God exists or he does not. There is no third possibility. It is important because there is the possibility that we have immortal souls, and it is obviously of critical self-interest to determine in what environment that soul will spend eternity, if it exists. Sitting on the fence is not an option, because that position is the same as atheism, in that only persons who live in accordance with theistic requirements are eligible for the reward of paradise.

However, saying that it is rational to believe in God based on this argument implies that it is irrational to not believe in God. That is probably an overstatement, because the argument is fundamentally a wager. Some people are, by nature, risk-takers. We may be bemused by the apparent lack of wisdom in choosing a lifestyle that has little, if any, benefit over a lifestyle lived in accordance with theistic requirements, which thereby risks the loss of paradise, but it is not arguable that such a choice is irrational, because the evidence in support of the existence of God is not compelling. Accordingly, we can conclude that Pascal's wager itself does not compel the choice of a lifestyle according to theistic requirements, but it does appear to strongly recommend it.

2.3 The Arguments against the Existence of God

2.3.1 The Cosmological Arguments

The cosmological arguments against the existence of God essentially assert that the evidence as to how the universe came into existence supports the view that our universe came into existence naturally rather than being created.

The evidence tendered in support of these arguments is observational data from astronomers and cosmologists which supports the various theories of the origin of the universe. To consider those arguments, we should bear in mind that observational data is essential for the formulation of a hypothesis. If the hypothesis is then supported by sufficient further data, it becomes a theory. If the theory can explain and predict yet further data, then it usually becomes widely accepted by the scientific community. Of course, much more than this is required before a theory will be accepted as a proven fact or law of cosmological physics.

The theories involved in these arguments are primarily the Big Bang theory, the theory of relativity, Hawking's wave function of the universe theory, and the theories of quantum cosmology. The arguments proceed on the assumption that the relevant theory involved is true and correct. And while we, as laypersons to cosmology, can abide the general acceptance of the Big Bang theory and the theory of relativity, it cannot be conceded that Hawking's theories or quantum mechanics have sufficient acceptance by the scientific community to warrant serious consideration. Even with acceptable theories, the arguments fall far short of proof.

The science of these theories has already been identified and need not be repeated here. For the purposes of these arguments, the science is the same, but the conclusions drawn from the data and theories are the opposite of the conclusions drawn in the arguments in support of the existence of God.

These arguments came to the conclusion that God probably does not exist. That appears to be an objective assessment of the persuasiveness of their argument. The existence of God is a matter of fact, and it can only be 100 per cent true or 100 per cent false. To say that God probably does not exist is to say that the chance that God exists is less than 50 per cent. The existence of God is not a matter of chance. It is a fact that either is true or is not true. What the scientists who express these arguments are really saying is that the evidence that they have identified has persuaded them that our universe came into existence spontaneously and therefore was not created by God, and thus, God, whether or not he exists, did not create our universe. The scientists who have expressed these arguments—such as Victor J. Stenger, Theodore Schick Jr, and Quentin Smith—are certainly reputable scientists, but they are expressing only their personal levels of persuasion, not some objective probability of the truth of a fact. Of course, there are other scientists of equal repute who are not persuaded by their arguments.

There are two further impediments to acceptance of these arguments. Firstly, for their arguments to have even logical validity, it must be shown that the *only* conclusion that can be drawn from the data is the conclusion that they propose. Bear in mind that the data cited is supportive of theories. It would be a brave scientist who asserts that there will never be any other theory that fits the data. Consequently, these arguments are tied to current state-of-the-art science in these areas. That is not inappropriate or necessarily invalid, because we need scientists to explain data on the basis of current knowledge. But it does mean that their argument is conditional on the relevant theory not being overturned or replaced by other theories which would not allow the same conclusions. Hence, these arguments cannot have any compelling persuasive value.

Secondly, some of the data relied on is negative in nature. In particular, it is alleged that the evidence of the origin of the universe does not indicate that there was any violation of the natural law of the conservation of energy. Bearing in mind that if God exists, then he is a spiritual being who created energy, from which he proceeded to construct the universe, we can question the logical necessity of God leaving some evidence of his creation of energy. The law of the conservation of energy does not explain the source of energy, and thus, its creation by God is not precluded. The argument that energy always existed is the same as the argument that matter always existed before the Big Bang theory! Accordingly, the absence of evidence of God's creation of energy does not prove that he did not create it, nor is it unreasonable to require scientists to specify what evidence should logically exist and be discoverable if God did create all energy.

2.3.2 The Teleological Arguments

These arguments generally follow the teleological method of examining part of our material realm. The conclusion that they reach is that what they examined does not display evidence or characteristics of intelligent design. From this, these arguments generalise that the universe is essentially chaotic and therefore not intelligently designed. Since God is accepted as being intelligent, it follows that the universe was not designed by God, and therefore, God probably does not exist.

Some of these arguments are fairly superficial and may be summarily considered. The anthropic principle argument is essentially a teleological argument but warrants separate consideration because it is relatively new and has appeared in popular literature. Perhaps the most credible argument of this type is the argument based on the theory of evolution, which is considered hereunder.

Of the minor teleological arguments is the one proposed by Nicholas Everitt. He postulates that if God exists, then he created humanity as the centrepiece of his creation. But science shows us that humanity has only existed during a tiny portion of time since the universe began and occupies only a tiny portion of space in an unimaginably vast universe. If this is part of God's design, then all that extra time and space is extremely wasteful, which suggests inefficiency to the point of incompetence. But God cannot be inefficient or incompetent; therefore, God did not create the universe and probably does not exist.

The flaws in this argument are obvious. Theists do not assert that humanity is the centrepiece of God's creation, and science tells us that our Earth could not be the way it is today if the universe were not as old as it is. From the scientific evidence, we can take the view that God has chosen to use natural processes to develop his creation, and since God is eternal and space is unlimited, haste and spatial economy are unnecessary.

A less credible argument of this type has been separately expressed by Wesley C. Salmon and Michael Martin. A composite of their argument is that, based on human experience, all designers have bodies, use pre-existing materials, collaborate with peers, are limited in power, and make mistakes. These characteristics are contrary to the normal concepts of God, and therefore, God did not design and build our universe and probably does not exist.

It is obviously incorrect to compare and limit God's capacity to design and create to our human capacities. Nor is there any evidentiary basis for the proposition that a spiritual entity is incapable of creating anything material. But that, of course, is a two-edged sword.

More substantial are two arguments based on the theory of evolution using the process of natural selection. Firstly, scientists have discovered fossils of species that had vestigial organs and various other anatomical inefficiencies. Most of these species are extinct, although some current species, like humans, also have vestigial organs. These findings suggest that the process of natural selection actualised a number of experiments with what turned out to be inferior survival attributes, leading to the extinction of the experimental species. This would not have occurred if the development of life, or even the process of evolution, had been intelligently designed, which would not require experimentation. This suggests no design and therefore no designer.

Secondly, fossil evidence and other biological evidence suggests that all creatures on Earth today descended from a common ancestor. If this is correct, then God did not directly create any species other than the single ancestor species, and not even this if the ancestor species came into existence spontaneously.

The first argument is difficult to refute, but it must be kept in perspective. Many species are extinct that had vestigial organs but also had optimum survival characteristics. That modern species are their descendants suggests that they had the ability to adapt and transmit their essential genetic code. Furthermore, other scientists tell us that nature exhibits design that is not merely intelligent but is actually at the level of genius.

The second argument is based on the comprehensive theory of evolution as popularised and expounded by Richard Dawkins. Essentially, this version of the theory asserts that evolution explains everything, given some origin of life and the eukaryotic cell. This version of the theory of evolution is not that widely accepted and remains only a theory. This argument has problems with explaining the origin of life, the development of the eukaryotic cell, the development of consciousness, and the development of human intelligence. While the evidence that supports the theory of evolution generally, to an extent, is acceptable as true and correct, there is other evidence that this version of the theory of evolution does not satisfactorily explain. Accordingly, this aspect of this argument cannot have significant persuasive value until these problems are satisfactorily resolved. But even then, this argument does not exclude the possibility that God designed and created the ancestor species and also designed and created the environment, which evolved to reach our present condition.

2.3.3 The Argument from Non-Belief in God

These are relatively minor arguments. The basic argument is that because most of the people in the world do not believe that God exists, then he probably does not exist.

There are a number of academic refinements to this argument. Theodore M. Drange argued that the God of Christians apparently wants all the people in the world to come to worship him. After 2,000 years, he has still not achieved this; therefore, he probably does not exist. He suggests that the same applies to the God of Orthodox Judaism.

Criticism of this argument has centred on the assumption that God wants everyone to believe in him and that Jesus is the saviour of the world. It was suggested by Christopher McHugh that God not merely allows a disbelief in him but actually causes such disbelief. This has been rejected by other theists who claim biblical support for Drange's assumption. Drange supplements his argument with the further assumption that God wants a personal relationship with humans and thus would want us to know him. He argues that the history of Christianity demonstrates confusion and even conflict about the nature of God. He further observes that the Bible, which is alleged to be God's Word, or at least is divinely inspired, is replete with ambiguities, errors, and contradictions. On this evidence, he concludes that God probably does not exist.

There are several flaws in this argument. The primary flaw is the assumption of what God wants. We do not know what God wants, and it is somewhat arrogant to make such an assumption. What we do know is that God loves us. We also know that he wants us to love him in return and that he has given us the free will to reject his love and to not love him in return. From this, the highest assumption that we can make is that God wants all men to be made aware of him and Jesus and to be given the choice to worship him or reject him. Jesus instructed his disciples to go and 'teach all nations' about him. In our time, the Catholic Church has an official presence in every nation on earth. Accordingly, this argument can have little persuasive value because it is based on an unfounded assumption.

Another aspect of the argument from disbelief is put by Walter Sinnott-Armstrong, who argues that if God exists, then he would provide strong evidence of his existence, because the benefits to God would greatly exceed the disadvantages. He then asserts that such evidence does not exist.

Again, asserting knowledge of what is in God's best interests appears to be somewhat presumptuous, given the limits of human intelligence and experience. To date, there has been no compelling proof that God exists, nor has there been any compelling proof that he does not exist. This balance must necessarily be maintained if the free will to worship or reject God is to be preserved. Furthermore, there is sufficient evidence to enable belief in God to the degree of basing one's life on this belief, as is apparent by the many intelligent and educated people who hold belief in God, although true free will requires that there can be disbelief based on reasonable grounds.

This argument of lack of evidence has been extended with a suggestion that God should manifest himself to comfort the needy and enable seekers to find him. It is argued that because God does not manifest himself, he probably does not exist.

Again, this argument presumes to suggest what God should do or what, by comparison with the love of a human parent for his or her child, he might be expected to do. This raises the big question of the purpose or meaning of life. The sympathetic and loving option is not necessarily supportive to God's purposes, because we do not know God's purposes. Accordingly, this argument cannot be considered logically valid.

2.3.4 The Anthropic Principle

Most of the arguments for and against the existence of God were devised many years ago, although new expressions and criticisms of such arguments are ongoing. A relatively new argument competing with arguments for the existence of God is based on the anthropic principle and was presented by Richard Dawkins in Chapter 4 of his book *The God Delusion*. Richard Dawkins is a biologist and, amongst other qualifications, is the Charles Simonyi Professor for the Public Understanding of Science at Oxford University. He is a fundamental atheist and is completely persuaded that the theory of evolution explains the diversity of life on Earth. He is a published vehement critic of all religions and is particularly opposed to the religious education of children.

It is not the purpose of this work to criticise Dawkins's views or to review his book. That has been done by others in other works. Our purpose is to carefully consider his argument based on the anthropic principle. This is important because his argument has not yet survived the test of time and because it may be encountered in various guises, which could generate doubts if it is not fully understood. Also, Dawkins, at the end of Chapter 4 at page 157, reiterates his argument in summary form and says that this chapter *'has contained the central argument of my book'*. From this, it follows that if the argument contained in this chapter is unsustainable, then all his criticisms of religion, based on the belief that God does not exist, are also unsustainable.

Before looking at Dawkins's argument, it may be helpful to know a bit more about the anthropic principle. The anthropic principle essentially is that life on Earth is so sensitive to the values of fundamental scientific constants that the smallest change in the value of any of these constants could mean that life could not exist in our universe. This view flows from what are known as the anthropic coincidences, some of which are as follows:

(a) The ratio of electromagnetic force to the gravitational force is 10^{39} (N_1).
(b) The number of particles in the world is 10^{79} (N). This is known as the Eddington number and is approximately the square of N_1.
(c) The ratio of a typical stellar lifetime to the time it takes light to traverse the radius of a proton (N_2) is of the same order of magnitude as N_1.

There are a number of consequences that flow from these numbers being what they are, and these are as follows:

(a) Stellar evolution requires billions of years. If N_1 were not as large as it is, stars would have burned out much sooner, and no heavy elements could have been formed.
(b) If the weaker force of gravity were slightly stronger than it actually is, then the entire universe would be hydrogen. If it were slightly weaker than it actually is, then the whole universe would be helium.
(c) If the difference in mass between a neutron and a proton was slightly different to what it actually is, then there would be no deuterium.
(d) Carbon has an excited energy level of 7.66 MeV. If this were any different, then carbon-based life forms could not exist.

Briefly, the history of the development of the anthropic principle is that in 1974, Brandon Carter introduced the principle by hypothesising that these constants were not random but somehow built into the structure of our universe. Thereafter, Barrow and Tipler formulated three forms of the anthropic principle as follows:

(a) *The strong anthropic principle (SAP).* The universe must have those properties which allow life to develop within it at some stage of its history. The implications of this are as follows:

   (i) There exists one possible universe 'designed' with the goal of generation and sustaining observers. This is generally the theists' view.

   (ii) Observers are necessary to bring the universe into being. This is generally regarded as New Age mysticism.

   (iii) An ensemble of other different universes is necessary for the existence of our universe. Current cosmological speculation is that there may be multiple universes, but there is no evidence of this, although it makes some 'mathematics' work.

(b) *The weak anthropic principle (WAP).* The observed values of all physical and cosmological quantities are not equally probable but take on values restricted by the requirement that there exist sites where carbon-based life can evolve and by the requirement that the universe be old enough for it to have already done so. The second requirements lead to the axiom that if the universe were not as old as it is, then we would not be here.

(c) *The final anthropic principle (FAP), otherwise known as the completely ridiculous anthropic principle (acronym not specified).* Intelligent information processing must come into existence in the universe, and once it has come into existence, it will never die out. Tipler thought that this would lead to humankind building robots with intelligence that will replicate themselves and populate the universe, and that at the end of time, they will merge with God and all humans that ever existed will be resurrected.

The *Oxford Dictionary of Science,* sixth edition, to which Professor Dawkins is not credited as a contributor, defines the anthropic principle as follows:

anthropic principle: *the principle that the observable universe has to be as it is, rather than any other way, otherwise we would not be able to observe it. There are many versions of the anthropic principle. The* weak anthropic principle *is specifically concerned with the conditions necessary for conscious life on earth and asserts that numerical values found for fundamental constants, such as the gravitational constant, have to hold at the present epoch because at any other epoch there would be no intelligent lifeform to measure the constants. The* strong anthropic principle *is concerned with all possible universes and whether intelligent life could exist in any other universe, including the possibility of different fundamental constants and laws of physics. The anthropic principle is viewed with considerable skepticism by many physicists.*

In the first part of Chapter 4, from pages 113 to134, Dawkins argues that the existence of God is highly improbable. He begins by citing the analogy of the Ultimate Boeing 747. This analogy is that *'the probability of life originating on Earth is no greater than the chance that a hurricane, sweeping through a scrapyard, would have the luck to assemble a Boeing 747'*. That remark is attributed to the renowned astronomer Fred Hoyle, who apparently made the remark as hyperbole, as it is obviously impossible. Dawkins appears to have fallen into the error of thinking that one can apply the laws of probability to something that is actually impossible. Apart from this, there is nothing new, surprising, or substantial in his arguments in this regard, and accordingly, they do not warrant special consideration. These arguments are essentially negative, so Dawkins goes further and offers a positive argument based on the anthropic principle as an alternative to creationism. Creationism in this context means attributing the creation of all that exists to some initial action by God, and it does not mean the book of Genesis version of Creation.

Dawkins presents two applications of the anthropic principle. The first is his planetary version, which appears to be the weak anthropic principle, and the second is his cosmological version, which appears to be the strong anthropic principle. It is the planetary version that is the essence of his argument, because it is his explanation of the origin of life on Earth, which is the starting point for the theory of evolution. He makes this point at the top of page 137, where he says:

Darwinian evolution proceeds merrily once life has originated. But how does life get started? The origin of life was the chemical event, or series of events, whereby the vital conditions for natural selection first came about.

He explains the anthropic principle by saying at page 135:

We exist here on Earth. Therefore, Earth must be the kind of planet that is capable of generating and supporting us, however unusual, even unique, that kind of planet might be.

What Dawkins is asserting here is that it must be possible for life to have come into existence spontaneously on Earth through some chemical process or event. To assess the validity of this assertion, we need to have a clear concept of what is meant by the words *possible* and *probable*. To clarify these concepts, we can consider the following scenario. There is a lottery in which 100,000 tickets were sold. We ask our friend, a mathematician, 'What are our chances of winning this lottery?' The first thing that our friend would ask us is 'How many tickets have you bought?' If we bought 1 ticket, then our probability of winning is 1 in 100,000. If we bought 100 tickets, then our probability of winning is 100 in 100,000, which reduces to 1 in 1,000. If we bought no tickets, then it is not possible for us to win this lottery, and accordingly, our chance of winning this lottery has no meaningful value. From this, it is clear that before we can calculate the probability of some event occurring, we need to know that it is possible for the event to occur. While the tickets in this lottery were still on sale, we had a conditional possibility of winning the lottery, which would have evolved into an actual possibility if we had bought any tickets but which would have devolved into impossibility if we did not buy any tickets before all the tickets were sold.

To clarify a related point, let us pursue this example a little further. Suppose that the prize in this lottery is $100,000 and that the payment of the prize is to be by an anonymous transfer into the bank account of the winner. Suppose that we bought a ticket, and after the lottery was drawn, we checked our bank account and found that $100,000 had been transferred into our account anonymously. From these facts, we might assume that we won the lottery. But this assumption is not necessarily the truth. It is possible that the money could have been transferred into our account by a wealthy friend who wished to remain anonymous, or it could have been transferred into our account by the bank as the result of some untraceable error by the bank. Of course, winning the lottery is most probably the true fact, but the proof of the truth of this fact is not compelling unless we can trace the transfer or eliminate all other possibilities. The point is that the conclusion that we draw from the evidence may well be what we can call a conditional conclusion if we cannot eliminate all other possibilities that would lead to a different conclusion.

Dawkins then explains that life as we know it needs water and a relatively narrow temperature range to survive. This means that any planet that can sustain life must orbit its sun in a nearly circular orbit at a range of distances from its sun that does not produce lethal temperatures. This range of different distances is referred to in astronomy as the Goldilocks zone. Dawkins then states that there are relatively few planets in the Goldilocks zone. He says:

The great majority of planets in the universe are not in the Goldilocks zones of their respective stars, and not suitable for life. None of that majority has life. However small the minority of planets with just the right conditions for life may be, we necessarily have to be on one of that minority, because here we are thinking about it.

He goes on to explain the application of the anthropic principle at page 137 and the top of 138, where he says the following:

Again, as with Goldilocks, the anthropic alternative to the design hypothesis is statistical. Scientists invoke the magic of larger numbers. It has been estimated that there are between 1 billion and 30 billion planets in our galaxy, and about 100 billion galaxies in the universe. Knocking a few noughts off for reasons of ordinary prudence, 1 billion billion is a conservative estimate of the number of available planets in the universe. Now suppose the origin of life, the spontaneous rising of something equivalent to DNA, really was a quite staggeringly improbable event. Suppose it was so improbable as to occur on only one in a billion planets . . . even with such absurdly long odds, life will have arisen on a billion planets—of which Earth, of course, is one.

This conclusion is so surprising; I'll say it again. If the odds of life originating spontaneously on a planet were a billion to one against, nevertheless that stupefyingly improbable event would still happen on a billion planets.

Towards the end of the section dealing with the planetary version of the anthropic principle, Dawkins acknowledges that the origin of life is not the only gap in the theory of evolution. He identifies the development of the eukaryotic cell as having possibly just as low a probability of developing as the spontaneous origin of life, and also that the origin of consciousness may be another gap of similar improbability. He disposes of these major difficulties as follows:

Nevertheless, it may be that the origin of life is not the only major gap in the evolutionary story that is bridged by sheer luck, anthropically justified. For example, my colleague Mark Ridley in Mendell's Demon *. . . has suggested that the origin of the eukaryotic cell (our kind of cell, with a nucleus and various other complicated features such as mitochondria, which are not present in bacteria) was an even more momentous, difficult and statistically improbable step than the origin* *of life. The origin of consciousness might be another major gap whose bridging was of the same order of improbability. One-off events like this might be explained by the anthropic principle, along the following lines. There are billions of planets that have developed life at the level of bacteria, but only a fraction of these life forms ever made it across the gap to something like the eukaryotic cell. And of these, a yet smaller fraction managed to cross the later Rubicon to consciousness. If both of these are one-off events, we are not dealing with a ubiquitous and all-pervading* process, *as we are with ordinary, run of the mill biological adaptation. The anthropic principle states that, since we are alive, eukaryotic and conscious, our planet has to be one of the intensely rare planets that has bridged all three gaps.*

The cosmological version of the anthropic principle is summarised by Dawkins as follows:

This objection can be answered by the suggestion, which Martin Rees himself supports, that there are many universes, coexisting like bubbles of foam, in a 'multiverse' (or megaverse as Leonard Susskind prefers to call it). The laws and constants of any one universe, such as our observable universe, are by-laws. The multiverse as a whole has a plethora of alternative sets of by-laws. The anthropic principle kicks in to explain that we have to be in one of those universes (presumably a minority) whose by-laws happen to be propitious to our eventual evolution and hence contemplation of the problem.

We need not consider this application of the anthropic principle further, as it is clearly based on some sheer speculation as to the existence of multiple universes. Cosmologists and science fiction writers may find such speculation entertaining, but until there is at least some evidence to support such speculation, this type of argument has no place in a serious search for the truth of what really exists.

The essence of this argument has been presented in Richard Dawkins's own words to avoid inadvertent misrepresentation of his argument. However, to carefully consider the argument and to assess its persuasive value, we should also consider any apparent flaws in his argument.

The first apparent flaw in Dawkins's argument is his assertion that it is possible that life originated spontaneously on Earth. His opening assertion at page 135 has already been quoted. His error here is saying that Earth is capable of 'generating' life. We do not know this to be true. We agree that Earth is capable of sustaining or supporting life, because we are here, so that part of his statement is axiomatic. **But his assumption that the Earth is capable of generating life spontaneously is the very conclusion that he is trying to prove.**

If we refer back to our lottery example, the logical invalidity of Dawkins's assertion becomes apparent. Dawkins is in the position of our mathematician friend, who has assumed that we have a ticket in the lottery, just as Dawkins has assumed that it is possible for life to have originated spontaneously on Earth. That is logically invalid. One cannot simply assume that a particular fact is possible without some evidence to support the possibility. It gets worse for Dawkins because he acknowledges that scientists have not been able to create life in a laboratory. He says at page 137:

The expertise required for it is chemistry and it is not mine. I watch from the sidelines with engaged curiosity, and I shall not be surprised if, within the next few years, chemists report that they have successfully midwifed a new origin of life in the laboratory. Nevertheless it hasn't happened yet, and it is still possible to maintain that the probability of its happening is, and always was, exceedingly low—although it has happened once!

In our lottery example, this is the same as saying that he does not know whether or not we have a ticket, because scientists' inability to create life in the laboratory means that he does not know whether or not this is possible. His optimism that it may happen soon does not validate his assumption. Here again he asserts with emphatic exclamation that life did arise spontaneously on our planet. There is simply no evidence that it happened this way. He then acknowledges that his anthropic principle is, at best, an alternative to creationism when he says:

Just as we did with the Goldilocks orbits, we can make the point that, however improbable the origin of life might be, we know it happened on earth because we are here. Again, as with temperature, there are two hypotheses to explain what happened—the design hypothesis and the scientific or anthropic hypothesis. The design approach postulates a God who wrought a deliberate miracle, struck the prebiotic soup with divine fire and launched DNA, or something equivalent, on its momentous career.

Again, we see the assumption that life originated spontaneously. The fact that we are here is not compelling proof that life *originated* here spontaneously. Referring to the second part of our lottery example, the money in the bank does not prove that we won the lottery. Atheists must necessarily believe that life did arise spontaneously. But this does not necessarily have to be on Earth. So just as the money could have come from elsewhere, life could have arisen elsewhere in our universe, and Earth may have been seeded with life from an asteroid containing life or by extraterrestrial life forms—perhaps even Tipler's robots!

Dawkins has repeated this assumption several times in this chapter and then goes on to apply probability mathematics on the basis that life can arise spontaneously on every earthlike planet. He concludes that life will still have arisen on 1 billion planets.

In short, Dawkins has assumed throughout that it is possible for life to arise spontaneously. He applies this assumption to the anthropic principle and ends up asserting that life has arisen on 1 billion planets and that our Earth is one of those planets. His only mention of the possibility of life arising spontaneously is to concede that scientists have not yet been able to replicate this process. He concedes that evolution cannot explain how life originated on our planet. Our belief in creationism holds that life originated on our planet as a result of a direct and personal act of God. Dawkins does not believe in the existence of God, so he must necessarily have an explanation for the origin of life on our planet that is a consequence of natural processes in the material realm and does not involve God. Dawkins argues the improbability of the existence of God, but he knows that this is not compelling proof that God does not exist, and that the best that he can do is to provide a further argument that life on our planet began spontaneously as a result of natural processes. Such an argument is then an alternative to creationism and justifies belief in the non-existence of God if one prefers this explanation to creationism.

The second flaw lies in the way that the mathematics and statistics are applied. It appears that the conclusions drawn from the application of probability theory to large numbers is misconceived. To understand this point, it may be helpful to consider an example. Suppose someone (X) shows us a bag said to contain thirty marbles. We look inside the bag and see twenty-nine red marbles and one blue marble. X then takes this to an airport, where he has placed 1 million bags each said to contain thirty marbles on a runway in an area equivalent to eight football fields. X places the bag shown to us containing the blue marble amongst the million bags on the runway and then asks us how many blue marbles there are in the bags on the runway.

Each bag is tied off at the top, so we do not know what is in any bag beyond what X has told us and what we have seen. The bags are all about the same size as the bag containing the blue marble which we saw. The bags on the runway are also lumpy, which is consistent with them containing marbles, but they could, in fact, contain pebbles, small lumps of green cheese, or any similar substance imaginable. We simply do not know what is in any of the bags except for the one that we looked into.

We could open every bag, look inside, and count the number of blue marbles that we see. But if it takes 1 minute per bag to open and inspect, this process would require 1 million minutes, which is 16,667 hours or roughly around 2,083 eight-hour working days, which reduces, allowing for weekends and public holidays, to just over eight years of work. This is obviously impractical and not worth the effort, so we would have to make an estimate if we want to answer the question.

Let us now project this example on Dawkins's planetary version of the anthropic principle. The bag first shown to us by X represents our galaxy. We looked into this bag and saw thirty marbles. The marbles represent the planets in our galaxy, with the blue marble being our own blue planet, Earth. Scientists have observed things in our galaxy beyond our own solar system that appear to be planets, so the number of marbles in the bag was set at a number higher than the number of planets known to exist in our solar system but not much higher than the number of planets so far observed in our galaxy.

The runway represents a universe. It is simply a flat place, so we can see the other bags of marbles. Analogously, it represents the space of our universe, most of which scientists can see through telescopes. The million other bags on the runway said to contain marbles represent the other galaxies in our universe. The bags are tied at the top so that we do not know what is in these bags. This represents our present level of technology, in that our telescopes are not yet able to penetrate other galaxies to the extent of detecting planets, and accordingly, we do not know whether there actually are any planets in any other galaxies. However, the apparent laws of physics applicable to the formation of the universe suggest that there are planets and other galaxies, which is projected by X telling us that all the bags on the runway contain marbles.

X asks us how many blue marbles there are in the bags on the runway. This represents asking us how many planets capable of sustaining life there are in our universe. To sustain life, the planet must have an orbit around its sun which does not travel outside its sun's Goldilocks zone; must have water; and must be otherwise earthlike in its composition—i.e. it cannot be gaseous like most of the other planets in our solar system. Also, it must have some mechanism to neutralise the cosmic radiation, which is lethal to life and emanates from suns, such as an atmosphere or magnetic core capable of deflecting such radiation. Of course, we do not know whether any sun other than our own has any planets in its Goldilocks zone or whether any planets that may be in the Goldilocks zone of other suns meet all the requirements necessary to sustain life as we know it.

From this example, it is fairly easy to see that Dawkins's estimate of there being life on 1 billion planets in our universe is technically misconceived. It is mathematically incorrect to assume that there is more than one blue marble in all the bags on the runway when X has not even told us that there is more than one blue marble there. All X has told us is that there are marbles in all the other bags. Likewise, science tells us that there are planets in other galaxies, but it does not tell us that any of them are earthlike and thus capable of sustaining life as we know it.

The 'magic of large numbers' does not rescue this application of the anthropic principle. The numbers used in our example were kept small so that the point it makes may be more easily conceptualised. It would make no difference to the identification of this flaw in Dawkins's argument if, instead of 1 million bags of marbles on the runway, we were presented with 7 trillion bags of marbles. We still would not know that there is more than one blue marble. Of course, the footprint of 7 trillion bags of marbles would occupy 56 million football fields, and it would take approximately 56 million working years to open each bag and look for blue marbles. This observation is not made as an attempt at humour but to legitimise the use of estimates based on statistics and the laws of probability, in situations where the actual counting process is impractical. This flaw in Dawkins's argument is not his use of statistics and probability but rather the assumption he has made that there are other earthlike planets in our universe, to which he has then applied the mathematical principles. In passing, it may be noted that Dawkins's statement that there are about 100 billion galaxies in our universe has been overtaken by recent observational data from the Hubble Telescope, which now puts the estimate of the number of galaxies in our universe at 7 trillion.

The same flaw applies to the cosmological version of the anthropic principle. In fact, the cosmological version is even more obviously flawed, because we do not even get to the runway. From the runway, we can see the million other bags, just as scientists can see the other galaxies in the universe. But no scientist has ever seen any other universe, and thus, the anthropic principle has no basis in known reality.

A third flaw in Dawkins's argument is that his statistical/probabilistic analysis is incomplete. From what Dawkins says on page 138, we are asked to accept that life will have arisen spontaneously on 1 billion planets in our universe. This is basic cellular life. He later says that the development of the eukaryotic cell is of the same order of improbability as the spontaneous development of this basic cellular life. He does not factor this into his calculations, so if we apply his one chance in a billion to this process, the result is that the chance of the evolution of the eukaryotic cell from the basic cell is that it can occur on only one planet in our entire universe.

Dawkins has also stated that the probability of the evolution of consciousness from the eukaryotic life form is of the same order as the evolution of the eukaryotic cell, i.e. one chance in a billion. If we apply this factor to Dawkins's calculations, the result is that the chance of conscious life developing in our universe are a billion to one *against*. In other words, we need a billion times the number of planets that Dawkins has estimated to exist in order to have one instance of conscious life in our universe.

But conscious life is not the end of it. We are also intelligent, and we are the only species of about 10 million species on our planet that is intelligent. Many other species have consciousness, which we can define for these purposes as having natural states of unconsciousness and being able to see and move when conscious. If we assess the probability of intelligent life developing from conscious life as low as one chance in 1 million and apply this to Dawkins's probability calculation, the result is that the chance of intelligent life developing in our universe is a million billion to one *against*. In other words, we need a million billion times the number of planets that Dawkins has estimated to exist in order to have one instance of intelligent life in our universe.

It is a little disappointing that Dawkins did not factor these contingencies into his calculations but instead simply dismissed them with a wave of his misconceived version of the anthropic principle.

Conclusions

Dawkins's version of the anthropic principle is fundamentally only the assertion that if life did not develop spontaneously on Earth, then we would not be here. The acceptable version of the anthropic principle is that if certain scientific constants of cosmology and chemistry were not as they are, then we would not be here. It is axiomatic that Earth has been a planet capable of supporting human life for as long as human life has existed on this planet.

The anthropic coincidences, from which the anthropic principle is derived, can be seen by theists as legitimate instances, amongst many other instances, of the teleological approach to the question of the existence of God, in that they suggest design. Furthermore, if the probability of sentient life elsewhere in the universe is calculated, it may well be so low as to provide substantial support for the teleological argument.

Dawkins's argument is intended to provide an alternative to creationism by showing that life on our planet could have come into existence spontaneously through the action of natural processes. His argument is mathematically misconceived, because it assumes that there are other earthlike planets in our universe although there is no evidence as yet of other earthlike planets in our own galaxy and no evidence that there exist any earthlike planets in any of the other galaxies in our universe. It is also logically invalid, because it assumes that it is possible for life to come into existence spontaneously, when this is the very possibility that the argument attempts to prove. To prove that it is possible for life to come into existence spontaneously through natural processes, scientists must actually create life in a laboratory experiment that is repeatable by other scientists. It must then be shown that the environment and the processes in the experiment existed on Earth at about the time that life first appeared on our planet. Dawkins acknowledges that scientists have not yet been able to create life in a laboratory, although he would not be surprised if they are successful in such an experiment soon. He must also be aware that scientists have been trying to do this for some time, and it is surprising that he proceeds to assume that they will succeed, as the invalidity of making this assumption is obvious. If scientists do succeed in creating life in a laboratory, then atheists can validly argue the spontaneous generation of life as an alternative to creationism, even though the exact particulars of such spontaneous generation may never be known.

If scientists do succeed in creating life in laboratory, it becomes immediately apparent that both versions of the anthropic principle are pointless. If scientists can prove that life on Earth could have arisen spontaneously, then the probability that life could have come into existence spontaneously on other planets does not strengthen the argument that life on Earth could have arisen spontaneously. Nor does it in any way diminish creationism, although it may claim from creationism some adherents who previously had no logically valid alternative.

Nor does the existence of life on other earthlike planets, if any are found, exclude creationism from having occurred on those planets. If, according to creationism, God has the power to create 7 trillion galaxies and the power to create life, he could easily have created life not only on Earth but on many, even 1 billion, other planets. And even if spontaneous generation of life on Earth and other planets becomes a scientifically acceptable explanation, there is still the creationist argument that God designed and implemented all the processes that created life.

But until science can persuade us that the spontaneous generation of life is possible, the anthropic principle may be regarded as premature, logically invalid, and mathematically misconceived and incomplete at this time.

2.3.5 The Argument from the Existence of Evil

Atheistic philosophers and writers have presented this argument in many different ways, focusing on different aspects of the argument. Essentially, all versions of this argument are based on logic having the following premises:

1. If God exists, then he has the following attributes: he is omnipotent, he is omniscient, and he is omnibenevolent.
2. From our evidentially based knowledge of the world, it is clear that widespread horrendous evil exists in our world.
3. Through his omniscience, God must be aware of such evil. Through his omnipotence, God could have created a world where such evil does not exist, or he could have prevented it from occurring. Through his omnibenevolence, God must have created a world without evil or in which he acts to prevent it from occurring.

Conclusion   Because evil does exist, it is probable that God is not omnipotent, omniscient, and omnibenevolent. If God does not have these three attributes, then he is not God, and therefore, God probably does not exist.

The conclusion is put as a probability rather than certainty, because the proponents of this argument concede that a God who is omnipotent, omniscient, and omnibenevolent may have created a world containing evil and permitted it to occur in order to enable a good which outweighs the evil to occur. But they maintain their conclusion on the basis that there is no evidence of any greater good flowing from evil. Theistic philosophers and writers have suggested that the existence of evil is necessary to enable moral decisions, because a knowledge of good and evil is fundamental to morality, and that evil must necessarily exist to enable a free choice. But the atheists reject these explanations as speculative and not evidentially based.

There are other aspects and explanations of this argument which will be considered hereunder. At this point, it is worth noting that in our everyday lives, we encounter atheists, some of whom base their non-belief on the essence of this argument. Since most of us are laypersons to philosophy and theology, we usually hear this argument expressed in something like the following terms:

I don't believe in God because I have seen too many bad things happen to believe that a loving God exists. If I had the power to prevent these bad things from happening, I would have done so. God must love everyone far more than I do, so why does he not prevent bad things from happening?

The essence of the academic version of the argument is clear from the obvious assumptions in the lay version.

In order to carefully consider this argument, it is necessary to define the term *evil*. The *Collins Concise Dictionary*, third edition (Australian edition), defines *evil* as

'1. morally wrong or bad; wicked. 2. causing harm or injury'.

On this definition, the atheists' use of this term is legitimate and accurate. The problem is that in modern times, the word *evil* has connotations of the supernatural. We Catholics generally understand the word *evil* to mean 'that which offends God'. It is not entirely a synonym for sin, because sin has the additional elements of voluntarily doing something knowing that it offends God. No doubt many people of other faiths have a similar understanding of the concept of evil.

The dictionary definition of *evil* is inadequate because it is based on the notion of morality. The difficulty here is that the parameters of morality are not universal. What is regarded as morally wrong by some people may not be regarded as morally wrong by other people. Of course, there are some things, such as stealing, that are regarded as morally wrong in virtually every culture. The thrust of this argument is not on the moral status of some event but rather is on the harm or injury caused by the event which makes the event evil. Thus, it is not necessary that God regards such an event as morally wrong, given that through his omniscience, God knows the harmful consequences of such event and, through his omnipotence, could have prevented such consequences either in his initial design of the world or by direct intervention.

As has already been noted, atheists concede that there may be some greater good flowing from some evil event causing harm or injury, but if such greater good is beyond human apprehension, then the harm or injury appears pointless to humans. And if God created or permits pointless harm or injury, then he is not omnibenevolent and is therefore not God.

Having regard to a common understanding of the meaning of the word *evil*, it seems that the academic atheists may have done themselves a disservice in using the word *evil* without clearly indicating that it is limited to the human perception of pointless suffering arising from the harm or injury consequent to some evil event. Perhaps the word *bad* is more appropriate, because something bad may have harm or injury as a consequence without having the implication that it also necessarily offends God. Of course, we do not know what offends God other than what he has revealed as being offensive to him, in particular human conduct contrary to the Ten Commandments. And there are many events that have bad consequences that are not within the actions proscribed by the Ten Commandments. To avoid confusion, the word *evil* will be used in this context, but it should be understood as subject to the above qualifications. For the sake of clarity, we can now define *evil* as used in this context as *'something that humans regard as reprehensible because it causes harm or injury'*.

The atheists who support this argument allege that evil is widespread and horrendous in our world. The mere allegation of something does not make it true, even if many people make the allegation. To understand this argument, we must know what these things are that the atheists say are evil. From the writings we can discern four main categories of evil as follows:

(a) evil natural laws
(b) natural disasters
(c) natural things
(d) evil human actions.

Each of these warrant a separate consideration.

Regarding Evil Natural Laws

Natural laws are not commonly regarded as evil, but it warrants consideration because it was argued in a 1991 paper by Quinton

Smith, a person who has written widely in support of atheism. One night, Smith heard one animal savagely attacking and killing another animal. From this experience, he said: '*It seemed to me self-evident that the natural law that animals must savagely kill and devour each other in order to survive was an evil natural law.*' Smith then goes on to construct a convoluted logical supposition that for every carnivorous animal that exists, there could exist a counterpart in another world that is a vegetarian. From this, it follows, he argues, that an all-powerful god could have made our world so that all species are vegetarians and the law of predation does not operate. Since this natural law is evil, according to Smith, it could not have been created by an omnibenevolent god; therefore, God probably does not exist.

The first issue for consideration about this argument is whether we agree that the law of predation is evil. Obviously, the predator kills its prey to eat it in order to survive. Studies of animal behaviour suggests that predators usually kill their prey quickly and efficiently, having regard to the means at their disposal, although it must be conceded that the prey feels some pain if it has a nervous system sufficiently developed to feel pain. So clearly, the killing of the prey is injury or harm within the meaning of the definition of *evil*. But is it reprehensible or morally wrong? Obviously, it must be the moral code of the predator which is breached. So far as we know, animals do not act in accordance with any moral code. We see them act in accordance with patterns of behaviour that are conducive to their survival and the survival of their offspring. It would be vexatious to suggest that predators are doing something reprehensible or morally wrong when they kill their prey for their own or their offspring's survival.

We humans do have a moral code, and we do kill animals in order to eat them. We are omnivores, so we could survive as vegetarians. Mostly we do try to kill animals humanely, but the death of an animal is still harm or injury within the meaning of the definition of *evil*. Then there are hunters who are not skilled enough to kill their prey quickly and efficiently, leading to the animal living with a painful wound or dying a slow, agonising death. And some hunters kill merely for sport. Thus, if we agree that the law of predation is evil, we should all become vegetarians, and our laws should ban any form of hunting.

But Smith's argument is not really about us. Essentially, he is saying that an omniscient God, if he exists, must regard the law of predation as evil because it causes injury or harm. Therefore, if he is God, he is also omnibenevolent and, accordingly, would not create a world in which the law of predation operates. To suggest that God must regard the law of predation as evil because it is self-evident to Smith that it is evil is not a sustainable proposition, especially since many people, in particular meat eaters and hunters, would disagree with Smith on the self-evident 'evil' nature of the law of predation.

Indeed, we might expect that atheists who support the theory of evolution would not support Smith's argument, because they recognise the need for predation in the process of natural selection, survival of the fittest, and environmental adaptation. Furthermore, evolutionists would probably agree that Smith's argument that all species could be vegetarians is nonsense. A tiger would not be a tiger without its fangs and claws, and the same applies to most predator species in our world. Our world would be much different and poorer in the diversification of species without the law of predation.

To theists, it is axiomatic that God would not create something that offends him by its very existence. We believe that God created us humans with the capacity to offend him and with the free will to choose whether or not to offend him. The law of predation does allow humans and animal predators to cause harm and injury to other life forms. From this, it is logically open to conclude that the law of predation does not offend God. Some humans do harm or injury to other humans, contrary to his revealed commands, but they do not do this under the control of the law of predation. Even if we limited the definition of *evil* to only such events that cause injury or harm, ignoring the moral aspects of *evil*, we humans can see that the law of predation is a necessary evil in a world that was created to be as it is. We do not presume to know the mind of God or to suppose that our logic binds him, but we can see the invalidity of the argument that God does not exist because the law of predation exists.

Regarding Natural Disasters

The next category of what the atheists claim to be evil may be described as a natural disaster. This category includes such things as volcanic eruptions, earthquakes, tidal waves, floods, droughts, plagues of insects, tornadoes, cyclones and other fierce and destructive storms, forest and bush fires, etc. Insurance underwriters call these events acts of God, but atheists say that they are just the opposite.

Another noted atheist academic, William L. Rowe, in his 1979 paper entitled 'The Problem of Evil and Some Varieties of Atheism', put his argument in relation to this type of evil in the following terms:

'Intense human and animal suffering, for example, occurs daily and in great plenitude in our world. Such intense suffering is a clear case of evil.'

The example he gives is as follows:

'Suppose in some distant forest lightning strikes a dead tree resulting in a forest fire. In the fire a fawn is trapped, horribly burned and lies in terrible agony for several days before death relieves its suffering. So far as we can see the fawn's intense suffering is pointless.'

In a later paper, Rowe specifies that this example is invented, although he asserts that this sort of thing occurs 'not infrequently' in nature.

Obviously, such an event does cause harm or injury to the fawn, and under the atheists' definition, the forest fire is evil. But can a forest fire be reprehensible? A criticism that can be made of Rowe's example is that it has an unwarranted emotive persuasive component. The fawn is a young, harmless, and even lovable creature. To imagine it suffering in agony for several days before dying may well be distressing to that generation of readers who grew up knowing and loving *Bambi*. A contrasting example might be as follows: a volcano erupts, and lava flows downhill, trapping an old ten-metre man-eating crocodile in a pool. The lava slowly flows into the pool, raising the water temperature, so that the crocodile is slowly boiled to death. That example would probably not distress many people, especially those who were brought up with the injunction to 'never smile at a crocodile'.

Again, if this argument is to be used to deny the existence of God, then it must be shown that if God exists, he must necessarily consider the suffering and death of the fawn to be evil. Rowe concludes that God may allow some evil to occur in order to achieve some greater good, but he sees the suffering and death of the fawn as pointless and cannot conceive any good coming from this event. Other atheists acknowledge that God's reason, if he exists, is greater than human reason and knowledge. An atheistic evolutionist might argue that the forest fire is nature's way of culling the weakest of the various species living in the forest and also enables a new growth of vegetation. Possibly, this could be regarded as sufficient good to outweigh the death of some animals, but this is mere speculation; we do not actually know why God allows lightning to strike the dead trees, nor can we conclude that God necessarily regards the death of the fawn as evil simply because some humans regard the event as evil.

Another issue raised by atheists is based on the love that parents have for their children. They assert that when parents cause their children to suffer for some greater good, they explain their reasons to their child so that the child can obtain some comfort from the suffering and not merely regard it as pointless or vindictive. No doubt some parents do give their children some explanations for the necessity of punishment and suffering, but it is not conceded that this occurs universally for all suffering endured by children. The atheists then argue that if God exists, he loves us in the same way, but more than parents love their children, so why does he not reveal to us his reasons for apparently pointless suffering? Of course, we cannot answer that question without knowing the mind of God, but it is clear that if God did reveal his reasons to us, then we would have no doubt as to his existence and, accordingly, lose our free will to not believe in him.

From these considerations, it is open to us to reject Rowe's assertion that the consequences of natural disasters, which inflict harm or injury on humans or animals, are necessarily regarded as evil by God, even though we may regard such consequences as tragic.

Regarding Natural Things

This category is really a subcategory of the natural disaster category. Essentially, it refers to things that exist which do not appear to have any benign or beneficial reason to exist. This category contains such things as bacteria and viruses that cause death or illness. Some people have phobias about some forms of life, like spiders and snakes, and regard these creatures as inherently evil because of the harm they do and the danger they occasion. Some people regard rats as evil because of their association with various plagues. The contents of this category is really a miscellany of those things that exist that cause harm or injury, as distinct from the processes, such as floods, that also cause harm or injury.

One of the most obvious examples of this type of thing is the Ebola virus. It does not appear to have any reason to exist other than to kill people in a horrific manner. The atheists ask, why would a loving God create such a thing? Again, our answer must be that we do not know God's reasons. However, if the question of whether or not God exists is necessarily uncertain either way, then God had to create a sufficient number of ways for our bodies to die so as to avoid the inference that God exists arising from an insufficient number of ways to die. By way of contrast to the many ways we have of dying, we can argue that God did not create every possible way for us to die in the natural order of things. This argument gathers validity when we look at human history and count the number of ways that humans have devised to kill other humans, which cannot occur in nature. For example, guns do not occur in nature, but many people have died from gunshot wounds.

Another example of a thing which some people regard as evil is the AIDS virus. It does not kill people directly but destroys the human immune system, which then enables the human to die from otherwise relatively minor infections. Interestingly, when it first emerged, some people, undoubtedly theists, believed that this was God's punishment for homosexual activity. We no longer believe that God punishes conduct that offends him in the material realm, but rather, he leaves such punishment to be applied in the spiritual realm. The point is that some people believed that God deliberately created and inflicted this virus on mankind. In contrast, atheists regard this virus in the same way that they regard the Ebola virus, and our response is accordingly similar. We do not know why God created the AIDS virus, but we can regard the efforts of medical professionals to overcome the harm or injury caused by this virus as a worthwhile human endeavour. Nor can we regard the very existence of the AIDS virus as inherently evil. It is the interaction of that virus with the human immune system that causes the harm or injury, which, while it is a bad thing to happen, cannot be described as morally wrong or reprehensible.

Another example worth considering is the Alzheimer's virus. While this virus does harm or injury to the person it infects, it does not cause them much suffering, except perhaps in lucid intervals when they might regret the loss of their mental capacities. The most significant harm that this virus causes is to the relatives or carers of the persons infected. Those of us who have not experienced it can well imagine the emotional pain of a person whose parent has Alzheimer's disease and, because of that, has lost the capacity to recognise even their own children. Although such pain is psychological as distinct from physical, it is nonetheless pain and no doubt qualifies under the atheist definition of *evil*.

Of course, many people feel emotional pain when one of their loved ones suffers any harm or injury. However, God's reasons for creating the thing that causes the harm or injury can be explained and justified using only human reasoning. This explanation is that God appears to be testing the people suffering the emotional pain, to determine to what extent they will honour their father or mother as he has commanded or to determine the extent to which the person being tested will help their friend or relative who is in need. Naturally, we do not know that this is God's reason, but it may be; it is certainly a sustainable reason on purely human behaviours or morals.

The atheist argument in relation to evil things is that it would be totally senseless for God to create something which offends him by its very existence, and we can be certain that God would not create such a thing. Yet some things exist that have no discernible benefit to humans and do nothing but harm to humans. The atheists cannot imagine any possible justification for the existence of these things and conclude from their reasoning process that probably not even God could have a valid reason for creating such a thing. From this, it follows that probably God does not exist.

The flaw in this reasoning process is the application of probability theory to a fact that definitely either is or is not. We can argue that God would not create anything that offends him by its very existence. But if God does exist, then he must have a reason for creating anything that appears to be inherently evil to us, even though that reason has not been revealed to us and may be beyond our comprehension. If God does not exist, then the atheist argument is understated as a mere probability. With these considerations in mind, it becomes clear that the argument against the existence of God from the existence of evil things is dependent on the actual existence or non-existence of God and, accordingly, does not advance our knowledge on this issue.

Regarding Evil Human Actions

Human beings frequently do things that are morally wrong and wicked which cause harm or injury to other humans or animals. Such actions not only meet the atheists' definition of *evil* but also meet the broader definition of offending God. Most of the crimes specified in the laws of most countries are instances of such evil, and many other actions that are not punishable by law for various reasons.

An example of the atheist argument was given by William L. Rowe in his 1988 article 'Evil and Theodicy'. His example is an actual event that occurred in Flint, Michigan, USA, on New Year's Day of 1986. On that day, a five-year-old girl was found raped, severely beaten, and strangled. In his argument on these facts, Rowe does not rely on God being omnibenevolent. His argument is that it would be morally wrong for a being who is omnipotent and omniscient to permit such a thing to happen. Since God cannot, by act or omission, offend himself and since events that offend God do happen, probably God does not exist.

There can be no doubt that the murder of the girl offended God. It is clearly against the fifth commandment. And obviously God cannot offend himself. It was not God who murdered this girl; it was a man. Not preventing the crime from being committed is a different issue. Most of us would agree that any human being who knew that the crime was about to be committed and who had the power to prevent it from being committed would have a moral duty to prevent the crime from being committed. But it does not follow that God is under the same moral obligation, even though he actually did know that the crime was about to be committed and he had the power to prevent it.

Our human reasoning powers are insufficient to understand why God is not under such a moral obligation, although the reason depends on whether or not we believe that we humans have free will.

Our free will allows us to choose to do or not do something. That something may be a mundane thing, or it may be an important thing. The choices we make may be predictable, given the knowledge of our nature and the factors that are likely to affect our choice, and taking into account the weight we are likely to give these factors. But we also do or omit to do things on an impulse or out of passion. If we know that the act or omission we choose offends God, then our belief in God and the certainty of punishment for offending him will be a factor, although we may still choose the usually selfish alternative. Similarly, if we do not believe in God but see the act or omission as contravening our moral sense of propriety we are still free to choose the selfish alternative, but this choice does not attract any punishment.

Some people believe that we do not have free will and that all our actions are predetermined and compelled by who and what we are. If that is so, then there can be no crime, for if we have no choice, then we have no responsibility for our actions. If God exists, then nothing we can do can offend God, because he gave us no choice; therefore, we have no responsibility. If God does not exist, then we are merely automatons in a pointless manifestation of our universe.

The existence of our free will and the existence of God are inextricably linked, because obviously God would not create a universe in which we had no free will. Thus, if God exists, then he created us with the free will to choose to do that which pleases him or that which offends him. Furthermore, the free will from God cannot be conditional, because God would not have created us to have free will to choose to do that which offends him and then prevent us from implementing our choice if it offends him. That would be a sham of free will, and we humans, even with our limited intelligence, would quickly perceive that we cannot implement a choice that offends God; consequently, we would not make that choice because it is not a real option.

The essence of this argument is that if God exists, then he is and was bound by what we humans see as moral imperatives in creating our world or preventing what we see as evil from happening by direct intervention. This raises the question of the nature of God. The nature of an infinite God is not knowable by a finite human mind, but there are a few things about God that we can confidently believe. Relevant to this issue, we can believe that God is not dishonest with us. If he gave us free will unconditionally, then he will not take back that gift or render it impotent, even though we may use our free will to do that which offends him. God has not expressly revealed that we have free will, but it is abundantly evident that he has given it to us from his promises to reward good and to punish evil, which implies our responsibility for our actions and, accordingly, a genuine choice.

The argument that God does not exist from the existence of evil is based on strong emotion. Imagine the feelings of a mother of a young girl who was horribly murdered. She would probably be incredulous that a loving God would allow such a crime to be committed. She might even resent a God who knew it was going to happen and who had the power to stop it but did nothing. The consideration that God has to allow choices to be implemented in order to determine whether love and obedience to God is real to the extent of being more than mere words or intentions would probably not diminish the pain felt by the girl's mother or change her view that God should have done something to prevent this crime. The point is that strong emotions of grief will generally obscure the rational consideration that the reality of free will prevents God from intervening. It is likely that this explanation will not be appreciated until after the grieving process has run its course, and even then, it may not be accepted. However, empathy and sympathy for the victims of evil should not obscure the perceptions and reasoning process of persons not personally involved, and thus, we should be able to perceive the flaw in this argument.

To this point, we have been considering the modern version of the argument as formulated by respected atheist academics. But this argument is not new. Many philosophers and theologians have expressed views on this argument over the years. It is beyond the scope of this work to outline the historical development of this argument, but it appears worthwhile to explore one of the earliest written works that deals with the existence of evil, to determine whether it can shed any light on the modern version of the argument. That work is the book of Job in the Old Testament of the Bible. We do not know who wrote that book, but it was written between the fifth and seventh centuries BC. It is clearly a didactic work or parable, and it does not document actual events, although it does give the full names and partial genealogy of some of the protagonists, as was the literary style of the time when it was written. It is considered by many to be a literary classic.

The story begins by introducing Job as an extremely wealthy man living in the land of Uz (Edom or Arabia). In those days, wealth was measured by the number of livestock owned and the number of children a person had. Job had seven sons and three daughters. Wealth was considered to indicate God's favour, and Job is also described as a pious man, which supports the view that he was favoured by God.

The next phase of the story is a conversation between God and Satan. God mentions Job is a good man, but Satan argues that Job is only good because he enjoys God's favour and that if God allows harm or injury to befall Job, then Job will surely curse God. God then allows Satan to inflict harm or injury on Job's possessions, animals, and family, but he prohibits any injury to Job personally.

Next, we are told that the Sabeans (people from South Arabia) stole his oxen and asses and killed the herdsman, and that Chaldeans stole his camels and killed their herdsmen. These are evil events in the nature of human evil, as considered above. Also, lightning destroyed all Job's sheep and their shepherds, and a strong wind collapsed the house in which all his children were eating and drinking, and killed all of them. These are evil events in the nature of natural disasters, considered in an earlier section. Job accepted these disasters as God's will and did not blaspheme.

The conversation between God and Satan is resumed, and God points out Job's fidelity after these disasters. Satan argues that the test was insufficient and suggests that if Job is afflicted personally, then he will surely blaspheme. God allows Satan to afflict Job personally but prohibits killing Job. Satan then afflicts Job with some boils all over his body. Job's wife tempts Job to 'curse God and die', but Job refuses, saying: 'We accept good things from God; and should we not accept evil?' Boils are obviously caused by a virus or bacteria, so this evil can be regarded as a type of evil considered as natural things in the previous section.

The next phase of the story begins when three friends of Job visit him to console him. Job laments his fate and tells them that he wishes that he were dead and that he had never been born. In a number of lengthy speeches, Job's friends try to console him, saying that God is just and that Job must have done something to deserve his fate. In those days, it was believed that God rewarded good people with wealth and happiness and punished wicked people with desolation. In his responses, Job steadfastly maintains his innocence of doing anything to offend God, and he calls on God to explain to him why these disasters have been inflicted on him. In his final speech (chapters 29 to 31), Job summarises all the good things he has done in his life and denies any failings.

A youth named Elihu, who had been listening to the speeches, then spoke and roundly condemned Job on the then traditional view of the nature of God. God then speaks to Job (chapters 38 to 41). God does not explain to Job his reasons for allowing evil to befall Job, but rather, he exemplifies his own omnipotence and omniscience, suggesting to Job that Job has lost the true perspective of man's relationship to God in calling God to account. Job then apologises to God and disowns what he said, resuming his former humility. In the epilogue of this story, Job's wealth is restored to the extent of double what he had initially, he is given another seven sons and three daughters, his health is restored, and he is given another 147 years of life.

It might have been interesting if the book had concluded with another conversation between God and Satan, in which God points out that even in great personal affliction, Job did not blaspheme or curse God. We can speculate as to what Satan might have replied, but perhaps the story does not end this way because there is nothing of substance that Satan could say.

In the light of Job's story, the fundamental flaw in the modern argument becomes apparent. That flaw is the premise that God is omnibenevolent. That premise is simply not true on the traditional view of the nature of God. We know from other sacred writings, dogma, and saintly expositions that God loves us. Job's story identifies a number of ways in which God has actualised that love, but there are many additional wonderful things in nature which can be attributed to God's design, even accepting modern cosmology.

Job's story also answers the modern criticism that God fails to console the victims of evil by telling them why they must suffer. Job's failure to understand why this has happened to him is one of the main strands of the story. God does not personally inflict evil on Job but allows Satan to do so. The story does not tell us why God allows this, but we might regard Satan's words as a challenge to God based on the premise that humans are weak and that in adversity, they will reject God. God presumably accepted this challenge on the premise that humans can tolerate adversity and that a true love of God will not fade into oblivion just because of adversity.

Job's story of fidelity to God and the traditional view of the nature of God assumes surprising potency in the light of some historical facts. The story was written at least five centuries before Jesus. It was Jesus who brought the Good News that there is a heaven and that God will reward fidelity to Jesus with eternal life in that heaven. In the time of Job's story, there was no concept of heaven or hell. Death was entry into the netherworld, from which there was no return. God rewarded the good and punished the wicked by giving or taking the things in our material world. Job's argument may well have been different if he had believed in an afterlife and that God would reward him in the afterlife. Also, the arguments of Job's friends would be much different if they believed, as we now do, that God does not inflict punishment in the material realm but does so only in the spiritual realm.

Belief in the existence of God was not an issue in Job's story. Job's friends and Elihu all took the existence of God for granted and argued the infallibility of God's justice. Job calling God to account was disrespectful and futile. That lesson has been learned by modern humans. So how can anyone respond to God for allowing evil to happen to them? God's first commandment is to believe that he is the one and only god. Obviously failing to believe in God offends or disappoints God, so it is not futile. If Job had been set in modern times, then he would have been tempted to deny that God exists rather than curse God, and the consoling arguments of Job's friends would have focused on the argument for the existence of God. In this light, Job's story can be applied to the modern argument and can answer many of the atheist arguments on this issue.

In the modern version of this argument, we have included Quentin Smith's assertion that the law of predation is an evil natural law. As we have seen, this view has little popular support. The story of Job does not identify any natural law as a type of evil, so Job could not complain that the operation of any natural law caused him harm or injury. The argument that the law of predation is evil attacks the alleged omnibenevolence of God in his creation of laws that govern our world. God's final speech to Job points to God's omnipotence and omniscience as being beyond challenge, which leads to the conclusion that God's will is supreme because it flows from limitless power, supported by awareness of everything that is knowable. So even if Smith's argument had been included in the story—for example, if some of Job's animals had been killed by predators—the argument would still have been refuted by the substance of God's last speech to Job.

William L. Rowe's argument about human evil does not attack God's omnibenevolence. His argument is that because of his omnipotence and omniscience, God knows of evil that is about to occur and has the power to prevent it. The fact that he does not prevent it is morally wrong. And since God cannot do anything morally wrong because he is the perfection of goodness, God does not exist. This argument limits God's omnipotence by requiring that it must be used to prevent evil. The illogic of this argument is apparent if we acknowledge that God created humans with the capacity to do evil, but he must then negate free will if he is under a moral obligation to prevent human evil. Again, God's final speech to Job, declaring his will to be supreme, disposes of this argument. If God created humans with the capacity to do evil, then clearly he intended humans to have free will, and it cannot be immoral for God to not circumvent his own will.

Conclusion

Consider the logic of the following argument:

Major Premise
If something (A) exists, then it has three properties (X, Y, and Z). If something else (B) exists, then it has two properties (X and Y).

Minor Premise
From evidence, we know conclusively that property Z does not exist.

Conclusion
Therefore, A (as defined) does not exist.

This argument is logically correct. Obviously, we cannot come to the conclusion that B does not exist, because there is no minor premise relating to it. Equally obvious is the fact that A becomes identical to B if A is redefined as having only properties X and Y, at which point B becomes redundant in the argument.

The atheist's argument for the non-existence of God based on the existence of evil is precisely this form of logical argument when we substitute the concepts for the letters:

A is God.
X is God's omnipotence.
Y is God's omniscience.
Z is God's omnibenevolence.

The minor premise is established by the undisputed existence of evil as defined and considered above. The conclusion that the atheists assert is that God does not exist. They omit the qualification (as defined). The correct way to express their conclusion is as follows:

A does not have property Z.
Pertinently, 'if God exists, then he is not omnibenevolent', and this is all that their argument proves.

If the atheists want to prove to us that the God that we believe in does not exist, then they must refer to the God that we conceptualise and not to some unsupported concept of God. Historically, the story of Job clearly shows that the God conceptualised by the Jews is not omnibenevolent. The God of Islam permits his followers to do harm and injury to infidels. In our Catholic faith, we have the atrocities of the Crusades and the Spanish Inquisition, which were perpetrated in the name of Jesus. We no longer believe that Jesus wanted these atrocities to occur, but they are nevertheless evidence that our concept of God does not regard him as omnibenevolent. And how could an omnibenevolent God punish evil? Would such punishment not itself be evil?

Modern atheists appear to regard God's omnibenevolence as undisputed. This is not the case. We believe that God loves us and that he has actualised that love by giving us life and more than sufficient means to survive, plus many wonderful things in this world. We believe that we have the free will to choose to do or not do evil that offends God. The reality of our free will makes the existence of evil necessary and inevitable. Perhaps modern theists have misconstrued the nature of God's love for us, equated it to omnibenevolence, and conceded God's omnibenevolence in arguments with the atheists. Presumably, the atheists would accept that arguing the non-existence of a God that does not accord to our concept is pointless and lacking credibility, so they must have perceived that we believe that our God is omnibenevolent, as they understand this concept. With respect, theists must disown the atheists' concept of God as omnibenevolent, even if this means that references to God's love for us must be expressed using more words, even if this seems tedious and pedantic.

William L. Rowe's argument about human evil, while not based on God's omnibenevolence, requires that God be bound by a moral duty to prevent evil. This duty can be regarded as property Z in the logical argument outlined above. And as we have seen, the will of God is supreme, and there is no valid argument that any human concept of morality binds God. The argument that God is under some duty to console the victims of evil is similarly unsupported, as well as being shown to be presumptuous in the story of Job.

Our world is not utopia. The argument that God does not exist because evil exists is little more than a complaint that our world is not utopia. Imagine our world if all species were vegetarian, there were no natural disasters, nothing existed which could cause disease or harm, and there was no crime or any evil action by humans that could cause harm or injury to other humans or animals. Life would be very dull indeed, and this is the nature of the world that atheists say God must necessarily create if he is omnibenevolent. It is such a world that can only come about at the expense of our free will to choose to do good rather than evil. Without that free will, we might justifiably question whether our existence is worthwhile. So why would God create a world like that?

2.4 Conclusion

As has already been stated, the existence or non-existence of God is a matter of fact. Our considerations are a search for the truth about this fact, and not some academic mind game or exercise. We have not considered every bit of evidence that relates to this issue or every argument that exists for belief one way or the other. Nor have we even done a close analysis of all the arguments that were raised for consideration. What we have done is outline the essential elements of the arguments on both sides and then identify and objectively consider the strengths and weaknesses of these arguments in order to assess their persuasiveness.

Whether or not any reader was persuaded by any of the arguments considered is entirely a matter for each individual reader. But for anyone still uncommitted, a brief review of the persuasiveness of the arguments considered may help.

- The Catholic Church's dogma on this issue is not an argument or evidence. It merely states that we can be persuaded to the degree necessary to make a commitment to believe in God. Of itself, it has no persuasive value, although it does refer to the teleological argument as the means through which such persuasiveness can be found.
- The Five Ways of Aquinas have been superseded by modern versions of the arguments, although the enduring aspects of Aquinas's reasoning are incorporated in the modern arguments. Consideration of the modern arguments should be preferred.
- The ontological argument is purely analytic in nature and is now not considered to be substantial, in addition to being rejected by the Catholic Church.
- The cosmological argument is about the origin of 'all that is' and incorporates Aquinas's reasoning about cause and effect and infinite regression. It has some logical appeal. But atheists claim it supports their view in the light of the

Big Bang theory, which limits regression to 13.7 billion years. However, the Big Bang theory is still only a theory and does not explain how the singularity source of all matter came about. Ultimately, the bipartisan nature of this argument diminishes its persuasiveness either way.

- The teleological argument is not really an argument or evidence. It is a reference to the process of analysis of any or all natural things in our world, viewing their complexity, construction, composition, and function in order to detect design beyond human capacity, which necessitates the existence of a superhuman designer. This process can lead to the requisite degree of persuasion to justify belief in the existence of God, but only if the process is implemented by actual analysis of a cross-section of natural things. Some atheists claim that the teleological argument supports their view that God does not exist. That assertion has no reasonable basis, but we must concede that applying the teleological process will not necessarily persuade us that God exists—i.e. the process of analysis of natural things with a view to the genius of their design will not compel us to believe that God exists.

- The arguments from the existence of consciousness and morality are merely applications of the teleological process to the abstract natural things of human consciousness and morality or conscience. They have some persuasive value in their obvious necessity for the ability of human beings with free will to recognise and choose between good and evil, but this is a circuitous argument because it presupposes the existence of God. Accordingly, it has little persuasive value.

- The argument from the existence of miracles has substantial evidentiary weaknesses. However, until science can provide acceptable rational explanations for the objective phenomena reported (if ever), some miracles can have a substantial persuasive value.

- The argument from religious experience is totally subjective and has little objective persuasive value. Also, the evidentiary weaknesses of this argument give what little persuasive value it has to only those who have experienced the event.
- The argument against the existence of God based on the non-belief of many people and the inefficiency of God's supposed plan to obtain universal worship is patent nonsense.
- The anthropic principle is flawed in logic, and its mathematics depends on human science proving that life could generate spontaneously. This has not happened yet and may never happen. Until then, this argument has no persuasive value.
- The argument from the existence of evil is based on the premise that God is omnibenevolent. The atheists' concept of God as omnibenevolent is a misconceived understanding of God's love for us. Theists do not and have not throughout history asserted that the nature of God prevents him from creating or allowing the existence of evil. Accordingly, this argument has no persuasive value.

The question of whether or not God exists is important if it is possible that we have an immortal soul. If we do have an immortal soul and God exists, then the choices of good or evil that we make in this life will determine the future of our immortal souls. Every individual must make the choice of whether or not to believe in the existence of God. It is not the purpose of this work to proselytise the existence of God. That is the function of the clergy. Our purpose has been to raise the most substantial of modern considerations about this issue to assist each individual in thinking clearly and sufficiently about this issue to enable an informed commitment one way or the other.

Many public figures and no doubt some of our personal acquaintances openly admit that they do not believe in the existence of God. When asked why they do not believe, a common answer they give is something like this:

I am not convinced [or persuaded] by the evidence that God does exist.

It is rare for such people to specify the nature and extent of the evidence that they have considered, and it may be that many such persons are not aware of the arguments and issues even to the extent outlined in this work. If we could cross-examine them on the nature and extent of the evidence and arguments that they have considered, we might be able to form a view as to whether or not their belief is informed.

The point is that there are many people who are not persuaded one way or the other. The problem with sitting on the fence or with agnosticism is that it is not a commitment, and God's existence or non-existence is a fact that requires a commitment. No commitment either way is effectively the same as a commitment to the belief that God does not exist. To make this clear, consider this hypothetical situation:

An agnostic has the view that God may or may not exist. He is not persuaded to make a commitment either way. What he decides is that when he is tempted to do evil or break any of the Ten Commandments, he will give in to the temptation only every second time and will resist the temptation the other times to prove his love of God, if he exists.

Obviously, God, if he exists, will not forgive the agnostic for the times that the agnostic has offended him, because the agnostic cannot have true contrition for offending God. So the agnostic may as well make a full commitment to atheism, because he is wasting his time in resisting any temptation in the hope that this will make him acceptable to God.

Pascal's wager, while not an argument or evidence for the existence of God, identifies the prudent commitment, having regard to the potential gains as against the potential losses.

The arguments and evidence we have considered make it clear that there is no argument or evidence one way or the other which can *compel* us to believe in the existence or non-existence of God. It all comes down to each individual's choice as to what to believe. An informed choice can only come from a clear perception of the arguments and evidence which generates persuasion, which in its turn enables commitment, in a situation in which non-commitment either way is not an option.

PART 3

THE DIVINITY OF JESUS CHRIST

3.1 Overview

To come to a view as to the persuasive value of the evidence concerning the divinity of Jesus Christ, we can start by applying the modern parameters relating to the persuasive value of evidence to the available evidence. We will see that the available evidence has numerous shortcomings by these standards. We can then consider factors operative at the time the available evidence was created, to come to a balanced view of the persuasive value of this evidence.

3.1.1 Significance

If a person has chosen not to believe in the existence of God, then there is no purpose in further consideration of religious issues, and the remainder of this work does not contain anything intended to influence such a choice. Accordingly, such a person can obtain no benefit from further reading this work, except perhaps to satisfy some curiosity as to the nature of the issues that concern us.

On the other hand, if a person has chosen to believe in the existence of God, then a number of questions arise which require consideration and further choices. The fundamental question is 'Why did God create us?' We do not know the answer to this question because we cannot know the mind of God, and God has not revealed his reasons to us. Using human reasoning, we can suppose that God created us because he wants something from us. God is completely self-sufficient, so he does not *need* anything from us. The question then becomes 'What is it that God *wants* from us?'

Again, we do not know the answer to this because we cannot know the mind of God. But in relation to this question, God has revealed a generalised code of how he wants us to behave. In addition, it is clear from God's treatment of us humans and the wonderful things that he has created that God loves us. Our human experience is that if we love someone, then what we want in return is for the loved person to love us. Even if the loved person cannot do anything of material benefit for us, we accept as love that person doing voluntarily that which the loved person knows pleases us.

'The sun shines and the rain falls on all of us equally.' From this aphorism, it is clear that God loves all of us equally, and we need not labour this point further.

At this point, our reasoning allows us to conclude that what God wants from us is for us to love him. We do this by obeying his generalised commandments. And because he loves all of us, we should love one another to the extent of treating others as we want to be treated by them. That is also one of God's commandments.

How we should behave in some particular situations is not always clear from the above generalisations. To help us make the best choices, most of us have the human wisdom to seek the counsel of persons more qualified than ourselves in the issues of concern, such as experts, elders, shamans, priests, etc. The source and the development of human wisdom is an issue of only academic theological relevance, because in modern times we have a substantial number of religious denominations which all have detailed rules, regulations, and devotional customs which address in detail the majority of situations we can encounter, including most of those where the best choice is not that obvious. In the most difficult situations, we have clerics to interpret and apply the precepts of their denomination.

Many of these denominations have similar precepts of what is considered by them to be correct moral conduct, but there are differences to the extent that the precepts of some denominations contradict the precepts of other denominations. There are obvious benefits in having access to the wisdom of religious denominations, so the issue that confronts us is 'Which denomination is the right one?'

It is beyond the scope of this work to analyse the various denominations, assess their credibility, and compare them in order to choose the most believable. As Catholics, we have our faith. The main difference between Christianity and all other denominations is our belief in the divinity of Jesus Christ. This difference allows us to reason as follows: if Jesus Christ is divine, then all denominations that deny Christ's divinity are necessarily wrong and vice versa. **There is no compelling argument or proof that God exists; therefore, there cannot be any compelling argument or proof that Christ is divine. If it were otherwise, the arguments for Christ's divinity would be used to prove the existence of God.**

However, if we are persuaded that Christ is divine, then we need not consider any non-Christian denomination in our search for the denomination that truly or most nearly has the tenets which accord with God's will in particular situations. Our reasons for preferring Catholicism over other Christian denominations will be considered in a later section of this work, but in relation to the present issue, it is sufficient to consider whether we can be satisfied to the degree that enables us to choose to believe that Jesus Christ is divine. If we cannot believe this, then we should look elsewhere for the right religion (assuming that we believe that God exists). It follows that if we believe that Christ is divine, then we are Christians, and if we reject Christ's divinity, then we are non-Christians. The reasons some people have for not practising their faith is another issue which will be considered later.

3.1.2 Belief Justification

In order to carefully consider the divinity of Jesus Christ, we must have regard to and apply the reasoning process principles set out earlier in this work, as we did in considering the existence of God. Accordingly, we must examine the relevant arguments and evidence and then assess the persuasive value of the totality of the arguments and evidence examined.

These issues are substantially easier to consider than the arguments for the existence of God, because in relation to Jesus Christ, the premise is that he was a real person who lived about two thousand years ago, who is divine in his existence as the second person of the triune being we believe our God to be. Naturally, the triune nature of God is meaningless to those denominations that conceive God as a single entity, and no polytheistic religion has accepted or claimed Jesus Christ as one of their pantheon of gods. Also, the concept of divinity assumes that divinity exists, and to consider Christ's divinity, we must look at the arguments and evidence to determine whether they meet the criteria of divinity. It is for this reason that the consideration of the existence of God precedes the consideration of the divinity of Christ, so that the divinity of Christ rests on the foundation of the existence of God, although we must concede that our consideration of the existence of God did not focus on the nature of God, in particular his triune nature.

Because Jesus Christ was a real person, we can have regard to natural evidence of what he did and said that is relevant to the issue of his divinity. As with all our considerations, we want to consider the best available evidence. The best possible evidence would be to hear from Jesus Christ himself and to have him demonstrate divinity. But since Jesus Christ ascended into heaven about two thousand years ago, this is not available. We believe that Christ is risen and still alive, and accordingly, he could come back and demonstrate his divinity; however, this has not happened, and it would necessarily have to happen for every generation, due to the uncertainty of historical records. Arguably, if Jesus Christ is divine, he could now appear and provide such evidence, but this would amount to compelling evidence, which would eliminate our free will to choose to believe in him and voluntarily love him. As already considered, it appears to be God's will that we may freely choose to believe in him and to love him or not.

Accordingly, the best available evidence is the records of what he did and said. And since Jesus Christ did not personally write a record of his life, we must look to records created by or based on the accounts of eyewitnesses. This must be our primary source of evidence. In this category, we can consider the four Gospels and some of the letters contained in the New Testament.

A secondary source of evidence is what was said or written about Jesus Christ by people who never met him or witnessed anything done by Jesus Christ. In this category, we can consider some of the letters in the New Testament and the works and writings of St Paul.

A tertiary source of evidence is what can be referred to as expert opinion. These are generally the beliefs of archaeologists and biblical scholars based on their findings and researches. Proper presentation of such opinions requires that the experts disclose their sources and reasoning. We could carefully analyse their reasoning and check the validity of all the sources, but in the final analysis, such opinions are only statements of an individual's belief and not a sound basis for any other person's belief unless that person has verified all disclosed sources and agrees with the expert's reasoning. We may, from time to time, hear things like 'Most biblical scholars agree that the massacre of the 200 innocent infants by Herod the Great, set out in Matthew's Gospel, never happened'. Even if you canvassed all biblical scholars and confirmed that most of them believed as stated, you would still need an explanation of why Matthew would falsely allege that Herod the Great had committed such an atrocity. From this example, it is clear that while the works of experts can provide valuable insights, their opinions and conclusions must be viewed with caution and, accordingly, have limited persuasive value.

A less natural source of evidence is some of the predictions about Jesus Christ in the Old Testament. In science, the prediction of the outcome of some experiment based on some hypothesis lends credibility to the hypothesis if the outcome is as predicted, subject to the elimination of experimental bias producing the predicted outcome. Biblical prophecies about Jesus Christ generally predict some particulars in the life of the Messiah. If these particulars are manifested, then the particular is referred back to the prophecy to support the argument that Jesus Christ was the Messiah. The form of such prophecy is usually cryptic, and accordingly, correlation is usually very tenuous at best. Nevertheless, some such prophecies are remarkable and, subject to the prophecy's clarity and translation issues, may be of some persuasive value.

3.1.3 Biblical Validity Issues

Logically, we could proceed to look at the evidence, and if it is relevant, we could then consider the validity and reliability of the evidence. However, the bulk of the available evidence is contained in the Bible. It seems inefficient to look at what the Bible says, form a view, and then look at issues going to the accuracy of the Bible, and to then review and reconsider the original views formed in the light of these biblical validity issues. It is obviously more appropriate to consider the biblical validity issues first and then to look at what the Bible says relevant to our present concern and then form a view of the persuasiveness of the evidence. Accordingly, the first part of this section will consider the biblical validity issues.

3.1.4 The Nature of the Bible

The Bible is a diverse collection of books written by various (mostly unknown) persons about events and thoughts of people from the beginning of life on earth till about two thousand years ago. The Old Testament is essentially about the Jewish people, and the New Testament is about the establishment of Christianity.

Most of the books of the Old Testament were clearly written as history. Modern 'best practice' principles about writing history require disclosure of sources, identification of principal persons involved, identification and credentials of the author, chronologies, objectivity, contemporaneous event cross references, observations about implications and consequences, and various other elements. The Old Testament books largely failed to meet the modern criteria of a historical record. This is not a criticism of the Old Testament books, because it is clearly unreasonable to expect the older works to contain the benefits of several thousand years of human development in historical recording. But it does show the older works as inadequate histories by modern standards and consequently less acceptable as to their truth and accuracy than a modern historical record.

The New Testament is comprised of the four Gospels, the Acts of the Apostles, various letters, and the book of Revelation. Except for Revelation, they can be regarded as historical documents with the same shortcomings as the Old Testament books, although they were clearly not written primarily as history but rather as a record of Christ's life and teachings for teaching purposes of the current and future generations.

For our purposes of considering the divinity of Jesus Christ, the four Gospels are the most important and useful parts of the Bible. Regardless of the purpose for which they were written, they are evidence. In fact, there is very little evidence concerning the life and teachings of Jesus Christ other than what is in the Bible and certainly nothing outside the Bible evidencing his divinity. The issue for us then is 'How persuasive is the evidence of the Bible?'

3.1.5 Evidentiary Value of Written Words

A definition of the purpose of words may be as follows: 'to transmit the thoughts, concepts or ideas that are in the mind of the speaker to the mind of the listener'. Words can be spoken or written. It is amazing that electrical impulses in one person's brain can be expressed by sound or the written word. But the expression is not always understood in the mind of the listener with the same meaning that it had in the mind of the speaker. The expression can be distorted or varied because of the following:

- speech or hearing impediments
- different understanding of the meaning of words between speaker and recipients
- ambiguity in meaning of the words
- different languages may not contain words with exactly the same meaning
- phrases can carry concealed, implied, or inferred meanings
- allegory and metaphor used may be unfamiliar to the recipient or not intended by the speaker
- the speaker failed to express the intended concept clearly.

Every word belongs to at least one of many different languages. Languages change over time, and some fall into complete disuse for various reasons. The Bible was written in Hebrew, Aramaic, and ancient Greek. These languages are now in disuse, and only scholars know how to use them. That means that their present form is unchanging, although they did change from time to time over the period in which the Bible was written. These languages each had their own idioms, slang, and colloquialisms, and different grammar, poetry, allusions, style, metaphors, similes, etc. There are even different ways of expressing tense in different languages. And while there are many words in most languages that have an exact equivalent word in another language, there are a substantial number of words that do not have an exact equivalent, although there are usually words with similar meaning.

Modern languages have the same attributes as the old languages, but they are still in a state of change or flux. Because of developments in technology, social sciences, mathematics, and other sciences, the modern languages have a vast number of words for which there is no concept in the old languages, and our modern languages have more developed expressions of some concepts that were within the old languages. For example, the modern concept of God is substantially different from the ancient concept of God, due to thinkers like St Thomas Aquinas.

3.1.6 Translation Issues

The language of Old Testament times was Hebrew and Aramaic. As the Jews were invaded and dispersed into other lands, they acquired the language of the invading nations, with their own language contracting, as happened with the Greek invasion about 200 years BC. Accordingly, all of the New Testament was written in Greek. It has been said that every translation is an interpretation.

The fundamental translation issues are as follows:

(i) All current languages are in a constant state of flux, due to usage, experience, and development in the arts and crafts, including social sciences. Words change in meaning, significance, and associations. A dictionary is out of date the day that it is published, so there is a need for constant revision of translations.

(ii) There are two paradigms of translation:
   (a) preserve the meaning of the original words or text, *word for word*
   (b) present the original *meaning* in clear and precise terms of the current form of the recipient language.
   A literal translation can be totally misleading, as a literal translation of words may not carry the intended meaning. The form and structure of the source language should be copied to the recipient language as closely as possible without mangling the recipient language. This makes the translation and interpretation of poetic writing very difficult.

(iii) There are two approaches to translation:
- (a) formal equivalence, i.e. word-for-word translation
- (b) dynamic equivalence, i.e. thought-for-thought translation.

  Modern theory prefers an approach somewhere between the two ends of the continuum of these two approaches.

(iv) No translation, even formal equivalence, can be the same as the source text. Information is lost from the original, added to it, or altered. Words in each language 'have a multiplicity of meanings and shades of nuance that do not permit a one-to-one correspondence into other languages'. For example, idioms must be expressed in a contemporary idiom in the recipient language.

(v) Cultural parameters—cultural differences must be taken into account in translations. For example, it is inappropriate to translate what a shepherd does into languages in which the culture has no knowledge or experience of sheep.

3.1.7 Modern Usage Issues

The Bible texts were written in patriarchal cultures. Feminists want more inclusive language, especially where it is clear that both males and females are being referred to or addressed. There is also pressure on translators to avoid language which denigrates or emphasises handicap, disability, or ethnicity based on colour. Most translators prefer to preserve the integrity of the original text. The gender of God is an issue for some translators. We know that there is no gender of spiritual beings and that there is no pronoun for such a being in English, so we simply use *he*, the male pronoun for God the Father. Perhaps 'God the Progenitor' or 'God the Creator' is more appropriate, but since Christ referred to him as 'My Father' it seems inappropriate to refer to him in any other way. Of course, the English language is constantly changing, so we could invent a pronoun for God; however, this seems inefficient, since the word *God* has only three letters.

3.1.8 Translation Differences

Some translations are intended for different denominations with different theological views. Some are intended for private or scholarly study. Some are intended for public worship, which is usually called a lectionary. In some translations, the translators have used different modern idioms to convey an idiom in the source text. In some translations, the translators have translated the text word for word because the meaning is obscure, while others have given their view as to its meaning in modern terms.

An ideal translation of the Bible should fall somewhere between formal and dynamic equivalence, but as close to formal equivalence as the equivalence of word-for-word translation allows. The translation should take into account recent archaeological findings, such as the Dead Sea Scrolls, and the current scholarship on the issues raised in a particular translation. It should also interpret the use of a particular word in the old language consistently into the new language. It should also include modest politically correct language. It should also avoid modern terms that are also expressed in the old text but that have a different modern meaning, such as the word *holocaust*. It should also have official approval.

3.1.9 Translator Issues

With all occupations, there is a range in the level of skill amongst the practitioners. So also with translators. There are translators with superior skills, merely competent ones, and some whose skills leave something to be desired. We laypeople have no way of knowing which is which. Qualifications and experience may be a guide, but our confidence generally resides in officially approved translations, on the assumption that a panel of experts has carefully considered the translation before approving it. However, even panels of experts can get it wrong.

Translation of original biblical text is an extremely difficult and exacting task. We know from experience with difficult tasks that we undertake that there is often the possibility that with a little more effort, we might have produced a better outcome. So too with translators. They must be very diligent in their thinking and research, because with such important documents, 'near enough is not good enough'. Realistically, we cannot expect exhaustive diligence, because the discovery of sources is incomplete and ongoing. Furthermore, the process of translation is more of an art than a science, depending greatly on the skill of the translator. In this regard, the translator's qualifications and experience are a guide. But only the translator knows whether his or her diligence during the task was satisfactory.

We would normally assume that the integrity of the translator is not in question. This is a safe assumption, but there are integrity-related issues to consider. The primary function of the translator is to express the things said in the source language as nearly as possible in the recipient's language. But as we have seen, there is a variety of uses to which a translation can be applied, and these different uses sometimes require different translation approaches. That is certainly legitimate, but it raises the question of the translator's agenda. Usually, this agenda is apparent from the intended usage of the translation. The caveat here is to not use translations for other purposes than intended.

It has also been recognised that bias can appear in the translation, no matter how hard the translator tries to be objective. This is probably inevitable, particularly in translating, because it is more of an art than a science. This can manifest itself in the way things are expressed, based on assumptions and underlying beliefs. This is not necessarily a bad thing in a Catholic Bible intended to be read by Catholics, but we should be aware of it and take it into account in considerations where it is relevant.

3.1.10 The Importance of Truth

Faith is believing something to be true. Faith is justified and justifiable if the evidence supporting the truth of the facts underlying the faith is reasonably persuasive. Compelling evidence compels belief and, accordingly, is irrelevant in any consideration of the justification of faith.

So what does *true* mean?

Truth generally refers to a fact. The fact is said to be true or not true. If something is said to be true, does this mean that it is also correct? Some argue that it does, but this is probably too broad a meaning to give to the word *true*. *Correct* refers to the logical validity of inferences, implications, and conclusions drawn from evidence, or the correlation between the intended or objective meaning of evidence and the comprehended meaning.

There are various types of facts that we encounter in our considerations.

(i) The first type of fact we call an *axiomatic* fact. Such a fact compels belief in its truth. An example of this is the fact that the sun rises in the east and sets in the west.

(ii) The second kind of fact is a *proven* fact. Such facts are proved to varying degrees or standards of proof.

(iii) The third type of fact is an *alleged* fact. This type of fact refers to facts that, at the time of the *allegation*, were either unproven or unprovable.

(iv) The fourth type of fact is a *contingent* fact. This is one that is assumed to be true for the purposes of an argument but is subject to proof.

3.1.11 Relevant Evidence

The function of truth is to persuade. The key question in this area is, how are facts proved? The answer is by *evidence*. Even axioms have to be proved by evidence.

So what is evidence? Evidence can be of various types, as was outlined earlier in this work. To briefly recap:

(i) The first type of evidence is the *eyewitness accounts*. This is generally called direct evidence.

(ii) The second kind of evidence is *circumstantial evidence*. This is called indirect evidence and corroboration. Indirect evidence can be merely a statement of surrounding circumstances, or it can be a statement of the evidence of an eyewitness as stated to a non-eyewitness, i.e. hearsay evidence.

(iii) The third kind is *documentary evidence*. This is also a type of indirect evidence and includes historical materials.

(iv) The fourth type of evidence is *scientific laws and theories*. These are also circumstantial but may well contain contingent facts, depending on the evidentiary support for the hypothesis or theory. Scientific *laws* are generally regarded as axiomatic.

The next consideration is the identification of what is *not* evidence. There are three broad categories of this type of material.

(i) The first is theological rhetoric. This is not evidence and has no persuasive value. It is inappropriate in a truth-seeking dialogue. It is legitimate as a teaching device. It is also legitimate as the starting point of devotional or explanatory homilies to congregations that already believe the rhetoric. It is inappropriate to prove the rhetoric in such homily or dialogue. Theological rhetoric can be axiomatic. For example, 'God never tells lies'. Such a fact is clearly unprovable but logically self-apparent. Theological rhetoric may be a conclusion drawn from sound argument based on highly persuasive evidence, an axiom, a conclusion based on questionable evidence, a devotional opinion, or a theological opinion unsupported by argument or evidence. Theological rhetoric may be true and correct, or it may be untrue and mistaken. It is inappropriate as dialogue in evangelisation, which is essentially a truth-seeking dialogue.

(ii) The second is arguments and hypotheses.

(iii) The third is inference, assumptions, conclusions, suppositions, deductions, and implications.

3.1.12 The Historical Jesus and the Jesus of Testimony

Many historians have written about the historical Jesus, and there are many different versions. These versions are generally factual, independent of dogma and devotional views of Jesus. The question is 'What does the historical Jesus mean?' Three aspects have been proposed:

(i) The first is purely factual, relating to his earthly human life.

(ii) The second relates to his actions, miracles, and teachings as the core of Christian faith.

(iii) The third relates to the concept of Jesus the divine, as he is and shall be on his return.

All the facts of the life of Jesus are not available to modern man. What is available are the Gospels. There are three Synoptic Gospels, but there are differences between them; arguably, they are biased, being the later basis of the Christian faith. Thus, historians are reluctant to accept the Gospels without independent verification or corroboration. All the versions of Jesus are constructs. The purpose of these constructs is to know him better in order to understand what he did and said. The question is whether the non-religious and religious versions of Jesus can be compatible to the extent of enabling a true understanding of Jesus.

3.1.13 The Gospels as Testimony

Testimony must be distinguished from historiography. Testimony is not acceptable uncritically but may be acceptable even if not capable of independent verification or corroboration. Viewed as history, the Gospels can indicate a true history. Viewed as testimony (with explanations of reasons and meanings), they underlie Catholic theology. The form of the Gospels is essentially eyewitness testimony that has been edited and interpreted, as distinct from accounts that have become traditions and then transmitted anonymously over several generations. Current scholastic argument is that the story of Jesus, what he said and did, passed through a long tradition of the early Christian communities to the writers of the Gospels, suggesting that the Gospels are not that accurate. The book *Jesus and the Eyewitnesses* (Bauckham, 2006) challenges that. It argues that Mark's Gospel was written during the lifetime of the eyewitnesses on which it is based and that the others were also written towards the end of the lifetime of such witnesses, because one would expect them to make such records so that the truth is not lost with their death.

The best historiographical practice is for the history to be written by eyewitnesses, preferably involved in the events, but supplemented by other evidence, as a single author may have bias or may not be aware of all relevant circumstances or may have flawed understanding of the events. The form of the Gospels as narrative and meaning was the historiographical best practice at the time they were written. However, modern historiographical practice appears to be somewhat different. The conclusion is that the Gospels still fall short and leave unanswered many questions, which affect their persuasive value.

3.1.14 The Gospels as Evidence

Here are some of the questions and issues that we need to consider that affect the persuasive value of the Gospels as evidence.

(i) Who wrote the Gospels?
 (a) What was their relationship to Jesus or the apostles?
 (b) Did they know Jesus personally?
(ii) When did they write the Gospels? Was it a unified document or a compilation of notes over a period?
(iii) What were the sources?
 (a) Was it the Q? (The common Christian knowledge about the life and teachings of Jesus is called the Q.)
 (b) Was it hearsay from the apostles?
 (c) Was it hearsay from others?
 (d) Was it documentary evidence, such as letters?
(iv) Why were they written?
 (a) Was it as testimony?
 (b) Was it as a teaching document?
 (c) Was it as theology?
 (d) Was it to preserve the knowledge of the facts?
 (e) Who were they written for?
 (f) How relevant are the standards of literacy at the time?
(v) In what language were they written?
 (a) Who translated them?
 (b) Where were they translated?
 (c) How often was the translation revised, and when?
 (d) Have the words used retained their original meaning?
 (e) Are there concepts in the translations that did not exist then?
(vi) Did any author or translator have any motives for falsification or exaggeration?
 (a) How could they possibly know some of the things written?

    (b) Was there any spin to support or promote some theological view?

    (c) Was it factual or a construct?

(vii) There are inconsistencies amongst the Gospels.

    (a) Was there a comparison of sources?

    (b) Why were these four Gospels approved and not others?

    (c) Are there inconsistencies with non-approved Gospels?

(viii) What is the effect of the interpretation of the meaning of the Gospels?

    (a) What was the role of the clergy in the process of the evangelisation and pastoral care of illiterate people?

    (b) What is the role of the clergy today with more literate communities?

3.1.15 Current Views on Gospel Origins

Bearing in mind all the types of information about the Gospels which are relevant to their authenticity and persuasive value, we can now consider scholarly opinions about the four Gospels with regard to the questions we have in mind. Little is actually known about the Gospels, thus the best information available is scholarly opinion.

The Gospel According to Mark

Reference: *The Oxford Companion to the Bible*
Oxford University Press   Page 492 et seq.

It is not known for certain who Mark was, but in about 130 CE, Papias, the bishop of Hierapolis, reported that this Gospel was written by Mark, 'the interpreter of Peter'.

It is not known when this Gospel was written, but it is believed to have been written somewhere between 65 CE and 75 CE. In Chapter 13 of this Gospel, the destruction of the Temple in Jerusalem, which occurred in 70 CE, is predicted. Most scholars agree that it was almost certainly written after the death of Peter, which occurred in 64 CE. It is probably the first of the three Synoptic Gospels written.

It is not known exactly where this Gospel was written, but it is thought likely by many scholars that it was written in Rome after Peter died there. Presumably, it was written for the gentile Christian community of Rome.

The sources of this Gospel are also unknown, but it appears to be based on oral tradition. However, if Mark was the interpreter of Peter, it is arguably based on the teachings of St Peter. The format of this Gospel is unclear as to whether it was intended as a theological presentation or a historical record.

The Gospel According to Luke

| Reference: | *The Oxford Companion to the Bible* |
| Oxford University Press | Page 469 et seq. |

It is not known who Luke was or what his relationship was to the Catholic Church. There was a sometime companion of St Paul called Luke who is believed to be the author of the Acts of the Apostles, and many scholars accept that this Gospel is Part 1 of the work of this man and that the Acts is Part 2.

It was probably written around 80 CE to 85 CE. This Gospel refers to the destruction of Jerusalem, which occurred in 70 CE, but this reference could also be a reference to the earlier desolation of Jerusalem by Nebuchadnezzar. However, it is clearly written after the Gospel of Mark.

It is not known where this Gospel was written. The Gospel appears to be written for Greek-speaking Gentiles, which is suggested by the language and the absence of strictly Jewish issues and controversies.

The sources of this Gospel appear to be the Gospel of Mark, part of the Q, and some material exclusive to Luke (L) which appears to be based on accounts from 'eyewitnesses' and 'servants of the word'.

The Gospel According to Matthew

Reference: *The Oxford Companion to the Bible*
Oxford University Press   Page 502 et seq.

It is not known who this Matthew was, but it appears that he was a Jewish Christian with rabbinic training and a good command of Greek. It is known that Matthew the Apostle helped establish the Christian church in Antioch in Syria. This Gospel appears to have been written about 85 CE to 90 CE, which would make it too late for Matthew the Apostle, but it is believed to have been written in Antioch in Syria. The destruction of Jerusalem in 70 CE was, by then, history. It appears to have been written for the local church in Antioch, which was comprised of both Jewish and Gentile Christians. There was persecution of Christians there at that time by both other Jews and Gentiles, although the church there was by then largely autonomous and self-sufficient.

The sources of this Gospel are most likely the Gospel of Mark, Q, and some oral traditions unique to Matthew. It was written in a coherent story/history/theology form.

The Gospel According to John

Reference: *The Oxford Companion to the Bible*
Oxford University Press   Page 373 et seq.

Once again, it is not known who this John was. It appears to have been written about 135 CE to 150 CE, and accordingly, it is far too late for John the Apostle.

This Gospel appears to have been written in stages. There are differences in language style, and there are repetition and sequence anomalies which suggest that it may have been a compilation from several authors or over a certain period. The history appears to be that John the Apostle and his disciples moved to Ephesus, where John established the church. It is likely that his followers recorded what he taught, and after his death, they published an edited version.

The sources of this Gospel appear to be the Q, which by then may have included the previous Gospels. The purpose of the work appears to be for the worship and teaching of John's community, which was composed of 'excluded Jews' and Gentiles.

3.1.16 A Balanced View

In any consideration as to the truth of some past matter of fact, we can rely only on the best of available evidence to persuade us that such fact is true. If the evidence does not persuade us that it is true, this does not mean that the fact is untrue. Similarly, if we were considering evidence that something is untrue and we are not persuaded that it is untrue, this does not mean that the fact is true. In other words, we can believe that a fact is either true or untrue, or we are not persuaded either way. But in any case, we can only have regard to the best available evidence.

Our consideration is of the fact of Jesus Christ's divinity. If the ministry and the death of Jesus Christ had occurred within the last few years, we would expect there to be a great deal of relevant evidence, such as eyewitnesses, public records, video recordings, sound recordings, photographs, etc. But Jesus Christ died about two thousand years ago. All the eyewitnesses are long dead. There was no audio or video technology in those days, no Internet, and in the remote areas where Jesus Christ conducted his ministry, there were practically no public records. This does not mean that we have no evidence to consider and should therefore abandon our consideration or conclude that we cannot be persuaded as to the truth of this fact. What we have left to consider is the kind of materials that historians use to propose the view of history they believe most likely to be true. And some historical facts, even from before the time of Christ, have been established to the degree of near certainty.

The main historical materials in our consideration are the four Gospels. There are other accounts of the life of Jesus Christ in the nature of the four Gospels, such as the gnostic gospels, the writings of other authors, or materials from the Dead Sea Scrolls, but they will not be considered here because they are not approved by our clergy and also because they do not add significantly to the evidence of the approved Gospels for our purpose.

The evidentiary shortcomings of the four Gospels have already been identified above. The arguments against the reliability of the Gospels based on these shortcomings are valid and must be conceded as valid. But that does not mean that they have no persuasive value, because we can legitimately consider the effect of these shortcomings on the overall reliability of the Gospels. An encapsulation of the argument against the reliability is as follows:

What weight can you give to a modern translation of the writings about Jesus Christ by an unknown author, written in an unknown place, for an unknown readership, written between 40 and 120 years after the death of Jesus Christ in the then current language, which was not the language spoken by Jesus Christ?

The first of these major shortcomings is the identity of the author. The question is *'How does the identity of the author impact the reliability of the Gospel written by that person?'* Obviously, the name alone is of no assistance. But if the same name appears in other places, we may have some indications of the author's qualifications, experience, associates, religious persuasion, etc. These attributes can enhance or diminish the reliability of the relevant Gospel if, for example, the Gospel purports to be an eyewitness account or contains some expert opinions.

However, the three Synoptic Gospels are clearly not eyewitness accounts, nor do they contain any expert opinions. They are simply an account, in story form, of the life of Jesus Christ. These stories detail where he went, what he said, and what he did that was relevant to his religious mission. Taking into account when they were written, it is clear that the authors were not themselves eyewitnesses but rather were merely putting into writing what they had heard from others who themselves may or may not have been eyewitnesses to the events set out in the Gospels. The Gospel according to John is essentially the same but is historically even further removed from the life of Jesus Christ and contains more commentary on the meaning and significance of Christ's teachings.

Essentially then, the authors of the Gospels were functionally only scribes of what they had heard. It is probably safe to assume that they were Christians and believed what they wrote, but it is also possible that they were paid translators and scribes, having regard to the high level of illiteracy in those days, especially amongst the classes of society that were the first Christians. Thus, if there was any bias, it was the bias of the Christians who told the story rather than any bias on the part of the scribes. There is, of course, little room for bias in setting out factual matters, especially where the need for truth and not some other motivation prevails. But human perception of factual matters is fallible.

Accordingly, if, with respect, the Gospel authors were merely scribes, then their identity neither enhances nor diminishes the reliability of their Gospels.

The second major shortcoming of the Gospels is when they were written. As a matter of common knowledge, it is accepted that the sooner after an event that the details of the event are recorded, the more accurate the record is likely to be. Modern psychologists and memory experts tell us that all memory is reconstruction, and accordingly, a contemporaneous record is the best possible record but is still subject to perception fallibilities.

The four Gospels were written between 40 and 120 years after the death of Jesus Christ, and accordingly, it is accepted that they were not written by eyewitnesses setting out their personal recollections. The problem with having such a long time between the event and the creation of a written record of the event is the reliability of the sources when all actual eyewitnesses are deceased. Essentially, the sources are the facts and teachings, as they have been handed down, possibly over several generations. Some may regard such material as folklore or tradition. This type of information in biblical studies is commonly called the Q by biblical historians and scholars.

In modern times, we tend to regard history based on oral tradition as fairly unreliable because of our knowledge about the unreliability of memory after long periods. However, at the time these Gospels were written, there were very few literate people. Businesses only kept records of the most important matters. Consequently, memory was more relied on in those times and was arguably far more reliable than modern memory. Consequently, it is justified in giving some reliability to the substantial content of the Q, although a detailed semantic analysis of such material may be very tenuous.

Another consideration in support of the reliability of the Synoptic Gospels, having regard to when they were written, is the argument that the first Gospel to be written was that of Mark. If we accept that Mark was the interpreter of St Peter, then it is likely that Mark's Gospel was based almost entirely on the testimony and teachings of St Peter. The case in support of this view is cogently argued by Richard Bauckham in his book *Jesus and the Eyewitnesses*. It is also believed by many scholars that the Gospels of Luke and Matthew are based largely on the Gospel of Mark, with some additional material from the Q and some additional materials exclusive to Luke (called 'L') and some material exclusive to Matthew (called 'M'). And if this Mark travelled with St Peter for some time, then it is likely that he made ongoing personal notes, wrote homilies and letters for St Peter, and kept other records of their travels and meetings. It seems likely that Mark would have used such materials as an aide-memoire in compiling the Gospel that he wrote.

Perhaps we can lament that Jesus Christ himself did not write down his works and teachings, but we do not know whether Jesus Christ was literate. Almost certainly none of the twelve apostles were literate. Nor could they have foreseen the invention of the printing press and the widespread literacy of modern times. No doubt they held the view that the details of the life of Jesus Christ could best then be spread by word of mouth. In the light of these considerations, it seems reasonable to accept the view that the creation of a written record of the life and teachings of Jesus Christ immediately was not necessary in order to spread the faith. It subsequently became necessary for other reasons.

Consequently, although there was no record of the life and teachings of Jesus Christ proximate to the time of his life, there is justification in regarding the accounts that were later created as having some reliability. We should also bear in mind that the Gospels are the most detailed and reliable records now available and cannot simply be dismissed because of shortcomings apparent by modern standards.

The third major shortcoming of the evidentiary value of the Gospels is our ignorance of where they were written. At first glance, the location of the place where the Gospels were committed to writing does not appear to be very important. We know that they were written in Greek and that Greek was then widely spoken throughout what was then the Roman Empire.

But because travel and communications were then very limited, there were colloquialisms, literary styles, and culturally relevant metaphors that were unique to various places. If we knew where they were written, our translators and experts may have more insights into the intended meanings of the Gospels by reference to these unique factors, especially if we know whether the actual scribe was a local disciple speaking with local knowledge and experience or a visiting evangelist speaking from a broader base of knowledge and experience.

This third shortcoming is closely linked to the fourth shortcoming, which is the purpose for which they were written. It has already been suggested that in those days, because of widespread illiteracy, it was not considered necessary or appropriate to spread the faith via the written word, especially since the first evangelists were the apostles, who were eyewitnesses. But even in those days, it was recognised that memories fade and that truths can become distorted by word-of-mouth transmission over several generations, despite the best efforts for fidelity. Obviously, they had writing in those days, and the purpose of writing then was the same as it is today—that is, to preserve the accuracy of recollection and to communicate where word of mouth is not available. Accordingly, we can legitimately form the view that the primary purpose of putting the Gospel stories in writing was to preserve the truth of the facts related in the Gospels.

However, literacy did not significantly increase during this period. In addition, the original texts are believed to be written on scrolls. A later form of written records was the codex, which was in book form. These scrolls were handwritten, and it is probable that only a few copies were made, at least initially. Since only a few members of any congregation were literate, they being most likely the local presbyters or visiting evangelists, clearly the written word was intended to be read by them to the broader illiterate congregation. Thus, the record created in writing was also intended as a means of telling or teaching subsequent generations about the life of

Jesus Christ. For this purpose, some commentary and explanation is legitimate, and we see this in the Gospels, especially the Gospel according to John.

Another inference that can be drawn from the small number of copies initially made is that the written account created was primarily intended to be read by the presbyters of the congregation where it was written, to that congregation. In the foreseeable future, it would aid the memory of existing members of the congregation, and for the distant future, it would preserve the fidelity to truth for future generations of that congregation. No doubt, as Christianity spread over the centuries after the writing of the Gospels, the evangelists came from communities that had the written Gospels, and they would have made more copies to take with them or to send to other congregations.

It is likely that the forgoing analysis is correct, because we can be confident that the Gospels were not written for financial gain, self-aggrandisement, or any other selfish motive, since the scribes are essentially anonymous.

Jesus Christ spoke the Aramaic of 2,000 years ago. The Gospels were written in the Greek of 2,000 years ago. The ancient Greek was translated into Latin, and from that, there have been translations from time to time into other languages. Most of the modern translations are of the Latin translations, and some are of the Greek versions. There is no Aramaic version of the Gospels, so we do not have the actual words used by the Jesus Christ.

The language of the earliest translations was, of course, confined to the syntax, idiom, metaphors, similes, and style current at that time of writing. All these things have changed over time. In addition, the meanings of words within any language have changed, although the meanings of words in any 'dead' languages have not changed since those languages died. It is also known that with many words, there is no word with an identical meaning in another language, although there are words with very similar meaning. One of the most obvious examples of this appears in the Gospel of Luke, Chapter 14, verses 25–26, which read as follows:

Great crowds accompanied him on his way and he turned and spoke to them. 'Anyone who comes to me without hating father, mother, wife, children, brothers, sisters, yes and his own life too, cannot be my disciple.'

Clearly, Jesus Christ would not have meant what we today understand from these modern English words. Christ's message was that we should love one another as he loved us. Also, the Fourth Commandment is that we honour our mother and father, and hating them is a clear breach of this commandment. Presumably, what Christ meant was that we must subordinate our love for our family to our love of God, giving the highest priority to doing his will. Why the translator chose the word *hating* is unclear, but our church has accepted it.

In addition to that, many words have a range of meaning, in that they mean different things to different people in different situations. For example, the word *love* means different things depending on the relationship between the persons who love each other, and what people do to express or implement their love for each other often covers a vast range of conduct. These are some of the difficult issues confronting the translators, which we have already mentioned.

Factual matters, such as where Jesus Christ went and what he did there, can be fairly reliably translated. But as we have seen, the Gospels were also written for teaching purposes. This means that in some instances, factual fidelity has been subordinated for teaching effectiveness. An example of this is the account of the Sermon on the Mount in Matthew Chapters 5–7. Many scholars believe that Jesus Christ never gave any sermon on any mount and that Matthew invented this scenario in order to list in one place all the beatitudes and some other relevant teachings of Jesus

Christ. The fidelity to truth in such a literary device is in the fact that Jesus Christ did pronounce each of these beatitudes and teachings, but at various other times and in other places.

Mindful of all these difficulties impeding reliance on the truth and factual accuracy of the Gospels, we could become apprehensive about the persuasive value of the Gospel. However, we should also take into account what we can describe as 'essence equivalence'. This concept means that the essence of truth and meaning expressed in one language, even in an ancient or dead language, can be accurately expressed in any modern language. For example, the ancient words for 'the poor, the blind, and the lame' mean exactly the same in the ancient languages as they mean to us today in our languages. In addition, the meaning of the parables told by Jesus Christ, such as 'The Good Samaritan' or 'The Prodigal Son', in our modern translations contain the same moral teachings and implications for us as Jesus Christ intended to convey to his listeners. Where Jesus Christ went and what he did in any particular place is not particularly relevant, so long as it is true that he did say and do the essence of the things reported in the Gospels.

For our purposes of considering the divinity of Jesus Christ, the Gospels are the primary and most important source of potentially persuasive evidence. The translation difficulties make it clear that a detailed analysis of any particular word in our modern language is not a reliable basis for a belief that Jesus Christ said or did something as we understand it from our modern word. But it is equally clear that the *essence* and truth of what Jesus Christ said and did is faithfully recorded in the Gospels. Accordingly, we can now consider the essence of the Gospels in seeking evidence of the divinity of Jesus Christ.

3.2 Man or Myth

In the theological debates, it has often been argued that there is no proof that Jesus was a real person. This argument acknowledges that much has been written about a man named Jesus, who was a wondering rabbi in Israel about the time of Caesar Augustus. The argument goes on to assert that there were many wandering rabbis at that time and that the story of Jesus is a composite construct of the works and teachings of a number of such rabbis. The construct was presumably made by Jewish people as part of the evolution of Judaism, which may have been perceived by them as having become so convoluted and cumbersome that it required codification and simplification.

There are several insurmountable flaws in this argument, so much so that today most theologians and even some outspoken atheists give it no credibility. However, it must be considered, because when it is raised, it is done so seriously; we cannot simply dismiss this argument without reason.

One of the major flaws in this argument is that a composite construct of the Jesus of the Gospels would have required some highly sophisticated organisation in a conspiracy involving many persons. Having regard to the level of education of the apostles and disciples, the rarity of literacy and writing and the dispersion of the evangelists with the difficulties of communication those days, the practicability of such a conspiracy is so fraught with difficulty that it becomes unlikely in the extreme. And with so many persons involved, that such a conspiracy could remain unexposed for about two thousand years reduces its probability to insignificance.

Another major flaw in this argument is that there is no evidence to support the composite construct argument. Even if there were numerous wandering rabbis in those days, it is unbelievable that they all had the power to work the miracles recorded in the

Gospels. Accordingly, this argument necessitates the assertion that the miracles recorded in the Gospels are fabrications. So while it is possible that Jesus is a composite construct, there is no evidence of any conspiracy, and the argument that the miracles are fabrications is unsupported. Unsupported speculation has no persuasive value, even if it is remotely possible.

The most substantial and yet misleading aspect of this argument is the underlying assumption that there is no proof that Jesus was a real person. This is misleading because as we have seen that proof is merely the degree of persuasion that can reasonably be drawn from the available evidence. Some people argue that proof can only come from compelling evidence, but that cannot be correct if we have such things as proof on the balance of probabilities, proof to comfortable satisfaction, and proof beyond reasonable doubt.

There is a substantial amount of evidence about the life and teachings of Jesus that has persuaded most people, to one degree or another, that Jesus was a real person. Accordingly, the assertion that there is no proof that Jesus was a real person is simply untrue.

The above assertion that there is evidence that Jesus was a real person should be supported by a brief identification of that evidence. The primary evidence that Jesus was a real person is in the Gospels. It has been argued that the Gospels are not historical documents, and as we have seen, they were not created as histories. They were created to preserve the authenticity of the testimony of the eyewitnesses about the teachings of Jesus and the events in his life. Testimony is what people say they perceived or understood, and it is the fundamental nature of evidence. We can compare this with what is regarded as a historical document, such as the history by Flavius Josephus called *The Antiquities of the Jews,* written in Rome about AD 94. Josephus was a non-Christian Jew who had fled to Rome and lived and worked under Roman patronage. The impartiality of parts of his history may be suspect due to the earlier events in the life of Josephus and also the obvious pressure on him to not write anything to antagonise his patrons. In any event, he also mentions Jesus as a real person who was crucified by Pilate at the request of the then Jewish leaders. There is no evidence that Josephus ever met Jesus, so his statement of this fact is, at best, hearsay evidence.

There is not even the faintest suggestion in any of the Gospels that Jesus was not a real person or that any of the teachings and actions attributed to him really came from some other rabbi. As a record of testimony, the Gospels clearly have evidentiary value, and as such, they have more persuasive value than other evidence, such as histories, which are invariably based on hearsay evidence. Indeed, even the works and letters of St Paul are subject to the hearsay impediment because it is known that he never met Jesus and thus cannot be regarded as an eyewitness giving testimony, even though he is regarded as the greatest evangelist in Catholic Church history.

In addition to the direct testimony of the Gospels, there are the letters of St Peter and parts of the Acts of the Apostles. Also, in the New Testament, there is indirect or hearsay evidence by Christians, such as the letters of St Paul. In addition to that, there are mentions of Jesus Christ in secular historical documents, such as those by Pliny the Younger and Celsus.

All the documents and records created close to the time of Jesus evidence that Jesus was a real person, and the primary evidence of the Gospels has overwhelming persuasive value. The proposition that Jesus was not a real person but a composite construct of various wandering rabbis is not supported by any evidence and therefore may be fairly regarded as a vexatious argument. This topic has been included for the sake of completeness and because this argument is seriously raised from time to time.

3.3 Evidence of the Gospels

3.3.1 Old Testament Biblical Prophecies

To assess the persuasive value of prophecy, we need to be aware of the nature and function of prophecy. We do not need to inform ourselves about this in depth, because the type of prophecy relevant to the issue of the divinity of Jesus is well known, being the fundamental, biblical Old Testament predictions of the prophets. But even in modern times, there are different types of prophecies, and we need to be able to recognise them to ensure that any prophecy that may be evidence of Jesus's divinity is a relevant type of prophecy.

The definition of *prophecy* in *Collins English Dictionary* is as follows:

A message of divine truth revealing God's will; a prediction or guess.

The *Shorter Oxford English Dictionary* (third edition, 1968) defines *prophecy* as follows:

The foretelling of future events; originally as an inspired action; extended to foretelling by any means.

From this, it can be seen that prophecy can be as trivial as a mere pronouncement of someone's opinion as to something that will happen in the future, or it can be as serious as a divine revelation in a vision, dream, or some other type of occult religious experience. And it can be many degrees in between.

We should also be mindful that a prophecy may not be honestly stated. Throughout history, there have been cases of people who prophesied for financial gain. The most obvious example is the fairground fortune teller. Others have deliberately stated as prophecy some matter that furthers their hidden agenda, without any prophetic basis.

Then there are prophecies made by persons who are delusional or under the influence of some substance. They may honestly believe their predictions, and unless we know the circumstances of their prophecy, we cannot easily discount such predictions. Prophecy is real in that there have been prophecies that predicted certain events that subsequently happened exactly as predicted. Accordingly, there have been, and may still be, people who have religious experiences in which they 'see' future events and then document their visions. These are genuine prophecies and, as such, can have some persuasive value. But what they can persuade us about must be considered within the parameters of the probative value of evidence.

An informative illustration of prophecy can be found in the writings of Nostradamus. He predicted in his Century 1, Verse 35, as follows:

The young lion will overcome the older one,
in a field of combat in single fight:
He will pierce his eyes in their golden cage;
two wounds in one, then he dies a cruel death.

Nostradamus was a French apothecary and seer who first published his prophecies in French in 1555. The event to which this prophecy refers occurred in 1559. King Henry II of France participated in a joust against the Comte de Montgomery. Both men had sigils of a lion on their shields, and King Henry was six years older than the Comte. This fits the reference to the younger and older lions, and it suggests the younger one will win. A joust is single combat where two knights charge towards each other on horseback with lances, intending to knock the other off their horse. It is clearly a fight but was often done for sport with non-lethal lances. What happened on this occasion was that the Comte's lance broke on impact with the king's armour, and two shards of the lance went through the visor of the king's helmet. One shard went through the king's eye and the other into his temple. The king was wearing a golden helmet. The king died from these injuries, an undoubtedly painful and cruel death, ten days later.

The facts clearly fit this prophecy. But if we had read this prophecy before the events happened, we would have found it difficult to precisely predict this event and outcome. Prophecy is typically cryptic, with the verification of the prophecy coming from application of the prophecy to past events. We do not know why prophecies are cryptic, but it appears reasonable to suspect that if a prophecy such as this were more precise and the persons involved knew of the prophecy and had some belief that it may occur, then they would exercise their free will to avoid the event, thus rendering the prophecy as false. In other words, prophecy is necessarily cryptic if it is to be fulfilled. No doubt King Henry would not have participated in this joust if he had known of the prophecy and believed that it could apply to his joust with the Comte.

One of the interesting things about this prophecy is that it is said to be historical fact that Queen Catherine de' Medici, the wife of King Henry II, summoned Nostradamus to Paris in 1556 to discuss this particular prophecy. By that time, Nostradamus had a reputation as a successful healer and as a proven seer. If this fact is true, then clearly Queen Catherine associated the reference to the lion in the prophecy with King Henry's sigil and took the prophecy seriously. We do not know what Nostradamus told Queen Catherine or whether King Henry knew of the prophecy. Even if he knew of it, he clearly did not regard it as applying to his joust with the Comte.

Another interesting point that arises from this prophecy is that some scholars have argued that this particular quatrain did not appear in the first edition of the published prophecies in 1555 but was first published in 1614, some fifty-five years after the event and about forty-eight years after the death of Nostradamus in 1566. If this is correct, then clearly there must be some doubt about the validity of this quatrain as a prophecy. It is possible that Nostradamus made this prophecy only verbally and that Queen Catherine was aware of this prophecy, because Nostradamus had some contact with the royal family prior to 1556. It is also possible that someone who stood to gain financially from the sale of Nostradamus's prophecies contrived this quatrain in order to lend credibility to the prophecies, thereby increasing sales. The point we can note from this is that the credibility of a prophecy depends on clear evidence that the prophecy was made before the prophesied event occurred. That does not mean that the prophecy was not verbally made before the prophesied event occurred, but an undocumented prophecy clearly has less persuasive value than a documented one.

It is a fact that throughout history many events have been prophesied, usually in cryptic terms. The validity of these prophecies is invariably established by applying the prophecy to some event that has subsequently happened. If the interpretation of the prophecy is tenable and a good fit to the events prophesied, then the prophecy is regarded as valid. Of course, not every interpretation of a prophecy is tenable, and in many cases, the event selected as fulfilment of the prophecy is not a good fit to the prophecy. But that does not lead to the conclusion that the prophecy is invalid, because it can still be argued that the prophecy must relate to some other event which may not have happened yet. Only a prophecy that clearly specifies some event, and a time and place at which the event is to occur, can be regarded as invalid if the facts of the event do not match the prophecy. Obviously invalid prophecies have no value, and we rarely hear about them. But it is reasonable to suspect that there have been many invalid prophecies over the years.

We do not know how a valid prophecy can be made. Thus, we classify prophecy as occult phenomena. The word *occult* simply means 'unknown'. But we do know that valid prophecies have been made. The key question in our consideration is 'What can a valid prophecy evidence?' Once an event has occurred, we have normal evidence of its occurrence, and any related prophecy does not add further proof. Before the prophesied event occurs, the cryptic terms of the prophecy make it uncertain which event is being prophesied, so it cannot be evidence that some particular event will occur. If the terms of the prophecy are not cryptic, then it is possible, and even likely for undesirable events, that human action to avoid the prophecy will be taken. Accordingly, prophecy is not evidence that some event has occurred or will occur.

However, it has been argued that prophecy can assist in identifying who will be involved in some prophesied event. In the case of the prophecy of Nostradamus considered above, the reference to the young and old lions may have alerted Queen Catherine that this may be a reference to her husband, because she would have been aware of the lion sigil on his shield, and she would also have been aware of the cryptic nature of prophecy. She was certainly astute if this was the case; however, clearly, she did not do anything to change the event, so it is more likely that she did not have any clear perception of the event prophesied. Another example of the identification of the subject of a prophecy is the reference to the number 666 as the number of the Beast in the book of Revelation in the Bible. Over the years, many men have been identified as the Beast, but none of these interpretations have been persuasive, even with the benefit of hindsight. So the present position is that the Beast has not yet appeared on earth. Accordingly, using prophecy to identify the persons involved is tenuous at best and therefore of little persuasive and evidentiary value.

So what is the point or function of prophecy? The prophecies of Nostradamus largely concerned predictions of undesirable or negative events. The same can be said of many biblical prophecies. The Old Testament of the Bible also contains prophecies of the coming of a messiah, who would restore the liberty and the pre-eminence of the Jewish people. This is not a disaster but the giving to the Jewish people of hope. There are prophecies which identify this messiah, and since we believe that Jesus was the prophesied messiah, we can consider whether these prophecies support the argument that Jesus is divine.

At this point, we can consider some of these prophecies as evidence of Christ's divinity. The texts quoted are from the New Jerusalem Bible on the Internet.

3.3.1.1 The Virgin Birth of Jesus

The Lord will give you a sign in any case: It is this: the young woman is with child and will give birth to a son whom she will call Immanuel.

Isaiah 7:14

The context of this prophecy is that Yahweh (God) was speaking to Ahaz about a war being waged, and he made a prediction of the outcome. He then said that there would be a sign that this prediction was happening and said the above prophecy. The term *young woman* is the translation of the Hebrew word *almah*. Those who wrote Matthew's Gospel in Greek translated this word as *virgin*, presumably because Matthew had interpreted the word to mean *virgin*. The context of Matthew's Gospel, where he quotes this prophecy, is where an angel appeared to Joseph in a dream and told him to take Mary as his wife and to name her son Jesus. How Matthew knew of Joseph's dream is not known. The fact that Jesus was named Jesus and not Immanuel contradicts the application of this prophecy to the birth of Jesus. It is not clear from the context of Isaiah's prophecy that he was referring to the Messiah. The interpretation that Immanuel means 'God is with us' is understood in modern terms more in the nature of God being on our side (in the war) than 'God is amongst us', although some other translations of the Bible do translate the name Immanuel as 'God is amongst us'.

These observations raise some doubt about applying this prophecy to the birth of Jesus, and clearly, the translation and interpretation issues may well be responsible for raising these doubts, along with the cryptic nature of the prophecy. This does not in any way diminish the other evidence of the virgin birth of Jesus, but it does indicate that this prophecy has little persuasive value towards proof of the divinity of Jesus.

3.3.1.2 The Birth of Jesus

Micah 5:1

But you (Bethlehem) Ephrathah, the least of the clans of Judah, from you will come for me a future ruler of Israel whose origins go back to the distant past, to the days of old.

We know Jesus was born in Bethlehem, and to that extent, this prophecy fits the facts. However, Jesus never became 'ruler of Israel' in the normal meaning of these words. The context of Micah goes on to mention things about this ruler clearly unrelated to Jesus. This application of this prophecy is tenuous at best and has no persuasive value to prove the divinity of Jesus.

Daniel 9:24

Seventy weeks are decreed for your people and your holy city, for putting an end to transgression, for placing the seal on sin, for expiating crime, for introducing everlasting uprightness for setting the seal on vision and on prophecy, for anointing the holy of holies.

Know this, then, and understand: From the time there went out this message: 'Return and rebuild Jerusalem' to the coming of an Anointed Prince, seven weeks and sixty-two weeks, with squares and ramparts restored and rebuilt, but in a time of trouble.

And after the sixty-two weeks an Anointed One put to death without his . . . city and sanctuary ruined by a prince who is to come. The end of that prince will be catastrophe and, until the end, there will be war and all the devastation decreed.

This prophecy has been interpreted by biblical scholars to mean that the Messiah would die about 480 years after the edict ordering the reconstruction of Jerusalem. This edict was made by Artaxerxes, the king of Persia in about 454 BC, so the prophecy fits the facts. The full context of this prophecy is cryptic and reads much like a summary of the apocalypse in the book of Revelation. The seventy weeks is seventy weeks of years, which is 490 years, with one week being seven years. The prophecy refers to the death of the Messiah and does not refer to his age at the time of his death. We know that Jesus was about thirty-three when he died. This prophecy is not a good fit to the life of Jesus other than to approximate the time of his birth and has no support for a belief in the divinity of Jesus.

Hosea 11:1–7

When Israel was a child, I loved him, and I called my son out of Egypt.

But the more I called, the further they went away from me; they offered sacrifice to Baal and burnt incense to idols.

I myself taught Ephraim to walk, I myself took them by the arm, but they did not know that I was the one caring for them,

that I was leading them with human ties, with leading-strings of love, that, with them, I was like someone lifting an infant to his cheek, and that I bent down to feed him.

He will not have to go back to Egypt, Assyria will be his king instead! Since he has refused to come back to me,

the sword will rage through his cities, destroying the bars of his gates, devouring them because of their plots.

My people are bent on disregarding me; if they are summoned to come up, not one of them makes a move.

This prophecy, on its face, appears to refer to the exodus from Egypt. To suggest that this prophecy refers to Joseph returning from Egypt with Mary and Jesus seems to be extremely tenuous. It was clearly Joseph who made the decision to move to Nazareth and not Jesus, so the argument that God called his son out of Egypt has little support, because if anyone was called out of Egypt, it was Joseph and not Jesus. Accordingly, this prophecy has little persuasive value.

Matthew 2:23

There he settled in a town called Nazareth. In this way the words spoken through the prophets were to be fulfilled: He will be called a Nazarene.

We know from the Gospels that Jesus grew up in Nazareth. There are a few references in the Gospels to Jesus as a Nazarene, but not many. He was better known as a wandering rabbi, and our concern is with his divinity, not with the town where he grew up. The prophecy that Matthew refers to has not been identified, even by biblical scholars, so this remark by Matthew cannot be verified as a prophecy documented before Jesus became a Nazarene. It has no persuasive value.

Daniel 7:13–14

I was gazing into the visions of the night, when I saw, coming on the clouds of heaven, as it were a son of man. He came to the One most venerable and was led into his presence.

On him was conferred rule, honor and kingship, and all peoples, nations and languages became his servants. His rule is an everlasting rule which will never pass away, and his kingship will never come to an end.

This is not specifically a prophecy about Jesus, but it identifies the divinity of this Son of Man. The relevance is that Jesus spoke of himself as the Son of Man on a number of occasions, and it is argued that he was referring to the same person identified by Daniel in his vision. This passage has no relevant value as prophecy, but it is evidence that Jesus was asserting his divine nature when he referred to himself as the Son of Man, although the reference was probably too obscure and cryptic to be understood by his listeners at the time.

Isaiah 35: 4–6

God himself will come and save you. Then the eyes of the blind shall be opened, and the ears of the deaf unstopped; then shall the lame man leap like a hart, and the tongue of the dumb sing for joy.

This prophecy is cited in an article entitled 'I Believe in Jesus Christ the Son of God', written by a monk of St Joseph de Clairval Abbey, with the imprimatur of Michel Coloni, Bishop of Dijon, 19 March 2000, and published on the Internet in the Catholic Encyclopedia. The prophecy appears to refer to Jesus by reference to the miracles that he performed, and it leaves no doubt as to his divinity by saying that it is God himself who will come. Which translation of the Bible this comes from is not specified in the article. Compare this with the same passage from Isaiah in the New Jerusalem Bible (standard edition) of 1995, which reads as follows:

And say to the faint-hearted, 'Be strong! Do not be afraid. Here is your God, vengeance is coming, divine retribution; he is coming to save you.'

Then the eyes of the blind will be opened, the ears of the deaf unsealed, then the lame will leap like a deer and the tongue of the dumb sing for joy.

Clearly, Jesus did not come to bring vengeance and divine retribution. In this version of the prophecy of Isaiah, the prophecy has nothing to do with Jesus and must refer to some other event.

Why the text specifying vengeance and retribution was omitted from the version used by the monk is unknown. The reference to vengeance and retribution also appears in the Douay–Rheims version of the Bible.

The wisdom that we can take from this inconsistency is that even intelligent men of good faith can see support for an argument where, in truth, there may not be any. We have already brought to mind the difficulties surrounding translation and interpretation of biblical texts. Add to that the necessarily cryptic nature of prophecy, and we are left with little support for the argument that this prophecy supports the view that Jesus is divine. It is certainly not evidence against this view, but it has little persuasive value in support of this view.

3.3.1.3 Conclusion

The word *messiah* is Hebrew and means 'anointed one'. In the Old Testament times, there were many anointings, as part of the process of installation of some person to a position of prominence. However, the sense in which it is used in the Old Testament is as the 'anointed one of God'. There are many prophecies in the Old Testament that predict the coming of the anointed one of God. Many anticipate him as a king and a conqueror or a great military leader. Jesus does not fit these conceptions, and again, it is the cryptic nature of prophecy that probably led the Jewish religious leaders of the time to expect something more than a wandering rabbi. *Christ* is the Greek translation of the word *messiah*.

Judaism was and remains a monotheistic religion. The concept of a triune God was completely unknown before Christ, being Catholic theology developed in the light of Jesus's teachings. It is therefore not surprising that the anointed one of God was not described in the Old Testament prophecy as being divine and part of God. The above brief analysis of some of these prophecies makes it apparent that the divinity of Jesus is not a part of any such foretelling. Prophecy does have a legitimate function, but it is clear that it does not provide any evidence of the divinity of Jesus, even though many Old Testament prophecies support the argument that Jesus was the Messiah.

3.3.2 The Miracles of Jesus

Definition: a miracle is an event which cannot occur naturally and which cannot have been caused to occur by any known human capability.

The obvious question that arises from this definition is, who or what can cause a miraculous event to occur? The answer is that by definition, nothing that exists in nature can break the laws of nature; therefore, the cause of a miraculous event must be supernatural.

The laws of nature have been known to humankind since human life began on the planet. Initially, our knowledge of the laws of nature was essentially based on recurring natural phenomena and the limitations of human abilities. Over the centuries, our knowledge expanded into the modern era, where we have the scientific method and detailed descriptions and names for various laws of nature. Also, we humans have extended our intellectual capacity through better diet and information storage techniques.

Some people argue that there are no limits to human or intelligent life's capacity to achieve with the aid of technology and that nothing is impossible. That is not an issue that can ever be decided one way or another, and it is therefore not helpful. We have today's technology and human capacities. Science fiction writers propose further technological advancements. In the past, science fiction writers proposed technologies that are now real. It does not follow that all speculations of future technology will become real or that they are even possible. Accordingly, any realistic consideration of an alleged miraculous event must be considered within the confines of current technology and current human capacities.

Reports of miraculous events 2,000 years ago were legitimately regarded as miracles at that time. Modern technology may be able to achieve the same effect as the older miracles, but we must also take into account the manner and speed with which the old miracle is alleged to have occurred before we can regard it as a genuine miracle. Thus, if modern science cannot achieve the same effect in the same way as the old miracle, then the old miracle remains validly regarded as a miracle.

The evidence that Jesus caused some miracles is almost exclusively contained in the Gospels. As we have seen, the Gospels are a record of the testimony of eyewitnesses to the words and teachings of Jesus but created at such a substantial time after the occurrence of the events recorded. In addition, they were written in Greek, which was not the language spoken by Jesus. **The original records have been lost, and the oldest extant copies of these originals date from about AD 400.** As we have also seen, there are translation difficulties, and the versions we read have gone through several translations and revisions.

Over the centuries, some of the world's greatest minds have developed the parameters of proof, largely for the improvement of various legal systems. These we call the Rules of Evidence. The evidence required to prove miracles are necessarily required to be extremely persuasive, because the starting point in any allegation that a miracle occurred is that we are already persuaded beyond reasonable doubt that what is alleged to have occurred is not naturally possible.

As evidence, the Gospels fall far short of proving, by modern standards, that Jesus performed any miracles, and the Gospels are the only evidence of the occurrence of the miracles performed by Jesus. There are other gnostic gospels which also evidence them, but they have no greater probative value than the authorised Gospels.

Some would argue that this situation renders the best available evidence of the miracles of Jesus as totally unsatisfactory, and accordingly, any consideration of this issue is futile. However, it is also arguable that the Gospels are the best available evidence of eyewitness testimony of persons who were persuaded that what they were reporting was not naturally possible. They persisted in this reporting, apparently to present the truth as they believed it to be and not for any reward or hidden agenda, in spite of the ridicule and the disbelief that such reports inevitably attract. On this basis, mindful of the evidentiary shortcomings of the Gospels, it is worthwhile considering the reports of the miracles of Jesus contained in the Gospels.

Before proceeding to consider some of the miracles in detail, there is another point to note. This point is the question of what a miracle can prove. From the above definition, it follows that whoever can cause a miracle to occur must have supernatural powers. But supernatural does not mean divine. It could be argued that angels and demons (if they exist) have supernatural powers, but they are, by definition, not divine. Also, there are reports in the Gospels and other parts of the New Testament of the apostles working miracles. Clearly, they were not divine but were merely exercising supernatural powers given to them by God. So even if we concluded that Jesus did cause some miracles to occur, they do not, in themselves, prove his divinity. But they do have some persuasive value towards this conclusion and are not the only evidence but rather an aspect in a larger case containing other evidence.

The miracles attributed to Jesus are substantially diverse in nature and display an unprecedented range of supernatural power. Let us then consider some of the different types of miracles performed by Jesus.

3.3.2.1 Water into Wine

John 2:1–11

On the third day there was a wedding at Cana in Galilee. The mother of Jesus was there, and Jesus and his disciples had also been invited. And they ran out of wine, since the wine provided for the feast had all been used, and the mother of Jesus said to him, 'They have no wine.' Jesus said, 'Woman, what do you want from me? My hour has not come yet.' His mother said to the servants, 'Do whatever he tells you.' There were six stone water jars standing there, meant for the ablutions that are customary among the Jews: each could hold twenty or thirty gallons. Jesus said to the servants, 'Fill the jars with water,' and they filled them to the brim. Then he said to them, 'Draw some out now and take it to the president of the feast.' They did this; the president tasted the water, and it had turned into wine. Having no idea where it came from—though the servants who had drawn the water knew—the president of the feast called the bridegroom and said, 'Everyone serves good wine first and the worse wine when the guests are well wined; but you have kept the best wine till now.' This was the first of Jesus' signs: it was at Cana in Galilee. He revealed his glory, and his disciples believed in him.

Miraculous Aspects

Six stone jars holding about twenty or thirty gallons each is the equivalent of over one thousand 750-millilitre bottles. Turning water into wine is essentially the transmutation of matter, something that alchemists have been trying, unsuccessfully, to do for thousands of years. The quantity of wine involved shows that this was no small-scale experiment in a laboratory. The quality of the wine produced is consistent with divine benevolence, since it would be questionable if the wine produced were cheap rubbish.

This was the first miracle performed by Jesus, and it signalled the start of his public ministry. However, clearly his public ministry had commenced before this time, because he already had disciples at this function. Presumably, these disciples informed John of this miracle, unless John himself was one of the disciples. It is presented as an account of an event that actually occurred, which persuaded his disciples to believe in him.

Probative Issues

Can this miracle be attributed to Jesus? According to this account, Jesus did nothing other than to tell these servants to fill the jars with water and then to take some of the water to the chief steward. He said no prayer and made no invocation or gesture that activated the transmutation of the water into wine. Nor is it stated when this transmutation occurred, although by the time the chief steward tasted the sample, that sample had turned to wine. Nor do we know where the water came from and if it was really water that was poured into the jars.

Rationale

Jesus was clearly reluctant to perform this miracle, but he did so because he understood that his mother wished him to do so. She obviously already knew that Jesus had the ability to do such things. If the water had really been wine before being poured into the jars, the chief steward would have known about it, and there would have been no point in Jesus ordering these servants to fill the jars with water. The entire context of the life of Jesus is not one of wizardry and magic but rather the real purpose of life and human relationship with the divine. This type of miracle is not magic and does not require invocations or casting spells. Divine power can accomplish such things with a mere thought, since there cannot logically be any higher power to invoke. It is worth noting that other persons who have apparently performed miracles invariably invoke the higher power. The fact that Jesus made no such invocation suggests that he did not need to do so, which is consistent with him being the higher power, i.e. divine.

3.3.2.2 Healings: The Leper

Matthew 8:2–4

Suddenly a man with a virulent skin-disease came up and bowed low in front of him, saying, 'Lord, if you are willing, you can cleanse me.' Jesus stretched out his hand and touched him saying, 'I am willing. Be cleansed.' And his skin-disease was cleansed at once. Then Jesus said to him, 'Mind you tell no one, but go and show yourself to the priest and make the offering prescribed by Moses, as evidence to them.'

Similar accounts appear in Mark 1:40–45 and Luke 5:12–15.

<u>Miraculous Aspects</u>

Jesus did not give this man any salve or ointment to put on his skin. He simply commanded him to be cleansed, and the skin disease disappeared immediately. Even modern medicine cannot duplicate the cure of a skin disease in such a way. It is not possible and, as reported, is clearly a miracle.

<u>Probative Issues</u>

Was this disease leprosy? It is not identified as such in any of the Gospel accounts. If it was not leprosy, then what was it? We know that leprosy was common in those days and that the Jewish priests would exile lepers from the community because it was highly contagious. We do not know what training or qualifications such priests had to enable them to diagnose leprosy. The fact that Jesus told this man to show himself to the priest suggests that it was leprosy that he had cured, especially when linked to the prescriptions of Moses. But we cannot be sure.

<u>Rationale</u>

It does not really matter whether it was leprosy or not. We know it was a virulent skin disease and that any such disease cannot be cured instantly. Jesus simply commanded the man to be cured and did not call on any higher power to effect the cure. Jesus touched the man, presumably to show that he was not in any fear of the man's disease. In this instance, it was appropriate for Jesus to articulate the command to cure, because it was in reply to the man's request to be cured. This cure could not have been psychosomatic, because there is no medical evidence that a virulent skin disease can be cured by a psychosomatic process, although even today the powers of the mind are not fully known.

3.3.2.3 Healings: The Withered Hand

Matthew 12:10–14

Now a man was there with a withered hand. They asked him, 'Is it permitted to cure somebody on the Sabbath day?' hoping for something to charge him with. But he said to them, 'If any one of you here had only one sheep and it fell down a hole on the Sabbath day, would he not get hold of it and lift it out? Now a man is far more important than a sheep, so it follows that it is permitted on the Sabbath day to do good.' Then he said to the man, 'Stretch out your hand.' He stretched it out and his hand was restored, as sound as the other one. At this the Pharisees went out and began to plot against him, discussing how to destroy him.

Similar accounts of this event appear in Mark 3:1–6 and Luke 6:6–11.

<u>Miraculous Aspects</u>

We do not know what caused this man to have a withered hand, but a withered hand is generally shrivelled up to be smaller than the non-withered hand and usually flexed into a clawlike position. The instant restoration of such a hand to normal size and position is clearly impossible to modern medicine, and therefore, this event may be considered a miracle.

Probative Issues

We do not know the extent to which this man's hand was withered. Possibly, this miracle was only a restoration of flexion of the muscles of the hand, which could have been effected psychosomatically. This man did not ask to be cured, but we know why Jesus did it.

Rationale

It is virtually axiomatic that the man wanted to be cured; otherwise, he would have asked Jesus to not restore him to his former condition. And obviously, the cure was spectacular enough to be recorded in the three synoptic Gospels, although there is clearly a teaching aspect to this incident. There is no record that Jesus touched this man or uttered any words of invocation or called on some higher power.

3.3.2.4 Healings: Blindness

Luke 18:35–43, Mark 10:46–52, and Matthew 20:29–34.

Matthew 20:29–34

As they left Jericho a large crowd followed him. And now there were two blind men sitting at the side of the road. When they heard that it was Jesus who was passing by, they shouted, 'Lord! Have pity on us, son of David.' And the crowd scolded them and told them to keep quiet, but they only shouted the louder, 'Lord! Have pity on us, son of David.' Jesus stopped, called them over and said, 'What do you want me to do for you?' They said to him, 'Lord, let us have our sight back.' Jesus felt pity for them and touched their eyes, and at once their sight returned and they followed him.

Miraculous Aspects

These were men who were previously able to see but had lost their sight and were now blind beggars. Restoring the sight of someone legally blind is possible in modern medicine but usually involves surgical intervention of some sort. There have been cases of spontaneous psychosomatic restorations of vision. We do not know the nature and extent of these men's blindness, but we do know that the cure was instantaneous. It is reported as a miracle, but without further information, we cannot say that the cure was miraculous. However, the cure was clearly consequent to intervention by Jesus.

Probative Issues

These men wanted to be cured. Perhaps having someone who had a reputation as a healer tell them that they were cured stimulated a psychosomatic process to restore their vision, but it is extraordinary that this could happen to two men at the same time. Matthews says that there were two blind men there and that Jesus cured them both. He also reports that Jesus touched them, but not that he said anything to them. Both Mark and Luke report that there was only one man, identified by Mark as Bartimaeus, and that Jesus spoke to him, but they did not say that he touched him.

Rationale

The differences between the Gospels are minor. The essence is that a blind man's sight was restored. Again, Jesus did not call on any higher power but simply commanded the restoration of vision or touched the eyes in response to the request to be cured. The cure may have involved the psychosomatic powers of the human mind, but at the very least, this process was precipitated by Jesus and, accordingly, can be regarded as a miracle attributable to him.

3.3.2.5 Demons Cast Out: The Capernaum Synagogue

Mark 1:21–28

They went as far as Capernaum, and at once on the Sabbath he went into the synagogue and began to teach. And his teaching made a deep impression on them because, unlike the scribes, he taught them with authority. And at once in their synagogue there was a man with an unclean spirit, and he shouted, 'What do you want with us, Jesus of Nazareth? Have you come to destroy us? I know who you are: the Holy One of God.' But Jesus rebuked it saying, 'Be quiet! Come out of him!' And the unclean spirit threw the man into convulsions and with a loud cry went out of him.

A similar account of this event appears in Luke 4:31–37.

Miraculous Aspects

Casting out demons is not a natural human capability. The demon spoke to Jesus and acknowledged that he was the Christ. Jesus simply commanded the demon to come out of the man, and the demon obeyed. This suggests that Jesus had the authority to do this.

Probative Issues

To believe that this was a miracle, we must first believe that such beings as demons exist and, secondly, that what appears to be demonic possession is actually that and not merely some form of mental illness in the persons appearing to be possessed.

Demons are, by definition, beings of the spiritual realm, and as such, they have no physical substance. We cannot see or hear them or perceive any physical evidence of their presence. However, well-documented cases of demonic possession report impossible occurrences, such as levitation and the spontaneous movement of objects. As Catholics, we believe that demons are real, and our church has specialist priests who still perform exorcisms, even in modern times. Since demons are beings of the spiritual realm, there can be no compelling evidence that they do not exist. Accordingly, it is open to us to believe that they do exist.

Modern medicine has identified a number of mental illnesses which have symptoms or behaviour events which appear to be similar to the behaviour of persons possessed by demons. But modern demonic possession cannot be cured with drugs or psychotherapy, and in most cases, it cannot even be diagnosed as a specific mental disorder. However, even in cases that are clearly not demonic possession, the persons suffering from the mental disorder often display strange abilities, such as speaking different languages or claiming to be possessed or hearing voices in their heads. Medical science is not yet sufficiently advanced to explain all these phenomena; however, it is clear that these are not a modern development in humans but are part of our basic human nature.

Medical science did not include mental disorders at the time of Jesus, so the problem with miracles reporting the expulsion of demons is that there is no evidence or even consideration of whether or not the person involved was actually possessed or merely had some mental disorder. And once again, psychosomatic processes could explain the apparent expulsion of demons.

Rationale

Jesus performed a number of similar expulsions of demons. A blind and dumb demoniac healed is recorded at Matthew 12:22–24 and Luke 11:14. A dumb demoniac healed is recorded at Matthew 9:32–34. The lunatic demoniac boy is recorded at Matthew 17:14–21, Mark 9:14–29, and Luke 9:37–43.

It is not unreasonable for us to believe in demons, especially since our church clearly believes in them. In these cases of demonic possession, we do not know whether they were real demonic possession or some form of mental disorder. The fact that Jesus commanded the demons to leave is not conclusive, because there was no knowledge of mental disorders in those days, so to activate the psychosomatic process in our healing, it would have been necessary to appear to be casting out demons. It is therefore open to us to believe that Jesus did actually cast out demons in that instance or that he performed miracles of healing which were well beyond the knowledge of medical science at that time. The doubt as to which it really was diminishes the persuasive value of the evidence, but it is still leaves substantial support for these events as miracles.

3.3.2.6 Demons Cast Out: The Pig Demoniacs

Mark: 5:1–20

They reached the territory of the Gerasenes on the other side of the lake, and when he disembarked, a man with an unclean spirit at once came out from the tombs towards him. The man lived in the tombs and no one could secure him any more, even with a chain, because he had often been secured with fetters and chains but had snapped the chains and broken the fetters, and no one had the strength to control him. All night and all day, among the tombs and in the mountains, he would howl and gash himself with stones. Catching sight of Jesus from a distance, he ran up and fell at his feet and shouted at the top of his voice, 'What do you want with me, Jesus, son of the Most High God? In God's name do not torture me!' For Jesus had been saying to him, 'Come out of the man, unclean spirit.' Then he asked, 'What is your name?' He answered, 'My name is Legion, for there are many of us.' And he begged him earnestly not to send them out of the district. Now on the mountainside there was a great herd of pigs feeding, and the unclean spirits begged him, 'Send us to the pigs, let us go into them.' So, he gave them leave. With that, the unclean spirits came out and went into the pigs, and the herd of about two thousand pigs charged down the cliff into the lake, and there they were drowned. The men looking after them ran off and told their story in the city and in the country round about; and the people came to see what had really happened. They came to Jesus and saw the demoniac sitting there—the man who had had the legion in him—properly dressed and in his full senses, and they were afraid. And those who had witnessed it reported what had happened to the demoniac and what had become of the pigs. Then they began to implore Jesus to leave their neighborhood. As he was getting into the boat, the man who had been possessed begged to be allowed to stay with him. Jesus would not let him but said to him, 'Go home to your people and tell them all that the Lord in his mercy has done for you.' So the man went off and proceeded to proclaim in the Decapolis all that Jesus had done for him. And everyone was amazed.

Miraculous Aspects

This is clearly a case of real demonic possession, because of the actions of the pigs. In the conversation with the demon, the demon was clearly using the voice of the person possessed, and there is nothing supernatural about that. However, both accounts reported that Jesus was identified as the Son of God by the demon, which is consistent with demons being able to identify God, although Jesus himself had not claimed this title, preferring to refer to himself as the Son of Man.

Probative Issues

The facts of this event are clearly and concisely reported. What we do not know is why the pigs drowned themselves. And what happened to the demons when the pigs died? Did the demons cause the pigs to commit suicide so that on death, the demons would be free to occupy someone else? And why did the people of that locality ask Jesus to leave?

Rationale

The unanswered questions leave us wondering what really went on. If we do not believe in demons, then this incident makes no sense. If we accept that it was a real casting-out of demons, then it becomes clear to us that there is much about demons and what

God allows demons to do that is unknown to us. In any event, this is not a case of psychosomatic healing. It is a serious report in the Gospels, and as such, it is evidence that demons are real.

3.3.2.7 Feeding the Multitudes: The 5,000

Matthew 14:13–21

When Jesus received this news he withdrew by boat to a lonely place where they could be by themselves. But the crowds heard of this and, leaving the towns, went after him on foot. So, as he stepped ashore, he saw a large crowd; and he took pity on them and healed their sick. When evening came, the disciples went to him and said, 'This is a lonely place, and time has slipped by; so send the people away, and they can go to the villages to buy themselves some food.' Jesus replied, 'There is no need for them to go: give them something to eat yourselves.' But they answered, 'All we have with us is five loaves and two fish.' So, he said, 'Bring them here to me.' He gave orders that the people were to sit down on the grass; then he took the five loaves and the two fish, raised his eyes to heaven and said the blessing. And breaking the loaves he handed them to his disciples, who gave them to the crowds. They all ate as much as they wanted, and they collected the scraps left over, twelve baskets full. Now about five thousand men had eaten, to say nothing of women and children.

Similar accounts of this event appear in Mark 6:31–44, Luke 9:10–17, and John 6:5–14. A similar miracle involving feeding 4,000 is reported in Matthew 15:32–39 and Mark 8:1–9. In that account, there were seven loaves and a few small fish.

Miraculous Aspects

To feed 5,000 men would require, say, 1,000 loaves (assuming that each man was satisfied with a fifth of a loaf) and, say, 1,000 fish (assuming that each man was satisfied with a fifth of a fish). We do not know the size of the loaves or the size of the fish, so these assumptions are based on the size of the oven dishes around that time and the size of table fish generally. This miracle then alleges that 5 loaves turned into about 1,000 loaves and 2 fish turned into 1,000 fish. This is clearly impossible even today, and it is on such a scale that it could not possibly have been done by any sleight of hand. The essence of this miracle is that much food was created out of a small amount of the same type of food.

Probative Issues

This miracle is presented in all four Gospels as a serious reporting of an incident that really occurred. It is not suggested as a parable or teaching metaphor or as some theological proposition. Science tells us that matter cannot be created or destroyed (except by nuclear reaction), and alchemists cannot explain how air can be transmuted into loaves and fish. Accordingly, in our material realm, this miracle is absolutely impossible and therefore unbelievable.

Rationale

Our faith is that God created all matter out of nothing and that nothing is impossible for God. This miracle clearly requires divine intervention. Jesus said a blessing over this food before distributing it. We do not know what this was, in that it may have asked God to multiply the food, which would suggest that Jesus was not causing this miracle through his own power. In any event, this miracle is clearly attributable to Jesus and at least shows that he had divine support. It is believable by us on the basis that God can do such things.

3.3.2.8 The Tempest Stilled

Mark 4:35–41

With the coming of evening that same day, he said to them, 'Let us cross over to the other side.' And leaving the crowd behind they took him, just as he was, in the boat; and there were other boats with him. Then it began to blow a great gale and the waves were breaking into the boat so that it was almost swamped. But he was in the stern, his head on the cushion, asleep. They woke him and said to him, 'Master, do you not care? We are lost!' And he woke up and rebuked the wind and said to the sea, 'Quiet now! Be calm!' And the wind dropped, and there followed a great calm. Then he said to them, 'Why are you so frightened? Have you still no faith?' They were overcome with awe and said to one another, 'Who can this be? Even the wind and the sea obey him.'

Miraculous Aspects

There is no documented evidence of any human being ever having the power to command the weather elements of nature. To command a storm to cease mid-stride, as it were, is beyond all human experience and capability; therefore, it must be caused by some supernatural power. There have been instances of persons coming into the eye of a storm, where suddenly all is calm, and modern technology can accurately predict the location and movement of the eye of a storm. But the storm resumes after the eye of the storm has passed. In the report of this miracle, there was no suggestion that the storm resumed, so we may conclude that this was not the eye of the storm.

Probative Issues

It could be argued that this storm was some sort of meteorological anomaly and that the sudden cessation of the storm was attributed to Jesus by zealous disciples simply because he was there. Disproving such an argument is difficult, because this event is recorded only in the Gospels. However, the account of the facts is consistent in all three Synoptic Gospels, so the argument that it is a fabrication also requires some evidence of collusion and conspiracy between the authors of the Synoptic Gospels. No such evidence has ever been produced.

The fact recorded in the Gospels asserts that the storm ceased immediately on the command of Jesus. There was no prayer or request to some higher power. But again, this does not prove the divinity of Jesus, because the higher power could have enabled Jesus to use such power. We do not have an answer to this argument, but if Jesus was given such power by God, then clearly, he had God on his side and was chosen by God to have such power, which surely makes him the Messiah.

Rationale

This extraordinary event was preached by eyewitnesses and eventually recorded in the Synoptic Gospels. The point of the story is to at least show that Jesus had supernatural powers and to demonstrate what Jesus was teaching about the power of faith. The power to cause storms to cease suddenly is clearly within the power of the God who created all things, and there is nothing impossible in God giving some human the power to do this. Accordingly, this event may reasonably be regarded as a miracle attributable to Jesus.

3.3.2.9 Jesus Walks on Water

Matthew 14:22–33

And at once he made the disciples get into the boat and go on ahead to the other side while he sent the crowds away. After sending the crowds away he went up into the hills by himself to pray. When evening came, he was there alone, while the boat, by now some furlongs from land, was hard pressed by rough waves, for there was a head-wind. In the fourth watch of the night he came towards them, walking on the sea, and when the disciples saw him walking on the sea, they were terrified. 'It is a ghost,' they said, and cried out in fear. But at once Jesus called out to them, saying, 'Courage! It's me! Don't be afraid.' It was Peter who answered. 'Lord,' he said, 'if it is you, tell me to come to you across the water.' Jesus said, 'Come.' Then Peter got out of the boat and started walking towards Jesus across the water, but then noticing the wind, he took fright and began to sink. 'Lord,' he cried, 'save me!' Jesus put out his hand at once and held him. 'You have so little faith,' he said, 'why did you doubt?' And as they got into the boat the wind dropped. The men in the boat bowed down before him and said, 'Truly, you are the Son of God.'

Miraculous Aspects

Walking on water is not possible for human beings. Physically, humans are dense solids, and water is fluid. An unsupported dense solid above a fluid of less density will sink into fluid due to the force of gravity acting on both solid and fluid on this planet. In other words, we cannot walk on water. Jesus appeared to the disciples to be walking on water, and they immediately recognised him and believed that it could not possibly be the human named Jesus—so it must be a ghost. Jesus clearly knew of their fear and confirmed that it was really him to allay their fears. This may clearly be regarded as a miracle. At least one modern illusionist has appeared to be able to walk on water, but he does not claim to be anything more than an illusionist.

Probative Issues

The part of this incident involving Peter is reported only in Matthew. John reports that as soon as they were ready to take him into the boat, they had reached the other side. There are discrepancies, but having been written by unknown disciples many years after the events, some discrepancies are not surprising. However, the fundamental aspect of the event remains consistent.

Rationale

Again, the point of recording this incident in the Gospels is to teach that Jesus had supernatural powers and to illustrate what Jesus meant in his teaching about the power of faith. It is not difficult to believe that God dispensed the ability to do such things to Jesus. This can easily be accepted as a miracle attributable to Jesus, although it does not directly prove his divinity.

3.3.2.10 Raising the Dead: The Widow's Son

Luke 7:11–17

It happened that soon afterwards he went to a town called Nain, accompanied by his disciples and a great number of people. Now when he was near the gate of the town there was a dead man being carried out, the only son of his mother, and she was a widow. And a considerable number of the townspeople was with her. When the Lord saw her he felt sorry for her and said to her, 'Don't cry.' Then he went up and touched the bier and the bearers stood still, and he said, 'Young man, I tell you: get up.' And the dead man sat up and began to talk, and Jesus gave him to his mother. Everyone was filled with awe and glorified God saying, 'A great prophet has risen up among us; God has visited his people.' And this view of him spread throughout Judaea and all over the countryside.

Miraculous Aspects

We are told in this Gospel that this man was dead. Jesus simply told him to arise, and the man did so and began to talk, which indicated life rather than an animated corpse. Raising people from the dead is not a human capability, even with the best of modern medical science and equipment.

As a miracle, this event was not unprecedented. In the Old Testament, at I Kings 17:17–24, it is recorded that Elijah raised a widow's son from the dead. He did so by praying at length to God to restore the life of the son, and eventually God answered his prayers. There are also some other accounts of raising the dead in the Old Testament, and some by people other than Jesus in the New Testament. These are all regarded as miracles.

Probative Issues

The main probative issue in any resurrection is the question of whether the person resurrected was actually dead before the time of resurrection. In the days of Jesus, medical science was not sufficiently advanced to be able to distinguish between a deathlike coma and actual death, even if they then knew that there was such a thing as a deathlike coma. Even a few centuries ago, this difference was not always correctly identified, and there are many documented cases of persons being buried; later, exhumation marks were found on the inside of the coffins, indicating that they had revived and tried to escape the tomb.

Rationale

We are simply told that the man was dead. We can accept that everyone there believed him to be dead. Jesus did not say that the man was not dead, and he simply told him to arise. Jesus did not pray to the Father to restore life to the widow's son. He did this with the power within himself to do this. Again, this does not prove the divinity of Jesus, but it is evidence that he possessed supernatural powers.

3.3.2.11 Raising the Dead: Jairus's Daughter

Matthew 9:18–26

While he was speaking to them, suddenly one of the officials came up, who bowed low in front of him and said, 'My daughter has just died, but come and lay your hand on her and her life will be saved.' Jesus rose and, with his disciples, followed him. Then suddenly from behind him came a woman, who had been suffering from a hemorrhage for twelve years, and she touched the fringe of his cloak, for she was thinking, 'If only I can touch his cloak I shall be saved.' Jesus turned round and saw her; and he said to her, 'Courage, my daughter, your faith has saved you.' And from that moment the woman was saved. When Jesus reached the official's house and saw the flute-players, with the crowd making a commotion, he said, 'Get out of here; the little girl is not dead; she is asleep.' And they ridiculed him. But when the people had been turned out he went inside and took her by the hand; and she stood up. And the news of this spread all round the countryside.

Miraculous Aspects

This event has commonly been classified as a raising from the dead. All three Synoptic Gospels give a similar account, and all three include the healing of the woman with the haemorrhage on the way to Jairus's house, although that miracle is not our present concern. Raising someone from the dead is clearly a miracle, but again it was done by Jesus simply telling the girl to arise.

Probative Issues

Clearly, everyone there believed that the girl was dead and that Jesus could do nothing to change this. However, when Jesus saw the girl, he proclaimed that she was merely asleep, and he was ridiculed for this assertion. Obviously, if she had been merely asleep, the family and medical practitioners involved would have tried to wake her. But Jesus would not have lied about her condition, nor could he have been mistaken. Nor was his use of the Aramaic word for *asleep* a euphemism for death, as it sometimes is in modern language, because he was ridiculed for saying it. He used the word for *asleep* to distinguish it from death, because there was no Aramaic or Greek word which translates to our modern word *coma*.

Rationale

The argument that this event was a raising from the dead is not highly persuasive. Furthermore, rousing someone from a deathlike coma is not a human capability, so this event can still be regarded as a healing miracle in which Jesus woke the girl from a coma.

3.3.2.12 Raising the Dead: Lazarus

John 11:1–46

There was a man named Lazarus of Bethany, the village of Mary and her sister, Martha, and he was ill. It was the same Mary, the sister of the sick man Lazarus, who anointed the Lord with ointment and wiped his feet with her hair. The sisters sent this message to Jesus, 'Lord, the man you love is ill.' On receiving the message, Jesus said, 'This sickness will not end in death, but it is for God's glory so that through it the Son of God may be glorified.' Jesus loved Martha and her sister and Lazarus, yet when he heard that he was ill he stayed where he was for two more days before saying to the disciples, 'Let us go back to Judaea.' The disciples said, 'Rabbi, it is not long since the Jews were trying to stone you; are you going back there again?' Jesus replied: Are there not twelve hours in the day? No one who walks in the daytime stumbles, having the light of this world to see by; anyone who walks around at night stumbles, having no light as a guide. He said that and then added, 'Our friend Lazarus is at rest; I am going to wake him.' The disciples said to him, 'Lord, if he is at rest he will be saved.' Jesus was speaking of the death of Lazarus, but they thought that by 'rest' he meant 'sleep'; so Jesus put it plainly, 'Lazarus is dead; and for your sake I am glad I was not there because now you will believe. But let us go to him.' Then Thomas—known as the Twin—said to the other disciples, 'Let us also go to die with him.' On arriving, Jesus found that Lazarus had been in the tomb for four days already. Bethany is only about two miles from Jerusalem, and many Jews had come to Martha and Mary to comfort them about their brother. When Martha heard that Jesus was coming she went to meet him. Mary remained sitting in the house. Martha said to Jesus, 'Lord, if you had been here, my brother would not have died, but even now I know that God will grant whatever you ask of him.' Jesus said to her, 'Your brother will rise again.' Martha said, 'I know he will rise again at the resurrection on the last day.' Jesus said: I am the resurrection. Anyone who believes in me, even though that person dies, will live, and whoever lives and believes in me will never die. Do you believe this? 'Yes, Lord,' she said, 'I believe that you are the Christ, the Son of God, the one who was to come into this world.' When she had said this, she went and called her sister Mary, saying in a low voice, 'The Master is here and wants to see you.' Hearing this, Mary got up quickly and went to him. Jesus had not yet come into the village; he was still at the place where Martha had met him. When the Jews who were in the house comforting Mary saw her get up so quickly and go out, they followed her, thinking that she was going to the tomb to weep there. Mary went to Jesus, and as soon as she saw him, she threw herself at his feet, saying, 'Lord, if you had been here, my brother would not have died.' At the sight of her tears, and those of the Jews who had come with her, Jesus was greatly distressed, and with a profound sigh he said, 'Where have you put him?' They said, 'Lord, come and see.' Jesus wept; and the Jews said, 'See how much he loved him!' But there were some who remarked, 'He opened the eyes of the blind man. Could he not have prevented this man's death?' Sighing again, Jesus reached the tomb: it was a cave with a stone to close the opening. Jesus said, 'Take the stone away.' Martha, the dead man's sister, said to him, 'Lord, by now he will smell; this is the fourth day since he died.' Jesus replied, 'Have I not told you that if you believe you will see the glory of God?' So, they took the stone away. Then Jesus lifted up his eyes and said: Father, I thank you for hearing my prayer. I myself knew that you hear me always, but I speak for the sake of all these who are standing around me, so that they may believe it was you who sent me. When he had said this, he cried in a loud voice, 'Lazarus, come out!' The dead man came out, his feet and hands bound with strips of material, and a cloth over his face. Jesus said to them, 'Unbind him, let him go free.' Many of the Jews who had come to visit Mary, and had seen what he did, believed in him, but some of them went to the Pharisees to tell them what Jesus had done.

Miraculous Aspects

Raising someone from the dead is clearly a miracle, because such action is not a natural human capability. In this case, there can be little doubt that Lazarus was actually dead, because Jesus himself said that Lazarus was dead. Also, Lazarus had been buried and wrapped in burial cloth, having died four days earlier. There is also no doubt that Lazarus lived after coming out of the tomb.

Probative Issues

This miracle is recorded only in the Gospel of John and is a lengthy account. It was clearly an event of major significance, and the apostles were there and witnessed it. Why was it not recorded in the other Gospels? We cannot know the answer to this question now, and speculation is unproductive; however, this omission from the Synoptic Gospels does raise the question as to whether this event actually happened.

We cannot be certain that Lazarus was actually dead, because Jesus was not with Lazarus at the time he said that Lazarus was dead; he only travelled to him two days later. We also know that deathlike comas can last for many days, and in modern times, with intravenous feeding and other care, it can even last for years. But even if Lazarus was not actually dead, this still remains a miracle healing as the waking of Lazarus from a deathlike coma.

Why did Jesus weep? Jesus said before going to the tomb that Lazarus was dead and that he was going to wake him. Was this a silent prayer? Before calling Lazarus to come out, Jesus thanked the Father for hearing his prayer. Does this mean that Jesus did not perform this resurrection with his own power?

Rationale

This account of this miracle is typical of the Gospel of John, which generally expresses the theological significance of events and reports the facts and dialogue which support the theology. Bearing in mind that this Gospel was written possibly as much as one hundred thirty years after the death of Jesus, it is arguable that this incident was presented as a metaphor to teach the theology of the resurrection of the body and life after death. Nevertheless, it is presented as an account of an actual event, with the persons and places involved being named and identified. On this basis, a belief that Jesus did actually perform this miracle is justified, although there are some reservations which diminish the persuasive value of this account.

3.3.2.13 Raising the Dead: The Resurrection of Jesus

Matthew 27:45–60

From the sixth hour there was darkness over all the land until the ninth hour. And about the ninth hour, Jesus cried out in a loud voice, 'Eli, eli, lama sabachthani?' that is, 'My God, my God, why have you forsaken me?' When some of those who stood there heard this, they said, 'The man is calling on Elijah,' and one of them quickly ran to get a sponge which he filled with vinegar and, putting it on a reed, gave it him to drink. But the rest of them said, 'Wait! And see if Elijah will come to save him.' But Jesus, again crying out in a loud voice, yielded up his spirit. And suddenly, the veil of the Sanctuary was torn in two from top to bottom, the earth quaked, the rocks were split, the tombs opened and the bodies of many holy people rose from the dead, and these, after his resurrection, came out of the tombs, entered the holy city and appeared to a number of people. The centurion, together with the others guarding Jesus, had seen the earthquake and all that was taking place, and they were terrified and said, 'In truth this man was son of God.' And many women were there, watching from a distance, the same women who had followed Jesus from Galilee and looked after him. Among them were Mary of Magdala, Mary the mother of James and Joseph, and the mother of Zebedee's sons. When it was evening, there came a rich man of Arimathaea, called Joseph, who had himself become a disciple of Jesus. This man went to Pilate and asked for the body of Jesus. Then Pilate ordered it to be handed over. So Joseph took the body, wrapped it in a clean shroud and put it in his own new tomb which he had hewn out of the rock. He then rolled a large stone across the entrance of the tomb and went away.

Matthew 28:1–10

After the Sabbath, and towards dawn on the first day of the week, Mary of Magdala and the other Mary went to visit the sepulchre. And suddenly there was a violent earthquake, for an angel of the Lord, descending from heaven, came and rolled away the stone and sat on it. His face was like lightning, his robe white as snow. The guards were so shaken by fear of him that they were like dead men. But the angel spoke; and he said to the women, 'There is no need for you to be afraid. I know you are looking for Jesus, who was crucified. He is not here, for he has risen, as he said he would. Come and see the place where he lay, then go quickly and tell his disciples, "He has risen from the dead and now he is going ahead of you to Galilee; that is where you will see him." Look! I have told you.' Filled with awe and great joy the women came quickly away from the tomb and ran to tell his disciples. And suddenly, coming to meet them, was Jesus. 'Greetings,' he said. And the women came up to him and, clasping his feet, they did him homage. Then Jesus said to them, 'Do not be afraid; go and tell my brothers that they must leave for Galilee; there they will see me.'

There are also accounts of the death and resurrection of Jesus in Mark 15 and 16, Luke 23 and 24, and John 19, 20, and 21.

Miraculous Aspects

There is no precedent or subsequent occurrence of any human being raising himself or herself from the dead. There are many cases of people believed to be dead subsequently showing signs of life and even resuming life. Invariably, in these cases, it is assumed that the person thought to be dead was not actually dead and revived either spontaneously or through some medical intervention. There has never been a substantiated case of a person who has been certainly killed resuming life.

In the case of Jesus, the evidence that he was really dead is highly persuasive. Jesus himself said that 'it is finished' and commended his spirit into the hands of the Father. Jesus was nailed to the cross, weakened after being scourged, and would have suffered fatal blood loss. He was also stabbed in the side with a spear by a soldier who was trained to kill. This evidence is overwhelming but is not as conclusive as a beheading.

It is argued that this miracle proves the divinity of Jesus. However, it remains possible that if God exists and Jesus was not divine but was merely the human messiah, God could have raised him from the dead. Nevertheless, if we accept that Jesus did rise from the dead, this miracle is highly persuasive of his divinity, because there is no evidence of any intervention by any human or even by the Father. Also, accepting this miracle proves that there is a spiritual realm containing the human spirit after the death of the body.

Probative Issues

The main issue here is not whether Jesus was actually dead but whether he actually rose from the dead. There is no account in any of the Gospels of any witnesses to the resurrection or to Jesus coming out of the tomb. There are several accounts of disciples meeting and having dialogue with Jesus after his death, but in most cases, they did not recognise the person they met as Jesus; rather, they concluded that it was Jesus when he gave them some sign. This failure to recognise Jesus is curious, because the disciples in the boat were able to recognise Jesus when he walked on the water, so much so that they thought he was a ghost.

However, the apostles did recognise him when he appeared amongst them in the locked room, and they did not think it was a ghost, because he wanted to eat something to demonstrate his materiality. The account of the disbelief of Thomas also evidences that Thomas recognised Jesus without having to tactilely examine the wounds Jesus suffered in the crucifixion.

The Jewish scholar Simcha Jacobovici, in his documentary *The Lost Tomb of Jesus*, which has already been considered, argues that Jesus did not actually rise from the dead, but that the disciples simply stole the body and conspired to allege his resurrection to promote their religious agenda. It is correct to say that without the resurrection of Jesus, there would have been less support for the divinity of Jesus, especially since he claimed to be divine, and Christianity may have deteriorated into oblivion. As has already been considered, the argument and evidence presented by Simcha Jacobovici is unconvincing and has little, if any, persuasive value.

<u>Rationale</u>

As Catholics, we believe that Jesus rose from the dead and that this belief is fundamental to our faith. The evidence that Jesus died by crucifixion is highly persuasive, and the evidence that he rose from the dead is also highly persuasive, not only because he predicted it but also because there were too many witnesses to the resurrected Jesus for this to have been a conspiracy which has remained unexposed for about two thousand years. The resurrection is cogent evidence of the divinity of Jesus but is not compelling.

3.3.3 His Teachings

3.3.3.1 Overview

The purpose of the teachings of Jesus was to provide knowledge of the way God wants us to live our lives. It is not their function to provide evidence of the divinity of Jesus, and accordingly, they do not warrant detailed consideration for this purpose. A more appropriate source of evidence about the divinity of Jesus is what Jesus himself said about this issue. To consider the testimony of Jesus about his divinity, we need to assess the reliability of his testimony. We must consider whether Jesus was being truthful, whether he may have been mistaken, and even whether or not he was sane. The life and teachings of Jesus provide an insight into the nature of Jesus that can assist us in our assessment of his testimony, and therefore, it warrants some generalised consideration.

The fundamental principle in the teachings of Jesus is that we must love God above all else and our neighbour as ourselves.

The expression of this principle in these terms codified and rationalised much of the old Jewish law, without diminishing its currency and validity. Certainly, Jesus did abandon some of the old laws—for example, the dietary laws and sacrifice laws—giving reasons for such abandonment. His life and teachings were essentially a demonstration and explanation of the requirements for love of God and our neighbour. He presented his teachings in direct instruction, parables, metaphors, and some cryptic statements. His parables and metaphors were drawn from the culture and environment in which he lived, and they still carry the intended meaning today in our language, despite the difficulties of translation already identified. His direct teaching is clear and consistent, and again it has survived translation. His cryptic statements were usually explained to the apostles privately in clear terms, but some remained inscrutable. From this, we can justifiably form the view that Jesus was extremely intelligent.

There is no evidence or suggestion in any of the Gospels or other parts of the New Testament that Jesus ever told a lie. Certainly not everyone has believed everything that Jesus is reported to have said, but this is the choice of the persons considering what Jesus said. What we can say with certainty is that nothing that Jesus said has ever been proven to be false. Jesus himself said, *'I am the Way; I am Truth and Life'* (John 14:6). This makes it clear that of all the attributes Jesus could have claimed, his focus on truth indicates the importance that he placed on truth. From this, we can justifiably form the view that Jesus was invariably truthful.

In his life, Jesus performed healing miracles reportedly out of compassion for the sufferers of some ailment. The Gospels simply state that Jesus felt compassion for the sufferer and then performed some miracle. They do not tell us what Jesus said or did which indicated the feeling of compassion within him. How the Gospel authors knew what Jesus was feeling is unknown, but we can understand compassion as a normal feeling in us humans when we encounter someone suffering from some ailment. Of course, some people are insensitive to such feelings, but since the Gospel authors did mention Jesus having such feelings, we can justifiably form the view that Jesus was a compassionate man.

The Gospels also show us other attributes of Jesus which do not directly impact the reliability of his testimony about his divinity. For example, Jesus valued peace so highly that it was his greeting and blessing, in accordance with Jewish custom at that time and still extant today. None of the teachings of Jesus endorsed violence, although he was clearly aware that conflict between people is inevitable, and his teaching was that we should choose the way of unselfishness and love in conflict situations. Jesus was very much a peacemaker, but he did not hesitate in criticising hypocrites, even when they were persons of authority in the community. This demonstrates that Jesus was courageous and consistent in his integrity.

3.3.3.2 Conclusion

The teachings of Jesus do not provide any evidence of his divinity, but they do show that he was an intelligent, honest, and caring man who abhorred violence and hypocrisy. The Gospels document his public life and do not provide any evidence of what could be considered eccentric behaviour.

3.3.4 His Testimony

3.3.4.1 Overview

What Jesus said about his own divinity is the best evidence in the consideration of this question. The actual words he used 2,000 years ago are no longer known, and furthermore, he spoke in Aramaic, a language which is unknown to most people in the world today. The records of his words are further obscured by the translation difficulties already identified, plus the fact that they were not recorded until many years after his death. These records were copied, and the oldest copies of these records date from about AD 400; therefore, there is a further question as to the accuracy of these copies and possibly editing of them, the extent of which is unknown. However, as has already been noted, we can assume the substantial competence of the translators and their integrity from the fact that our modern English versions of the Gospels are very close in meaning to the earliest extant copies, which cover a time span of about 1,600 years.

It is also clear that the words Jesus spoke were not uttered specifically as testimony. The modern concept of testimony is that it is said or written, under oath or affirmation that it is the truth, and that the statement has legal significance. With the benefit of hindsight, we have seen that Jesus placed the highest priority on truth, so much so that he would undoubtedly be regarded as a witness of truth if he were giving evidence today. The key statements that Jesus made about his divinity were made to the Sanhedrin and Pilate; thus, there can be no doubt that Jesus was aware that his statement would attract legal consequences.

3.3.4.2 John's Question

One aspect of the testimony of Jesus that warrants consideration is the fact that in response to some of the allegations and questions that were put to him, he made no reply or gave a cryptic answer. A good example of this is John's question of Jesus, set out in Matthew 11:2–6. This question is as follows:

Matthew 11:2–6

Now John had heard in prison what Christ was doing and he sent his disciples to ask him, 'Are you the one who is to come, or are we to expect someone else?' Jesus answered, 'Go back and tell John what you hear and see; the blind see again, and the lame walk, those suffering from virulent skin-diseases are cleansed, and the deaf hear, the dead are raised to life and the good news is proclaimed to the poor; and blessed is anyone who does not find me a cause of falling.'

It is initially puzzling why Jesus did not simply say a plain yes or no. We cannot be sure why he did anything regarding which he did not explain his reasons. However, if we consider the surrounding circumstances, we can make an educated guess as to his reasons.

If we look ahead to the trial of Jesus before the Sanhedrin, which will be considered in more detail shortly, we see that this was the first time that he made a clear and unambiguous declaration of his divinity. The Sanhedrin immediately regarded his statement as blasphemy, which was the most serious type of heresy, and condemned him to death under Jewish law, although they could not implement this sentence because of the Roman occupation. Prior to this, the Sanhedrin had heard from other witnesses, with a view to obtain evidence that Jesus had preached heresy, but no witness was able to give such evidence.

Looking back, we see that on a number of occasions, the Pharisees and other agents of the Jewish clergy had attempted to trap or provoke Jesus into making heretical statements or teachings, but Jesus knew their plans and avoided their traps.

Clearly Jesus was aware that when he declared his divinity, the Jewish clergy would regard it as blasphemy and that they would then have grounds to have him put to death. But he also had to perform a public ministry, the mission of which was to proclaim the Good News, to establish his credentials through his miracles and teachings, and to die for the forgiveness of our sins. Any declaration of his divinity would terminate his ministry by his death, so it seems most likely that Jesus was deliberately cryptic about his divinity until he determined that his mission was accomplished, save for the final phase of his passion, death, resurrection, and ascension.

If this reasoning is correct, then the answer Jesus gave to John's disciples is clearly appropriate. It can be seen as inferring that Jesus was the Messiah without him actually saying so. The disciples of John were not bound to Jesus in any way; any statement to them was a public statement, and Jesus could not require them to keep it secret. The answer is also more positive than a mere yes, because not only is his reply a positive answer to the question, but it also refers to proof that his answer is true.

3.3.4.3 At the Baptism of Jesus

Against this background, we can now consider some of the other statements that Jesus made regarding his divinity. The first incident that can be considered occurred at the start of his public ministry: his baptism by John the Baptist. The Gospels relate this event as follows:

Matthew 3:16–17

And when Jesus had been baptized he at once came up from the water, and suddenly the heavens opened and he saw the Spirit of God descending like a dove and coming down on him. And suddenly there was a voice from heaven, 'This is my Son, the Beloved; my favor rests on him.'

Mark 1:9–11

It was at this time that Jesus came from Nazareth in Galilee and was baptized in the Jordan by John. And at once, as he was coming up out of the water, he saw the heavens torn apart and the Spirit, like a dove, descending on him. And a voice came from heaven, 'You are my Son, the Beloved; my favor rests on you.'

Luke 3:21–22

Now it happened that when all the people had been baptized and while Jesus after his own baptism was at prayer, heaven opened and the Holy Spirit descended on him in a physical form, like a dove. And a voice came from heaven, 'You are my Son; today have I fathered you.'

John 1:29–34

The next day, he saw Jesus coming towards him and said, 'Look, there is the lamb of God that takes away the sin of the world. It was of him that I said, "Behind me comes one who has passed ahead of me because he existed before me." I did not know him myself, and yet my purpose in coming to baptise with water was so that he might be revealed to Israel.' And John declared, 'I saw the Spirit come down on him like a dove from heaven and rest on him. I did not know him myself, but he who sent me to baptise with water had said to me, "The man on whom you see the Spirit come down and rest is the one who is to baptise with the Holy Spirit." I have seen, and I testify that he is the Chosen One of God.'

The Gospels of Mark and Luke suggest that this was a private vision given to Jesus alone, because the words of God are in the second person, as in a private conversation. How the authors of these two Gospels knew what occurred and what was said is unknown, but it seems logical to assume that Jesus told his apostles of this event. If this version of the event is correct, then the unrecorded account given by Jesus to his apostles is clearly a statement by him affirming his divinity.

The Gospel of John relates the events as a private revelation given to John the Baptist as Jesus approached him for baptism. If this version of the event is the correct account, then this is not a statement by Jesus about his divinity but merely the testimony of John the Baptist based on his vision. Again, we do not know how the scribes of this Gospel knew of this event, but it has been suggested that the apostle John was formerly a disciple of John the Baptist, so it may be assumed that John the Baptist related his account in the presence of the apostle John.

The Gospel of Matthew relates the incident as a public vision or manifestation and portrays the words of God in the third person, speaking about Jesus to the public present at this event. Again, we do not know how the scribes of this event knew about it, but if it was a public event, then the apostles (particularly Matthew) who were not present as they had not yet been chosen by Jesus to be his apostles could have been informed of this event by the actual witnesses. The significance of this account is that while it was not a statement by Jesus about his divinity, clearly he was present and heard the words said about him. What is significant is that he did not deny or contradict these words, which can be seen as a tacit acceptance and acknowledgement of their truth. This tacit acknowledgement at this stage of his ministry is consistent with Jesus deliberately not publicly making a statement which could be seen as blasphemy by the Jewish clerical hierarchy at that time.

In the three Synoptic Gospels, we have assumed that the words spoken from heaven were spoken by God the Father. In the Gospel of John, the words were clearly from God, if not actually spoken by God the Father. It is appropriate to acknowledge this assumption as such, even though there is no evidence in support of it. However, none of these Gospels would make any sense in the absence of this assumption.

3.3.4.4 Cure of the Paraplegic

The next event to be considered is the cure of a paraplegic. The Gospel accounts of this event are as follows:

Matthew 9:1–8

And suddenly some people brought him a paralytic stretched out on a bed. Seeing their faith, Jesus said to the paralytic, 'Take comfort, my child, your sins are forgiven.' And now some scribes said to themselves, 'This man is being blasphemous.' Knowing what was in their minds Jesus said, 'Why do you have such wicked thoughts in your hearts? Now, which of these is easier: to say, "Your sins are forgiven," or to say, "Get up and walk"? But to prove to you that the Son of man has authority on earth to forgive sins,'—then he said to the paralytic—'get up, pick up your bed and go off home.' And the man got up and went home. A feeling of awe came over the crowd when they saw this, and they praised God for having given such authority to human beings.

Mark 8:29

When he returned to Capernaum, some time later word went round that he was in the house; and so many people collected that there was no room left, even in front of the door. He was preaching the word to them when some people came bringing him a paralytic carried by four men, but as they could not get the man to him through the crowd, they stripped the roof over the place where Jesus was; and when they had made an opening, they lowered the stretcher on which the paralytic lay. Seeing their faith, Jesus said to the paralytic, 'My child, your sins are forgiven.' Now some scribes were sitting there, and they thought to themselves, 'How can this man talk like that? He is being blasphemous. Who but God can forgive sins?' And at once, Jesus, inwardly aware that this is what they were thinking, said to them, 'Why do you have these thoughts in your hearts? Which of these is easier: to say to the paralytic, "Your sins are forgiven" or to say, "Get up, pick up your stretcher and walk"? But to prove to you that the Son of man has authority to forgive sins on earth'—he said to the paralytic—'I order you: get up, pick up your stretcher, and go off home.' And the man got up, and at once picked up his stretcher and walked out in front of everyone, so that they were all astonished and praised God saying, 'We have never seen anything like this.'

Luke 5:20–24

But as they could find no way of getting the man through the crowd, they went up onto the top of the house and lowered him and his stretcher down through the tiles into the middle of the gathering, in front of Jesus. Seeing their faith he said, 'My friend, your sins are forgiven you.' The scribes and the Pharisees began to think this over. 'Who is this man, talking blasphemy? Who but God alone can forgive sins?' But Jesus, aware of their thoughts, made them this reply, 'What are these thoughts you have in your hearts? Which of these is easier: to say, "Your sins are forgiven you," or to say, "Get up and walk"? But to prove to you that the Son of man has authority on earth to forgive sins,'—he said to the paralyzed man—'I order you: get up, and pick up your stretcher and go home.' And immediately before their very eyes he got up, picked up what he had been lying on and went home praising God. They were all astounded and praised God and were filled with awe, saying, 'We have seen strange things today.'

This incident is not recorded in the Gospel of John. The three Synoptic Gospels are very similar. In each of these, Jesus asserts that the Son of Man himself has the power to forgive sins. The scribes who heard this thought that this was blasphemy, because only God has the power to forgive sins, and to them, the reference by Jesus to himself as the Son of Man appeared to be a statement of his humanity. However, as we have already seen, when Jesus referred to himself as the Son of Man, he was using this description in the sense portrayed in the prophecy of Daniel, where Daniel's reference to the Son of Man is clearly a reference to a divine being.

The Gospel of Matthew allows the insight that even the ordinary people who witnessed this event misunderstood Jesus's reference to himself as the Son of Man, for they then thanked God for giving the authority to forgive sins to human beings. This is consistent with Jesus asserting his divinity in a cryptic way to avoid the premature allegation of blasphemy. If we accept that Jesus was using the phrase 'Son of Man' in the sense given by Daniel, then this is clearly a statement by Jesus asserting his own divinity.

3.3.4.5 Peter's Confession of Faith

The next item of evidence for consideration is Peter's revelation. This is recorded in the Gospels as follows:

Matthew 16:16–19

Then Simon Peter spoke up and said, 'You are the Christ, the Son of the living God.' Jesus replied, 'Simon son of Jonah, you are a blessed man!

Because it was no human agency that revealed this to you but my Father in heaven. So I now say to you: You are Peter and on this rock I will build my community. And the gates of the underworld can never overpower it. I will give you the keys of the kingdom of Heaven: whatever you bind on earth will be bound in heaven; whatever you loose on earth will be loosed in heaven.' Then he gave the disciples strict orders not to say to anyone that he was the Christ.

Mark 8:29

'But you,' he asked them, 'who do you say I am?' Peter spoke up and said to him, 'You are the Christ.' And he gave them strict orders not to tell anyone about him.

Luke 9:20–21

'But you,' he said to them, 'who do you say I am?' It was Peter who spoke up. 'The Christ of God,' he said. But he gave them strict orders and charged them not to say this to anyone.

Again, this event is not recorded in the Gospel of John. It is clear in all three Synoptic Gospels that Jesus acknowledged the truth of Peter's statement. The Gospels of Mark and Luke can be strictly read as limiting Jesus to being the messiah. But the word *messiah* means the 'anointed one of God', which could mean that God anointed a human to be the messiah. Thus, being the messiah is not necessarily being divine. However, the Gospel of Matthew has Peter saying that Jesus is also the Son of God, which can only be read as a clear recognition of the divinity of Jesus.

The instruction that Jesus gave the apostles to keep this incident secret is consistent with him wishing to withhold any assertion of his divinity attributable directly to himself until the appropriate time. Indeed, the requirement for secrecy is puzzling for any other reason. It is also clear from subsequent events that the apostles did, in fact, keep this incident secret until after the ascension of

Jesus, but then they revealed it in their teachings, as recorded in the Synoptic Gospels.

3.3.4.6 Institution of the Eucharist

The next incident for consideration is the institution of the Eucharist. This is recorded in the Gospels as follows:

Matthew 26:26–28

Now as they were eating, Jesus took bread, and when he had said the blessing he broke it and gave it to the disciples. 'Take it and eat,' he said, 'this is my body.' Then he took a cup, and when he had given thanks, he handed it to them saying, 'Drink from this, all of you, for this is my blood, the blood of the covenant, poured out for many for the forgiveness of sins.

Mark 14:22–26

And as they were eating he took bread, and when he had said the blessing he broke it and gave it to them. 'Take it,' he said, 'this is my body.' Then he took a cup, and when he had given thanks, he handed it to them, and all drank from it, and he said to them, 'This is my blood, the blood of the covenant, poured out for many.

Luke 22:14–20

When the time came he took his place at table, and the apostles with him. And he said to them, 'I have ardently longed to eat this Passover with you before I suffer; because, I tell you, I shall not eat it until it is fulfilled in the kingdom of God.' Then, taking a cup, he gave thanks and said, 'Take this and share it among you, because from now on, I tell you, I shall never again drink wine until the kingdom of God comes.' Then he took bread, and when he had given thanks, he broke it and gave it to them, saying, 'This is my body given for you; do this in remembrance of me.' He did the same with the cup after supper, and said, 'This cup is the new covenant in my blood poured out for you.

Again, this is not recorded in the Gospel of John. While the Gospels do not attribute to Jesus any words directly asserting his divinity on this occasion, the words creating the new covenant between God and man can only be seen as Jesus taking the part of God in this covenant. It is Jesus giving his body and blood to God for the benefit of mankind.

Some Christian religions do not accept the truth of the transubstantiation. They believe that the bread and wine are merely symbols of the divine spirit and that communion is merely a religious ritual. We should be cautious about using several-times-removed translations of words written down long after the occasion on which they were said. However, the concept of symbolism was clearly present in the Aramaic that Jesus spoke, as they had scribes. It would have been easy for Jesus to say something like 'This is the token of my body and blood' if that was what he meant. The words recorded in the Gospels are evidence, and it appears to be erroneous to attribute any meaning other than their plain meaning simply because we cannot understand how transubstantiation works. Accordingly, this event should be regarded as evidence of Jesus declaring his divinity through the natural meaning and effect of his words and actions.

This occurred shortly before he was put on trial before the Sanhedrin, where he admitted his divinity. The Last Supper was in private with his apostles, thus there was no need for secrecy at this time.

3.3.4.7 Jesus before the Sanhedrin

We can now consider the evidence of the words of Jesus at his trial before the Sanhedrin. This is recorded in the Gospels as follows:

Matthew 26:63–65

But Jesus was silent. And the high priest said to him, 'I put you on oath by the living God to tell us if you are the Christ, the Son of God.' Jesus answered him, 'It is you who say it. But, I tell you that from this time onward you will see the Son of man seated at the right hand of the Power and coming on the clouds of heaven.' Then the high priest tore his clothes and said, 'He has blasphemed. What need of witnesses have we now? There! You have just heard the blasphemy.'

Mark 14:60–63

But he was silent and made no answer at all. The high priest put a second question to him saying, 'Are you the Christ, the Son of the Blessed One?' 'I am,' said Jesus, 'and you will see the Son of man seated at the right hand of the Power and coming with the clouds of heaven.' The high priest tore his robes and said, 'What need of witnesses have we now? You heard the blasphemy. What is your finding?' Their verdict was unanimous: he deserved to die.

Luke22:66–71

When day broke there was a meeting of the elders of the people, the chief priests and scribes. He was brought before their council, and they said to him, 'If you are the Christ, tell us.' He replied, 'If I tell you, you will not believe, and if I question you, you will not answer. But from now on, the Son of man will be seated at the right hand of the Power of God.' They all said, 'So you are the Son of God then?' He answered, 'It is you who say I am.' Then they said, 'Why do we need any evidence? We have heard it for ourselves from his own lips.'

John 18:19–24

The high priest questioned Jesus about his disciples and his teaching. Jesus answered, 'I have spoken openly for all the world to hear; I have always taught in the synagogue and in the Temple where all the Jews meet together; I have said nothing in secret. Why ask me? Ask my hearers what I taught; they know what I said.' At these words, one of the guards standing by gave Jesus a slap in the face, saying, 'Is that the way you answer the high priest?' Jesus replied, 'If there is some offence in what

I said, point it out; but if not, why do you strike me?' Then Annas sent him, bound, to Caiaphas the high priest.

The account in John's Gospel refers to the questioning of Jesus by Annas, a high priest, and ends with Jesus being sent to Caiaphas, another high priest. The Synoptic Gospels appear to relate to the questioning of Jesus by Caiaphas. In all three of these accounts, it is absolutely clear that Jesus stated that he was the Son of God, i.e. divine. In each account, Caiaphas tore his robes on hearing what Jesus said, this being the Jewish protocol when a high priest heard a blasphemy. The words Jesus said are reported with slight differences in each account. Matthew has Jesus giving an indirect answer to the question of whether he is the Son of God. Mark has Jesus stating clearly 'I am' in answer to this question, and Luke also has Jesus giving the indirect answer. In any event, it was clear that Jesus conveyed from his own lips that he was the Son of God.

As Catholics, we do not regard what Jesus said as blasphemy. It is somewhat puzzling that Caiaphas immediately tore his robes on hearing Jesus say this. It appears not to have occurred to him that Jesus may be telling the truth. On the other hand, Caiaphas was a senior Jewish religious authority with a responsibility to oppose blasphemy. All he saw before him was a bound man. It may also be that he was concerned about the general popularity of Jesus and perceived his teachings as undermining traditional Jewish theology.

We do not know how the apostles became aware of what was said by Jesus at this trial. Perhaps some of the witnesses informed them, which seems likely and accounts for the minor variations in the Gospels. We know that Peter was in the grounds and could have heard what Jesus said, because his later denial of Jesus places him there. This gives the Gospel of Mark the greatest credibility. Or perhaps Jesus informed them after his resurrection. In any event, this event is evidence that Jesus clearly and unambiguously stated that he was the Son of God.

3.3.4.8 Jesus before Pilate

The next event for consideration is the trial of Jesus before Pilate. This is recorded in the Gospels as follows:

Matthew 27:11

Jesus, then, was brought before the governor, and the governor put to him this question, 'Are you the king of the Jews?' Jesus replied, 'It is you who say it.'

Mark 15:2–5

First thing in the morning, the chief priests, together with the elders and scribes and the rest of the Sanhedrin, had their plan ready. They had Jesus bound and took him away and handed him over to Pilate. Pilate put to him this question, 'Are you the king of the Jews?' He replied, 'It is you who say it.' And the chief priests brought many accusations against him. Pilate questioned him again, 'Have you no reply at all? See how many accusations they are bringing against you!' But, to Pilate's surprise, Jesus made no further reply.

John 18:29–40

So, Pilate went back into the Praetorium and called Jesus to him and asked him, 'Are you the king of the Jews?' Jesus replied, 'Do you ask this of your own accord, or have others said it to you about me?' Pilate answered, 'Am I a Jew? It is your own people and the chief priests who have handed you over to me: what have you done?' Jesus replied, 'Mine is not a kingdom of this world; if my kingdom were of this world, my men would have fought to prevent my being surrendered to the Jews. As it is, my kingdom does not belong here.' Pilate said, 'So, then you are a king?' Jesus answered, 'It is you who say that I am a king. I was born for this, I came into the world for this, to bear witness to the truth; and all who are on the side of truth listen to my voice.' 'Truth?' said Pilate. 'What is that?' And so saying he went out again to the Jews and said, 'I find no case against him.'

This event is recorded in the Gospel of Luke, in Luke 23:1–25, but this account appears to have little relevance to this issue. The Gospel of Matthew, Mark, and Luke give little information of any substance, although they reported Jesus as giving a cryptic answer to the question of whether he was the king of the Jews. The Gospel of John contains the information worth considering. In this account, Jesus clearly states that he is a king but that his kingdom is not of this world. That can only mean that he is a king in the spiritual realm and that as a king in this realm, he is divine. These are the words of Jesus, and they are evidence.

It could be argued that Jesus did not say these words or that Pilate did not grasp their meaning, on the basis that Pilate ordered the execution of Jesus because he claimed to be the king of the Jews. The answer to this argument is that Pilate clearly ordered the execution of Jesus under political pressure from the Jewish religious leaders. Executing Jesus on the grounds that he claimed to be a king of the Jews gave Pilate some legal justification under Roman law, because Rome had appointed Herod the Great and his successor, Herod Antipas, as kings of the Jews. John's Gospel goes on to show that Pilate did this under such political pressure.

It is also clear from all the Gospels that Pilate did not find that Jesus was an insurrectionist claiming kinship of the Jews, because he clearly stated in all the Gospel accounts that he found no fault in Jesus. Presumably, when Jesus told him that his kingdom was not of this world, Pilate formed the view that Jesus was a harmless lunatic. He even went so far, in Matthew's account, as to physically wash his hands of any guilt over the death of Jesus. If this is correct, then Pilate had Jesus executed as king of the Jews to justify the legality of the execution on the grounds that Jesus had told Pilate that he was a king and he was clearly Jewish. Pilate may also have found that the public statement of this basis for the execution was an appropriate way to mock the Jews in response to the political pressure they had put on him. It appears that this basis for the execution certainly pleased Herod Antipas.

Any criticism of Pilate is not relevant to the issue of what Jesus said about his divinity. What remains factual is that Pilate did order the death of Jesus on the basis that Jesus claimed to be a king, and that Pilate did not consider this claim to be deserving of any punishment. We do not know how the apostles knew about what Jesus said to Pilate, but the facts recorded in the Gospels strongly suggest that the account in John's Gospel is true and correct.

3.3.4.9 Jesus on the Cross

The final evidence for consideration is the words Jesus said just prior to his death. This is recorded in the Gospels as follows:

Matthew 27:45–50

From the sixth hour there was darkness over all the land until the ninth hour. And about the ninth hour, Jesus cried out in a loud voice, 'Eli, eli, lama sabachthani?' that is, 'My God, my God, why have you forsaken me?' When some of those who stood there heard this, they said, 'The man is calling on Elijah,' and one of them quickly ran to get a sponge which he filled with vinegar and, putting it on a reed, gave it him to drink. But the rest of them said, 'Wait! And see if Elijah will come to save him.' But Jesus, again crying out in a loud voice, yielded up his spirit.

Mark 15:33–39

When the sixth hour came there was darkness over the whole land until the ninth hour. And at the ninth hour Jesus cried out in a loud voice, 'Eloi, eloi, lama sabachthani?' which means, 'My God, my God, why have you forsaken me?' When some of those who stood by heard this, they said, 'Listen, he is calling on Elijah.' Someone ran and soaked a sponge in vinegar and, putting it on a reed, gave it to him to drink saying, 'Wait! And see if Elijah will come to take him down.' But Jesus gave a loud cry and breathed his last. And the veil of the Sanctuary was torn in two from top to bottom. The centurion, who was standing in front of him, had seen how he had died, and he said, 'In truth this man was Son of God.'

Luke 23:44–47

It was now about the sixth hour and the sun's light failed, so that darkness came over the whole land until the ninth hour. The veil of the Sanctuary was torn right down the middle. Jesus cried out in a loud voice saying, 'Father, into your hands I commit my spirit.' With these words he breathed his last. When the centurion saw what had taken place, he gave praise to God and said, 'Truly, this was an upright man.'

What Jesus said at this time is worth considering for two reasons. Firstly, the words attributed to Jesus here in Matthew and Mark's Gospels are the words actually spoken by Jesus in Aramaic and are as near as we come to his exact words. Secondly, as can be seen in these excerpts, Jesus appeared to be calling out to his God, which suggests that Jesus is 'below' his God. This suggestion is strengthened by the observation that these were his actual words. Accordingly, this event can be argued to weigh against the divinity of Jesus, and we should be aware of it.

The response to this argument is that calling on God does not make Jesus any less divine. We saw that when Jesus taught the multitude the Our Father and when he was in his agony in the Garden of Gethsemane, Jesus was submissive to the will of his Father. This does not make him subordinate or inferior to his Father, because he does so out of love for his Father. Logically, there is nothing inconsistent in Jesus calling his Father 'my God', given the triune nature of the God of our Catholic theology.

However, the question Jesus asked as to why God had abandoned him raises the question of the extent to which the humanity of Jesus limited his access to divine knowledge. Death is a solitary experience, even for those who die with family and friends around them or at the same instant as many others die, because only the person dying can truly and personally experience the end of his or her life. Jesus knew that he was going to die before he came to Jerusalem, and he predicted his own death on several occasions.

He also knew that his death would be agonising. Having been scourged, crowned with thorns, made to carry his cross, crucified, and left hanging there for about three hours, it was obviously worse in actuality than his foreknowledge of these events, and it is an understandable human emotion to feel abandoned as the solitude of death approaches.

Our theology is that Jesus was both fully human and fully divine, and this display of human emotion can be seen as his final statement of his fully human nature. A point to ponder about this event is that Jesus did not call on God to end his suffering. He merely expressed his desolation in the duration of his suffering and the death of his human body. Seen this way, the last words of Jesus only confirmed his true humanity without in any way diminishing any of the other evidence of his divinity.

3.3.5 The Legacy of Jesus

Jesus was a wandering Jewish rabbi in Israel, a reasonably arid backwater of the world, about two thousand years ago. He wrote nothing. Today there are more than 1 billion Catholics in a world of just over 7 billion people. The church that he founded has an officially accepted presence in every country of the world.

It can be argued that there are principles of sociocultural dynamics at work which explain this growth of a religion that has significant social popularity and appeal, along with very effective evangelisation by some very extraordinary people.

The 'big five' religions are Christianity, Islam, Judaism, Hinduism, and Buddhism. It can also be argued that the other four of the big five religions have a similar legacy in terms of number of adherents and geographical distribution.

The point being made here is that Christianity is not a minor religion with only few adherents in some limited parts of the world. What this means is that for the last two thousand years, many generations of people have believed that the teachings of Jesus are truly the way God wants us to live. The same is true of the other major religions, but that does not diminish our faith in our religion as a religion of Catholic appeal; it presents this as the legacy of the most extraordinary life of Jesus. As such, it cannot be simply dismissed and warrants consideration as a factor going to the divinity of Jesus.

3.3.6 The Search for Truth

3.3.6.1 The Meaning of 'Truth'

The foundation of our faith is the underlying belief that what is written in the Gospels is a true account of the life and teachings of Jesus. Jesus said, *'I am the way, the truth and life'* (John 14:6), and later Pilate asked him, *'What is truth?'* (John 18:37–38). So before we can consider the evidence as to the truth of the Gospels, it seems appropriate to review our understanding of the nature and meaning of truth. Philosophers and theologians may have deep and meaningful discussions about the nature of truth, but for our consideration, we need only a fundamental understanding of the concept.

In our reality, we humans live in a universe which is composed of what we call matter, ranging in size from subatomic particles to galaxies. Some matter is inorganic, and some is organic and may be alive, like us humans. All matter is in continuous motion, and the motion of some matter can affect the motion of other matter. Such an occurrence is called an event. Some events involve only inorganic matter, and these are called natural phenomena. Events can also affect organic matter and may even be caused by organic matter.

We humans have words, intelligence, and emotions, which are certainly part of our reality. But words, intelligence, and emotions have no material existence and therefore do not exist outside the human mind. The word *truth* refers to a concept which is a property of another group of words which we call a statement. The statement to which the concept of truth can be applied may be—but is not limited to—an assertion about the present condition of something or an account of a past event or condition. A proposition of reason or mathematics is more appropriately said to be correct or incorrect. Truth, then, is whether or not the event actually happened or whether the condition actually exists or existed. If the event actually happened or the condition actually exists or existed, the statement has the property of being true. If not, then it has the property of being untrue. It should be noted that truth can only apply to what presently is or what was, because the future has no actuality until it becomes present or past.

The problem with applying the concept of truth is that we cannot always be certain that the subject of the statement actually exists or existed as asserted. There are several reasons for this, which may be briefly outlined as follows.

Firstly, there is the imprecision of human memory. Any statement of a past event or condition or a present condition that is beyond the sensory capacity of the receivers of that statement comes from a human brain and is based on the speaker's recollection of the event or condition. The human brain stores information digitally. The appearance of a person's face, the sound of his or her voice, and what was said or done is all information that is recorded digitally by our brains. When we recognise someone, our brains have subconsciously redigitised that person's appearance and have compared that data to the data in our mental database of a person's appearance. Then our brains select the closest match and make our conscious mind aware that we know that person from other information associated with that person's profile in our mental database. Clearly, this is a reconstruction from digital data. There are no photo albums or recording machines in our heads! This is a wonderful ability that we have, but it is not always accurate. People with photographic or eidetic memories appear to store more information input from their sensory organs and have the ability to recall at will all this information for long periods. Most of us do not have this ability, and over time, we lose some of the details of the sensory input. So then, when our brains act to recall someone's appearance, our brains extrapolate the missing data to give us a complete picture. That extrapolation may be based on presently available data and may consequently be an inaccurate recollection. Most of us have had the experience of mistaking someone for someone else or being mistaken for someone else ourselves. This illustrates the concept sought to be outlined above and supports the proposition that this is how our memory works. It must make us mindful that recollection is a process of reconstruction which at times is not accurate.

Secondly, our human sensory organs do not always register or record input accurately. Why this happens need not concern us for our present purpose. Again, most of us have had the experience of believing that someone said a particular word when, in fact, that person actually said something completely different. Often such misperception is corrected on the spot, but not always, which can leave us with an honest memory of something that was not actually said. Such misperceptions can occur in all our senses. For example, we can misperceive the colour of something, especially if we are colour-blind. Or we can mistaste something if we have just prior tasted something very pungent. Or we can mishear something in a crowded room or if we are partially deaf. The same applies to our sense of smell and touch. An awareness of the fallibility of our own senses must make us mindful of the possible inaccuracy of the sensory content of a statement presented as true because of the sensory fallibility of the person making the statement.

Thirdly, most statements about events or conditions are presented as being true based on the knowledge or belief of the person making the statement. If the statement is the speaker's memory of his own sensory input, then we must be mindful of the potential for error set out in the two preceding paragraphs. If the statement is based on the speaker's belief based on statements made by others, then we should examine whether that belief is justified, by enquiring as to the source of that belief. Usually, the source will be statements made to the speaker by some other person, sometimes collated or pieced together to come to a conclusion, which is the statement being considered. It can be a long and tedious process to trace a long chain of prior statements, and it may still end in uncertainty as to the truth. In such cases, we often rely on the opinions of experts, whose credentials should certainly be checked.

Fourthly, some persons make statements that they do not honestly believe to be true. This is called a lie. Within this category of statements is fiction, which, if presented as fiction, is not regarded as a lie but is certainly untrue. There are also illusionists who present events in a deliberate attempt to deceive our senses, mostly to make us believe that we have perceived something that is impossible. This is done for entertainment purposes, with the audience being fully aware that what they are perceiving is an illusion. This is not a lie, but it is certainly untrue. Then there are confidence tricksters who knowingly present false information or illusion as true, usually for the purpose of obtaining some benefit, financial or otherwise, from their victims.

3.3.6.2 The Likelihood of Error

The truth of the events that concern us occurred many centuries ago, and the evidence that they occurred is only available in documents and records, principally the Gospels, written centuries ago. These documents and records were written in ancient languages which have been frequently transcribed in those languages and then translated into modern languages by experts. We all know that human error can occur in the process of transcription and translation. We do not know whether there was any human error in the transcriptions, or the extent of them, if any. We also know that there are meaningful differences between the translations of the same source documents by various experts and that these differences accord with the theology of the various translators. With these difficulties in mind, we have read the Gospels and formed the belief that is currently the basis of our faith, although for many of us, it involved being brought up as Catholics, with the uncritical acceptance of the truth of the Gospels we had as children. As adults, we have become more critical and aware of the need for evidence to support our beliefs. The evidence provided by the Gospels is essentially unchanging, subject to the need to translate the Gospels into the current language. This process is ongoing because our modern languages are in a constant state of flux, with new words, concepts, and idioms occurring every day.

But the Gospels do not stand alone. The expert translators and archaeologists have discovered other documents describing historical events relevant to the events described in the Gospels which can affect the meaning of the Gospels and, accordingly, their translation. Indeed, there were several other gospels, which are still extant, which were rejected by our church when it fixed the four existing Gospels as canonical. In more recent times (1946), there has been the discovery of the Dead Sea Scrolls. These scrolls were written around the time that Jesus lived and may have some value in our modern understanding of the Gospels. Most of them were written in ancient Hebrew, and many of them have not yet been fully translated. The experts tell us that a complete translation may not be available for many years yet. However, most of the major scrolls have been translated and these translations published.

3.3.6.3 Thiering's Interpretation

Based on some of these scrolls, Barbara Thiering has presented and published an interpretation of the Gospels which fundamentally contradicts our understanding of the Gospels. Her views, although very controversial, are worth considering, because she was an eminent expert and devoted about twenty-five years of her life to forming her views.

Barbara Thiering (1930–2015) was academically qualified in modern languages and theology. She lectured in the School of Divinity at Sydney University and did private research on the Dead Sea Scrolls and may appropriately be regarded as an expert in this field. Based on about twenty years of her research on the Dead Sea Scrolls, she formed a view about the interpretation of the Gospels and published her views in academic journals prior to 1990. In 1990, she presented her views in a television documentary called *The Riddle of the Dead Sea Scrolls*, which is still available on YouTube. In 1992, she published her views in a book called *Jesus the Man: Decoding the Real Story of Jesus and Mary Magdalene.* This work has subsequently (2006) been republished. She also published other books supplementing her views and also, in 2006, established a website devoted to explaining the pesher technique, which she uses in her interpretation.

Our consideration will be confined to her major work, i.e. *Jesus the Man*. It is not the purpose of this work to present a refutation of her theory or to review her book but rather to illustrate the process of critical consideration, which is necessary in relation to any theory that contradicts our understanding of our faith. Critical thinking about such theories is necessary, because if our faith is fragile, we might precipitously accept such a theory as valid and lose our faith, whereas a mature consideration gives us a more reasonable basis for any views that we may form about such a theory.

To consider Barbara Thiering's theory, it is necessary to at least have an outline of what it is about. Of course, an outline cannot do justice to the full text of her work, and it is not presented as a substitute for further reading if her theory stimulates interest.

But before we can outline her theory, it may be helpful to know a little about the Dead Sea Scrolls and the Essenes.

3.3.6.4 The Dead Sea Scrolls

The Dead Sea Scrolls were discovered in caves near Qumran, which is about two kilometres north-west of the Dead Sea in Israel. There are about nine hundred eighty scrolls, and they were discovered between 1946 and 1956. Most experts agree that they were written between about 100 BC and AD 70. They were written mostly on parchment, vellum, and papyrus, and mostly in Hebrew, with some in Aramaic, Greek, and other minor obscure languages. Obviously, the materials on which they were written have significantly decayed over the last 2,000 years, leaving many gaps in the documents, making translation difficult even for the experts.

There is still some academic diversity of opinion as to who wrote the scrolls and where they were written. It is generally agreed that they were hidden in the caves in about AD 70, when the Romans destroyed the Temple in Jerusalem, to prevent them from also being destroyed by the Romans. The vast majority of the texts are Jewish religious writings. They have been classified into two main groups: biblical and non-biblical. The biblical texts are copies of the Hebrew Bible and make up about a quarter of the scrolls. Some of these scrolls contain differences from the Hebrew Bible that were settled in modern times. The non-biblical scrolls are further divided into non-canonical biblical texts and sectarian writings in approximately equal parts. It is the sectarian writings that contain information that was previously unknown and that are essentially the source of Barbara Thiering's theory.

The Essenes, Pharisees, and Sadducees were the main sects of Judaism, with the Pharisees having the most popular support and numbers in ancient times. The origins of these sects are obscure. The Jewish historian Josephus, whose writings have survived, mentions them as first existing during the rule of the Hasmoneans (Maccabees), after the Jews won their independence from the Greek kings of Syria in 165 BC. The standard model of their origins shows that the Sadducees, a priestly conservative sect, supported the priestly family of the Hasmoneans, while the liberal Pharisees opposed them. Both sects had both a religious and political agenda, and their animosity towards each other was essentially a civil war. That civil war ended when the Romans invaded and annexed Judea as a Roman province in 63 BC.

The Essenes were essentially a male-dominated monastic sect with a mostly religious agenda. They had been largely rejected by the other two sects, which occupied the main population centres, so they established their headquarters at Khirbet Qumran. The scrolls relate to events about a Teacher of Righteousness who is believed to be the founder of the Essenes sect. The archaeology of Khirbet Qumran indicates that it was constructed in about 150 BC, which would date the Teacher at about 170 BC. On this timing, the Wicked Priest, also referred to in the scrolls, would be a contemporary of the Teacher, and the identity of this person was probably Jonathan Maccabee, who 'ruled in Israel' at about this time.

3.3.6.5 The Controversy

Against this background, we can now outline Barbara Thiering's views. The primary view is that she identifies the Teacher of Righteousness as John the Baptist and Jesus as the Man of the Lie, who, according to Thiering, was also the Wicked Priest. She ends her book by asserting that Jesus was about seventy years old in AD 64 and probably died of old age in seclusion in Rome sometime after this date. This means that the scrolls, from which she obtained her information, had to be written between AD 64 and AD 70, when the Temple in Jerusalem was destroyed by the Romans and the scrolls were hidden in the caves. Most scholars agree that the scrolls referring to the Teacher and the Wicked

Priest were written, at the latest, about 65 BC, which makes it impossible for the Teacher to be John the Baptist and for the Wicked Priest to be Jesus. The dating of the scrolls by the experts is based on carbon-14 dating and palaeographic analysis. Carbon-14 dating is imprecise enough to allow Thiering's views, but the palaeographic analysis is more precise. Thiering argued that the palaeographic analysis was not valid, on the grounds that young scribes could be seated with and learn styles from older scribes, so that styles typical of an earlier period could anomalously appear in later writings. This argument has not persuaded the majority of experts who adhere to their view.

The fundamental basis of Thiering's reinterpretation of the Gospels is her discovery of the use of what she calls the pesher technique in scroll 1QpHab 7:1–5, which she says explicitly states this technique. This does not appear to be correct. This scroll was also translated by Wise, Abegg, and Cook in their book *The Dead Sea Scrolls*, published by Hodder Headline Australia in 1997. In this book, the authors say that this scroll must have been written shortly after 63 BC, which was when the Romans arrived and began their invasion of Israel. They support this dating from palaeographic analysis, carbon-14 dating, and the content of the scroll. The scroll is essentially a lament about the depredations of the Kittim, which most scholars agree is an oblique or coded reference to the Romans. There are also oblique references to the Teacher of Righteousness ('the righteous man') and to the Wicked Priest ('the wicked man'). The word *pesher* means 'the process of the interpretation of dreams', and in this scroll, this process is used in interpreting the prophecy of Habakkuk, which was made in the sixth century BC, and applying it to the present situation of the invasion by the Romans. The obliqueness of the references is itself a form of code.

The first rule of interpretation of any document is 'plain words, plain meaning'. But people do use code in some types of communications. For example, the military uses coded communications to prevent an enemy from knowing their secrets if the enemy intercepts the communication. Poets use allegories, metaphors, and arcane references, usually for aesthetic reasons. Nostradamus used cryptic references to protect himself from being declared in league with the devil. This scroll demonstrates that even in ancient times, the Jews were well aware of the prudence of using code in some communications.

Thiering argues that the Gospels are written in code. Presumably, the teachings of Jesus are in plain language, but what he did—i.e. his actions, miracles, etc.—is essentially a story of his political struggles to be both the spiritual and temporal head of the Jewish people. She then uses the pesher technique to decode the Gospels using the information mainly from what she calls the Temple Scroll as the key to unlock the code.

Thiering's interpretation of the Gospels contradicts fundamental dogmas of the Catholic Church and most other Christian denominations. Her book is the most appropriate source of her interpretations, and while it is not our purpose to consider them in detail, her most startling interpretations can be outlined as follows:

(a) Jesus was not conceived by God. Joseph fathered Jesus out of wedlock.
(b) Jesus worked no miracles. He did not turn the water into wine at Cana, he did not walk on water, and he did not raise anyone from the dead.
(c) Jesus did not die on the cross. The drink he was given on the cross was a poison which made him appear to be dead, and he was given an antidote while in the tomb. The crucifixion took place at Qumran, not in Jerusalem.
(d) Jesus married Mary Magdalene and had two sons by her. He lived until he was well over seventy and was the de facto author of John's Gospel.

To illustrate how Thiering's interpretation works, we can consider the first interpretation (a) above. She presents this interpretation in Chapter 8 of her book. Briefly, she says that *virgin* was the word for a type of nun. If a virgin became pregnant, then it could be said that a virgin had conceived. Joseph, according to his genealogy in the Gospels, was a descendant of King David, making him the king of the Jews and an Essene. The priests and Levites of the Essene sect believed themselves to be and were regarded in their sect as incarnations of gods and angels, while lower priests, kings, and princes were regarded as spirits. Mary was a virgin. Where the Gospel says that she 'conceived of the holy spirit', it means that Joseph made her pregnant. And where the Gospel says that Joseph had a dream in which an angel advised him to proceed with the marriage to Mary, it means that Joseph discussed the matter with a Levite, who advised him to proceed with the marriage. Accordingly, Jesus was not conceived by God; he is not the Son of God, and therefore, he is not divine.

The above example illustrates the process Thiering applied. In other interpretations, she used archaeological data and literary references to decode the Gospels, in addition to the pesher technique. The question for us is, how do we assess the likelihood that her interpretations are true and correct? To do this, we must identify and explore some of the questions that may reasonably be asked about her interpretations.

3.3.6.6 Obstacles to Thiering's Interpretation

The first question is 'What evidence is there to support her interpretations?' Evidence is essential for each individual interpretation, so let us consider the virgin birth interpretation, as outlined above. The interpretation asserts that Mary was a virgin, i.e. a type of nun. We have no evidence of this. It also asserts that Joseph was an Essene. We have no evidence of this. It also asserts that Joseph was either the king of the Jews or the prince-heir to this title. The Gospels give us the lineage of Joseph back to King

David. This is a lineage and not a chain of inheritance, because it does not tell us that each of Joseph's ancestors was the firstborn of his respective generation or otherwise entitled to the kingship of David. His lineage does not evidence the royalty of Joseph, and there is no other evidence. In passing, it may be noted that the lineage given in the Gospels specifically says that each of Joseph's ancestors 'fathered' or 'begat' their respective sons, but in relation to Joseph, it does not say that Joseph fathered Jesus. Rather, it says that Joseph married Mary, who 'bore' Jesus. This can be read as a specific denial that Joseph fathered Jesus, but it may also be an instance of the theological bias of the translators. That the hierarchy of the Essene sect were considered by sect members to be gods, angels, and spirits appears to be evidenced in the Temple Scroll, relied on by Thiering. Such a perception suggests that the Essenes were somewhat elitist, to say the least. The sequence of events contained in Thiering's interpretation is clearly mostly supposition based on the Gospels' account of the birth of Jesus, using the pesher technique to reverse-engineer an account of the events. This version of events is clearly possible, but it is unsupported by evidence and may properly be regarded as having little persuasive value and therefore being highly unlikely.

The next question we can explore is whether other experts on the Dead Sea Scrolls agree with Thiering's interpretations. A substantial part of Thiering's interpretations is based on the scrolls' account of the activities of the Teacher of Righteousness and the Wicked Priest. For the writings in the scrolls about these persons to be about the activities of John the Baptist and Jesus, they must necessarily have been written after Jesus began his public ministry. The problem for Thiering is the dating of the scrolls. Most of the experts hold the view that the relevant scrolls were written before the birth of Jesus, and accordingly, they reject the validity of Thiering's interpretations for this reason and also for the lack of supporting evidence. Of course, it is possible that Thiering is correct and all the other experts are wrong, but it would require very persuasive evidence to overturn the view of the majority on the dating from the palaeographic evidence. Thiering's argument on this issue falls well short of being persuasive.

Another question we can consider is why the evangelists would have written the Gospels in this Essene code. Thiering argues that this was done because the majority of the people to whom they preached the Gospels were 'babes in Christ' and would not understand the significance of the Essene sect and of the actions of Jesus, but those people with knowledge of the Essene sect would understand.

This argument is lame at best. It assumes that all the apostles were Essenes and that they all conspired to preach the truth to only those knowledgeable about Essene culture. This truth was essentially that Jesus was not divine. But they were prepared to construct a whole body of lies to deceive non-Essenes into believing that Jesus was divine. There is no evidence that all the apostles were Essenes. And what would be the point of only the Essenes knowing the truth and the rest of the world being deceived? From the scrolls themselves, it is clear that while some of the teachings of Jesus were consistent with Essene teachings, there were some of his teachings that contradicted Essene teachings. Why did the supposedly Essene evangelists not sanitise the teachings of Jesus to be consistent with the Essene teachings? There may be speculative answers to some of these questions, but the incongruities raised make the argument that the Gospels were written on two levels—one for Essenes and one for the babes in Christ—highly unlikely. In passing, it is worth noting that despite the difficulties of translation, the texts of the Gospels have been dealt with on the 'plain words, plain meaning' basis for the past nearly two thousand years, and no one has slipped up and let the cat out of the bag, as it were, neither accidentally nor deliberately revealing the secret meaning of the Gospels to the Essenes.

In the introduction to her book, Thiering says that Christianity does not stand or fall by these as literal events. That assertion is incredibly naive. What her book does is argue that Jesus was not divine, that he worked no miracles, and that he did not die on the cross and resurrect himself. This is the core belief of Catholicism and most other Christian religions. If the churches were to accept Thiering's reinterpretation of the Gospels, they would be admitting that virtually the whole of the New Testament is a lie and that the supposedly immutable dogma of our church is false because it is based on lies. If our church did this, the church would lose all credibility with every Catholic. No one would ever attend Mass again or give any money to the church. It would probably go into worldwide voluntary liquidation. Catholicism cannot survive an acceptance of Thiering's theory, and it is fairly obvious that such acceptance is not going to happen.

Barbara Thiering was a reputable expert in relation to the Dead Sea Scrolls and theology. From the presentation of her interpretation of the Gospels in her television documentary, it appeared that she genuinely believed that her interpretations had merit. The theory was essentially her life's work. When we come across a theory such as hers from a reputable expert, we must take it seriously and consider it at least as thoroughly as in the above outline. We may not agree with her theory, but it is important because it does give us an insight into Essene culture and politics. It is valuable to us because it clearly demonstrates that new archaeological discoveries can enable a totally new and different legitimate interpretation of even settled documents. In these respects, we should be thankful for her contribution.

In our religious lives, we may well come across theological views that are different from official Catholic teachings. If the theory does not contradict Catholic dogma or the source of the theory is not a recognised and reputable expert, then we need only consider it on a superficial level. But if we do respect the source of the theory or views which raise important dogmatic issues, then we should embark on a serious search for truth before forming any views as to the persuasive value of such a theory.

3.3.6.7 Conclusion

The question we have been considering is whether or not Jesus is divine. We started by identifying the shortcomings and the difficulties surrounding the nature of the available evidence. The conclusion that we must come to on this aspect is that we cannot assess the potentially persuasive value of the evidence by applying modern standards of persuasiveness. Nor can we abandon modern standards and apply the standards that were current at the time that the events under consideration occurred. The available evidence is all we have to help us in choosing to believe on an issue in respect to which we must make a choice. Our best option is to consider the evidence by applying a balanced view of the standards which countenance practical realities within modern standards.

The evidence we considered began with a look at some of the least obscure prophecies about the coming Messiah, contained in the Old Testament. These prophecies are real and were certainly made well before the time of Jesus. As with most prophecies, they are couched in obscure and ambiguous language, and their application to subsequent events is a more or less tenuous construct. That does not mean that the prophecies have no evidentiary value, as they may well be true and correct applications to the facts. But it does mean that we cannot regard the considered prophecies as having been conclusively proven. We can believe, but not without caution.

A number of miracles were attributed to Jesus in the Gospels, and our consideration of these dealt with the reliability of the recorded accounts, the miraculous nature of the event, and the probative value of the miracle in relation to the divinity issue under consideration. The consistency of the accounts and their purpose, along with other aspects, were also considered. Belief in a miracle is essentially belief in the unbelievable. Modern technology and the science of illusion may be able to appear to duplicate some of the reported miracles, but that technology and science did not exist at the time Jesus lived. Miracles are seriously reported as facts, not fiction or hyperbole uttered for teaching or other purposes. Again, the evidentiary uncertainties suggest caution in our assessment, but it remains clearly open to us to choose to believe that some or all of them happened essentially the way they were recorded.

The life and teachings of Jesus do not provide any substantial evidence of his divinity. Nevertheless, we can conclude from the evidence that he was a good and holy man who taught the highest of human values and who never did anything wrong. His ministry did not bring him fame, fortune, or political power. Indeed, it brought him only an agonising death after a relatively short life, as he knew it would. His motives for undertaking this ministry are clearly altruistic and, accordingly, strongly support the conclusion that he only said what he believed to be true.

His truthfulness is a key aspect of our consideration of his testimony. Again, there are evidentiary uncertainties as to what he actually said, but even so, it is clear that Jesus claimed to be the Son of God and, accordingly, divine. His actual words, although somewhat obscured by time and language issues, are the best evidence of his divinity. His testimony is corroborated and supported by the other aspects considered—the prophecies, his miracles, and his truthfulness.

Each of these aspects on their own have some persuasive value, but together they make a believable case in support of the divinity of Jesus. Arguably, in this case, the whole is greater than the sum of its parts. Then there is the legacy of Jesus, which, while not direct evidence of his divinity, certainly supports this proposition.

As was stated at the outset, belief in the divinity of Jesus necessarily depends on belief in the existence of God. The effect of belief in the divinity of Jesus is to allow us to choose Christianity as the true religion. We have seen that the evidence for the existence of God is not compelling but is sufficient to enable us to choose to believe in the existence of God. That is a logically valid and available choice on the arguments and evidence considered, and any criticism or disparagement of this choice as unreasonable or ignorant is sheer humbug. Equally, we cannot criticise or disparage the choice to not believe in the existence of God, despite our emotional attachment to our own choice.

The same applies for choice as to the divinity of Jesus. The evidence, necessarily, cannot be compelling, but as has hopefully been considered, there is a strong case in support of this belief which justifies the choice to believe it. Any criticism of our choice to believe can be summarily dismissed, just as our criticism of the choice to not believe in the divinity of Jesus can be summarily dismissed.

Belief in the divinity of Jesus is really an all-or-nothing choice. Some people believe that Jesus was a good and holy man or even a great prophet, but they reject the proposition that he is divine. From the evidence of his testimony, it is clear that Jesus claimed to be divine. If we accept that Jesus did really make this claim, then the only conclusion that can be drawn by non-believers in his divinity is that Jesus was wrong when he claimed to be divine. He could only be wrong if he was deliberately lying or was honestly mistaken. We have examined the evidence of his life, and it is virtually unarguable that Jesus was an honest man who told no lies.

For Jesus to have been honestly mistaken about his divinity, it is necessary to conclude that Jesus was insane, for it is inconceivable that a sane person could believe that he or she is divine. Normal, sane human beings cannot do all those supernatural things attributed to Jesus in the Gospels which gave him sound reasons to believe in his own divinity. There is simply no evidence anywhere that he was in any way insane, and accordingly, any view that he was a great prophet but not divine is simply untenable.

The prophecies, miracles, teachings, and testimony of Jesus considered in this work are not exhaustive of materials relevant to this issue, many other pieces of evidence being discoverable in the Gospels. However, enough has been raised for consideration to fully justify the choice to believe in the divinity of Jesus. Our theologians teach us that we have the gift of faith. Another way of looking at it is that our faith, the church and all it does for us, is the gift we receive when we choose to believe.

PART 4

THE CATHOLIC CHURCH

4.1 The Nature of the Church

The *Shorter Oxford English Dictionary*, third edition, gives several meanings of the word *church*, which are as follows:

I. *A building for public Christian worship. Applied to public places of worship of any religion as Mohammedan mosque etc.*

II. *The Christian community collectively; a particular organized Christian society, separated by peculiarities of doctrine, worship or organization, or confined to limits territorial or historical; the ecclesiastical organization of Christianity or of a great Christian society: esp. the clergy etc. of this society as a corporation having continuous existence and as an estate of the realm.*

III. *A congregation of Christians locally organized.*

The above definitions are so general that it is difficult to know the intended meaning when one speaks of 'the church', unless the intended meaning is specified, which is not usual. For the purposes of this work, it is appropriate to specify the intended meaning. The church referred to herein is the Catholic Church. The fundamental meaning of the church in this work is that it is a corporation.

To support this meaning, it may be helpful to apply the parameters of a body corporate to our church's attributes. A large multinational corporation usually has a chief executive officer, a board of directors, senior executives, middle management, and workers. The pope is our chief executive officer. The Curia is the board of directors. Cardinals and bishops are our senior executives. Monsignors are our middle management, and ordinary priests are the workers. Our church is indeed large and multinational. In fact, it has a presence in every country of the world, and accordingly, it can fairly be described as catholic, which means 'universal'.

Corporations are usually owned by shareholders. Our church was founded by Jesus and belongs entirely to him. Shares in a corporation are heritable, and thus, corporations can exist across multiple generations. Since Jesus is the only shareholder and is eternal, our church can and has existed across the generations since its founding. We humans are not shareholders in our church, but we are stakeholders, which is a different thing. The clergy and religious are high-level stakeholders because they have devoted their lives to the service of the church. We, the Catholic laity, are the clients of the corporation and, as such, are also stakeholders to this extent.

Corporations usually have a constitution and rules which govern the structure and operations of the corporation. Our church has this attribute, as it is embodied in the canon law.

Corporations usually own property in the nature of premises, plant and equipment, money, and the stock in which it trades, whether it is manufactured by it or purchased. Our church also owns property. Our church's buildings, also usually simply called churches, are facilities which usually have a presbytery attached. The plant and equipment are the church pews, altars, decorations, et cetera. Our church is said to be the wealthiest non-government organisation in the world, so it clearly has money. Of course, our church does not trade in any material stock, but rather in education, counselling, services, and rituals. The clergy does not own this property. It belongs to the corporate entity that is our church. Our priests are the custodians and guardians of church property, with all the legal entitlements, responsibilities, and authority of such status, just as the employees of a corporation do not own the corporation's property but are custodians and guardians of it. We, the laity, have no rights or responsibilities for church properties and assets, even though as parishioners, we may have paid for or donated such property to the church.

Legally, a corporation is merely a conceptual entity, and as such, it cannot have any moral responsibility. However, a corporation can be fined for unlawful acts committed by its servants or agents in the course of their employment, and in some jurisdictions, they can even have punitive damages awarded against them for the negligence of its servants or agents. Our church is all about exhorting its clients (us) and potential clients to behave according to the highest standard of morality. But that does not mean that servants or agents of the church cannot do anything unlawful or immoral in the course of their duties. The accountability of the clergy will be considered later in this work. For the present, the point is that it is wrong to criticise or blame the church generally for the wrongdoing of its servants or agents. Any criticism or blame should be directed at the servants or agents concerned.

Some Catholic theologians have proposed that the church is the 'mystical body of Jesus Christ'. It follows from this that everyone who is baptised into the Catholic faith is a part of the church. Jesus said, *'I am the vine, you are the branches'* (John 15:5). Whether he was referring to the church is uncertain. No doubt there is a mystical body, but its mystical and theological nature obscures our understanding of it and adds nothing to our conceptual understanding of the nature of the church.

Another concept that has been raised to argue that we, the laity, are all part of the church is the Apostolate of the Laity. Briefly, this concept holds the laity responsible for the evangelisation of Catholicism through leading lives of good example. Naturally, any disciple of Jesus will live in accordance with the teachings of Jesus. Unless such disciple is ashamed of his faith or fearful of the consequences of being recognised as a disciple of Jesus, there is no reason to be secretive or furtive about how we live our lives. Jesus had twelve apostles whose successors are now our clergy. He also had numerous disciples whose successors are us, the laity. Perhaps the word *discipleship* is more appropriate than the word *apostolate*. Accordingly, this concept does not change our status as clients and stakeholders in our church.

The references to the clergy herein are intended to mean the hierarchical structure of the priesthood, from the pope to ordinary ordained priests. There are a number of quasi-clerical organisations, such as brothers and nuns, and lay religious groups, such as the Society of St Vincent De Paul, and some Catholic social groups. These, for the purposes of this work, are included amongst the laity.

4.2 The Authenticity of the Catholic Church

4.2.1 Overview

The question to be considered here is whether or not the modern Catholic Church remains the church that Jesus founded and that he said would last until the end of the world. The need to consider this issue arises from the fact that there are many churches in modern times, and all of them claim to be the 'true' church. There are, of course, non-Christian religions that have churches. However, having accepted the divinity of Jesus as truth, our concern is with the competing claims of the various Christian churches that split from the Catholic Church. There are several criteria which assist in our consideration of this question, and fortunately, there is sufficient biblical and historical evidence to enable a determination. These criteria are as follows.

4.2.2 Foundation

It has already been argued that Jesus clearly intended to found a church. This was argued on the basis of Peter's profession of faith, which was quoted earlier and recorded in Matthew 16:13–23, Mark 8:27–33, and Luke 9:18–22. So the words of Jesus clearly evidence his intentions. We can now consider what action Jesus took to implement his intentions.

We know that Jesus spent much time with his apostles and that he had many conversations with them that are not recorded. Some of these conversations were clearly instructional, because the Gospels tell us that in some of these unrecorded conversations, Jesus 'taught them many things'. They also called him rabbi, which means 'teacher'. And there are a number of instances in the Gospels where Jesus explains the meaning of a parable to them and that explanation is recorded.

Having equipped the apostles to teach his message, he then sent them out to do such teaching. Perhaps this was to give them some practical experience of teaching, but it was nevertheless bringing his message to real people and thereby spreading the Word. This can be seen from Jesus sending out the twelve, recorded in Mark 6:6–13 and Luke 9:1–6. Luke 10:1–16 also records the sending out of the seventy, so clearly Jesus instructed more than just the apostles in the work of evangelisation.

The return of the twelve is recorded in Mark 6:30–44 and Luke 9:10–17. The return of the seventy is recorded in Luke 10:17–20. How they performed their task is briefly recorded. Perhaps this is recorded to remind the apostles and disciples of their accountability to Jesus of how they performed the missions. In any event, the record shows that they were successful, which qualified them for more such work.

The most significant evidence of Jesus founding his church is recorded in Matthew 28:19–20, where Jesus, immediately prior to his ascension, commissioned the apostles to

go, therefore, make disciples of all nations; baptize them in the name of the Father and of the Son and of the Holy Spirit, and teach them to observe all the commands I gave you. And look, I am with you always; yes, to the end of time.

The accountability of the Catholic clergy to Jesus for their performance of their mission will come on the last day, when Jesus returns to this world (see Matthew 24:29–31).

4.2.3 Church Identity

The modern Catholic Church has a large repertoire of dogma, doctrine, canon law, liturgy, theology, and policy—far larger, in fact, than all that was taught by Jesus in his lifetime. This raises the question of whether Jesus intended to found a church that has evolved into what it is today. To answer this question, we need to consider two issues. Firstly, we can consider the scope of the beliefs of Jesus. Secondly, we can consider the justification for the evolution of a church in relation to cultural and technological developments.

In relation to this first consideration, we know with certainty that Jesus was a Jew. Indeed, he was a rabbi of the Jewish faith. He celebrated the traditional Jewish feast days and generally observed Jewish customs and traditions. There are a number of incidents recorded in the Gospels which evidence his adherence to the Jewish faith, which warrant mention.

(i)   At his baptism by John the Baptist, a voice from heaven was heard saying:

This is my Son, the Beloved; my favor rests on him.

This voice was believed to be the voice of Yahweh (the Jewish name of God) or God the Father in Catholic nomenclature (Matthew 3:16–17).

(ii) At the transfiguration, Jesus spoke to the prophets of the Jewish faith, as set out in Mark 9:1–8.

(iii) Jesus endorsed and explained the Ten Commandments, which are the essence of the Jewish faith. Much of this is set out in Matthew 19:16–22.

(iv) Jesus often spoke of 'my Father who is in heaven' or 'the One who sent me'. Clearly, he was referring to Yahweh, God the Father.

(v) Jesus was born of a Jewish mother and brought up in the Jewish faith. At age twelve, he impressed the temple scholars with the depth of his knowledge of Judaism (Luke 2:46–50).

(vi) We do not know what Jesus did between this incident at age twelve and when he began his public ministry, but it is clear from his many quotes from Jewish scripture that he had a thorough knowledge of Jewish scripture.

Jesus himself said that he had not come to abolish the law but to fulfil it (Matthew 5:17–20). What he actually did as the Messiah was reveal to the Jews how Yahweh wanted them to live. In this process, he identified and declared the basic principles underlying the Jewish religious laws, i.e. love of God and of each other. He endorsed the substantial Jewish laws and scriptures, but he dismissed some minor laws, particularly the ancient Jewish dietary laws. He said,

What goes into the mouth, does not make one unclean; it is what comes out of the mouth that makes someone unclean

(Matthew 15:10–11).

Naturally, the Jewish religious hierarchy challenged his authority to do this, because they did not accept that he was the Messiah. However, the point is that Jesus was fundamentally supporting mainstream Jewish faith.

The clearest indication of what Jesus intended his church to be comes from Jesus himself, where he said,

I am the Way; I am Truth and Life

(John 14:6).

Jesus spoke in Aramaic, and his followers and disciples were known as Wayists. That is a translation, but clearly there was an equivalent Aramaic and Greek word that means this. The way that Jesus was referring to is the way through the proliferation and complexity of Jewish law by following the fundamental principle of love of God and of one another.

From this, it becomes clear that Jesus did not intend to found a new church separate and distinct from Judaism, but rather to put Judaism into the next phase of its evolution, which begins with the coming of the Messiah—i.e. himself. On this view, we Catholics can authentically claim the Old Testament as our religious heritage through the teachings of Jesus.

4.2.4 Succession

To consider the aspect of succession on the issue of authenticity of the church, it may be helpful to identify the concepts of our consideration. The first concept is the nature of what is being passed on to successors.

4.2.4.1 The First Clerics

At Pentecost, a ragtag group of middle-class men were appointed as the first clerics of the Catholic Church by the supernatural appearance of tongues of fire coming to rest on each of their heads (Acts Chapter 2). They immediately went out and preached to a large number of people in different languages. The task given to them by Jesus was evangelisation and pastoral care, so they soon organised themselves and set out in different directions to perform their task.

The apostles travelled mainly from towns and cities to other towns and cities, preaching to those who would listen. They converted many and established communities to perpetuate the teachings of Jesus. They appointed presbyters (elders) to conduct the new liturgy in accordance with their teachings and then moved on to the next town or city. Initially, the presbyters were volunteers who performed these duties in addition to their normal occupation. However, this system eventually evolved to give the presbyters the necessary authority in a ceremony involving the laying on of hands. Also, as the number of such communities in a region increased, they started to communicate with one another. Differences and disputes inevitably arose, which led to the necessity of having a superintendent (bishop) of the entire region, usually the chief presbyter in the capital city of the region.

Thus, in the formative years, what was being passed on to the successors were the duties and responsibilities of clerical office. Initially, such duties were undertaken out of love and faith, with no financial reward. But in later times, when the office became lucrative, there was corruption, simony, and apostasy. Also developing were the ways in which persons were selected and appointed to such offices. The concept then is that clerical office is not something that can be passed on by inheritance or devised in a will, although throughout the 2,000-year history of the church there have been a number of instances of nepotism.

The second concept which is relevant is that this development of the clergy occurred against a background of persecutions, during which many Catholics were martyred. Accordingly, at least in the early years, most of the liturgy was conducted furtively, and there were no church buildings, with the liturgy being conducted in the homes of members of the community.

The next relevant concept is the recognition of the clergy as separate and distinct from the laity. Initially, it was the laity who undertook the function of pastoral care on a voluntary basis. By about the middle of the second century AD, it was perceived by those communities that there was a need for someone to represent Jesus in the liturgy of the Eucharist, who should also have authority to ordain others. These communities also needed a leader and spokesman who was authorised to communicate with other church communities, attend meetings representing his community, and be an arbiter of theological disputes internal to the community, on the basis of his knowledge and upholding of traditional teachings.

With these concepts in mind, we can now consider the life of Peter the Apostle, because the modern Catholic Church has a hierarchical structure in which our pope is the supreme cleric of the entire Catholic Church.

Jesus necessarily gave the apostles sufficient authority to perform their mission. Their mission is perpetual and, consequently, needs to be continued by the successors of the apostles, who accordingly inherit the necessary authority. The nature and extent of that authority will be considered elsewhere in this work. For the purposes of considering the authenticity of the Catholic Church, if we can trace a line of legitimate successors of the apostles, then we have sound reason to believe that the Catholic Church today is the authentic church founded by Jesus.

The line of succession begins with the apostles. To trace the succession of every apostle and the succession of every legitimate appointee of each of those apostles is a mammoth task well beyond the scope of this work. However, our modern church has a leader or chief whom we call our pope, and all modern lay Catholics and clergy acknowledge him as such. Thus, if we can trace his line of succession, then the legitimacy and authenticity of all who acknowledge him as such follows.

Jesus, in saying that Peter was the rock on which he would build his church, undoubtedly was conferring pre-eminence on Peter, and we can regard him as the 'first amongst equals'. After Jesus died, Peter preached in Jerusalem and Antioch for several years and eventually went to Rome because it was the seat of the empire and, accordingly, the best place from which to manage the 'teaching of all nations', which was the church's mission. Peter became the bishop of Rome and performed this function until he was martyred by the Roman authorities.

By the time Peter died, the position of the bishop of Rome had acquired de facto pre-eminence amongst the apostles and other communities of converts, mostly due to Peter's personal pre-eminence and the politically central position of Rome. Some scholars believe that Peter favoured Linus as his successor. In any event, Linus was elected as the bishop of Rome by the Catholic congregation of Rome at that time. Since that time, there has been substantial continuity in the position of bishop of Rome, and there are several excellent historical works that detail the line of succession from Linus to our present pope. However, there are four events that warrant further consideration. The first is the formal acquiring of pre-eminence. The second is the split with the Orthodox Church. The third is the Great Schism, and the fourth is the Reformation.

4.2.4.2 The Pre-Eminence of Rome

The de facto traditional pre-eminence of the bishop of Rome was expounded in writing by Irenaeus, the bishop of Lyon, in Gaul in about AD 185. This was accepted by most Catholics on the basis that the bishop of Rome was the successor of Peter and Paul, which guaranteed doctrinal fidelity to the teachings of Jesus. Of course, the bishops of other regions were also successors of the other apostles, with equal guarantees of doctrinal fidelity, and the bishops did communicate with one another. Having regard to the pre-eminence bestowed on Peter by Jesus, as recorded in the Gospels, the other bishops tended to follow the lead of the bishop of Rome and thus essentially taught with one voice.

Shortly before his death in AD 311, the Roman emperor Galerius issued an Edict of Toleration. After his death, Constantine, the son of the co-emperor Constantius Chlorus of Britain, crossed the Alps, intent on seizing the empire for himself. His rival was Maxentius, and they met near Rome in AD 312, with Maxentius having a clearly superior military force. The history is uncertain, but apparently, before the battle, Constantine had some type of dream or vision which informed him that he could win the battle in the name of Jesus. He then instructed his forces to mark their shields with the sign of the cross or the monogram of Jesus and then engaged in battle, which he won. Thereafter, Constantine favoured the Christian faith, bringing his children up in this faith, although he was not baptised until shortly before his death in AD 337.

The relevance of this to our present concern is that in order to settle an internal theological dispute raised by Arius, a presbyter in Alexandria, Constantine convened the Council of Nicaea in AD 325 and actively participated in the debates, although he had not yet been baptised. He had actually moved the seat of the empire from Rome to Byzantium (later called Constantinople) in AD 324. The council did not finally resolve the Arius issue, but of relevance here is that the fourth canon of the Council of Nicaea officially recognised the primacy of Rome, the translation of which is 'The church in Rome always holds primacy'. Not long after, St Augustine said, 'Rome has spoken, the case is settled.'

After Constantine inaugurated Constantinople, there was naturally a bishop of Constantinople, and there developed a rivalry between the bishop of Rome and the bishop of Constantinople. Rome was still pre-eminent, but the bishop of Constantinople, supported by the emperor, could clearly diminish Rome's pre-eminence, especially since Constantine was actively involved in religious affairs. This rivalry finally led to the Council of Chalcedon, which, in October AD 451, declared that the bishop of Constantinople had equal authority to the bishop of Rome.

Both Rome, which is now referred to as Western Christianity, and Constantinople, now referred to as Eastern Christianity, believed that they were orthodox in the sense that they held sound or good theology. The successors of the Eastern Orthodox Church have retained their self-proclaimed designation as orthodox, whereas the West has become the Roman Catholic Church, as *catholic* means 'universal'. However, over the ensuing millennium, theological differences emerged. The most obvious of these is the orthodox devotion to icons. The devotion to icons is, of course, part of Orthodox liturgy. But as form follows function in most human constructs, so liturgy follows theology. The theology of reverence of icons appears to have started during the reign of the emperor Justinian in the latter part of the sixth century AD and has survived to the present day despite substantial opposition over the years. In 1054, Rome excommunicated Constantinople.

Then in 1453, the Ottoman Turks conquered Constantinople, and the church eventually retreated to Greece and Cyprus. Also, both Boris, the king of Bulgaria, and Vladimir, the Grand Prince of Kiev and Russia, had earlier been converted, and thus, these areas also offered sanctuary. Eventually, Moscow saw itself as the third Rome both politically and religiously, because the first Rome had fallen to the barbarians and the Roman Catholic heresy, and Constantinople, the second Rome, had fallen to the Muslims.

The point of the above superficial excursion into history is to recognise the authenticity of the modern Orthodox churches as successors of the apostles, possibly even Peter. The modern differences in liturgy and theology are, in the final analysis, only the comprehension of humans of the implications of biblical texts and, for the most part, are beyond human comprehension.

4.2.4.3 The Great Schism

The next aspect for consideration as to the authenticity of the Catholic Church line of succession from Peter to our present pope is what is known as the Great Schism. Briefly, the facts of the matter are as follows:

Pope Gregory XI died in 1378, and the people of Rome wanted an Italian pope for financial reasons. Thus, in April 1378, sixteen cardinals elected Urban VI (Bartolomeo Prignano) as pope. His personality changed dramatically after election, and he became an intolerable tyrant. Thirteen cardinals fled to Fondi, where they declared Urban's election invalid and elected Clement VII (Robert of Geneva). Both popes received political support from various countries. Clement VII moved his seat to Avignon.

Urban VI declared a crusade against Clement VII, who responded with military force. Both had a Council of Cardinals. The war was expensive for both, which lead to extreme papal taxes and simony. Urban VI returned to Rome from the war, which remained undecided, in 1389 and died there in that year. His cardinals then elected Boniface IX (Pietro Tomacelli), but there were still two popes.

The people wanted Clement VII to resign, but he did not and died in 1394. Benedict XIII was elected as his successor by the Avignon cardinals. He had sworn to resign if elected, but he did not. France rebelled, but after about five years, it returned to his obedience.

In 1406, the Roman cardinals elected Gregory XII (Angelo Correr) after the death of Boniface IX. He swore to resign if Benedict XIII did the same. Both popes agreed to meet at a neutral place to jointly resign, and they even set out for this place; however, mutual distrust lead to manoeuvres that prevented any such meeting. The people wanted a resolution, so on 25 March 1409, a body of churchmen met at Pisa and deposed both popes and elected a new pope, Alexander V (Petros Philargos). There were now three popes, each of whom had substantial support within the church.

Alexander V died on 3 May 1410. His successor, John XXIII (Baldassare Cossa), arrived in Rome in 1411. Then the Holy Roman Emperor, Sigismund of Luxembourg, prevailed on John XXIII to convene a church council at Constance on 1 November 1414. On 1 March 1415, John XXIII declared that he would resign when the other two did, but he, with an entourage, fled to the Duke of Austria. On 6 April 1415, the council declared its superiority over the pope. John XXIII was abandoned by the Duke of Austria, captured, taken back to Constance, tried, and deposed. Gregory XII formally convoked the council to endorse its legitimacy and voluntarily resigned. The Avignon pope, Benedict XIII, refused to resign and fled to the fortress of Pensacola in Spain with a few of his cardinals. He eventually died, and the fiasco of his papacy

372 • Peter Mazurek

ended when his last remaining cardinal elected himself pope. The council tried him in absentia and deposed him.

On 9 October 1417, the council passed the decree of Frequens, which required the pope to call regular council meetings. On 11 November 1417, they elected Martin V (Oddo Colonna), and the Great Schism was over.

From the above outline, it is clear that this turmoil in the papal succession was an anomaly in the political history of the church. The line of succession was restored in Martin V, and there is now no church claiming legitimacy through the line of succession of any of the pretenders. Accordingly, we can rely on the line of succession of the popes to support the authenticity of our church as founded by Jesus.

4.2.4.4 The Reformation

The next aspect of this issue that warrants consideration is the Reformation. This is an extensive topic which cannot be briefly recounted. There are many excellent books that deal with just this topic. For our purposes of considering the authenticity of our church, all that is required is an overview of what happened and why. The issue we should consider is whether any of the Christian churches formed during the Reformation have any legitimate claim to being the authentic church founded by Jesus. A brief outline of the main churches formed during this period is as follows.

4.2.4.4.1 The Lutheran Church

This church was founded by Martin Luther in Wittenberg, Germany. As a consequence of a personal religious experience, Luther became a Catholic priest and became assigned to the chair of biblical studies at Wittenberg University. He was intelligent and thoughtful, and his religious insights led to the development of his theology that man is saved by faith alone. This contrasted sharply with the orthodox Catholic theology that salvation requires both faith and good works. For Luther, *faith* means faith in Jesus, and accordingly, the Gospels are the sole authority enabling this faith. As a consequence, any action by the church adding to or modifying the message of the Gospels is unauthorised and insignificant, although a church remains necessary to evangelise and interpret the Gospels.

The stimulus for Luther acting in accordance with his theology was the sale of indulgences. This practice was introduced during the Crusades as a means to fund those crusades and later as a preferred source of revenue for the church. Luther saw this practice as not authorised by scripture, and he criticised it in his sermons. In his capacity as the chair of biblical studies, he drew up ninety-five propositions or theses in a document, which he fixed to the door of the castle church on 31 October 1517. This was the conventional way of calling for a debate on such issues in that time and place. The propositions included a theological discrediting of the validity of indulgences, amongst other aspects of his theology. This action is now regarded as the action that started the Reformation.

Naturally, the church hierarchy rejected and opposed Luther's views. In 1519, Luther debated his views with Johann Eck at Leipzig in an eighteen-day debate. After this, Eck acted to have Luther declared a heretic. Luther responded by publishing three pamphlets for distribution amongst the German people, advocating reform in the church and creating a national German church. In June 1520, Pope Leo X issued a bull condemning Luther and giving him sixty days to recant. Luther burned the bull and was excommunicated. The emperor Charles V supported the pope and would have arrested and executed Luther, but Luther sought refuge with the prince of Saxony (Duke Frederick the Wise) and obtained sanctuary in Wartburg Castle, where he stayed for about one year. While there, he translated the New Testament into German.

In any event, and possibly partly due to Luther's pamphlets, the need for reform of the church became apparent to the German people and their leaders, and the reform movement gained substantial momentum, with some proposed reforms being far more radical than anything Luther had proposed.

In 1522, Luther returned to Wittenberg, where he put into effect the reforms appropriate to his theology. He abolished the office of bishop and abandoned the rule of clerical celibacy. He married in 1525. He revised the church's Latin liturgy and translated it into German. Politically, he supported the princes rather than the peasants. In 1530, Luther was still an outlaw, so the leadership of his reformed church passed to Philipp Melanchthon, who could take the new church to places where Luther could not go. Luther died in 1546, aged sixty-three, but by then there was a powerful group of German princes who had converted to his theology, who could and did ensure the survival of Lutheranism.

No doubt Luther regarded himself as a Catholic throughout his life, but a Catholic who had his own beliefs about how to achieve salvation. His beliefs allowed him to reject the authority of the pope, the hierarchical structure of the clergy, and the canon law, to the extent that it amended scripture. But he was excommunicated. Does that mean that anyone who believes as Luther did is also automatically excommunicated? Certainly, in relation to the issue of the sale of indulgences, the church had fallen into error, and Luther was justified in his criticism. But his theology on indulgences is flawed, and his theology on how to achieve salvation was and still is heretical to orthodox Catholicism. This begs the question of whether our faith is about what we believe or about how we live. As a Christian religion, it may be viewed as Lutheran Catholicism, just as orthodox Catholicism is generally referred to as Roman Catholicism. In any event, it is clear that Luther never intended to found a church separate and distinct from his Catholic faith but rather to implement a reform of Catholicism which was a new way of Catholicism, just as Jesus implemented a new reformed way of Judaism.

4.2.4.4.2 The Anabaptists

One of the things that Luther taught was that common people have the right to read the Bible for themselves. By the early sixteenth century, the printing press had been invented, enabling relatively widespread dissemination of Luther's teachings. It was also a time when the governance of the people came from a compound of church and state authorities.

The church, ever mindful of its duty to evangelise, had cultivated the tradition of baptising infants, thereby delegating some of the responsibility to evangelise the next generations to the parents, who were required to bring up their children as Catholics. Thus, everyone born into what was then the Christian world was immediately a Catholic, and church and state had an identical constituency.

In Zürich, Conrad Grebel and Felix Manz read the Bible and started holding Bible classes. They saw no fusion of church and state in New Testament times. They saw no infant baptism in the New Testament. They saw the original church as a fellowship of true believers, with baptism as adults being their profession of true belief. Infant baptism was, to them, invalid because the infant did not have the capacity to make a profession of belief. They wanted to return to apostolic Christianity.

In late 1524, Grebel's wife gave birth to a son, and the Grebels refused to baptise their son. Other couples followed this example. The city council arranged and conducted a public debate on this issue on 17 January 1525. The outcome of the debate was that the majority of the people supported the view that infants should be baptised. Accordingly, the city council required all parents who had not had their children baptised to have them baptised within a week or face banishment from Zürich.

Four days later, on 21 January 1525, the city council ordered Grebel and Manz to stop holding Bible classes. That night, at a prayer meeting in Manz's house, Grebel baptised George Blaurock, a former priest, who then baptised the others at the meeting. Essentially, this was a rebaptising, which is what the word *anabaptist* means, but which was attributed to them as a pejorative label.

Still refusing to baptise their children, Grebel and his like-minded companions moved to a nearby village called Zollikon, where they formed the first Anabaptist congregation, which had no ties with the state. The Zürich City Council arrested and imprisoned some of them for a time, but this did not deter them. On 7 March 1526, the city council ordered that anyone found rebaptising was to be put to death by drowning. On 5 January 1527, Manz was drowned in the Limmat River pursuant to this order.

The people who had converted to Anabaptism fled to Germany and Austria, but the Imperial Diet of Speyer proclaimed Anabaptism to be a heresy and required all such heretics to be put to death. During the Reformation years, between four thousand and five thousand Anabaptists were killed pursuant to this proclamation.

The Anabaptists dispersed. In the Tyrol region of the Swiss Alps, they were ministered to by Blaurock, who was there burned at the stake on 6 September 1529. In Moravia, they were ministered to by Jakob Hutter, who died in 1536. His modern disciples are known as Hutterites. In the lower Rhine area near Münster, Menno Simons ministered to them. In modern times, most orthodox Anabaptists are known as Mennonites.

The theology of Anabaptism quickly developed and was documented as early as 1527 at the Anabaptist synod in Schleitheim. This document is now known as the Schleitheim Confession. Briefly, the main tenants are as follows:

1. True Christianity requires daily adherence to the teachings of Jesus and a lifestyle based on his example.
2. The principal teaching of Jesus was love of God and of one another. This requires strict pacifism and communal sharing of wealth.
3. The personal confession of true belief meant that Anabaptists could have no ecclesiastical superiors or hierarchy, so moral issues were decided by consensus of the community, which extended to the significant affairs of the community.
4. True acceptance of God can only come from a free and informed choice by an individual, and the state exceeds its authority when it seeks to champion the Word of God with a fist. Hence, there must be a separation of church and state.

From the above brief historical outline, it appears that the Anabaptists were persecuted just as the Christians were persecuted in Roman times. But the Romans persecuted the Christians for clearly secular political reasons, while the Anabaptists were persecuted for principally ecclesiastical political reasons. It was the state that executed the Anabaptists, on the justification that they were religious heretics. It is difficult in modern times to believe that the entirety of the state hierarchy in those times was so fanatically Catholic that they perceived it to be their duty to execute heretics. A more pragmatic explanation is that the state saw in Anabaptism the germ of civil disobedience and recognised the destructive effect this could have on their power base. Accordingly, they were willing to be heavy-handed in crushing this movement.

If they did not act out of religious fervour, then the so-called heresy was merely an excuse for murder. Historians do not blame the ecclesiastical authorities at that time for these murders, but there was clearly persecution of the Anabaptists by the Catholic Church authorities. We cannot say that the Catholic Church instigated all four thousand or more murders, but we can say that allowing or tolerating the state to commit these murders without objection is a clear breach by the entire Catholic clergy of the teachings of Jesus and is one of the most shameful episodes in church history.

For the purposes of the authenticity issue that we are considering, we can see from the Schleitheim Confession that their beliefs were not contrary to New Testament teachings. They were contrary to church teachings at that time, but not to what is now regarded as church dogma. The Anabaptists did not declare themselves right in their understanding of the Bible and did not accordingly excommunicate the rest of the 'wicked world' as heretics. They merely lived their lives in accordance with their perceptions and beliefs. In a way, this is claiming to be the true faith, but the Anabaptists cannot and do not claim any legitimacy from any line of succession traced back to the apostles, although they do claim to practise the Catholic faith as it was in apostolic times.

4.2.4.4.3 Calvinism

John Calvin was born in a small town north of Paris in 1509. He attended Paris University, where he obtained his Master of Arts degree in 1528. He did further studies in law at the University of Orléans and the University of Bruges but returned to Paris in 1531 after his father died. Back in Paris University, he became aware of the Protestant movement and theology, and he had some sort of religious experience which led him to a career path in service of the Protestant cause. He clearly had a brilliant mind. After an incident at the university, he fled to Basel, where he wrote and published his work entitled *Institutes of the Christian Religion* in March 1536. This was an exceptionally clear and lucid explanation of Protestant theology, which gained him immediate recognition as a leader of the Protestant movement.

Zwingli had been proselytising the Protestant cause in Zürich and the surrounding Swiss cantons, but he was killed in a battle between Protestants and Catholics at Kappel in 1531. By 1536, the practice of Catholicism in Geneva had deteriorated to insignificance due to their rejection of the duke of Savoy and the pope and because of political hostility towards the bishop of Geneva. This soon became a fairly hedonistic community. The city council, knowing that religious observance was more conducive to an orderly and peaceful community, wanted a return to religious observance. With Catholicism in rejection, Protestantism offered an alternative.

In this situation, Calvin entered Geneva on his way to Strasbourg in July 1536. His fame as a Protestant leader had preceded him, and William Farel, who had been preaching in Geneva for several years, sought him out and persuaded him to stay in Geneva and help establish Protestantism there. The city council offered Calvin a position as professor of Sacred Scripture, which Calvin accepted.

Calvin's theology was essentially similar to Luther and Zwingli. However, he differed from Luther in that the core of his belief was the absolute sovereignty of God rather than Luther's justification by faith. This difference enabled Calvin to subordinate the authority of the state on religious issues, although his concept of minimal clerical hierarchy was similar to Luther's.

In his role as a religious administrator, Calvin drafted a very repressive constitution. Everyone who wanted to be a citizen of Geneva had to make a confession of faith, and those who did not live in accordance with high spiritual standards were to be excommunicated. A dispute arose between Calvin and the city council, who wanted the power to excommunicate via magistrates, whereas Calvin wanted the church to have this power. This dispute forced Calvin to flee Geneva in 1538, but he returned to Geneva in September 1541 and resumed his work there until his death in 1564.

Although Calvin saw his work as the administration of a community which provided a Christian environment to its members and was a sanctuary for persecuted Protestants, the real substance of his work was much broader. In effect, he built a model Protestant community which was visited and studied by persons from many lands who took the example back with them to their own countries. In modern times, those who have adopted many of Calvin's theology and methods include the Dutch and German reformed churches, Baptists, Congregationalists, and Presbyterians. Calvinism thrived in the Netherlands, and Scotland became staunchly Calvinistic largely due to the efforts of John Knox.

On the issue of the authenticity of the Catholic Church through succession, it is clear that Calvin did not intend to form a new church. He merely intended to build a community which lived and held as its values the teachings of the New Testament. He did not challenge the Catholic Church, but he clearly believed that the Catholic Church had fallen into error and corruption. He did not claim any legitimacy of the priests of his community greater than the legitimacy of any other properly ordained priest. In short, neither Calvin nor his modern successors make any claim to greater authenticity than the Catholic Church on the basis of the line of succession of its clergy.

4.2.4.4.4 Anglicanism

Henry VIII (1509–1547) was initially a staunch Catholic. When Luther criticised the seven sacraments in 1521, Henry wrote a scathing criticism of Luther in an article entitled 'Defence of the Seven Sacraments'. For this, the then pope bestowed on Henry the title of Defender of the Faith. In 1509, Henry married Catherine of Aragon, who was the aunt of Charles V, the oly Roman Emperor and king of Spain. She had also been previously married to Arthur, Henry's deceased brother. Marrying a brother's wife was prohibited under church law, but Henry obtained a dispensation from Pope Julius II for this marriage.

After eighteen years of marriage, Henry and Catherine had only one surviving child, who they named Mary. Henry wanted a male heir. He had also become enamoured with another woman, Anne Boleyn. Accordingly, in 1527, Henry asked Pope Clement VII for an annulment of the marriage to Catherine. Clement VII refused, probably because he did not wish to alienate Charles V.

In January 1533, Henry married Anne. In May 1533, an English ecclesiastical court declared the marriage to Catherine null and void. In September 1533, Anne gave birth to Elizabeth. Then the pope excommunicated Henry.

In response to the excommunication, Henry revived an old law forbidding dealings with foreign powers and required the English clergy to observe this law, effectively cutting the English clergy off from the authority of Rome. Also, in 1534, Henry procured the Act of Supremacy, which declared the king to be the supreme head of the Catholic Church in England. Of course, Henry was not an ordained cleric, so while he could, as head of the church, appoint bishops, he could not ordain them. Nor could he make decrees of dogmas of faith. These tasks fell to the Archbishop of Canterbury, who was naturally the king's appointee.

By these actions, Henry had effectively removed the pope from the clerical hierarchy of the Catholic Church in England while retaining fidelity to the doctrines of the Catholic Church and the authenticity of the English clergy through succession from legitimately ordained clergy.

Inevitably, the doctrines of the Roman Catholic Church and the Catholic Church in England diverged. Henry was keen to preserve doctrinal fidelity, and by the Statute of Six Articles of 1539, he retained the doctrines of clerical celibacy, private mass, and confession to a priest. Henry also authorised the widespread reading of an English translation of the Bible, which had the effect, presumably unintended by Henry, of stimulating Protestant and Reformation views and attitudes in its readers.

Henry died in 1547. His son by Jane Seymour, his third wife, ascended the throne as Edward VI (1547–1553) as a ten-year-old boy. The reins of government were then held by a group of advisers who were essentially Protestants. They repealed the Statute of Six Articles, allowed priests to marry, and replaced the Latin liturgy with the English Book of Common Prayer. In 1553, Cranmer produced the Forty-Two Articles, which essentially changed English Catholicism to Protestant theology.

Edward died in 1553. Then the daughter of Henry and Catherine of Aragon ascended the throne as Mary (1553–1558). She remained a devout Catholic and tried to restore Catholicism in England. Her method was to persecute and martyr Protestants, which proved to be wrong and counterproductive. She died in 1558. After Mary's death, the daughter of Henry and Anne Boleyn ascended the throne as Elizabeth I (1558–1603).

Elizabeth ended the persecutions and recognised that good order in the realm required legitimisation of both Catholic and Protestant observances in the one church. She recognised the Bible as the supreme authority and retained baptism and the Holy Eucharist as sacraments, but her Thirty-Nine Articles of 1563 were essentially the Protestant theology. The liturgy remained basically Catholic, and the clergy retained their legitimacy through apostolic succession.

The question for our consideration is whether the legitimate claim of the English clergy to apostolic succession gives the Church of England a legitimate claim to being the authentic descendant of the church founded by Jesus. Clearly, apostolic succession has occurred, but so has doctrinal deviation from Catholic dogma and rejection of the authority of the pope, which was conferred on Peter by Jesus. Accordingly, the Church of England cannot be regarded as the authentic descendant of the church founded by Jesus.

4.2.5 The Argument from Property

The Catholic Church owns the Vatican, a vast number of church buildings and the land they stand on, other property such as houses, and a vast amount of money. It is said to be the wealthiest non-government organisation in the world. The ownership of any particular piece of property has no evidentiary value in relation to the issue of the authenticity of the church, because property ownership can change. For example, the Hagia Sophia in Turkey was constructed in the year 537 and initially served as an orthodox cathedral which was the seat of the patriarch of Constantinople. In 1261, it was converted to a Roman Catholic cathedral under the then Latin Empire. In 1453, it was a mosque until 1935, when it was secularised and turned into a museum. Even the Vatican could one day be owned by another religion or government.

The function of the ownership of a church building is to identify it as a place of worship of the religion that owns it, so that members of any particular religion would not go to the wrong place to practise their faith. For example, a Catholic would not go to a mosque or synagogue expecting to attend a mass service.

However, the ownership of a significant amount of property by a religion, which services a significant portion of the population of a country, carries with it significant political power, especially if the proportion of the population that are members of that religion are in the majority of the population of that country. In such a situation, the religion concerned is seen by many as the establishment or de facto government of that country. Such a perception is a recognition of the authority of that religion, which implies the authenticity of that religion.

There have been many times in the history of the Catholic Church when the church leaders of the day have had and exercised the controlling political power of a country, sanctioning the use of such power with the threat or actual excommunication of the persons they wished to control. In those days, excommunication was very much an expulsion of the individual concerned from the Catholic faith and all its liturgical rites. Associated with this was the power to issue an interdict. The interdict applied to whole nations. It suspended all pastoral care except baptism and extreme action, and it was aimed at the rulers of the various lands by creating civil unrest. From time to time, the church also had the power to impose other penalties for disobedience, including execution. There were even ecclesiastical courts.

There are numerous instances of this throughout history, and a few examples are worth considering. In the fourth century, the church acquired de facto authority over certain territories of land within Italy. Pope Gregory the Great was instrumental in this acquisition. In the eighth century, the Lombards seized Ravenna, and the then pope Stephen (II or III) sought help from the king of the Franks, Pippin III. Pippin defeated the Lombards and made them return all the territory that they had seized from the church. This is recorded in a document in 756 known as the Donation of Pippin. This donation of land was subsequently supplemented in the Treaty of Pavia, the Donation of Constantine (believed to be a forgery), and further donations by Charlemagne and his son, Louis the Pious. The boundaries of the territories involved included the present-day Lazio (Latium), Marche, Umbria, and part of Emilia-Romagna. There was, of course, also Ravenna and, later on, Spoleto. The exact boundaries of the territories changed from time to time, but essentially, the sovereignty over these territories remained with the popes of Rome until 1870, when those territories were annexed to Italy. Eventually, in 1929, the Lateran Treaty set up the Vatican City as an independent state owned by the Catholic Church. The popes of Rome actually governed these territories as a sovereign nation, having full civil powers over the inhabitants of those lands. We need not consider here whether that power was abused in any way. Our concern is with the perception of the subjects of these lands. Clearly, they saw the pope as their monarch and also as the head of the church. The pope clearly had the secular authority to govern, and this supported the argument for the authenticity of the Catholic Church.

Another example relates to the sack of Rome in 455. In about 442, Gaiseric, the king of the Vandals, made a deal with the then Roman emperor Valentinian to marry their children to strengthen their alliance. Valentinian died, and his successor, Petronius Maximus, effectively repudiated the deal. Pope Leo persuaded Gaiseric to not destroy the ancient city or murder its inhabitants. Gaiseric agreed to this and was allowed unopposed entry into Rome, where he and his men plundered the city for fourteen days. Apparently, they did not burn many buildings or kill the local people, but they did loot vast amounts of treasure and, according to some historians, took a lot of people for sale as slaves in Africa. Clearly, the pope was the political leader of Rome, and his deal with Gaiseric was based on this authority. Again, his actions supported the authenticity of his church.

A third example is when Pope Innocent III had a dispute with King John of England (of Magna Carta fame) in relation to the appointment of the Archbishop of Canterbury. The pope then excommunicated King John and placed the whole of England under interdict. King John eventually capitulated and was forced to become Innocent's vassal, being granted England as his fief and having to pay a substantial annual tribute. Pope Innocent III applied or threatened to apply the sanction of interdict eighty-five times during his pontificate! This clearly demonstrates the extent of the political power that has been wielded by popes over the rulers and peoples of many nations. Of course, this was disgraceful conduct by the pope, in clear violation of his duty to provide pastoral care to all Catholics. Perhaps the perception of the ordinary people wrongly excommunicated was that this pope had acted unfairly towards them, but he appeared to have the authority to do what he did. Again, this supports the authenticity of the Catholic Church and was no doubt the reason that the people put pressure on the king to relent.

In modern times, there is a clear separation of church and state between the Catholic Church and Western states, even though many of the elected government are members of the Catholic faith. This does not appear to be the case in Muslim countries where religious leaders appear to control the government. Our church still has political influence, which it exercises in relation to some moral and social issues that affect Catholic life choices, but it has no actual power to determine government policy and laws; accordingly, it can no longer be regarded as 'the establishment'. The conclusion appears to be that in modern times, the property owned by the Catholic Church and the political influence that it has are not evidence in support of the argument for the authenticity of the Catholic Church as the one true church.

4.3 The Mission of the Church

4.3.1 Foundation

As we have already observed, Jesus intended to and did found our church.

Matthew 16:13–20

When Jesus came to the region of Caesarea Philippi he put this question to his disciples, 'Who do people say the Son of Man is?' And they said, 'Some say he is John the Baptist, some Elijah, and others Jeremiah or one of the prophets.' 'But you,' he said, 'who do you say I am?' Then Simon Peter spoke up, 'You are the Christ,' he said, 'the Son of the living God.' Jesus replied, 'Simon son of Jonah, you are a happy man! Because it was not flesh and blood that revealed this to you but my Father in heaven. So, I now say to you: You are Peter and on this rock I will build my Church. And the gates of the underworld can never hold out against it. I will give you the keys of the kingdom of heaven: whatever you bind on earth shall be considered bound in heaven; whatever you loose on earth shall be considered loosed in heaven.' Then he gave the disciples strict orders not to tell anyone that he was the Christ.

The obvious question that arises is 'Why did Jesus found a new church?' However, in his teachings and lifestyle, Jesus had clearly discarded and relaxed many of the teachings and practices of Judaism as it then was, most notably the dietary laws. Clearly, the innovative and possibly heretical oral teachings of Jesus would not long survive his death without some ongoing impetus. Perhaps this is why some of the Jewish leaders plotted to kill Jesus. In this light, it was clearly necessary for Jesus to found a new church if his teachings were to survive. Indeed, even during his lifetime, his followers were called the Aramaic term for Wayists, as Jesus was teaching a 'new way' to relate to God. These followers were the basis or core of the church he founded.

Structurally, the church Jesus founded was in accord with the normal paradigms of a church. His apostles were the clergy, with their ordination being selected and called by Jesus. The people he had preached to and who had accepted his teachings by baptism were the laity of the church, and his disciples were those members of the laity who had not been selected and called by Jesus but who wished to follow and serve him.

4.3.2 The Authority of Jesus

The chief priests and elders of Judaism approached Jesus and asked him for his authority to act and teach as he did. Jesus refused to tell them, because they would not acknowledge that John the Baptist was from God.

Matthew 21:23–27

He had gone into the Temple and was teaching, when the chief priests and the elders of the people came to him and said, 'What authority have you for acting like this? And who gave you this authority?' 'And I,' replied Jesus, 'will ask you a question, only one; if you tell me the answer to it, I will then tell you my authority for acting like this. John's baptism: where did it come from: heaven or man?' And they argued it out this way among themselves, 'If we say from heaven, he will retort, "Then why did you refuse to believe him?"; but if we say from man, we have the people to fear, for they all hold that John was a prophet.' So, their reply to Jesus was, 'We do not know.' And he retorted, 'Nor will I tell you my authority for acting like this.'

However, when commissioning the apostles at his ascension, he said:

Matthew 28:18

All authority in heaven and on earth has been given to me.

Historically, we know that no human had given Jesus all authority on earth, and all authority in heaven can only have been bestowed on Jesus by God. Therefore, the words of Jesus mean that he claimed to have been given his authority by God. It is implicit in the concept of authority that it can be transferred, shared, delegated, and even subdelegated.

4.3.3 Commissioning Imperatives

In commissioning the apostles to propagate and spread his church, Jesus told them what he wanted them to do in general terms. He did this at his ascension, and it is appropriate for us to consider his actual words (subject to translation issues) to understand the nature and extent of the church's mission. These are recorded in the Gospels as follows:

Matthew 28:16–20

Meanwhile the eleven disciples set out for Galilee, to the mountain where Jesus had arranged to meet them. When they saw him, they fell down before him, though some hesitated. Jesus came up and spoke to them. He said, 'All authority in heaven and on earth has been given to me. Go, therefore, make disciples of all the nations; baptize them in the name of the Father and of the Son and of the Holy Spirit, and teach them to observe all the commands I gave you. And know that I am with you always; yes, to the end of time.'

This text shows a clear imperative to the apostles to evangelise and expand the membership of the Catholic Church through baptism. From this, we may glean an insight as to the function of baptism. It appears that baptism forgives all previous sins of the person baptised (if any, which applies to infant baptisms) and enrols with Jesus the baptised person as a member of his church.

Mark 16:14–18

Lastly, he showed himself to the Eleven themselves while they were at table. He reproached them for their incredulity and obstinacy, because they had refused to believe those who had seen him after he had risen. And he said to them, 'Go out to the whole world; proclaim the Good News to all creation. He who believes and is baptized will be saved; he who does not believe will be condemned. These are the signs that will be associated with believers: in my name they will cast out devils; they will have the gift of tongues; they will pick up snakes in their hands, and be unharmed should they drink deadly poison; they will lay their hands on the sick, who will recover.'

This text from Mark is essentially similar to Matthew, but it goes on to refer to the signs for believers in relation to immunity from harm. It is unclear whether these immunities from harm are a prediction of miracles or simply the promise of a fortunate life. But obviously every human being must die.

John 21:14–17

This was the third time that Jesus showed himself to the disciples after rising from the dead. After the meal Jesus said to Simon Peter, 'Simon son of John, do you love me more than these others do?' He answered, 'Yes Lord, you know I love you.' Jesus said to him, 'Feed my Lambs.' A second time he said to him, 'Simon son of John, do you love me?' He replied, 'Yes, Lord, you know I love you.' Jesus said to him, 'Look after my sheep.' Then he said to him a third time, 'Simon son of John, do you love me?' Peter was upset that he asked him the third time, 'Do you love me?' and said, 'Lord, you know everything; you know I love you.' Jesus said to him, 'Feed my sheep.'

This is an account of the church's mission regarding pastoral care. These words of Jesus are clearly a metaphor by which Peter is directed by Jesus to provide pastoral care to the members of the church. By asking Peter three times whether he loved Jesus more than the other apostles did, Jesus was counterbalancing the three times that Peter denied him, and he thereby forgave Peter for his denial and restored Peter to his favour to the extent of giving him pre-eminence amongst the apostles. The metaphor of feeding the lambs and sheep is a clear reference to providing pastoral care to both young and old, and new converts and long-time followers of Jesus. The 'Look after my sheep' is less clear but probably refers to providing counselling, education, and guidance to followers with special problems, as part of pastoral care. It is unlikely that it was intended to be an instruction to support the material welfare of the laity of the church.

Luke 24:49

And now I am sending down to you what the Father has promised. Stay in the city then, until you are clothed with the power from on high.

This text is a foreshadowing of Pentecost by Jesus to his apostles at his ascension. A more detailed account of this conversation appears in Acts 1:7–12. Most biblical scholars hold the view that Luke was substantially the author of Acts, so we can regard this as part of Luke's Gospel.

Acts 1:7–12

Now having met together, they asked him, 'Lord, has the time come? Are you going to restore the kingdom to Israel?' He replied, 'It is not for you to know times or dates that the Father has decided by his own authority, but you will receive power when the Holy Spirit comes on you, and then you will be my witnesses not only in Jerusalem but throughout Judaea and Samaria, and indeed to the ends of the earth.' As he said this he was lifted up while they looked on, and a cloud took him from their sight. They were still staring into the sky when suddenly two men in white were standing near them and they said, 'Why are you men from Galilee standing here looking into the sky? Jesus who has been taken up from you into heaven, this same Jesus will come back in the same way as you have seen him go there.'

What instructions the Holy Spirit gave the apostles at Pentecost is not recorded, but the subsequent texts show that the apostles dispersed and performed evangelisation and pastoral care. Pentecost is now celebrated as the birthday of our church.

In saying that he would be with them till the end of time, Jesus was clearly saying that this mission of evangelisation was ongoing until the end of time. This means that the church must evangelise every generation in every nation. Naturally, there is no need for evangelisation in communities that have been evangelised and that have accepted the Catholic faith. The obligation of the church in such communities is pastoral care. However, there remains the duty to evangelise succeeding generations in such communities. This is usually done by imposing on parents a duty to bring up their children in the Catholic faith and by providing religious education in schools and youth groups.

The difficulty with this command of Jesus is the zeal with which men have implemented these instructions to 'make disciples of all nations', 'teach ye all nations', and 'proclaim the good news to all creation'. We know that one cannot force another to love anyone. We also know that God wants us to love him. Yet throughout history, men have tried to force others to love God. An example of this is the conquest of the New World by the conquistadors, who were mostly devout and zealous Catholics who often forced baptism on their conquered people 'at the point of the sword' (*Church History in Plain Language* by Bruce L. Shelley, Word Publishing, Second Edition, 1984, page 283). The great debate in those days was whether the faith should be spread by love or by force. For us, that debate has long been resolved, but not yet for some other religions.

The Gospel texts relating to evangelisation and pastoral care are clearly directed to the clergy of the Catholic Church. All the other commands and teachings of Jesus are directed to the laity of the church. This means that we, as the laity, must live our lives in accordance with the commands and teachings of Jesus. Jesus imposed no duty on the laity to evangelise or provide pastoral care. However, he did require that we must not conceal our faith and good works, as follows:

Matthew 5:13–16

You are the salt of the earth. But if salt becomes tasteless, what can make it salty again? It is good for nothing and can only be thrown out to be trampled underfoot by men. You are the light of the world. A city built on a hilltop cannot be hidden. No one lights a lamp to put it under a tub; they put it on the lampstand where it shines for everyone in the house. In the same way your light must shine in the sight of men, so that, seeing your good works, they may give the praise to your Father in heaven.

However, this must be considered in the light of what Jesus said about almsgiving:

Matthew 6:1–4

Be careful not to parade your good deeds before men to attract their notice; by doing this you will lose all reward from your Father in heaven. So when you give alms, do not have it trumpeted before you; this is what the hypocrites do in the synagogues and in the streets to win men's admiration. I tell you solemnly, they have had their reward. But when you give alms, your left hand must not know what your right is doing; your almsgiving must be secret, and your Father who sees all that is done in secret will reward you.

The rationale of these texts appears to be that it is the motive for charitable or good works that determines whether it is pleasing to God. So if we do some good works and display them in order to receive some kudos from other people, then they are not of any interest to God. But if we do them and display them so that other people may see the goodness and greatness of God, then God is pleased. Our reason for doing good works should therefore be that we do good works because we are Catholics and because our God wants all people to love one another.

Naturally, all the teachings of Jesus apply to the clergy just as much as they apply to us, because the clergy are still individuals who are responsible for saving their own souls.

4.3.4 How to Evangelise

Jesus did not simply command the apostles to go and evangelise after his resurrection. The apostles who travelled with Jesus certainly had the model and precedent of how Jesus went about his task of evangelisation, simply from observing him. Also, we can probably assume that Jesus had numerous unrecorded conversations with his apostles in which he explained the meanings of things he had said and trained them in his methods of evangelisation. Some such conversations are recorded in the Gospels, and it is also recorded that Jesus gave them practical training and experience before he died. This is evidenced in the following texts:

Matthew 10:1–16

He summoned his twelve disciples and gave them authority over unclean spirits with power to cast them out and to cure all kinds of diseases and sickness. These are the names of the twelve apostles: first, Simon who is called Peter, and his brother Andrew; James the son of Zebedee, and his brother John; Philip and Bartholomew; Thomas, and Matthew the tax collector; James the son of Alphaeus, and Thaddaeus; Simon the Zealot and Judas Iscariot, the one who was to betray him. These twelve Jesus sent out, instructing them as follows: 'Do not turn your steps to pagan territory, and do not enter any Samaritan town; go rather to the lost sheep of the House of Israel. And as you go, proclaim that the kingdom of heaven is close at hand. Cure the sick, raise the dead, cleanse the lepers, cast out devils. You received without charge, give without charge. Provide yourselves with no gold or silver, not even with a few coppers for your purses, with no haversack for the journey or spare tunic or footwear or a staff, for the workman deserves his keep. Whatever town or village you go into, ask for someone trustworthy and stay with him until you leave. As you enter his house, salute it, and if the house deserves it, let your peace descend upon it; if it does not, let your peace come back to you. And if anyone does not welcome you or listen to what you have to say, as you walk out of the house or town shake the dust from your feet. I tell you solemnly, on the day of Judgment it will not go as hard with the land of Sodom and Gomorrah as with that town. Remember, I am sending you out like sheep among wolves; so be cunning as serpents and yet as harmless as doves.'

Mark 6:7–13

He made a tour around the villages, teaching. Then he summoned the Twelve and began to send them out in pairs giving them authority over the unclean spirits. And he instructed them to take nothing for the journey except a staff—no bread, no haversack, no coppers for their purses. They were to wear sandals but, he added, 'Do not take a spare tunic.' And he said to them, 'If you enter a house anywhere, stay there until you leave the district. And if any place does not welcome you and people refuse to listen to you, as you walk away shake off the dust from under your feet as a sign to them.' So, they set off to preach repentance; and they cast out many devils, and anointed many sick people with oil and cured them.

Luke 9:1–6

He called the Twelve together and gave them power and authority over all devils and to cure diseases, and he sent them out to proclaim the kingdom of God and to heal. He said to them, 'Take nothing for the journey; neither staff, nor haversack, nor bread, nor money; and let none of you take a spare tunic. Whatever house you enter, stay there; and when you leave, let it be from there. As for those who do not welcome you, when you leave their town shake the dust from your feet as a sign to them.' So, they set out and went from village to village proclaiming the Good News and healing everywhere.

These instructions are fairly clear and specific. What is remarkable from these texts is that Jesus gave the apostles the power to cast out demons and to cure illness. In modern times, specially trained priests can still cast out demons in exorcisms, but the power to cure illness appears to have been abandoned by the church. Perhaps this is because modern medicine has come so far or because miraculous cures fell into disrepute when the church started persecuting people for witchcraft.

It is clear from these texts that what Jesus required was that the apostles go peacefully to people, tell them the Good News, and move on. If they listened and accepted, then they were blessed. If they refused to listen, then the apostles should have nothing more to do with them. In essence, it is up to the people told the Good News to make a free choice to accept or reject it, and the apostles should not use force, bribery, seduction, or any other means that suborns free will.

The difference between the mission given to the apostles in Matthew 10:1–16 and Matthew 28:16–20 is that in Matthew 10:1–16, the mission was to the Jewish people only, whereas in Matthew 28:16–20, it was to the whole world. The mission in Matthew 10:1–16 was the first mission given to the apostles by Jesus, and his instructions were properly specific. Repeating these instructions for the second mission appears to be superfluous, and it is reasonable to assume that Jesus intended that the same instructions apply to the second mission.

Another difference between the first and final missions given by Jesus is that the first mission was limited in time and location. The final mission was given by Jesus just before he ascended and was to the whole world for all time until the end of the world. This means that the apostles and their successors were commissioned to evangelise all generations of all nations.

We tend to think of evangelisation as missionary work to remote and uncivilised parts of the world. That is certainly part of it, and even today, although the Catholic Church has a presence in every country of the world, there are still people who have never heard of Jesus. The need for missions to such people persists and will continue to persist because knowledge of Jesus is sometimes lost after several generations, especially in remote places where there is no established church community or where governments have repressed freedom of worship.

But missionary work is not all there is to evangelisation. When a missionary goes to a place where the people do not know of Jesus, he or she preaches to people of all ages and tries to establish a community of people who accept the teachings. If this occurs, then evangelisation of the community is complete, and pastoral care of the community begins to operate, subject to clerical resources. The evangelisation of subsequent generations of that community is left to the parents of those generations and to whatever Catholic education resources may have been established in that place.

4.3.5 How to Provide Pastoral Care

Jesus did not give the apostles any specific instructions regarding the how-to of pastoral care. His instruction to Peter to feed and care for his lambs and sheep is clearly a metaphor for providing spiritual sustenance to his 'flock', which is the laity of his church. But he did give the apostles knowledge of the nature of spiritual sustenance and authorised them to provide it. This spiritual sustenance is essentially the Mass and the seven sacraments.

The authority to perform baptisms is expressed in the text commanding evangelisation, considered above. The authority to say Mass and provide the Eucharist is expressed in the words of Jesus at the Last Supper, where he said:

Do this in memory of me.

The authority to provide the sacrament of penance is expressed in the words of Jesus when he said:

Whose sins you shall forgive they are forgiven and whose sins you shall retain they are retained.

The authority to bind people in matrimony and holy orders is expressed where Jesus said:

Whatever you bind on earth is bound in heaven.

The sacrament of confirmation is an innovation by the church which is essentially a personal commitment to our faith by a person who was baptised non-consensually as an infant or which serves as a precursor to essential mature education about our faith and some experience of life as a Catholic. The sacrament of extreme unction is essentially a combination of penance, the Eucharist, and anointing for an indulgence. Again, this is an innovation by the church and is not expressed in the words of Jesus.

The authority to provide counselling and guidance to individuals or communities with special problems is expressed in the evangelisation text considered above, because all such counselling and guidance is essentially drawn from the works and teachings of Jesus. A good illustration of this is the various letters found in the New Testament, most of which were written to various communities to address special problems that had arisen in those communities. There is also a more clearly implied authority from Jesus in the parable of the good shepherd, as recorded in Matthew 18:12–14 as follows:

Tell me. Suppose a man has a hundred sheep and one of them strays; will he not leave the ninety-nine on the hillside and go in search of the stray? In truth I tell you, if he finds it, it gives him more joy than do the ninety-nine that did not stray at all. Similarly, it is never the will of your Father in heaven that one of these little ones should be lost.

4.3.6 Evolution of the Mission

Our concern is with the nature and extent of the mission of the church in our modern times. We have considered the origins of the mission as established by Jesus some two thousand years ago. Since that time, there has been no amendment or variation of this mission by Jesus. Accordingly, the mission of the church today is the same as it was when it was established by Jesus. But time has changed things. The liturgy of the church has evolved. The requirement to provide ongoing pastoral care has led to the church acquiring property for the building of churches and residences for parish priests. The increase in the number of parishes around cities has required a city-based administration hierarchy of the clergy and has led to the acquisition of cathedrals by the church. The Catholic Church currently has a presence in every nation on earth and cathedrals in most cities of the Western world. Historically the church (the pope) was actually the secular ruler of substantial territories in Italy, which have since shrunk to the Vatican City, which is the seat of the pope and the apex of the Catholic Church administration for the whole world.

There are currently about 7 billion people on this planet. About 1 billion are Catholics requiring pastoral care. Another billion are Muslims who know about Jesus but reject his divinity. About 1 billion are Hindus, who worship a pantheon of gods. Another billion or so are members of other religions who know very little about Jesus or who have rejected Jesus, such as Judaism. The rest are atheists or agnostics. From these numbers, it is clear that the church has a massive task to evangelise these people who do not know Jesus, and 'the laborers are few' is even more applicable now than it was when Jesus said it.

The task of evangelisation is made more difficult because nowadays Catholic evangelists are not particularly welcome in some nations and are even prohibited from preaching in others. Also, some parts of the world are too dangerous to enter for evangelisation or any other purpose, because of brigands and terrorists. Other places are so sparsely populated and remote that it is wasteful of available resources to go there, but the duty to go there remains.

Evangelisation of children is and has been a controversial issue. Some outspoken atheists like Richard Dawkins believe that children should not be brought up in the religion of their parents and should be allowed to make a free choice when they are old enough to understand the issues. Of course, children need to be taught socially acceptable behaviour, but this can be and is done by many non-religious parents who teach their children social mores.

Historically, there has been an issue as to when a person should be baptised. In evangelisation, it is invariably adult baptism. Over the centuries, after the founding of the church, the tradition of giving baptism to infants arose. During the Reformation, some sects, which were called the Swiss Brethren, the Hutterian Brethren, and the Mennonites, arose and gained a substantial following. These sects were broadly labelled as Anabaptists. They held the view that only adults who had experienced personal spiritual regeneration were fit subjects for baptism and that infant baptism was merely a convenient device for perpetuating Christianity and, as such, was devoid of merit. That was not their fundamental belief, but it was integral to their essential belief of daily following the lifestyle of Jesus.

Today we see baptism as a sacrament which bestows grace. It signals membership of the Catholic Church which carries eligibility to receive other sacraments. It is not a declaration of belief in the dogma of the Catholic Church by the baptised. That always remains a personal choice in the mind of every Catholic, and as we know, some Catholics lose their faith. From these perceptions, the modern practice of infant baptism is completely justified. Naturally, there is still adult baptism of converts, and the adult renewal of baptismal vows is now a regular part of church liturgy.

However, baptism alone is not sufficient evangelisation of children. The church relies on parents to bring up their children as Catholics. Mostly, this is done by the parents taking their children to Mass every Sunday, letting their children know that they accept fundamental Catholic beliefs by their example, and teaching them Catholic morals where possible by sending their children to Catholic schools. Catholic schools are normal schools teaching required non-religious subjects but also teaching Catholic beliefs and morals. They are usually run by quasi-clerical sects, but in modern times, the number of such sects, like the Christian Brothers, is declining; there are mostly non-clerical teachers in such schools. Also, many Catholic parents send their children to non-religious schools, some of which allow voluntary religious education by catechists.

All these strategies work and are worthwhile, but there is still a major problem. Most young people leave school on the verge of adulthood and go to a totally secular workforce. Some go on to higher education in a totally secular scholastic environment. On coming into contact with sophisticated atheistic views and lifestyles, many Catholic youths abandon their faith. This appears to happen largely because they have only a simplistic and childlike knowledge of the Catholic faith. Obviously, the teaching of the Catholic faith to children must be presented in language and content within the range of comprehension of the age groups of the children. However, it is clear that they are not being equipped to deal with the mature anti-religious arguments and lifestyles that they will encounter in early adulthood. This is an issue that must be reviewed by our clergy, as it appears that their present action on this issue is insufficient.

Another development in the Catholic Church since the time of Jesus has been the development of non-priestly religious orders, such as brothers and nuns, who are not ordained members of the clergy. In this work, the word *clergy* refers to ordained priests, bishops, cardinals, and popes. These religious orders are mostly dedicated to teaching children or caring for the sick, poor, orphans, widows, and other needy persons. The religious education provided by such orders needs to be approved by the church, because it is part of the evangelisation process. The other services provided by such orders are generally classified as the sort of good works or charitable works that Jesus exhorted the laity to perform. Accordingly, such orders might appropriately be considered as part of the laity of the church even though they have some vows specific to their order.

Another development has been the formation of orders of monks and cloisters of nuns. These orders do not provide any services of evangelisation or pastoral care, and they are mostly dedicated to a life of prayer and austerity. The membership of such orders has declined in modern times and, accordingly, need no further consideration for our purposes.

Again, because of the number of people requiring pastoral care, the church has authorised the appointment of acolytes to assist parish priests in their duties. These acolytes are usually volunteers from the laity of a parish, who are then consecrated to assist in distributing Communion at Mass or even conducting Communion services in the absence of a priest.

Another development has been the formation of Catholic lay organisations whose purpose is to provide works of charity to needy persons. This is seen in organisations like the Society of St Vincent de Paul. Essentially, such groups assist in servicing the material needs of people in their area, even non-Catholics. There are also some international groups who work in missionary areas, providing services for the material needs of the people in these areas.

The church we see today is largely what men have made it, pursuant to the instructions to evangelise and provide pastoral care and do charitable works. **It is not the function of the clergy to do charitable works. That is the function of the laity.** However, the provision of some charitable works requires more money than can be raised by lay organisations, and consequently, the church has become involved in charitable works and has developed many sophisticated techniques to raise money. A current perception is that the Catholic Church is the wealthiest non-government organisation in the world.

4.3.7 Fidelity Issues

The fundamentalist view is that the mission of the church is defined by the words of Jesus recorded in the Gospels and that the church must do no more and no less than what Jesus commanded. What Jesus said is clear, so it follows that when the church does or teaches something beyond what Jesus said, it becomes important to consider what Jesus did not say. Leaving aside for the moment the question of express or implied authority from Jesus to act and teach beyond the parameters set by him, we may consider the sufficiency of his instructions and teachings.

The divinity of Jesus is fundamental to our faith. He is part of our triune God. It is axiomatic that God, who created all things and is omniscient, does not make mistakes. Accordingly, the instructions and teachings of Jesus are not in any way defective or insufficient, and it would be arrogant and stupid for any Catholic to assert otherwise.

However, Jesus had to work and teach in the circumstances of his time. For example, he could not have said anything about the modern phenomenon of road rage or computer crime, because these things did not exist in his time. Had he taught about them, his teachings would have been regarded as incomprehensible gibberish, and his general credibility would have been diminished.

But Jesus did give us the general command to love one another, and he also gave clear teachings about anger. Thus, in declaring road rage to be displeasing to God and contrary to the teachings of Jesus, the church is legitimately applying the teachings of Jesus to the changed circumstances of modern times.

In relation to pastoral care, Jesus gave no instructions as to how this was to be implemented. But he was a Jew, and the apostles had the paradigm of how the Jewish faith implemented pastoral care. The Jews had temples and synagogues, resident priests, financial support from donations or offerings, regular attendance, and a calendar of annual holy days. As the assets of the early church grew, they structured pastoral care in accordance with this paradigm. Clearly, the Jewish paradigm had worked for many centuries, and following this precedent was legitimate and appropriate.

In relation to the liturgy of the church, our fundamental liturgical observance is the Mass. In this regard, the apostles had clear instructions from Jesus at the Last Supper to *'do this in memory of me'*. Accordingly, the apostles structured the Mass around the format of the Last Supper, and it remains our fundamental liturgy to this day.

On the other hand, declaring it to be a mortal sin to eat meat on Fridays is well outside anything Jesus taught or any authority he gave to the church. Happily, this is no longer church law, but that it happened displays confusion amongst some of the clergy of the necessity to support dogmatic theology and the desirability to practise devotional works.

This example compels us to concede that our church has fallen into error in the past. Clerics who have made erroneous decisions are generally intelligent men motivated by love of God, although historically there have been bad popes and other bad clergy. The errors made may be considered in the light of Peter's argument with Jesus that he must not let himself be crucified. Jesus said to Peter, *'Get behind me, Satan.'* Clearly, Peter erred, yet later Jesus made Peter pre-eminent amongst the apostles.

It is, of course, not for us to judge whether any cleric has done something reprehensible. However, the Gospels make it clear that the clergy is accountable to Jesus for how they perform their ministry. This is clear from the texts in:

Mark 6:30–31

The apostles rejoined Jesus and told him all they had done and taught.

Luke 9:10–11

On their return the apostles gave him an account of all they had done.

These texts refer to the return of the apostles from the missions given them in the texts referred to above, being Mathew 10:1–16, Mark 6:7–13, and Luke 9:1–6. These texts clearly show that they reported to Jesus what they had done, which is accountability, and this accountability is, of course, in addition to the individual accountability for their own souls in their private lives.

4.3.8 Conclusion

Having considered the nature and extent of the mission given to the apostles by Jesus and how the apostles and their successors have implemented their mission, it appears that the church remains focused on the essence of its mission, although there have been mistakes. The current scope of church activity and involvement is far more extensive than basic evangelisation and pastoral care.

4.4 Authority of the Church

4.4.1 The Nature of Authority

The essence of the meaning of *authority* is that it legitimises, validates, or enables the words or actions of persons acting under the authority, whose words or actions affect other people and require their submission to these words or actions to the extent of the authority. Authority can only be exercised by persons either individually or within some corporation or other organisation. Any authority necessarily requires a legitimate source, and the authority of anyone acting under a claimed authority must be traceable back to the source, which is usually a chain of grants, appointments, or delegations of that authority.

A grant or delegation of authority is essentially a verbal conferring and acceptance of the authority, usually conferred, evidenced, and defined in writing and operative as of the date of the writing. All the rights, duties, and powers which may be regarded as the extent of the authority are not always clearly and fully set out in the verbal grant or the written evidence of the grant. Thus, to clearly perceive the extent of an authority, it is often necessary to regard some rights, duties, powers, and limitations as implied in the grant. Such implied qualifications and limitations may be axiomatic, practical necessities, or apparent from other materials or evidence relevant to the grant, delegation, or appointment.

There are many forms of authority. For example, there is the authority of governments, police, judges, teachers, parents, etc. The relevant form of authority for our consideration is the authority of the church. The source of this authority is Jesus, who we believe was divine and therefore has the authority to form our church and to delegate some of that authority to the apostles. Jesus delegated such authority verbally and did not create or sign any document evidencing this delegation. However, the Gospels may be regarded as evidence of this delegation. We accept the

Gospels as true, but technically, this evidence is self-serving, because the Gospels were written by members of the church. In this context, *self-serving* means that it is, in effect, like the grantee of an authority claiming to have the authority on the basis of only his or her assertion that he or she has been granted the authority.

Jesus founded our church, and he delegated several forms of authority to the apostles, as is recorded in the Gospels. He died and rose from the dead and ascended into heaven. He is still alive, and he is coming back. There can be nothing mystical about the authority that Jesus delegated, because it is essential that the grantee of any authority know the nature and extent of such authority in order to exercise it properly. Accordingly, we can use human reasoning and understanding in regard to the nature and extent of the authority Jesus delegated. Using human understanding, the authority given by Jesus to the apostles is very much like what we know as power of attorney.

For a valid exercise of power of attorney, it is necessary that the persons in respect of whom the attorney is exercising his power are aware that the authority that the attorney is exercising is wide enough to legitimise the subject dealing—i.e. they must know the extent of the authority given in the power of attorney. Under the same reasoning, it is necessary that we, the laity and clients of our church, know the nature and extent of the authority of the church in relation to what the church requires of us, pursuant to the various authorities exercised by the church. This requires some consideration of the main types of authority exercised by our church, which are as follows.

4.4.2 Mission Authority

In the previous section, we saw the words of Jesus in assigning the work of the church to the apostles, and those words need not be duplicated here. The form of words used by Jesus is a directive or command. He did not use words that are typically used in a grant authority, such as 'I hereby authorise you to . . .' Therefore, the authority to teach and provide pastoral care must be implied in his words.

That such authority is implied is clearly axiomatic, because it would be nonsense for Jesus to have commanded the apostles to teach and provide pastoral care and then to have said something like 'but I do not give you the authority to do these things'.

There is a principle of comprehension and interpretation which is embodied in the Latin maxim *'expressio unius est exclusio alterius'*, which means that saying one thing excludes any other thing that is not said. However, this must be used subject to the principle that it is correct to imply anything that is necessary to give the clearly intended meaning and effect to the subject statement. In relation to the command to teach and provide pastoral care, it is clearly necessary for the church to have the authority to do this, and therefore, such authority may validly be regarded as implied in the commands of Jesus.

The next aspect of this authority to be considered is the extent of the authority. In relation to the command to evangelise or teach, the question arises: 'What is it that the apostles are authorised to teach?' Jesus said:

Matthew 28:18–20

Jesus came up and spoke to them. He said, 'All authority in heaven and on earth has been given to me. Go, therefore, make disciples of all the nations; baptize them in the name of the Father and of the Son and of the Holy Spirit, and teach them to observe all the commands I gave you. And know that I am with you always; yes, to the end of time.'

The plain meaning of these words is that Jesus commanded them to teach all that he had done, taught, and commanded during his ministry, no more and no less.

Currently, our church's primary teaching is the four Gospels, which contain, in the view of the clerics who canonised the four Gospels, all that Jesus taught, did, and commanded. However, the church also has a large body of other teachings that cannot be directly referred to anything that Jesus did, taught, or commanded. Under the principle of 'expressio unius est exclusio alterius', the authority to teach these things cannot be implied as necessary to give meaning and effect to the teachings and commands of Jesus.

In his encyclical entitled *Humanae Vitae*, Pope Paul VI said at Paragraph 4:

No believer will wish to deny that the teaching authority of the Church is competent to interpret even the natural moral law. It is, in fact, indisputable as Our Predecessors have many times declared, that Jesus Christ when communicating to Peter and to the Apostles His Divine authority and sending them to teach all nations His commandments, constituted them as guardians and authentic interpreters of all the moral law, not only, that is, of the law of the gospel, but also of the natural law, which is also an expression of the will of God, the faithful fulfilment of which is equally necessary for salvation.

From this, it is clear that the church has long claimed that its authority to teach matters not dealt with by Jesus is implied in the general assignment of the mission of the church by Jesus to the apostles and is, in effect, authority to the church to teach what its clerics perceive to be the proper application of natural law. Such authority was not specifically given by Jesus, and under the principle of 'expressio unius est exclusio alterius', it is not necessary to imply such authority to give meaning and effect to the teachings and commands of Jesus. This claim is therefore substantially self-serving because the assertion that this authority is implied is, at best, tenuous. That does not mean that such additional teachings are wrong. We should be mindful that they are made by men who love God and are trying to provide guidance to us so that our actions and lifestyle are pleasing to

God. Accordingly, such teachings are legitimate as guidance, although the claim that they are authorised by Jesus is no less self-serving simply because it has been claimed by many of 'our predecessors' many times.

However, the authority to interpret and apply the teachings of Jesus in modern circumstances can clearly be implied from the teachings of Jesus. Jesus spoke in the local language, using figures of speech current and comprehensible to his audience. Had he spoken about things that were unknown to his audience or that did not exist at that time, he would have been regarded as talking gibberish, and his credibility would have been greatly diminished. For example, Jesus could not have taught about human cloning. That has only been possible in recent times. This is obviously something about which God has a view and about which the church should have a teaching. Essentially, the church should teach whether human cloning involves a killing, contrary to the fifth commandment. Since Jesus endorsed the Ten Commandments, it is clearly necessary to apply his teachings to circumstances about which Jesus could not have taught. The authority to teach on this can clearly be implied and may even be seen as a duty of the church.

As to pastoral care, again it is axiomatic that if Jesus commanded this to be given, then clearly the authority to do so is implied.

At the time when the apostles began their ministry, their primary task was evangelisation. Having established a core evangelised community, they needed to move on to evangelise other places, so the task of pastoral care was largely delegated to resident presbyters. But they did continue to provide counselling and guidance to such communities, as can be seen from the letters forming part of the New Testament. In these times, the extent of pastoral care was mostly an early form of Mass and counselling about the nature of our faith based on the teachings of the evangelists. Baptism was part of the evangelisation process, with the other sacraments being developed much later. The exception was the holy orders, which, while not a part of pastoral care, was immediately necessary to establish pastoral care. Eventually, the Gospels were written and canonised, after which the content of counselling and guidance became more uniform and authoritative.

In modern times, pastoral care consists mostly in the provision of Mass and the sacraments, counselling, and religious education of children and adults. Clearly, from the earliest times, counselling and guidance has been authorised. Naturally, the primary source of such counselling and guidance must be the Gospels and other parts of the Old and New Testament. However, not every issue in respect of which counselling is sought can be answered from these sources. Accordingly, the church has claimed natural law as an additional source. Clearly, divine law takes precedence over natural law, but what if divine law is silent on an issue of concern? Jesus did not specifically give the apostles authority to refer to natural law in counselling, nor did he specifically exclude such reference. His command of 'look after my sheep' is very general but countenances the churches giving counselling and guidance that it perceives to be in accordance with God's will.

The problem with natural law is that there is no authoritative statement as to what the law is or covers. Does it include the law of the jungle? Does it include evolution or survival of the fittest? To what extent can science claim authority to declare what is natural law? Can natural law change if new scientific discoveries change scientific opinion that was previously universally accepted?

We cannot answer these and other similar questions. What we, the laity of our church, can accept is that the church has done the best it can to guide us towards salvation. The modern *Catechism of the Catholic Church* contains a substantial amount of the best human wisdom that the church can offer. It is clearly authorised as counselling and guidance but is necessarily subordinate to relevant guidance that can be gleaned from the Gospels. And to what extent are these teachings of the church binding or dogmatic?

4.4.3 Authority to Bind and Loose

In order to consider this issue, we must first have a clear understanding of the natural human meaning of what Jesus said. Accordingly, we must understand what types of things can be bound or loosed, the extent of the authority given, and the sanctions attendant on any rejection of a ruling or decision made under this type of authority.

In our human experience, the types of things that can be binding are essentially contracts and laws. There are many types of contracts, most of them commercially oriented. There are also service contracts and relationship contracts. The church has no interest in commercial contracts between humans, but it does have an interest in service contracts made by humans with God, i.e. holy orders. It also has an interest in relationship contracts made between humans and supported by God—for example, marriage.

Obviously, if the mission of the church is perpetual, and because all humans must die, it is necessary that the church have authority to appoint successors to the work of the church. If there were any doubt, then the words of Jesus are sufficiently specific to overcome any such doubt.

Suppose a priest, on his ordination, takes a vow of obedience. Later in his ministry, he preaches something which his superiors in the clerical hierarchy consider erroneous. The superiors of the priest command him to cease such teachings, but he disregards this command. The superiors clearly have the authority to laicise the priest and probably have a duty to do so. In another example, suppose a bishop commands a priest under his authority to participate as a combatant in military action, and the priest refuses. The bishop then laicises this priest. Clearly, the Bishop has the secular power to laicise the priest, but the spiritual validity of the laicisation is another matter. The point of these two hypothetical examples is to illustrate the point that the authority to loose the vows of holy orders is spiritually limited to what is implied in the oath of obedience made on ordination, i.e. commands that are legitimately connected to the mission of the church or that are properly administrative regulations of the clergy of the church. Such an oath on ordination cannot be regarded as unconditional on the part of the ordinee.

Marriage is a contract between a man and a woman. That it is supported by God can be seen below:

Matthew 10:3–6

Some Pharisees approached him, and to test him they said, 'Is it against the Law for a man to divorce his wife on any pretext whatever?' He answered, 'Have you not read that the creator from the beginning made them male and female and that he said: This is why a man must leave father and mother, and cling to his wife, and the two become one body? They are no longer two, therefore, but one body. So then, what God has united, man must not divide.'

Such a contract made before God in the presence of a priest is blessed by God. That does not mean that any marriage contract made other than before God is not valid. Such a marriage is simply not blessed and supported by God, but this does not mean that such a marriage cannot be valid, happy, and enduring. It is also clear from the teachings of Jesus that a single person can commit adultery with a person married outside the church whose spouse is still alive.

Marriage is a sacrament which is clearly within the church's mission to provide pastoral care. The authority to perform marriages as agents of God is not specifically given to the church; however, Jesus did teach substantially about marriage, and from the passage set out above, it is clear that God is personally involved in some marriages. Accordingly, the church's authority to perform and annul marriages is arguably implied and included in the words of Jesus.

The church clearly has the authority to 'loose' marriages. What this means is that the church can say to the couple that their marriage is terminated. What the church has done over the centuries is annul marriages on the basis that they were void *ab initio*, i.e. from the beginning, meaning that there was never any marriage at all, for some reason. While such an annulment is clearly valid if the reasons are sound and not a mere rationalisation, such an annulment is not a loosing under these words of Jesus, because you cannot loose something that was not bound in the first place.

Historically, we know that the church granted such divorces to historically significant persons, often for political purposes. There is little evidence that any of the ordinary Catholic laity ever received a divorce, and that policy remains current in modern times. It is not our purpose to be judgmental of anyone involved in divorces that have been given or critical of the church's reluctance to loose marriages that have clearly failed. However, most lay Catholics regard their chances of getting a divorce from Rome as less than one in a million, so they are too discouraged to even apply. The church has the authority to both bind and loose marriages. To date, it has largely failed to use its authority to loose marriages. Performing and unbinding marriages is clearly part of the church's mission to provide pastoral care. Jesus spoke sternly about the sanctity and permanence of marriage, and the above passage clearly prohibits putting a marriage asunder. Arguably, Jesus was referring to the destruction of a marriage by adultery, slander, or any other way that a person can destroy the marriage of another. The issue that the church needs to address is how to apply God's mercy and love to people whose marriage has been irretrievably put asunder long before they tell any priest of the situation. To date, our church has failed those persons whose marriage is irreversibly asunder, by not enabling them to move on with God's blessing.

Law is another thing that is, by definition, made binding. Anyone who has the authority to make a law normally has the authority to repeal, i.e. unbind, the whole law. The hierarchy of laws is as follows:

(a) *Divine law.* This is law made by God and is the supreme law. For us, this is essentially the Ten Commandments of God and the teachings and commands of Jesus.

(b) *Natural law.* These are laws that are recognised by most legal systems in every era. This includes the principles of natural justice, such as the right of a person accused of some wrongdoing to a fair trial. It does not include natural phenomena or those parts of the law of the jungle observed in some animal behaviour, such as the killing of competitors for the selection of a mate. There is no universal agreement as to the entire contents of this type of law.

(c) *Human law.* This is primarily law made by the governing body of a community. In this context, a community can be a sovereign nation state or territory, a religion, an economic or commercial association, or a social group. The most important law is generally a constitution, followed by legislation setting out the principle laws of the community. A third level of law is called regulations. The authority to make regulations is generally delegated to the persons charged with the task of implementing particular legislation, and the regulations made deal with the processes and procedures with which the relevant legislation is to be implemented. Regulations do have the force and authority of law.

In this hierarchy, the higher law always prevails. For example, if there is an inconsistency between a regulation and its parent or other legislation, the legislation prevails, and the regulation is deemed *ultra vires*, which means 'beyond the authority or jurisdiction of the regulation makers'. Similarly, if legislation conflicts with the constitution, the constitution prevails. If any human law conflicts with natural law, then the natural raw prevails, provided the relevant natural law is recognised. Similarly, if there is any conflict between human or natural law and divine law, divine law prevails.

Only God can make, repeal, or change divine law, and therefore, it is preposterous to argue that the church has the authority to repeal, change, or add to any of the Ten Commandments or the teachings and commandments of Jesus. Nor can the church change any natural law, although it can decline to accept something as natural law.

Clearly, the words of Jesus giving the church authority to 'bind and loose' gives the church authority to make law, but as is abundantly clear, this authority is limited to making human law, with God recognising the validity of these as such.

The fundamental nature of any law is that it must be enforceable— i.e. it must have a sanction and a process for implementation. Some lawyers argue that a law can have a solely declaratory function. Such laws, while having a sanction or penalty, are not politically favoured and therefore not prosecuted. For example, abortion. In some jurisdictions, it is still on the books as a crime but is not prosecuted, because of political instructions to the police and prosecution departments. If a law can be ignored, then it is not a law. Another long-standing principle in most legal systems is that 'ignorance of the law is no excuse'. That principle is a practical necessity, but clearly not fair and just in situations where a person is genuinely unaware that what he is doing is against some law. This principle cannot be applied to moral laws. Consequently, moral laws must be promulgated so widely that it cannot be believably argued that an offender was unaware that what he did was against some moral precept.

From early times in the history of our church, clerics have made human laws. The aggregate of this body of law is called the canon law, which has been frequently revised, amended, and consolidated. The latest revision became operative on 27 November 1983 under the auspices of Pope John Paul II. The nomenclature *canon law* is a slightly inaccurate description, because this body of laws is more in the nature of regulations than legislation. But as has already been observed, regulations do have the force of law.

It is said that the canon law is all about church order and discipline rather than doctrine or dogma—i.e. it regulates behaviour and not beliefs. In promulgating the latest code, Pope John Paul II said, 'Its very purpose is to create an order in the ecclesial society.'

One of the key questions on this issue is whether the canon law applies to the laity of the Catholic Church. It is argued that by virtue of our baptism, we share in the priestly nature of Jesus and are therefore bound by canon law. Against this arcane theological argument, we see that the canon law is not widely promulgated amongst the laity. Very few of the laity have ever read or been taught the canon law. The canon law does have sanctions, but they cannot be enforced against the laity, except excommunication or interdiction. It is certainly arguable that these penalties are unchristian, having regard to the example and teachings of Jesus, and that these sanctions are unprecedented and unauthorised from anything Jesus did or said. Thus, if we do not know about it and can ignore any so-called penalties, such law cannot bind the laity.

However, the clergy of the church is clearly bound by canon law. They are taught the law, and the sanctions that can be applied to them are substantial and enforceable. The vexatious aspect of the church applying the sanctions of excommunication, interdiction, or suspension is that such action is, in effect, a deliberate refusal by the church to provide pastoral care to the subject of such action, even if this subject is one of its clerical members. This is contrary to the mission of the church, which was entrusted to the church without the discretion to refuse to provide it in any circumstances.

Thus, as we have already observed, the church has a duty to publicly disown scandalous conduct and unorthodox or radical teachings. If it is correct that excommunication and interdiction can never be regarded as an authorised sanction, then the church must use other means to deal with unacceptable public conduct or teachings. In relation to both members of the laity and the clergy, the most appropriate response appears to be public disownment of such conduct and public refutation of erroneous teachings. In relation to the clergy, in very serious matters, the sanction of suspension and laicisation may also be appropriate, but these are actions in relation to the binding and loosing of the cleric's holy orders rather than under the canon law. In any case, the public disownment should be officially promulgated and published widely enough to counteract the effects of the unacceptable conduct or teachings. Becoming aware of such conduct or teachings requires substantial vigilance on the part of the clergy of the church, and there is clearly a duty on the laity to report such unorthodox conduct or teachings to the appropriate clerical authority.

It is not the function of this work to review canon law, but in order to see it in perspective, it is worth noting that some experts tell us that some of the canon law comes from divine law, much of it is based on the church's view of natural law, some of it is in the nature of human legislation and regulation, and some parts are merely 'human opinion which warrants substantial respect'. All these sources are intermingled in various issues, which is obviously necessary to deal comprehensively with the respective issues. Consequently, if we, the laity, are simply told that something is canon law, we do not know whether the law is binding dogma, a natural law–based teaching, a procedural requirement, or a recommendation.

It seems reasonable that we be aware of the status of what our church asks of us or recommends to us. The church's practice in this regard may well be an appropriate issue for review and reform.

A legitimate prospective is that the church clearly has the authority to bind and loose marriages and holy orders, and it has authority to make binding rules for the administration of the clergy of the church. Whether the church has used this authority to the extent intended by Jesus and whether any or many such uses are *ultra vires* is another matter.

4.4.4 Authority to Forgive Sins

After saying this he breathed on them and said: 'Receive the Holy Spirit. For those whose sins you forgive, they are forgiven; for those whose sins you retain, they are retained.'

John 20:22–24

These words of Jesus give the church clear and expressed authority to forgive sins. In addition, it gives the church authority to exercise a discretion to decline to forgive a person's sins. This discretion is clearly necessary for the proper exercise of the power to forgive sins, because without it, forgiveness of sins would be available on demand, which would lead to insincere repentance. The discretion also enables the church to make absolution conditional on specific reparation and acts of penance.

Jesus gave this power to men for use amongst humans. Our comprehension of this sacrament is our comprehension of the human concept of forgiveness. The human concept of forgiveness requires that the person seeking forgiveness be genuinely and sincerely sorry for the act or omission in respect of which forgiveness is sought. That sorrow must be for the harm done to the person offended and not based on having been caught or discovered to be responsible for the offence. This involves voluntary restitution or reparation, if the nature of the offence is amenable to this. For example, if A stole some money from B and then became sorry for the harm caused to B. A then apologises to B, but A must also pay B an amount of money equivalent to the amount stolen. This concept is clear, but it can become complicated if the identity of B cannot be determined, if A does not want his identity to become known, or if the thing stolen is not money but something unique which has been disposed of and cannot be replaced.

It is also essential to the nature of sincere sorrow or contrition that there be a firm and binding intention on the part of the person seeking forgiveness to not repeat that offence or give any other offence to the person offended. If, in the above example, A apologises to B but says or implies that he may do it again or give some other offence to B, then B would certainly not forgive A, and accordingly, A should sincerely let B know that he will not repeat this offence or give any other offence to B if he wants forgiveness.

An act of penance is in the nature of compensation, and as such, it is in addition to restitution or reparation. In the human situation of offence, compensation is not always practical or even appropriate. If we have offended God, then compensating God is clearly impossible. The best we can do is say some prayers and do some act of self-denial or self-discipline as an offering to God and hope God finds this pleasing.

Although the church has the discretion to decline to give absolution for sins, actual refusal to forgive sins is essentially unheard of. Even excommunicants have the sacrament of penance available to lift their excommunication conditionally on negating the cause of their excommunication. Clearly, the church approaches the forgiveness of sins with mercy and compassion, which gives us reason to be thankful for the love our clergy has for us.

The church uses the power to forgive sins in the modern sacrament of penance. The procedure for administration has developed over the centuries, and today we have the option of the traditional private confession or a communal joint confession on special occasions. The communal format assumes that we all know that there must be true sorrow, reparation, and an act of penance, but it leaves it up to us to ensure the adequacy of these.

From our point of view, one of the greatest benefits of the church having the power to forgive our sins is the relief we feel when we know that our sins are really forgiven in a sincere confession. If our only option were to ask God in prayer to forgive our sins, we would not know whether our apology was accepted or whether our reparation and penance was adequate. Our church gives us certainty in these things. However, that does not mean that we cannot ask God directly for forgiveness. The authority given to the church is a delegation of authority, not a transfer. If it were a transfer, then the words of Jesus shown below would have no meaning, because God would no longer have the power to forgive sins.

Matthew 6:14–15

Yes, if you forgive others their failings, your heavenly Father will forgive you yours; but if you do not forgive others, your Father will not forgive your failings either.

This point is also supported by what Jesus said:

Mark 3:28–30

I tell you solemnly, all men's sins will be forgiven, and all their blasphemies; but let anyone blaspheme against the Holy Spirit and he will never have forgiveness: he is guilty of an eternal sin.

Obviously, the church cannot forgive an offence that Jesus has declared to be unforgivable.

Another issue is whether the church is using the power to forgive sins wisely. Most of us believe that a person grows in strength of character and wisdom when they accept the consequences of their mistakes. As structured in modern times, the sacrament of penance is more of an aid to avoiding the spiritual consequences of our mistakes than to their acceptance. There is a firmly held principle that anything confessed to a priest in confession must remain confidential forever. This must remain so; otherwise, we, the laity, would lose confidence in the sacrament and cease using it. But the church has a dilemma when a person confesses a serious crime; God gave the state or nation its authority, and the church must respect that authority and support its function of maintaining order. Perhaps the church could use its authority to specify an act of penance, as a condition of absolution, which requires the penitent to accept the secular consequences of his or her offence. This is a matter for our church.

From the forgoing it is clear that our church has the authority to forgive sins and the discretion to decline to do so if it thinks fit. This authority is endorsed by God, but the discretion to decline forgiveness does not bind God, who can nevertheless forgive that sin. The extent of this authority is limited only to not being available to forgive the unforgivable sin. Whether the church has used this authority wisely or whether it can improve its usage is a matter for our clergy and beyond the scope of this work.

4.5 The Church and Money

4.5.1 The Cost of Evangelisation

As we have seen, the mission of the church is evangelisation and pastoral care. The work of evangelisation which Jesus assigned to the twelve is as follows:

Matthew 10:5–15

These twelve Jesus sent out, instructing them as follows:

'Do not turn your steps to pagan territory, and do not enter any Samaritan town; go rather to the lost sheep of the House of Israel. And as you go, proclaim that the kingdom of heaven is close at hand. Cure the sick, raise the dead, cleanse the lepers, cast out devils. You received without charge, give without charge. Provide yourselves with no gold or silver, not even with a few coppers for your purses, with no haversack for the journey or spare tunic or footwear or a staff, for the workman deserves his keep. Whatever town or village you go into, ask for someone trustworthy and stay with him until you leave. As you enter his house, salute it, and if the house deserves it, let your peace descend upon it; if it does not, let your peace come back to you. And if anyone does not welcome you or listen to what you have to say, as you walk out of the house or town shake the dust from your feet. I tell you solemnly, on the day of Judgment it will not go as hard with the land of Sodom and Gomorrah as with that town. Remember, I am sending you out like sheep among wolves; so be cunning as serpents and yet as harmless as doves.

From this passage, we see that the apostles needed no money and were specifically instructed to not take any money with them on this mission. They were told to rely on the hospitality of the good people in the places they visited. Things were different in those days. The mission of evangelisation is ongoing and is still of primary importance in our church. In modern times, our church is worldwide, and the generations requiring evangelisation are vast in number. Visiting them and offering them information about the life and teachings of Jesus remains the appropriate procedure, but our evangelists no longer work miracles or cure the sick. Modern evangelisation requires substantial funding to be effective. This funding is mainly for the transport and living expenses of the evangelists.

4.5.2 The Cost of Pastoral Care

In the early history of the church, the process of evangelisation involved forming a community of people who accepted the teachings of the evangelists and appointing some presbyters to manage the ongoing liturgy in that community. The evangelists then moved on to the next place to be evangelised. The presbyters appointed were usually volunteers who had other occupations and who kept in touch with the evangelists when issues requiring their assistance arose, as is exemplified in the letters of St Paul. They also raised funds to support the expanding work of the evangelists. The presbyters were the forerunners of the parish priests we have in modern times. The presbyters had their own accommodation and conducted the liturgy in private homes, but over time, they became full-time presbyters who required the financial support of their communities and purpose-built venues for the conducting of the liturgy—i.e. churches. Thus, it is clear that the mission of pastoral care has required the church to have money from virtually the earliest times. In modern times, our parish priests need a church building, a residence for themselves, a vehicle for travel around the parish, food, clothing, some money to pay overheads and maintenance, and perhaps a housekeeper. All these require a reasonably substantial amount of money.

4.5.3 The Role of Canon Law in Money-Raising

The church does not deal in any commercial or marketable commodity. It is essentially a service industry that relies almost exclusively on cash donations from the laity of the church. It solicits these donations by preaching the virtues of generosity and love as taught by Jesus and by making it a canon law that the laity must support their pastors. Whether the church has the authority to make such a canon law is arguable but need not be considered here, because it is irrelevant, as it has no sanction. The laity of our church is not stupid. We give money to the church out of generosity and because we understand that our church needs money. No canon law can make us more or less generous or increase our understanding of its need for money.

4.5.4 Church Ways of Money-Raising

In addition to directly asking for money, our church has developed a variety of indirect ways of raising money. Some of these ways are now obsolete—for example, the sale of indulgences and taxation of the subjects in territories governed by the church. However, there are some modern fundraising initiatives that warrant consideration. The first of these is the weekly envelope or planned giving system used in places where donations to a church are tax-deductible. This system requires that every donation under this system be recorded by the church so that it can issue a receipt at the end of the tax year to the donor to verify the donation for tax deduction. This means that the government allows as a tax deduction the amount of money donated, thereby reducing the taxable income and giving credit against tax paid or a reduction of tax due.

The problem with this system is that it appears to be an indirect method of obtaining government funding for our church. No doubt most of us agree that the government ought to fund our church to an extent, because our church helps provide law and order to nations by teaching and encouraging a moral lifestyle. Nevertheless, allowing the deduction as a donation to a charitable organisation is misleading. Our church is not a charitable organisation. Its mission is evangelisation and pastoral care.

Another problem with this system is that it is not private. Jesus said:

Matthew 6:1–4

Be careful not to parade your good deeds before men to attract their notice; by doing this you will lose all reward from your Father in heaven. So when you give alms, do not have it trumpeted before you; this is what the hypocrites do in the synagogues and in the streets to win men's admiration. I tell you solemnly, they have had their reward. But when you give alms, your left hand must not know what your right is doing; your almsgiving must be secret, and your Father who sees all that is done in secret will reward you.

A legitimate understanding of these words is that donations to the church should be anonymous and confidential. For accounting purposes, it is usual to specify the amount intended to be donated weekly. Some priests regard this as a promise to donate, and it has happened that the priest has read out the names of parishioners who are in arrears of such 'promised' donations, in order to name and shame them into bringing their donations up to date. Such conduct by a priest is totally unacceptable and even reprehensible. Such conduct by a priest loudly proclaims that the church is no longer a loving guide to the salvation of our souls but has become a business devoted to extracting money from the gullible. Since this has actually happened, there can be little doubt that this perception of the apparent current function of the church has turned some people away from the church.

4.5.5 Inappropriate Aspects of Money-Raising

The planned giving system enables the parish priest to forecast the amount of income from this source, thereby indicating the cost of projects that the parish can afford to undertake. Having undertaken some projects, usually a building project, there is a legal obligation on the parish to repay borrowed money at the agreed rate. We can understand the pressure on the parish priest if planned giving donations fall short of the forecast amounts, but this does not excuse a name-and-shame response. Any donation that is not truly voluntary is not a work of charity and is of no value to the donor as such.

In many parishes, there are two collections of donations for the church at Mass on Sundays but no collections at other weekday masses. In addition, there are regularly appeals at Sunday Mass for financial support of charitable associations, usually collected by special envelopes, by a third collection, or by collectors outside the church after Mass. There are many such charitable associations, usually run by volunteers from the Catholic laity. All of them are worthy of support, and in some of the wealthier parishes, there is an appeal for such a charity almost every week. So for many of the laity who attend Mass on Sunday, the expectation is that we will be confronted with an appeal for money to support our church and a variety of charities. Eventually, this focus on money becomes tiresome, especially since money is definitely not what Jesus was all about. Little wonder that many Catholics have stopped attending Mass on Sundays. Clearly, our church would be far less wealthy if the church had not declared attendance at Sunday Mass to be compulsory.

Occasionally, the Sydney archdiocese conducts special appeals in all its parish churches, such as the Peter's Pence appeal and the Charitable Works Fund. The Charitable Works Fund is inappropriately named, as it is not primarily directed to funding charitable works. The proceeds of this appeal are used to fund the Aboriginal Ministry, CatholicCare, Chaplaincies, the Confraternity of Christian Doctrine, the Ephpheta Centre, and the Seminary of the Good Shepherd. A study of the work that these agencies do shows that their principal function is to serve pastoral care and evangelisation, although CatholicCare is clearly a charitable function. They are all important and worthwhile functions. Again, there are pressures on the archdiocese to meet the legal obligations and continuing viability of these functions, and accordingly, there is a quota put on each parish, relative to the size and wealth of the parish. If the quota is not met by donations, then the archdiocese requires the shortfall from other parish funds. The parish priest has no choice but to obey, but this is clearly wrong. If we give money to our parish to pay for the running costs of our parish, the archdiocese has no right to appropriate that money for one of its projects, even important projects like those included in the Charitable Works Fund. Accordingly, if any parish money is taken under this scheme, it is, in fact, a misappropriation.

4.5.6 The Church's Need for Wealth

It is said that the Catholic Church is the wealthiest non-government organisation in the world. This may or may not be correct, but there can be no doubt that our church is extremely wealthy. The wealth of our church lies principally in property assets, such as churches, cathedrals, clerical residences, and private properties. There is also the Vatican, which itself is very valuable and which contains many almost priceless church treasures. In addition, our church has vast cash resources in the custody of many wealthy archdioceses. The source of this wealth is readily apparent. The church, over the last twenty centuries, had the devoted and dedicated lifetime service of many priests who were paid little more than their keep. During the spread of our faith by evangelisation and the formation of communities requiring pastoral care, our presbyters, and later priests, built churches and residences with funds donated by their communities. Excess funds were distributed to assist further growth and evangelisation. Some philanthropists funded significant building or beautification projects. Many devout members of the laity left substantial property to the church in their wills. Sometimes governments have directly funded churches and religious schools. The church has even imposed direct taxes at various times in history. And some enterprising priests have produced some innovative schemes to raise money, like holding the Silver Circle (a raffle), selling Christmas cakes or

Easter eggs, and letting people 'buy a brick' for 'ownership' in a building project.

Certainly, the church has spent vast amounts of money over the centuries. Whether this money was wisely spent is not for us to judge, although funding the crusades and the personal extravagances of some clerics appears inappropriate. We are, of course, entitled to have an opinion. A more relevant issue for our consideration is whether it is appropriate for our church to have such great wealth and how this wealth may best be utilised, having regard to the mission of the church. As is apparent, most of the church's wealth is in property, so it can be regarded as being asset-rich. The use of such property as clerical residences, churches, cathedrals, and the Vatican is clearly appropriate and serves an ongoing need of our church. However, the church also owns many private properties which it lets for rental income, which adds to the church's cash reserves. The question that arises here is whether the church needs such large cash reserves. If not, then why does the church not make these properties available to lay charitable organisations, like the Society of St Vincent de Paul, who try to provide temporary accommodation to people who are temporarily homeless due to some negative life event? As to the treasures in the Vatican, Jesus said that our real treasure is in heaven. Our church's real treasure is in the ordinary parish priests, who selflessly give a life of service to the church, which increases the material wealth of the church and implements the mission of the church. The Vatican treasures would be better sold rather than being kept under lock and key until they eventually perish. But such sale is most unlikely. As to the cash reserves of the church, we know that as with governments, it is better to be in surplus rather than in deficit, although the ideal is neither surplus nor deficit. So if the situation is that our church has a large cash surplus, which appears to be the case, then it should spend so much of that surplus as is not needed to cover contingencies. But what to spend the money on? Here we can ask some questions that may assist, having regard to the fact that our church is not a charity but rather a church with a specific mission.

(a) Why does the church not take better care of retired priests?
(b) Why does the church continue to appeal to us for more money when it has large cash reserves?
(c) Why does the church not pay for the running of infrastructure agencies out of surplus rather than demanding ongoing 'donations'?

There are many other worthwhile ways for the church to spend surplus cash, such as promoting vocations to the priesthood, setting up appropriate facilities for the evangelisation of young people and adult education, etc. While some of the observations in this section of this work appear critical, the criticism is intended to be constructive. Our modern concern is that the church's apparent preoccupation with money fosters the perception that the church has become a commercially focused business and is not practising the morality that it preaches.

4.6 The Teachings of the Church

4.6.1 The Current Content of Church Teachings

4.6.1.1 Overview

The teachings of our church are about our faith, our morals, devotional practices, and church liturgy. Our faith is what motivates our moral behaviour, and the church liturgy in part requires and, in fact, recommends our devotional practices. The totality of our church's teachings is generally called the doctrines of the Catholic Church, and this can be divided into two parts, called the dogma of the church and the non-dogmatic doctrines.

The dogmatic doctrines of our church are those teachings which have been formulated by the collective of bishops of our church in the church councils over the centuries or have been pronounced by a pope ex cathedra. They are almost exclusively about matters of faith, and our church claims that these teachings are absolutely correct and immutable—i.e. the church claims magisterium and papal infallibility over such teachings and presents them to us as the essential articles of our faith. In essence, they are theological necessities.

The non-dogmatic doctrines of our church are the rest of our church's teachings. Some of these doctrines are so firmly believed by our church that they have nearly the status of dogma but are not yet proclaimed as such; meanwhile, others are less absolute, and some are only recommended. Most of the firmly held teachings concern morals. Those which are direct applications of the Ten Commandments are very clear and firm, while those dealing with peripheral issues less so. And, of course, liturgy and devotional teachings can and have changed from time to time and therefore are non-essential, although some liturgies, like the canon of the Mass, are essentially immutable.

A comprehensive review of the contents of church teachings, both historical and current, would require many volumes and is well beyond the scope of this work. What we can consider is how we can access those teachings that the church has promulgated as its official teachings.

Most of us ordinary adult members of the Catholic laity will have reasonably sufficient education in our faith. However, most of us will need to consider some religious issues from time to time in relation to which our churches may have some teachings of which we are not aware. Such issues may be a crisis of faith, with which parts 2 and 3 of this work are intended to assist, or it may involve some relatively obscure or complex teaching of our church. We want to do what is right by God, so we need some help from our church's teachings. What we need to know is how and where we can obtain such help that is both Catholic and authoritative.

In modern times, we have several resources for Catholic authoritative information about our church's teachings. We could ask a priest, read the *Catechism of the Catholic Church*, or do private research.

4.6.1.2 Ask a Priest

Asking a priest is obviously the easiest way to get some answers about an issue that concerns us. But this is not always the most expedient way to a solution, because it involves making an appointment and then considering what the priest has told us. If the issue of concern is clearly answerable within the dogmatic teachings of the church or the canon law, then we have our answer. But if the issue concerns some non-dogmatic doctrine, then the priest's answer may not satisfy us.

This can be the case because our priests are ordinary human beings. They are not all equal in intelligence and approachability, although they are all highly educated in theological issues and trained to provide pastoral guidance. Some may be passionate and understanding about the issues that concern us, while others may be dismissive or bombastic. If the issue of concern involves something about which the Catholic Church does not yet have an authoritative teaching, then the priest we consult may not be aware of our church's best thinking about such an issue. For example, consider if our concern is about stem cell research. Archbishop Anthony Fisher of Sydney is a recognised leader in our church because of his qualifications. But as archbishop of Sydney, his workload may not make him accessible to us. A priest in a rural parish may have only rudimentary knowledge about this issue, which may not satisfy our concerns. In such a situation, we would probably have to do some further private research.

4.6.1.3 Private Research

The type of private research that we can do is to go to a library or religious bookshop and browse for texts that deal with the issues that concern us. We can then borrow or buy any relevant book and study it at our leisure. This is not an efficient mode of research, because many libraries do not contain books on a comprehensive range of religious issues, especially if the issue involves current theological advances. Religious bookshops have a broader range than most libraries; however, there are not that many of them, and they are almost non-existent in rural areas and some countries. Probably the most efficient resource in our time is the Internet. Using a reliable and reputable search engine, we can rapidly find texts and articles on virtually all the church's official teachings, as well as articles by our church's leading thinkers on issues that have not yet been incorporated into the official church teachings. For example, an article by the then bishop Fisher on stem cell research is available at http://www.CatholicAustralia. com.au/links/stem-cells.

4.6.1.4 The Catechism of the Catholic Church

Undoubtedly, the best resource for most of our church's official teachings is the *Catechism of the Catholic Church*. Many of us already own a copy of this book, but for those who do not, the whole text is available on the Internet, in several languages. This really is a wonderful book. The decision to create and publish it came from a resolution of the Second Extraordinary General Assembly of the Synod of Bishops on 25 January 1985, and its construction was initiated by Pope John Paul II in 1986, when he appointed a team of cardinals, bishops, and theologians to do this work. The text was approved by Pope John Paul II on 25 June 1992, and he promulgated it on 11 October 1992. It was first published in French, but this was subject to a master version in Latin, from which all later translations were to be taken. On 15 August 1997, Pope John Paul II promulgated the official Latin version. The current official version is accordingly the second edition, which replaces the first English edition of 1994.

The text of the book is 675 pages long, not including the prologue and appendices. It is written in four main parts. Part 1 deals with what we believe as Catholics and is essentially a detailed theological summary of our creed. Part 2 deals with our liturgy, the sacraments, and pastoral care. Part 3 deals with general morality and the Ten Commandments. Part 4 deals with our need for prayer and devotion.

This book does not contain all Catholic teachings and obviously cannot contain issues warranting teachings that have arisen after its publication. But as our current best resource, it is state of the art and almost comprehensive. We can hope for further editions which will undoubtedly include new teachings on present or future issues that require them. Our English translation is in plain but good English, although many of the theological concepts are expressed in sophisticated terms which assume a substantial knowledge and acceptance of Catholic theology. This is a compliment to us as the laity because the book was made available to us, and the complexity of the text presupposes that we have the intelligence to understand it, even if this requires some study and cross-referencing. However, it is clearly beyond comprehension for undereducated and mentally handicapped Catholics.

Overall, the text on particular topics is concise and clear. It properly references sources which themselves are mostly available on the Internet. The book is well organised, with a very detailed Contents page. Particular issues are readily accessible with an excellent index which is about one hundred eight pages long. Accordingly, it is structured and useful as a reference work. We can regard this book as authoritative and helpful in dealing with issues that would most certainly be more disturbing without such a resource. We can be thankful that our generation has a work that clearly shows the love our church has for its laity.

4.6.1.5 The Dogmas of the Catholic Church

The *Catechism* does not directly identify and deal with every dogma of our faith. Presumably, this is because many of the dogmas that have been formulated over the past two millennia were formulated to deal with specific controversies or heresies throughout our church's history, with many such issues having been resolved and, accordingly, not being issues of concern in modern times. Another reason is obviously that dealing with each dogma requires substantial explanation and reference to source materials, which requires voluminous theological materials and is therefore clearly beyond the scope of the *Catechism*. The *Catechism* does deal with all essential dogma in modern times in Part 1, as indicated above.

However, it may be helpful to us as the laity to at least know what those dogmas are, where we can access an authoritative account of the history and development, and where we can access further source materials if our concern requires this.

Accordingly, set out hereunder is a list of 248 dogmas specified as being *'de fide'* (i.e. formally proclaimed as dogma), taken from a book by Dr Ludwig Ott called *Fundamentals of Catholic Dogma*. Dr Ott was a Catholic priest and a lecturer in theology. His book was published in 1955 with the imprimatur of Bishop Cornelius. There have been no new dogmas since its publication. The list is in the order in which Dr Ott presents them in his book, but the numbering is unique to this work for ease of reference. This list is as follows:

Book 1. The Unity and Trinity of God

Part 1:   Section 1:   The Existence of God

1   God, our Creator and Lord, can be known with certainty, by the natural light of reason from created things.
2   God's existence is not merely an object of rational knowledge, but also an object of supernatural faith.

Section 2:   The Nature of God

3   God's Nature is incomprehensible to men.
4   The blessed in Heaven possess an immediate intuitive knowledge of the Divine Essence.
5   The immediate vision of God transcends the natural power of cognition of the human soul, and is therefore supernatural.
6   The soul, for the immediate vision of God, requires the light of glory.
7   God's Essence is also incomprehensible to the blessed in Heaven.

Section 3:   The Attributes of God

8   The divine attributes are really identical among themselves and with the Divine Essence.
9   God is absolutely perfect.
10   God is actually infinite in every perfection.
11   God is absolutely simple.
12   There is only one God.
13   The one God is, in the ontological sense, the true God.
14   God possesses an infinite power of cognition.
15   God is absolute veracity.
16   God is absolutely faithful.
17   God is absolute ontological goodness in Himself and in relation to others.
18   God is absolute moral goodness or holiness.
19   God is absolute benignity.
20   God is absolutely immutable.
21   God is eternal.
22   God is immense or absolutely immeasurable.
23   God is everywhere present in created space.
24   God's knowledge is infinite.
25   God's knowledge is subsistent.
26   God knows all that is merely possible by the knowledge of simple intelligence.
27   God knows all real things in the past, the present and the future.
28   By the knowledge of vision, God also foresees the future free acts of rational creatures with infallible certainty.
29   God's Divine Will is infinite.
30   God loves Himself of necessity, but loves and wills the creation of extra-divine things, on the other hand, with freedom.
31   God is almighty.
32   God is the Lord of the heavens and of the earth.
33   God is infinitely just.
34   God is infinitely merciful.

35   In God there are three Persons, the Father, the Son and the Holy Ghost. Each of the three Persons possesses the one (numerical) Divine Essence.

Part 2:   Section 1:   The Trinity of God

36   In God there are two internal divine processions.
37   The Divine Persons, not the Divine Nature, are the subject of the internal divine processions (in the active and in the passive sense).
38   The Second Divine Person proceeds from the First Divine Person by generation, and therefore is related to Him as Son to Father.
39   The Holy Ghost proceeds from the Father and from the Son as from a single principle through a single spiration.
40   The Holy Ghost does not proceed through generation but through spiration.
41   The relations in God are really identical with the Divine Nature.
42   The Three Divine Persons are in one another.
43   All the *ad extra* activities of God are common to the three Persons.

Book 2. God the Creator

Section 1:   The Act of Creation

44   All that exists outside God was, in its whole substance, produced out of nothing by God.
45   God was moved by His goodness to create the world.
46   The world was created for the glorification of God.
47   The Three Divine Persons are one single, common principle of creation.
48   God created the world free from exterior compulsion and inner necessity.
49   God has created a good world.

50 The world had a beginning in time.

51 God alone created the world.

52 God keeps all created things in existence.

53 God, through His Providence, protects and guides all that He has created.

Section 2: The Work of Creation

54 The first man was created by God.

55 Man consists of two essential parts—a material body and a spiritual soul.

56 The rational soul *per se* is the essential form of the body.

57 Every human being possesses an individual soul.

58 God has conferred on man a supernatural destiny.

59 Our first parents, before the fall, were endowed with sanctifying grace.

60 In addition to sanctifying grace, our first parents were endowed with the preternatural gift of bodily immortality.

61 Our first parents in Paradise sinned grievously through transgression of the Divine probationary commandment.

62 Through sin our first parents lost sanctifying grace and provoked the anger and the indignation of God.

63 Our first parents became subject to death and to the dominion of the devil.

64 Adam's sin is transmitted to his posterity, not by imitation but by descent.

65 Original sin is transmitted by natural generation.

66 In the state of original sin man is deprived of sanctifying grace and all that this implies, as well as of the preternatural gifts of integrity.

67 Souls who depart this life in the state of original sin are excluded from the Beatific Vision of God.

68 In the beginning of time God created spiritual essences (angels) out of nothing.

69 The nature of angels is spiritual.

70 The secondary task of the good angels is the protection of men and care for their salvation.

71 The devil possesses a certain dominion over mankind by reason of Adam's sin.

Book 3. God the Redeemer

Section 1: The Two Natures of Jesus

72 Jesus Christ is true God and true Son of God.

73 Christ assumed a real body, not an apparent body.

74 Christ assumed not only a body but also a rational soul.

75 Christ was truly generated and born of a daughter of Adam, the Virgin Mary.

76 The Divine and human natures are united hypostatically in Christ, that is, joined to each other in one Person.

77 In the hypostatic union each of the two natures of Christ continues unimpaired, untransformed, and unmixed with each other.

78 Each of the two natures in Christ possesses its own natural will and its own natural mode of operation.

79 The hypostatic union of Christ's human nature with the Divine Logos took place at the moment of conception.

80 The hypostatic union was effected by the three Divine Persons acting in common.

81 Only the second Divine Person became Man.

82 Not only as God but also as man Jesus Christ is the natural Son of God.

83 The God-Man Jesus Christ is to be venerated with one single mode of worship, the absolute worship of latria which is due to God alone.

84 Christ's Divine and human characteristics and activities are to be predicated of the one Word Incarnate.

85 Christ was free from all sin, from original sin as well as from all personal sin.

86 Christ's human nature was passible.

Part 2:   The Work of the Redeemer

87   The Son of God became man in order to redeem men.
88   Fallen man cannot redeem himself.
89   The God-man Jesus Christ is a high priest.
90   Christ offered Himself on the Cross as a true and proper sacrifice.
91   Christ by His sacrifice on the Cross has ransomed us and reconciled us with God.
92   Christ, through His passion and death, merited reward from God.
93   After His death, Christ's Soul, which was separated from His Body, descended into the underworld.
94   On the third day after His death, Christ rose gloriously from the dead.
95   Christ ascended body and soul into Heaven and sits at the right hand of the Father.

Part 3:   The Mother of the Redeemer

96   Mary is truly the Mother of God.
97   Mary was conceived without the stain of original sin. Mary is the Immaculate Conception.
98   Mary conceived by the Holy Ghost without the cooperation of man.
99   Mary bore her Son without any violation of her virginal integrity.
100 After the birth of Jesus, Mary remained a Virgin.
101 Mary was assumed body and soul into Heaven.

Book 4. God the Sanctifier

Part 1:   Grace

Section 1:   Actual Grace

102 There is a supernatural intervention of God in the faculties of the soul, which precedes the free act of the will.

103 There is a supernatural influence of God in the faculties of the soul which coincides in time with man's free act of will.

104 For every salutary act, internal supernatural grace of God (*gratia elevans*) is absolutely necessary.

105 Internal supernatural grace is absolutely necessary for the beginning of faith and salvation.

106 Without the special help of God, the justified cannot persevere to the end in justification.

107 The justified person is not able for his whole life long to avoid sins, even venial sins, without the special privilege of the grace of God.

108 Even in the fallen state, man can, by his natural intellectual power, know religious and moral truths.

109 For the performance of a morally good action, sanctifying grace is not required.

110 In the state of fallen nature, it is morally impossible for man without supernatural Revelation, to know easily, with absolute certainty, and without admixture of error, all religious and moral truths of the natural order.

111 Grace cannot be merited by natural works either *de condigno* or *de congruo*.

112 God gives all the just sufficient grace for the observation of the divine commandments.

113 God, by His eternal resolve of Will, has predetermined certain men to eternal blessedness.

114 God, by an eternal resolve of His Will, predestines certain men, on account of their foreseen sins, to eternal rejection.

115 The human will remains free under the influence of efficacious grace, which is not irresistible.

116 There is grace which is truly sufficient and yet remains inefficacious.

Section 2:   Habitual Grace

117 The sinner can and must prepare himself by the help of actual grace for the reception of the grace by which he is justified.

118 The justification of an adult is not possible without faith.

119 Besides faith, further acts of disposition must be present.

120 Sanctifying grace sanctifies the soul.

121 Sanctifying grace makes the just man a friend of God.

122 Sanctifying grace makes the just man a child of God and gives him a claim to the inheritance of heaven.

123 The three Divine or theological virtues of faith, hope and charity are infused with sanctifying grace.

124 Without special Divine Revelation no one can know with the certainty of faith, if he be in the state of grace.

125 The degree of justifying grace is not identical in all the just.

126 Grace can be increased by good works.

127 The grace by which we are justified may be lost, and is lost by every grievous sin.

128 By his good works, the justified man really acquires a claim to supernatural reward from God.

129 A just man merits for himself through each good work an increase of sanctifying grace, eternal life (if death finds him in the state of grace) and an increase in heavenly glory.

Part 2:   The Catholic Church

130 The Catholic Church was founded by the God-Man Jesus Christ.

131 Christ founded the Catholic Church in order to continue His work of redemption for all time.

132 Christ gave His Church a hierarchical constitution.

133 The powers bestowed on the Apostles have descended to the Bishops.

134 Christ appointed the Apostle Peter to be the first of all the Apostles and to be the visible Head of the whole Catholic Church, by appointing him immediately and personally to the primacy of jurisdiction.

135 According to Christ's ordinance, Peter is to have successors in his Primacy over the whole Catholic Church and for all time.

136 The successors of Peter in the Primacy are the Bishops of Rome.

137 The Pope possesses full and supreme power of jurisdiction over the whole Catholic Church, not merely in matters of faith and morals, but also in Church discipline and in the government of the Church.

138 The Pope is infallible when he speaks *ex cathedra*.

139 By virtue of Divine right, the bishops possess an ordinary power of government over their dioceses.

140 Christ founded the Catholic Church.

141 Christ is the Head of the Catholic Church.

142 In the final decision on doctrines concerning faith and morals, the Catholic Church is infallible.

143 The primary object of the Infallibility is the formally revealed truths of Christian Doctrine concerning faith and morals.

144 The totality of the Bishops is infallible, when they, either assembled in general council or scattered over the earth propose a teaching of faith or morals as one to be held by all the faithful.

145 The Church founded by Christ is unique and one.

146 The Church founded by Christ is holy.

147 The Church founded by Christ is catholic.

148 The Church founded by Christ is apostolic.

149 Membership of the Catholic Church is necessary for all men for salvation.

150 It is permissible and profitable to venerate the Saints in Heaven, and to invoke their intercession.

151 It is permissible and profitable to venerate the relics of the Saints.

152 It is permissible and profitable to venerate images of the Saints.

153 The living faithful can come to the assistance of the souls in Purgatory by their intercessions.

Part 3:   The Sacraments

154 The Sacraments of the New Covenant contain the grace which they signify, and bestow it on those who do not hinder it.

155 The Sacraments work *ex opera operato*, that is, the sacraments operate by the power of the completed sacramental rite.

156 All the Sacraments of the New Covenant confer sanctifying grace on the receivers.

157 Three Sacraments, Baptism, Confirmation, and Holy Orders, imprint a character, that is an indelible spiritual mark, and, for this reason, cannot be repeated.

158 The sacramental character is a spiritual mark imprinted on the soul.

159 The sacramental character continues at least until the death of the bearer.

160 All Sacraments of the New Covenant were instituted by Jesus Christ.

161 There are seven Sacraments of the New Law.

162 The Sacraments of the New Covenant are necessary for the salvation of mankind.

163 For the valid dispensing of the Sacraments it is necessary that the minister accomplish the Sacramental sign in the proper manner.

164 The minister must have the intention of at least doing what the Church does.

165 In the case of adult recipients moral worthiness is necessary for the worthy or fruitful reception of the Sacraments.

Sacrament 1:   Baptism

166 Baptism is a true Sacrament instituted by Jesus Christ.
167 The *materia remota* of the Sacrament of Baptism is true and natural water.
168 Baptism confers the grace of justification.
169 Baptism effects the remission of all punishments of sin, both eternal and temporal.
170 Even if it be unworthily received, valid Baptism imprints on the soul of the recipient an indelible spiritual mark, the Baptismal Character, and for this reason, the Sacrament cannot be repeated.
171 Baptism by water (*Baptismus fluminis*) is, since the promulgation of the Gospel, necessary for all men without exception for salvation.
172 Baptism can be validly administered by anyone.
173 Baptism can be received by any person in the wayfaring state who is not already baptised.
174 The Baptism of young children is valid and licit.

Sacrament 2:   Confirmation

175 Confirmation is a true Sacrament properly so-called.
176 Confirmation imprints on the soul an indelible spiritual mark, and for this reason, cannot be repeated.
177 The ordinary minister of Confirmation is the Bishop alone.

Sacrament 3:   Holy Eucharist

178 The Body and Blood of Jesus Christ are truly, really, and substantially present in the Eucharist.
179 Christ becomes present in the Sacrament of the Altar by the transformation of the whole substance of the bread into His Body and of the whole substance of the wine into His Blood.
180 The accidents of bread and wine continue after the change of the substance.

181 The Body and Blood of Christ together with His Soul and Divinity and therefore, the whole Christ, are truly present in the Eucharist.

182 The Whole Christ is present under each of the two Species.

183 When either consecrated Species is divided, the Whole Christ is present in each part of the Species.

184 After the Consecration has been completed the Body and Blood are permanently present in the Eucharist.

185 The Worship of Adoration (*latria*) must be given to Christ present in the Eucharist.

186 The Eucharist is a true Sacrament instituted by Jesus Christ.

187 The matter for the consummation of the Eucharist is bread and wine.

188 For children before the age of reason, the reception of the Eucharist is not necessary for salvation.

189 Communion under two forms is not necessary for any individual members of the Faithful, either by reason of Divine precept or as a means of salvation.

190 The power of consecration resides in a validly consecrated priest only.

191 The Sacrament of the Eucharist can be validly received by every baptised person in the wayfaring state, including young children.

192 For the worthy reception of the Eucharist, the state of grace as well as the proper and pious disposition are necessary.

193 The Holy Mass is a true and proper Sacrifice.

194 In the Sacrifice of the Mass, Christ's Sacrifice on the Cross is made present, its memory celebrated, and its saving power applied.

195 In the Sacrifice of the Mass and in the Sacrifice of the Cross the Sacrificial Gift and the Primary Sacrificing Priest are identical; only the nature and the mode of the offering are different.

196 The Sacrifice of the Mass is not merely a sacrifice of praise and thanks-giving, but also a sacrifice of expiation and impetration.

Sacrament 4:   Penance

197 The Church has received from Christ the power of remitting sins committed after Baptism.

198 By the Church's Absolution sins are truly and immediately remitted.

199 The Church's power to forgive sins extends to all sin without exception.

200 The exercise of the Church's power to forgive sins is a judicial act.

201 The forgiveness of sins which takes place in the Tribunal of Penance is a true and proper Sacrament, which is distinct from the Sacrament of Baptism.

202 Extra-sacramental justification is effected by perfect sorrow only when it is associated with the desire for the Sacrament (*votumsacramenti*).

203 Contrition springing from the motive of fear is a morally good and supernatural act.

204 The Sacramental confession of sins is ordained by God and is necessary for salvation.

205 By virtue of Divine ordinance, all grievous sins according to kind and number, as well as those circumstances which alter their nature, are subject to the obligation of confession.

206 The confession of venial sins is not necessary but is permitted and is useful.

207 All temporal punishments for sin are not always remitted by God with the guilt of sin and the eternal punishment.

208 The priest has the right and duty, according to the nature of the sins and the ability of the penitent, to impose salutary and appropriate works for satisfaction.

209 Extra-sacramental penitential works, such as the performance of voluntary penitential practices and the patient bearing of trials sent by God, possess satisfactory value.

210 The form of the Sacrament of Penance consists in the words of Absolution.

211 Absolution, in association with the acts of the penitent, effects the forgiveness of sins.

212 The principal effect of the Sacrament of Penance is the reconciliation of the sinner with God.

213 The Sacrament of Penance is necessary for salvation to those who, after Baptism, fall into grievous sin.

214 The sole possessors of the Church's Power of Absolution are the bishops and priests.

215 Absolution given by deacons, clerics or lower rank, and laymen is not Sacramental Absolution.

216 The Sacrament of Penance can be received by any baptised person who, after Baptism, has committed a grievous or a venial sin.

217 The Church possesses the power to grant Indulgences.

218 The use of Indulgences is useful and salutary to the Faithful.

Sacrament 5:   Extreme Unction

219 Extreme Unction or anointing of the sick is a true and proper Sacrament instituted by Jesus Christ.

220 The remote matter of Extreme Unction is oil.

221 The form consists in the prayer of the priest for the sick person which accomplishes the anointing.

222 Extreme Unction gives the sick person sanctifying grace in order to arouse and strengthen him.

223 Extreme Unction effects the remission of grievous sins still remaining and of venial sins.

224 Extreme Unction sometimes effects the restoration of bodily health, if this be of spiritual advantage.

225 Only Bishops and priests can validly administer Extreme Unction.

226 Extreme Unction can be received only by the Faithful who are seriously ill.

Sacrament 6:   Holy Orders

227 Holy Order is a true and proper Sacrament which was instituted by Jesus Christ.

228 The consecration of priests is a Sacrament.

229 Bishops are superior to priests.

230 The Sacrament of Order confers sanctifying grace on the recipient.

231 The Sacrament of Order imprints a character on the recipient.

232 The Sacrament of Order confers a permanent spiritual power on the recipient.

233 The ordinary dispenser of all grades of Order, both the sacramental and the non-sacramental, is the validly consecrated Bishop alone.

Sacrament 7:   Matrimony

234 Marriage is a true and proper Sacrament instituted by God.

235 From the sacramental contract of marriage emerges the Bond of Marriage, which binds both marriage partners to a lifelong indivisible community of life.

236 The Sacrament of Matrimony bestows sanctifying grace on the contracting parties.

Book 5. God the Consummator

237 In the present order of salvation, death is a punishment for sin.

238 All human beings subject to original sin are subject to the law of death.

239 The souls of the just which in the moment of death are free from all guilt of sin and punishment for sin, enter into Heaven.

240 The bliss of Heaven lasts for all eternity.

241 The degree of perfection of the Beatific Vision granted to the just is proportioned to each one's merit.

242 The souls of those who die in the condition of personal grievous sin enter Hell.

243 The punishment of Hell lasts for all eternity.

244 The souls of the just which, in the moment of death, are burdened with venial sins or temporal punishment due to sins, enter purgatory.

245 At the end of the world Christ will come again in glory to pronounce judgement.

246 All the dead will rise again on the last day with their bodies.

247 The dead will rise again with the same bodies as they had on earth.

248 Christ, on His second coming, will judge all men.

Dr Ott defines the concept of dogma as follows: '*By dogma in the strict sense is understood a truth immediately (formally) revealed by God which has been proposed by the Teaching Authority of the church to be believed as such.*' In the text of his book, he gives an explanation of the meaning of each of the subject dogmas or other teachings, citing the sources of the dogma or teaching and quoting the key parts of the source document.

The work of Dr Ott will be sufficient for most of us Catholic laity, but if more detailed research is required, then there is a standard text that can be recommended. This is *Denzinger: Enchiridion Symbolorum*, forty-third edition, published in 2012 by Ignatius Press, updated from the first edition published in 1854.

From a reading of the above list, it is readily apparent that our dogmas are essentially articles of faith. As such, they are irrelevant to issues of morality, devotion, or liturgy that we may need to consider in our day-to-day lives. However, in dialogue with persons whose opinions warrant respect, we may hear a proposition that contradicts one or more of these above dogmas. The most common of these are 'I do not believe that God exists' or 'I do not believe that Jesus was divine'. It is in relation to such views that we need to know what our dogmas are and how our church requires us to respond to them. The status of dogma is that they are settled articles of faith and are not open to debate. We cannot question them or ignore them or contradict them. Privately, we must be satisfied that our church's dogma is true and correct to the degree that enables us to publicly, honestly profess belief in their correctness and to base our moral actions and decisions on our belief in the correctness of the relevant dogma.

To publicly contradict dogma is heresy, which was, in the past, a capital offence. These days, it is merely a self-exclusion from valid membership of the Catholic Church.

4.6.2 Challenges of Current Teachings

4.6.2.1 Magisterium

The most substantive and general challenge to the teachings of our church is as to their status. The church claims magisterium, i.e. authority and infallibility of all its teachings that can be classified as dogma. This is a self-serving dogma which warrants consideration. St Paul also claimed this in his teachings and writings, which are part of the New Testament. Magisterium, as it is understood today, was not specifically granted to the apostles by Jesus in commissioning them. Essentially, Jesus promised to send the Paraclete (John 44:15–17) to guide our church, which happened on Pentecost. But this does not mean that the Holy Spirit controlled those responsible for formulating church teachings to the extent of overriding their individual intelligence, free will, and the human vulnerability to error. There is a difference between guidance and control. If control had been promised by Jesus, we could accept the claim of infallibility, because obviously the Holy Spirit is infallible. What the Spirit gave to the apostles at Pentecost was the gift of tongues and the power to express themselves (Acts 2:4–5). Our modern-day successors of the apostles certainly have the power to express themselves well and to do so in many languages.

In relation to the concept of infallibility, our church teaches that the Holy Spirit will not allow our church to fall into serious error. We do not know how the Holy Spirit does this, but we do know that the Holy Spirit does not take over the bodies of popes or bishops and speak through them, nor does it appear to them in visions. We do know that our popes and bishops carefully consider and pray about serious matters before pronouncing any dogma. They do the same for serious non-dogmatic moral issues, and accordingly, teachings on these issues should be strongly regarded as correct, if not infallibly so.

To understand the nature of the church's claim to the infallibility of the magisterium teachings and the infallibility of a pope's ex cathedra teachings, we need to consider these concepts in relation to the church's and pope's authority. The word *infallibility* is unfortunate, because although it is the word which most nearly expresses the concept desired, it has aspects of meaning implying divinity or supernatural power in those claiming the infallibility.

Throughout human history, people have often been sceptical about claims of supernatural powers. Even the prophets of the Old Testament were often treated with scorn and rejection by some people they addressed. It is this human wisdom to not be naive or gullible that challenges the church's claim to the infallibility of its teachings. Our church does not claim that its bishops and the pope are divine or that they have supernatural powers. The infallibility claim stems from the church's authority. In commissioning the apostles to evangelise his commands and teachings, Jesus clearly delegated to them the authority to do this under his claim that *'all authority in heaven and on earth have been given to me'* (Matthew 28:18–19). Clearly, these teachings are infallible because Jesus is divine.

This specific grant of authority necessarily carries with it a number of implied authorities. Due to the vagaries of language and the generalised nature of Jesus's teachings, it is implied that the church can authoritatively interpret and apply his teachings as circumstances require. While the source teachings of Jesus are immutable and infallible, if specific circumstances change, so may the church's translations, interpretations, and applications change. Any such change does not make the source teachings any less infallible.

Another implication is that the church has authority to teach on collateral issues on which Jesus himself was silent. This does not suggest that the teachings of Jesus were insufficient or that Jesus overlooked any necessary issue. But it does make the status of such teachings by the church less infallible than the teachings of Jesus while remaining authoritative. This is the status of our church's doctrines that relate to such collateral issues. These are not the type of teachings over which our church claims papal infallibility or magisterium.

Clearly, the pope, as head of our church, and our cardinals and bishops, as its leaders, have authority from Jesus to proclaim as essential to our faith certain doctrines. Such doctrines are usually theological necessities. Many of these were settled in the first few centuries after the death of Jesus and required dogmatic pronouncement by our church because early theological thinking by some raised propositions which the orthodox theologians of the church considered erroneous and identified as heretical. Our church's authority and duty to reject heresy and to counter them with dogmatic statements is unarguable.

It is the church's dogma which is infallible, and this dogma is essentially the commands and teachings of Jesus and the counter-heresy proclamations of the head and leaders of our church.

To consider our church's claim to infallibility of its teachings, we should firstly consider whether our church presents the entirety of all its teachings as infallible. To this end, we can classify the church's teachings into the following categories.

4.6.2.1.1 The Ten Commandments

The Ten Commandments are God's laws, given to the Jewish people by God the Father. The church does not have the authority to repeal or amend or add to them. The commandments are generalisations, and the church has a duty to formulate and teach the particular types of conduct that breach or offend these commandments. For example, the church must teach whether abortion is a breach of the fifth commandment, at what stage in the process of procreation human life begins, and whether there are any circumstances in which a pregnancy can lawfully be terminated under God's law. This the church has done and teaches in the *Catechism*, in articles 1 to 10 of Section 2 of Part 3 of that work.

In relation to the example of abortion given above, the church has declared that human life begins at the moment of conception and that any termination of a pregnancy after this moment is prima facie contrary to the fifth commandment. The church's view is based on biological science, but there is also the spiritual mystery of when an embryo acquires a human soul. The church's determination to regard this acquisition as occurring at the moment of conception may be conservative, but there is wisdom in the approach that it is better to be safe than sorry, especially when the actuality is unknowable. Accordingly, we can be justified in accepting all the church's teachings about the Ten Commandments as absolutely correct without challenging the church's claim to infallibility.

4.6.2.1.2 The Four Gospels

The Gospels are not, strictly speaking, a teaching of our church. They are a record of the teachings of Jesus. If we accept that Jesus was divine, which we do as Catholics, then clearly the commandments and teachings of Jesus are absolutely correct and infallible. The teachings of Jesus are far more particular and specific than the Ten Commandments, and Jesus also endorsed and particularised the types of conduct that contravene the Ten Commandments. For obvious reasons, Jesus was silent on activities that were not possible during his lifetime because the technology had not then been discovered, so our church has to deal with issues that have arisen after the time of Jesus. Jesus also taught about issues not directly related to the Ten Commandments, such as the Beatitudes. Again, some of these teachings, which he exemplified in his parables, have warranted identification as principles of broader application requiring more specific teachings and explanation.

The *Catechism* deals with the life of Jesus in Chapter 2 of Part 1 and with some of his teachings in Chapter 3 of Part 1. Many of the teachings of Jesus were perfectly clear and require no further explanation. Those teachings which involved theological issues have been presented as part of our church's teachings in the *Catechism*. Again, our church is using the best theological thinking available. We, the laity, do not really need much theology. What we need is practical guidance as to what actions or decisions will support living a life that is pleasing to God. With this perspective, we can accept the teachings of Jesus as absolutely correct and infallible, and the churches supplementary teachings related to the Gospels are also absolutely correct. This we can regard as our church's teachings on divine moral prescriptions.

4.6.2.1.3 The Acts of the Apostles

The Acts of the Apostles and the other parts of the New Testament do not have as much weight or authority as the Gospels, because they are not a record of anything that Jesus said or did. They are a record of the history of the early church. They deal with events and teachings that occurred after the ascension of Jesus. It is believed that the author of Luke's Gospel also wrote the Acts of the Apostles, as can be seen in the introduction to the Acts of the Apostles in the Jerusalem Bible. The Acts is mainly a chronicle of events, which includes the texts of the teachings by St Paul and others.

The letters in the New Testament are key teaching documents because they show the early teachings of the church. They are often cited as sources of some of our church's modern teachings and, as such, demonstrate the temporal catholicity of our church's teachings. However, many of the letters were written to deal with issues of the time, many of which were resolved and are no longer of any concern, meaning that the teachings contained therein are no longer relevant.

Much of this part of the New Testament is about the conversion, travels, adventures, and teachings of St Paul. St Paul is arguably the greatest evangelist in the history of our church, but he never met Jesus, except in his uncorroborated vision. He was not with the apostles at Pentecost and had no official status in our fledgling church, although he was widely accepted and claimed authority from Jesus pursuant to his vision. Again, his teachings are a source of our church's current teachings. St Paul was clearly a highly intelligent man dedicated and zealous in the service of God, with an unblemished character after his conversion. The application of his views in our church's current teachings should justifiably be highly regarded and accepted, but they cannot carry the same status and infallibility as the words of Jesus. Not that there is any conflict or inconsistency between St Paul and Jesus, the point being that the teachings of Paul are secondary and subject to the teachings of Jesus and, accordingly, have a lower status. Some of the matters dealt with by Paul could not have been discussed or dealt with by Jesus.

4.6.2.1.4 Papal Encyclicals and Church Council Decrees

Our Catholic dogma of papal infallibility, seen as the authority of St Peter under the guidance of the Holy Spirit, has clearly existed since the assumption of Jesus but was only declared to be dogma by the First Vatican Council on 18 July 1870. Since that time, there has been only one instance of the use of this authority, and that was by Pope Pius XII when he declared the Assumption of Mary to be dogma in 1950. While it is a dogma, this proposition is mainly theological, with little impact on our daily lives other than as a devotional justification.

Throughout history, our popes have rarely used the authority to declare dogma ex cathedra (about seven times in all). In relation to issues of concern to our church that require a new dogma to be proclaimed, the popes have almost universally relied on church councils convened by the pope to make such proclamations as the assembly of the bishops considers correct.

Accordingly, the consternation that some Catholics feel in having as dogma the infallibility of the pope is really a storm in a teacup, because it is little used and will probably remain so in the foreseeable future.

But in our modern world, the pope is a prominent world figure whose views on faith-related issues are highly regarded and therefore substantially influential. Our popes know this and regularly express their views on faith-related issues in public statements and encyclicals. Most of us Catholics regard such pronouncements as the official teachings of our church, and some even misperceive them as dogma.

The current position appears to be that such pronouncements by a pope are not dogma unless specifically declared to be so. Nor do they have the same status as official church doctrine promulgated by church councils—i.e. they are lower in status. However, our popes are the head of the Roman Curia, which is a collection of bishops permanently stationed in the Vatican, organised into various departments, who assist the pope in formulating administrative decisions and doctrinal views. It would be unlikely and rare for the bishops of a church council to disagree with the expert bishops of the Roman Curia; therefore, the views of the popes, supported by the Curia, can, for practical purposes, be regarded as doctrine.

4.6.2.1.5 The Catechism of the Catholic Church

As already considered, the *Catechism of the Catholic Church* is a most valuable resource to the laity of our church in this age of literacy and education of the laity. It was initiated by Pope John Paul II on the twentieth anniversary of the close of the Vatican II, and as Pope John Paul II states in his introduction to the *Catechism*, it was inspired by the need for improvement identified in Vatican II. It is essentially a compilation of church teachings containing both dogma and doctrine. Although it was constructed by a synod of bishops, it does not formulate any new dogma or teachings. It is essentially a catechism.

From all the issues already considered herein and a basic familiarity with Catholic history, it is clear that our church has evolved over the last 2,000 years. There is no basis to conclude that the process of church evolution has now reached its zenith and that there will be no further development or improvement in church teachings. From this, it follows that our *Catechism* is not perfect and will require revision and amendment in the future, although it was state of the art when it was produced.

The status of the *Catechism* is that some parts of it contain the dogmatic teachings of our church. This is mainly Part 1, which deals with our creed; Part 2, which deals with the sacraments; and Section 2 of Part 3, which deals with the Ten Commandments. Section 1 of Part 3 is mostly church doctrine based on human wisdom, and Part 4 is largely devotional doctrine.

Of course, all our church's teachings are important and valuable to us, but the status of particular teachings becomes significant to us in the light of the concepts of papal infallibility and the magisterium of the assembly of bishops. The concept that some teachings are unarguably correct carries with it the corollary that those teachings that are not specified as unarguably correct may be incorrect or expired through current irrelevance or even optional as purely devotional. Unfortunately, but understandably, the *Catechism* does not identify all the dogmatic teachings as such. With the use of our intelligence, we can discern which teachings are purely devotional. These are clearly optional, although they are strongly recommended by our church as capable of increasing our love of God. That leaves other teachings which are based on the best human wisdom of our bishops, whose sole agenda was to help us save our souls, with the status of guidance and not dogma.

4.6.2.1.6 The Compendium of the Catechism of the Catholic Church

Another worthwhile and valuable resource for us is the *Compendium of the Catechism of the Catholic Church*. This compendium is a comparatively short book and is a synthesis of the *Catechism*, presented in question-and-answer format, dealing with all the topics in the Catholic catechism in the same order. The preparation of this work was initiated by Pope John Paul II in 2003, when he appointed a commission of cardinals presided over by the then cardinal Ratzinger, prefect of the Congregation for the Doctrine of Faith, to prepare the text. The work was completed on 28 June 2005. Pope Benedict XVI (formerly Cardinal Ratzinger) approved the publication of the compendium.

In his motu proprio approving the work, Pope Benedict XVI pointed out that the *Catechism* was primarily addressed to bishops as a reference work of authentic Catholic teaching and doctrine. It is clearly apparent from a reading of the catechism that the language of the catechism and exposition of issues and concepts presupposes higher education in Catholic theology. Nevertheless, the catechism was widely published and well-received by the Catholic laity. The need to make it more comprehensible to the less theologically educated laity became apparent, and Pope Benedict XVI also said in his motu proprio that the compendium, *'with its brevity, clarity and comprehensiveness, is directed to every human being'.*

4.6.3 Natural Moral Law

The main challenge to the status of the non-dogmatic teachings of the Catholic Church lies in the reliance of our church on its perceptions of the contents of natural law from which the 'natural moral law' is derived. To understand this challenge, we need some familiarity with the hierarchy of laws and the role of reason and intelligence in interpreting and applying these laws.

In the hierarchy of laws, the divine law is supreme. Then comes the natural law, and below that is human law. Canon law is not recognised as a type of law. It is more in the nature of the terms of employment of the Catholic clergy, and to the extent that they purport to rule the laity, they may be seen as ultra vires, i.e. beyond their authority. Of course, what priests are allowed to do or not allowed to do has an impact on the laity, but this is legitimate.

4.6.3.1 Divine Law

Divine law is the law made by God. Naturally, atheists deny the existence of this type of law. As believers, we accept that God has revealed as much of his divine law as we need to lead lives pleasing to him. This revelation has been through the prophets, the Ten Commandments, and the commands and teachings of Jesus. All our church's teachings, which are interpretations and applications of the divine law, can and should be accepted by us as absolutely correct, without reservation.

4.6.3.2 Natural Law

Natural law is expressed in the Catholic catechism, in Paragraph 1956, as follows:

The natural law, present in the heart of each man and established by reason, is universal in its precepts and its authority extends to all men. It expresses the dignity of the person and determines the basis for his fundamental rights and duties:

For there is a true Law: right reason. It is in conformity with nature, is diffused among all men, and is immutable and eternal; its orders summon to duty; its prohibitions turn away from offence . . . To replace it with a contrary law is a sacrilege; failure to apply even one of its provisions is forbidden; no one can abrogate it entirely.

Pope Paul VI, in his encyclical *Humanae Vitae*, said in Paragraph 4 as follows:

No believer will wish to deny that the teaching authority of the Church is competent to interpret even the natural moral law. It is, in fact, indisputable as Our Predecessors have many times declared, that Jesus Christ, when communicating to Peter and to the Apostles his Divine authority and sending them to teach all nations His Commandments, constituted them as guardians and authentic interpreters of all moral law, not only, that is, of the law of the gospel, but also of the natural law, which is also an expression of the will of God, the faithful fulfilment of which is equally necessary for salvation.

Certainly, many philosophers and theologians throughout history accept that there is such a thing as natural law. The problem is that what it is and what it prescribes and proscribes is not written anywhere. It is a totally abstract concept. What history and experience has shown us is that not everyone agrees that our church's version of the contents of natural law is correct. Some people even argue that there are natural moral laws that are clearly contrary to current church teachings.

For example, the pro-abortionists argue that a woman has an absolute right, discernible from natural law, to terminate a pregnancy if she wishes, because she has the right to control the reproductive process of her own body. By contrast, our church and other natural law proponents argue that natural moral law requires a person to do what is good, and killing a foetus or embryo cannot be good.

For atheists, humanists, and others, the natural law contains some sort of a bill of human rights, and for them, this is the highest law. But it is unwritten, so what these natural laws are is essentially a matter of opinion. If all the natural laws were *'written in the heart of every person'*, then there would be consensus amongst all persons as to what these laws are. But this is not the case. We humans have a tendency to rationalise, i.e. to find and argue reasons to let us do what we want to do, regardless of what our heart tells us.

The point is that arguing on the basis of our perception of what is a natural law is a two-edged sword because the opponents can argue persuasively from their contrary perception of natural law. The challenge to our church's teachings based on natural law is our church's claim that its view of what is natural law is necessarily the only correct perception of all natural law. Since it is not objectively discernible, the church cannot identify any source of its perception other than the consensus of all humans across all generations, which clearly does not exist.

We, the laity, accept that our church teachers, who have formulated their perceptions of natural law, are good, intelligent men whose main agenda is to help save our souls. We regard their teachings based on natural law as altruistic human wisdom.

Our church's claim that it has authority from Jesus to teach about natural law is obviously vacuous to atheists and humanists. Claiming that it has this authority does not make it so, especially since the authority is, at best, implied, and not necessarily so. Nor does it prove the correctness of the church's perceptions of what actually is the natural law. Even to us laity, the church's claim to have authority from Jesus to teach about natural law is less than persuasive, despite the frequency of this claim over the centuries from eminent clergy.

The fact is that there is no clear reference to natural law by Jesus anywhere in the Gospels. The Gospel texts giving the apostles and their successors authority to teach (quoted above) are crystal clear as to what they were authorised to teach, and that is to teach what Jesus himself taught and his commandments. The obvious question that flows from this is whether our church actually needs to teach anything based on natural law. Does the church hold the view that the teachings and commandments of Jesus were incomplete or inadequate to deal with the diversity of human conduct? We understand that in the work of evangelisation, it is often necessary to engage in dialogue with non-Catholics and to address their perceptions of natural law and to accommodate beliefs and practices that do not conflict with the teachings of Jesus. So our church should be armed with a comprehensive set of perceptions about natural law and views on how they relate to the teachings of Jesus. But is it necessary to incorporate natural law perceptions and teachings in the official teachings to us, the converted laity?

The forgoing is not a criticism of our church's reference to natural moral law; rather, it is more in the nature of a caveat. Such a caveat would not be helpful if our church had no alternative. But there is an alternative.

We already have a substantial body of divine law which has been revealed to us by God in the Old Testament and in the life and teachings of Jesus. We also have what may be called divine moral prescriptions, which can be known from the life and teachings of Jesus and the teachings of the prophets of the Old Testament. The combination of these two bodies of laws and prescriptions is necessarily sufficient to cover any proposition that can reasonably be argued to be a precept of natural moral law.

The difference between a divine law and a divine moral prescription is that the divine law has a sanction or punishment, whereas the divine moral prescriptions promise a reward. In other words, God will punish a failure to comply with his divine law unless it is forgiven, but he gives a reward if a divine moral prescription is complied with. Compliance with divine law is required, and compliance with divine moral prescriptions is optional. Compliance with divine law makes us acceptable to God, and compliance with divine moral prescriptions makes us pleasing to God. Both divine law and divine moral prescriptions can specify either some action or avoidance of some action.

Jesus became human to redeem us, which he did by his passion and death. We needed to know what we must do to take advantage of our redemption, so Jesus brought us the Good News of eternal life, God's love and mercy, what we must do to gain eternal life, and how we can love God in return. This is a theological aspect of Jesus, but in his life and teachings, he showed us the necessary divine laws and divine moral prescriptions. The divine laws that Jesus specified are seen in his commands and his statements about human conduct that offends God and warrants punishment. The divine moral prescriptions that Jesus revealed are seen in some of the incidents in his life, his teachings about the Beatitudes, and other teachings, especially those parables that resulted in some human or divine reward. His miracles were often a reward for faith. Clearly, there is a substantial number of divine moral prescriptions or moral lessons that can be learned from just the Gospels. In addition, there are also many moral lessons that can be learned from the Old Testament, especially from the teachings and lives of the prophets.

With the above perspective, the question we might ask our church is whether it is really necessary to look at natural law for more laws and guidance to influence our conduct. Are not the divine law and divine moral prescriptions enough? Or are the divine law and divine moral prescriptions somehow insufficient or inadequate? And is not natural moral law merely a synonym for right human reasoning on moral issues? Bear in mind that right human reasoning is thinking as men do, not as God does, and that Jesus said, *'For my yoke is easy, and my burden is light.'* (Matthew 11:30). So how can our church justify burdening us with human reasoning if divine law and divine moral prescriptions are sufficient?

To date, our church has not produced or compiled a comprehensive list of divine moral prescriptions. However, our priests are well educated and know what all these lessons to be learned from the life and teachings of Jesus are, and they are required to teach us about these precepts in the homily that they are required to present at Mass, explaining the text of the Gospel reading of the day. If our church were to compile a list of divine moral prescriptions, which undoubtedly our church has the resources to achieve, such a list may well be sufficient to encompass all the precepts of what is argued to be natural moral law. The benefit of this would be that the divine moral prescriptions based on the life and teachings of Jesus and the prophets of the Old Testament would be far more authoritative than the debatable precepts of natural moral law. Whether our church takes action to compile such a list is a matter for the church. In the light of the present adequacy of the Catholic catechism, it seems unlikely that such a list will be compiled any time soon. But in the fullness of time, the wisdom of avoiding the controversies involving arguing natural moral law precepts may lead our church along this path.

4.6.3.3 Human Law

There is relatively little that we need to consider about human law. Jesus endorsed the legitimacy of human law in saying *'give to Caesar what is Caesar's and give to God what is God's'* (Matthew

22:21–22). Jesus was talking about money, and this is almost universally what governments want from us. In return, they give us the ability to earn more money, which provides more taxes.

There is seldom any conflict between human law and divine law, since most human laws are based on the essence of the Ten Commandments. Commercial laws are based on honesty, fairness, and justice, while other laws, like traffic laws, are intended to provide peace and good order in the community.

Because human laws are legitimate, we as Catholics should obey them, unless they require or forbid us to do something that is forbidden or required by God's laws. That will rarely happen, but it has happened. For example, communism forbade religious worship. What is more common are human laws that allow some action or conduct that is forbidden by God's law. For example, it was the law in many countries that any abortion, except one necessary to save the life of the mother, was illegal. These laws have changed to the present situation, where abortion is available on demand without the requirement of any reasonable justification. Our church still teaches that any abortion is against God's laws, which means that we as Catholics cannot have, facilitate, or procure an abortion. Such human laws are permissive and not binding or compelling us to do anything, but we as Catholics simply cannot take advantage of the human permissiveness when it allows something that God forbids.

When human laws permit something that God forbids, we must consider whether we should express our views to our legislators before the law is made and whether we should endeavour to change the law if it is already law. Usually, the bishops of a jurisdiction that is proposing such laws will make our church's views known to the legislators. They sometimes ask us to sign petitions or participate in peaceful protests. We, the Catholic laity, are a legitimate part of our secular communities, and we have the secular right to be heard. Accordingly, we should support our bishops in any way that we can. We should do this because we accept the correctness of our church's teachings, especially if the relevant teaching involves dogma. There may also be social reasons. Again, in relation to abortion, we believe that abortion is the murder of innocent humans, and we do not want the community that we live in to condone or allow such conduct, even if most of the members of our community do not share our faith.

4.6.4 Conclusions

1. We, the Catholic laity, are disciples of Jesus. We believe that Jesus is divine and that all his teachings, and commands are infallibly correct. Jesus founded our church to spread our faith throughout the world for and to every generation to come, and to provide pastoral care to those who become his disciples.

2. The clergy of our modern church are the successors of the apostles and have the responsibility to implement the mission given by Jesus to the apostles. The teachings of our church are generally referred to as church doctrine.

3. Our church must have catholicity of its teachings in all places, in every generation. To this end, our church claims magisterium of the collective of bishops and cardinals, and infallibility of ex cathedra papal decrees on matters of faith and morals where such magisterium or infallibility are specifically claimed.

4. Those parts of the church doctrine that have claimed to be infallibly correct are called church dogmas. The non-dogmatic parts of church teachings have no special name but remain church doctrine. Some of those teachings may, in the future, be elevated to the status of dogma, while others are capable of being amended or withdrawn.

5. The divinity of Jesus is a dogma. The infallibility of the magisterium and the ex cathedra teachings of the pope are also dogmas. There are about two hundred fifty dogmas, but there have not been any new dogmas since 1950.

6. Some church doctrines dealing with pastoral care are dogmatic, while others have varied to accommodate the diversity of cultural development and differences. Doctrines dealing with purely devotional issues can be dogma, as some are; however, most are usually permissive or recommended, and accordingly, these are optional.

7. The non-dogmatic and non-optional doctrines of our church have a lower status than dogmas but should nevertheless be regarded by us as authoritative teachings by intelligent and good men.

8. Some of our church's doctrines are derived from a perception of natural moral law. None of these are dogma. Such doctrines have the weakness of being able to be challenged on rational grounds by opponents having a competing view of natural moral law. The sufficiency of divine law enables our church to retain all those teachings that can be inferred from divine law as being divine moral law. Our church does need knowledge and views on what are regarded as universally agreed principles of natural moral law, for evangelical purposes.

9. A comprehensive account of church doctrines was published in the *Catechism of the Catholic Church* in 1994. In authorising its publication, Pope John Paul II said that it is a *'statement of the Church's faith and of Catholic doctrine'*. It was primarily directed to bishops and Catholic educators but is usable by the laity.

10. Unfortunately, the Catholic catechism does not identify which of the teachings that it contains are dogma. Such identification was last done by Dr Ludwig Ott, a priest, in his book entitled *Fundamentals of Catholic Dogma*, published in 1954. There have been no new dogmas since this book was published.

11. *A Compendium of the Catechism of the Catholic Church* is a short and easily comprehended book, authorised by Pope Benedict XVI on 20 March 2005 and subsequently published. It is aimed at us, the adult laity of our church.

12. The Internet is a valuable and efficient reference tool to research issues relating to church doctrine, but the information provided on it is not always accurate; users should be cautious to ensure that they rely on only official Catholic websites.

PART 5

CONTEMPORARY ISSUES

5.1 Modern Views on Killing

5.1.1 Overview

Modern medicine has evolved from the chants and herbs of witch doctors to a high-tech science. The modern technology has done much to cure illness, extend life, and enhance the quality of life. As Catholics, we can see the current technology of medicine as a gift from the Holy Spirit to persons having a desire to medically help other people.

By comparison with earlier times, the extent of current medical technology is truly amazing. We have a plethora of pharmaceuticals which aid our bodies in overcoming illness and diseases. Modern surgical techniques are far less invasive than in the past, and we can achieve results previously thought impossible. Modern prosthetics can nearly duplicate the function of the part they replace. Modern diagnostic techniques and equipment are so advanced as to be beyond the understanding of non–medically educated people. Scientists have mapped the human genome; they know how DNA works and have developed techniques of gene therapy.

The development of even higher technology is ongoing. The pharmaceutical companies are engaged in constant research to develop new and better pharmaceuticals, and there are numerous other organisations engaged in medical research such as nuclear medicine and nanotechnology. We can be happy that we live in this wonderful age of medical knowledge, which our science fiction writers imagine will become even more wonderful.

But with the development of this technology has come the knowledge and ability to medically terminate life in more humane ways. Arguably, we have always had the means to destroy health and life by gross violent physical trauma, but now it can be done in a seemingly benign and scientific way. This aspect of modern medical technology raises a number of issues that we Catholics, living in modern times, need to consider, as we may well have to make some decisions involving these issues. These issues, which will each be considered hereunder, include the following: euthanasia, abortion, human cloning, and stem cell research.

There is nothing in the Ten Commandments or anything in what Jesus said which gives us specific guidance on these issues. Therefore, we must look to our church for guidance. As has already been observed, our church has a duty to have an official teaching about what acts or omissions amount to a breach of any of the Ten Commandments or contravene the teachings of Jesus. The church has such teachings, which will be briefly set out in relation to each of these issues, and they cannot be lightly disregarded. These teachings are made by intelligent men who are highly educated in religious issues and who have devoted their lives to serving God by helping us understand how God wants us to live.

The status of dogma is that we cannot ignore it, nor can we publicly reject or teach anything contrary to dogma. The idea that we can legitimately disregard a non-dogmatic teaching of our church may appear to be incongruous to some, but there are two points to be considered in relation to non-dogmatic teachings of our church.

Firstly, it is a fact that our church has made mistakes in the past. The self-serving claim by our church to papal infallibility in the pope's ex cathedra statements can only apply in relation to Catholic dogma. The argument that the Holy Spirit guides the church may well be correct in relation to issues that our church declares to be immutable, but clearly, there have been many instances, observable in any objective history of our church, where the clergy concerned have failed, deliberately or otherwise, to follow the Holy Spirit's guidance. We must necessarily regard such instances as non-dogmatic. For example, our church leaders (popes) promoted and funded the Crusades, which necessarily anticipated a massive amount of killing of other human beings. There can be little doubt that this contravened the fifth commandment of God, the teachings of Jesus, and whatever guidance the Holy Spirit provided to the popes involved.

From this, we can safely conclude that our church made errors in the past and that the guidance provided by the Holy Spirit is not always followed. This doctrine of guidance by the Holy Spirit is, in fact, that the Holy Spirit will not allow the church to fall into error in relation to serious issues of faith and morals, rather than a doctrine that the church is always right in whatever it says or does. We can then ask whether any modern teaching of our church is necessarily correct. Any cleric who argues that our modern church is perfect and that no current teachings will ever change cannot be taken seriously. Our church is growing in wisdom and evolving to meet a constantly changing environment. Accordingly, most of the current teachings of our church are most probably correct but not necessarily so, which requires that we carefully consider them before either accepting or rejecting them.

Secondly, the primary responsibility for our own souls is ourselves. Our church teaches this in paragraphs 1730 to 1734 of the Catholic catechism, dealing with freedom and responsibility. Our church is there to help us, but in the final analysis, to our own selves we must be true. The church is there to guide us, not to make our decisions for us or to rule us. In earlier times, before the spread of literacy, our church needed to be more domineering than it now is, because education about religious matters was largely limited to the clergy. That has changed. Today, certainly in the Western world, the laity of our church is both intelligent and reasonably well educated about religious matters. In fact, our church has largely contributed to that education. We, the laity, are now far better equipped to consider whether some particular act or omission offends God than ever in the past. We see the teachings of the church as the best opinions of intelligent and good men with the intention to help us, although we recognise that those teachings are very conservative where those teachings cannot be sourced to the Ten Commandments or the teachings of Jesus.

The essence of our church's teachings on the issues identified above are mostly referable to the fifth commandment. What follows will be a short description of the nature of the conduct involved in the issue, the church's teachings on the issue taken from the *Catechism*, an identification of some of the arguments involved, and some conclusions. It is not the purpose of this work to criticise or contradict any church teachings but to provide sufficient information to us to help us carefully consider the issue.

5.1.2 Divine Law and Human Law

In Paragraph 2273 of the *Catechism* is a quote from the encyclical *Donum Vitae*, as follows:

The inalienable rights of the person must be recognized and respected by civil society and the political authority.

With respect, that teaching is now politically naive.

When Constantine made Catholicism the official religion of the Roman Empire, the practical necessity was that the subjects of the empire needed to become Catholics. So it happened. With this, the clergy of our church acquired so much political influence that they were able to control significant aspects of the governance of the empire and later the city states and nations, because even emperors, princes, and dictators knew that they could not rule without the support of the people, and the church could direct the will of the people. In that situation, the church could assert that the rulers had a duty to make and enforce laws that endorsed the moral teachings of the church.

After the Reformation, the practical necessity to be a Catholic waned, and governments became more democratic. The essence of democracy is *'government of the people, by the people, for the people'*. Being a Catholic was not required to be a member of the government, and many people lost their faith when science produced alternative explanations for the origins of the universe and life, i.e. the Big Bang theory and the theory of evolution.

The way politics works in modern times is that the government will legislate what they perceive to be the will of the majority of the voting members of the community they govern. While there are Catholic members of many governments, they are usually in the minority in most countries, except those in which Catholicism is the religion of the majority. So while the minority of Catholic politicians may vote in accordance with the church's view of the moral law, their numbers are insufficient to determine the outcome of an issue involving moral law if the majority of the legislators perceive the will of the voters to be contrary to our church's view of the moral law, especially under the modern party system of government.

What this means is that our church no longer has the substantial influence on government that it once had. It still presents its views in public debates on moral issues, and while it does not tell us how to vote, it makes it clear which side Catholics should support.

The separation of church and state has not been achieved in all countries for all religions. For example, in some countries where the majority of people are Muslims, the secular law is, in fact, sharia law. The advantage of having the secular law endorse the moral views of the predominant religion is that many people regard the law as having a declaratory function, which means that if the law allows some sort of action, then that action must be morally acceptable. Even some prominent jurists have agreed that part of the function of law is the enforcement of morals.

These perceptions are important, and our church recognises and encourages us to be proactive in supporting its view of the moral law in relevant political debates, on the basis that we would rather that the community that we live in did not allow abortion or euthanasia or whatever the moral evil may be. However, we must also respect the rights of persons to choose to believe and act differently than in accordance with our beliefs. In addition, we should also appreciate that those laws that allow something forbidden by morals are essentially decriminalising or permissive and do not actually require us to act in any way contrary to our beliefs. When we compare this with sharia law, which, for example, requires its adherents to kill homosexuals, we can appreciate that our governments still allows us to live our lives in accordance with our beliefs and that the permissive elements of our laws are not something that we are required to accept or implement in our own lives.

5.1.3 Homicide

The fifth commandment of God the Father, as endorsed and explained by Jesus, is 'Thou shall not kill'. This is a clear and unconditional prohibition. Our church, pursuant to its authority and duty, has formulated teachings applying this prohibition to human behaviour and updating its teachings to take into account the new behaviour enabled by technological advances. The current version of those teachings is clearly and concisely set out in the *Catechism of the Catholic Church*, in paragraphs 2258 to 2317. It is not the province or function of this work to expound or review those teachings, but there are related issues which warrant consideration.

This category is essentially the deliberate killing of a separately living human being and, for our consideration, includes infants, but not embryos or foetuses. We generally know this type of killing as murder, which can be committed out of passion or for a variety of other motives. Murder has been considered a secular crime in all places throughout history, and there is no forum or lobby to change or vary the public perception of this as seriously morally wrong and a heinous crime. Our catechism makes it quite clear that murder mortally offends God, and accordingly, we need consider this issue no further.

5.1.3.1 Defences

Our church recognises that our strongest human instinct is self-preservation, which flows from a proper love of life, especially our own and that of our loved ones. Accordingly, it teaches that self-defence and the defence of our loved ones and others is legitimate and also not offensive to God. However, the degree of violence used in self-defence must be no more than sufficient to avoid the threatened harm. In such situations, there is what is known as the 'agony of the moment'. This recognises that there is usually not enough time to be cool, calm, and collected, enabling us to carefully and precisely measure the amount of force needed to avoid the threatened harm. Usually, people acting in self-defence or defence of others use whatever skills they have and whatever resources are available, in the hope that this will be effective. So long as killing the aggressor is not intended, unless there is no viable alternative, killing the aggressor in self-defence is legitimate. The secular laws in most jurisdictions essentially accept this defence.

Unintentional killing, as such, is not a breach of God's law, but if there was negligence, which led to the death, then clearly there must be some accountability to God for this. If the killing resulted from some action or inaction taken with reckless indifference to human life, such a killing may be regarded as a homicide. The secular authorities generally refer to negligent killing as manslaughter and provide penalties for this as a crime.

5.1.4 Suicide

Our church teaches that suicide is an offence against God and a breach of the fifth commandment. This teaching is set out in paragraphs 2280 to 2283 of the *Catechism*. In English history, suicide was once a criminal offence, which was punished by the forfeiture of all the deceased's assets to the Crown. Logically, this only punishes the heirs or beneficiaries of the deceased and, accordingly, has the flavour of a grab for money by the Crown.

In modern times, there is no secular prohibition on suicide. Statistically, most suicides are young persons, and there are also more suicides in rural areas than in city areas. There is a lobby of persons arguing for the legalisation of substances which can cause a painless and peaceful death. They call this 'assisted suicide', because the person wanting to commit suicide is either too ill to self-administer the substance or because the substance is only available on prescription or not legally available at all. This issue is more appropriately considered in the next topic of euthanasia.

5.1.5 Euthanasia

The church's teaching on euthanasia is set out in paragraphs 2276 to 2279 of the *Catechism*. These teachings are clear and consistent, with a proper respect for life. However, there is a lobby which argues for the legalisation of euthanasia of terminally ill persons. Representatives of this group tell stories in the media of how distressing it is for them to have to watch their loved ones endure a slow and painful death while their eyes plead for an end to the suffering. They argue that palliative care and painkillers do little to alleviate the suffering and indignity of a painful and helpless death. In most cases, the dying person does not want to be a burden to his or her family and friends, and has a genuine desire to die. Accordingly, they argue that the law should enable them to terminate the life in such circumstances. They present such a termination as assisted suicide rather than euthanasia.

It is difficult for even us Catholic laity to be unsympathetic to this argument, especially since the stories we hear are almost certainly true and sad enough to be heart-rending. We might ask why God allows such suffering, and from our experience, we know that it is our inability to answer this question that has caused many people to lose confidence in the goodness of God or belief in his existence, even if they initially believed that God exists. As Catholics, we must simply obey what our church teaches as God's commands, in the belief that God has his reasons, which have not been revealed to us, and consequently, we must endure the distressing dying of loved ones.

The secular law in most jurisdictions is that euthanasia is a serious criminal offence. However, the lobby has had some success in recent times to the extent that in some jurisdictions, euthanasia has been decriminalised subject to certain safeguards, such as documented consent and medical certificates that the illness was both terminal and painful.

The problem with such laws is that they are the thin end of the wedge. We know that secular law is in a constant state of flux and that, as time passes, unusual circumstances are presented to the courts and the safeguards specified in the legislation are relaxed by sympathetic judges. Any law is only ever as good as the judiciary's determination to enforce it, and laws and safeguards that are not enforced are eventually abandoned.

What this means is that eventually the safeguards will be ineffective in preventing the killing of terminally ill persons who do not want to die and even the killing of persons who are not terminally ill but have lost significant quality of life, such as persons institutionalised for severe dementia. Clearly, as Catholics, this development is not something that we can support.

5.1.6 Abortion

Our church's teaching on abortion can be found in paragraphs 2270 to 2275 of the *Catechism*. In Paragraph 2271, it is stated that the church has affirmed the moral evil of abortion since the first century and that this teaching is unchangeable.

Under secular law, abortion was a serious criminal offence. However, in modern times, abortion has been decriminalised in virtually every jurisdiction, to the point of being available on demand, i.e. available without the need to give any reason or justification for the procedure. This is the result of the pro-abortion lobby's argument that a woman has an absolute and inalienable right to control what happens to her body, from which it follows, so it is argued, that she has the moral right to terminate a pregnancy.

The anti-abortion lobby concedes the right of a woman to control what happens to her body, but it argues essentially that a pregnancy means that there is another human life involved and that the woman's right must be subject to the right to life of that other person, even though that other person is physically connected to the woman.

Another argument used by the anti-abortion lobby is that we must all accept the responsibility for and consequences of our actions and that this principle applies to women who have taken action resulting in their pregnancy. The reality is that most pregnancies in which an abortion is considered are unintended. The pro-abortion lobby has used this fact to argue that the seriously adverse social consequences of an unwanted pregnancy justifies termination of the pregnancy.

The essential moral law that flows from the fifth commandment is that every human being has an absolute and inalienable right to life, and our church teaches that this right is held even while that human is still in utero. *Inalienable* means that no human being can ever acquire the right to life of another human being. From this, it follows that any killing of a human being by another human being is, prima facie, a breach of the fifth commandment. Such a breach can only be excused in circumstances where there is a recognised defence, such as self-defence or in a just war. Adverse social consequences is not a defence recognised by our church or secular authorities in relation to homicide.

In any event, the pro-abortion lobby has won this argument, and the likelihood of a reversal of the law to its former effect is negligible.

5.1.7 Cloning

To consider this issue, we need to have a clear concept of what cloning is and how it is produced. *Cloning* may be defined as *'an asexual and agamic reproduction meant to produce individuals biologically identical to the adult which provided the nuclear genetic inheritance'*.

The process of creating a clone is medically and biologically complex, but for our purposes of considering the killing of human beings, a basic understanding is sufficient. Essentially, the process is as follows: an unfertilised human egg is isolated, and its DNA is removed from its nucleus. Then a cell, usually a skin cell, is taken from an adult donor, and the DNA from this cell is extracted and inserted into the egg from which the DNA was removed. That effectively creates an embryo, which is then placed in a female womb for development and normal birth of an individual.

In 1996, this process resulted in the birth of a cloned sheep named Dolly, which was cloned from a cell taken from the mammary gland of the donor sheep. The process did not have a high success rate at that time because Dolly was the only successful birth of a lamb in 277 trials of this process. So far as is known at present, this process has not been trialled on human beings, and scientists have not succeeded in cloning other primates, such as monkeys.

Scientists tell us that the feasibility of human cloning is a long way off technically, but it is not regarded as impossible. If scientists are allowed to trial this process with technical adjustments on human beings, then the ultimate success of human cloning would appear to be inevitable.

There is nothing in our *Catechism* about cloning. This is surprising, because one of the significant church documents, *Donum Vitae*, is cited as a source of some of the teachings in the *Catechism*. *Donum Vitae* says in Paragraph I.6, *'attempts or hypotheses for obtaining a human being without any connection with sexuality through "twin fusion" cloning or parthenogenesis are to be considered contrary to the moral law'*. Obviously, cloning in this document means human cloning.

In relation to the issue under consideration here, the removal of DNA from a human egg is not a killing of a human being, because conception in that egg has not occurred. However, the implanting of the DNA of a living human being effectively turns the unfertilised egg into a human embryo, which is, in essence, the same as conception. From this analysis, it is clearly apparent why our church condemns cloning. It is because it sees this as similar to homologous IVF, which is condemned in Paragraph II.5 of *Donum Vitae*.

There is no pro-cloning lobby because it is not yet possible. However, there are some scientists who argue that the ban on research about human cloning is an impediment to progress and the advancement of human knowledge. The church's answer is that science and scientists are not beyond or above human ethics, and those ethics clearly indicate that human cloning is not a morally justifiable process. However, the church permits scientific research in relation to cloning of animals and vegetables, provided that the animals and species' biodiversity are properly respected and observed.

To anticipate whether or not there will ever be a pro–human cloning lobby, we must consider the potential benefits to individuals and mankind generally. The abuses of human clones grown to adulthood that are portrayed in science fiction movies and novels are clearly speculative and unrealistic, and they do not warrant further consideration at this time. However, stem cell therapy (the subject of the next section of this work) has remarkable and very real substantial benefits for the health and medical knowledge of mankind. Human cloning and even human cloning research that fails to result in a normal human birth can still be a source of stem cells. If stem cells become readily available, they may well become the centrepiece and staple of modern regenerative medicine. If stem cell research shows that this capacity of stem cells is real, then the sources of stem cells will be in demand, and it seems likely that the human cloning source will be further argued, especially if medicine shows that there is less likelihood of cellular rejection of stem cells from a foetal clone of the patient needing the stem cells.

In 1987, in Part 3 of *Donum Vitae*, the magisterium of the church declared that it was the duty of public authority to ensure that its civil laws enforce the moral law. There are laws legalising artificial procreation in many countries, but today it appears that cloning has not been made legal under the laws of any country.

As we have already considered, laws change according to the will of the people. Our communities are becoming increasingly atheistic numerically. If stem cell research and cloning research can prove the potential benefits of stem cells, especially cloned stem cells, by demonstrating success and eventually a high percentage of success rate in other primates such as monkeys, the community attitude may well change to allow some human cloning experiments, and accordingly, the law will change. There is also the risk that there will be researchers, in places where there are no anti-cloning laws or where the laws are not efficiently enforced, doing human cloning research, and they may produce the evidence necessary to alter a community's view and laws. Accordingly, it is important that we, who accept our church's teachings on this issue, and the clergy of our church do not let our guard down simply because we appear to have won the battle on this issue for the present.

5.1.8 Stem Cells

Stem cells are a relatively recent (within the last fifty years) discovery of medical science, and we need some basic understanding of their nature and function to consider the issues arising from their use.

Basically, a stem cell is a cell that has not acquired the characteristics and functions of the cells that comprise any of the various parts of our bodies. Their value lies in the fact that when they become associated with a particular part of our body, such as the heart, lungs, skin, bones, muscles, et cetera, they acquire the functions and characteristics of the cells forming that part of the body. There are 220 different types of cells in our bodies, but not all stem cells can become one of any of the 220 different types. Those that can become any one of the 220 different types are called pluripotent.

The benefit of stem cells is that they replace worn-out, damaged, or diseased cells, thereby restoring our health and vitality, which is the natural function of our metabolism. The medical science of injecting the stem cells into that organ or part of the body that needs replacement cells is still in its infancy, although this therapy has already been used to restore health in a substantial number of cases. The need for such therapy arises from the fact that our metabolism cannot always function quickly enough to replace damaged or diseased cells, and accordingly, medical intervention is required.

Because the medical technology is still in its infancy, there is much medical research that needs to be done in order to realise the full potential of this medical innovation. Such research necessarily requires living human stem cells in its processes and experiments. The stem cells used are derived by placing a small number of donor stem cells into a culture where they multiply and grow into colonies. The issue for our consideration is the source of the donor stem cells. There are basically three sources of stem cells, which are as follows:

- *Embryonic stem cells.* As the cells of an embryo continue to divide, they become a *blastocyst*, which contains hundreds of stem cells. These cells are pluripotent. They are obtained from IVF embryos.
- *Embryonic germ stem cells.* These are obtained from the reproductive organs of aborted foetuses, because they are cells which have not yet acquired the sexual function. They are also pluripotent.
- *Adult stem cells.* These cells are obtained from various parts of the body of adults or children, and they include umbilical cords, placenta, and amniotic fluid. These cells are not pluripotent.

The harvesting of stem cells from embryos necessarily involves killing the embryo. Harvesting embryonic germ stem cells from an abortion begs the question of whether the abortion was procured for the purpose of such harvesting and also whether it is morally licit to benefit either research or therapy from something that our church condemns—i.e. abortion. The harvesting of adult stem cells is the appropriate and legitimate source of stem cells. The Catholic Church is *'profoundly in favor of stem cell therapy and research provided that it does not interfere with the inviolable right to life of a human person from conception to natural death'.*

Because adult stem cells are not pluripotent, it is argued that the embryonic and foetal stem cells have the greater potential for therapeutic use. However, there is a major problem with this argument. Every stem cell—embryonic, foetal, and adult—already contains the DNA of the donor. The primary purpose of stem cell therapy is to heal a separately existing human being. Inserting the DNA from one person into another person usually leads to the destruction of the DNA of the intruder by the recipient's immune system. Accordingly, the stem cell most likely to be effective therapy is an autologous stem cell, i.e. one that comes from the recipient rather than from another person. To date, there have been a number of documented cases of autologous stem cell therapy in which successful outcomes have been achieved in relation to Parkinson's disease, heart attack, multiple sclerosis, spinal cord injuries, vision, sickle-cell blood disease, and diabetes. There are no reports of cases of any successful outcomes using embryonic or foetal stem cells.

Because it has become clear to medical scientists that autologous stem cells are the future, they have intensified the argument that in vitro *cloning* to the embryonic stage should be legalised to enable harvesting of stem cells for autologous therapy to the donor, which appear to have greater potential than autologous adult stem cells.

Again, the problem for our consideration is that the harvesting of such stem cells involves the killing of the embryo. Our church teaches that the killing of an embryo, regardless of whether it is *in vitro* or *in utero* is a killing, against the fifth commandment, and a cloned embryo is still an embryo. Furthermore, if IVF cloning is allowed, then soon full reproductive cloning will be allowed; the undesirability of this has already been considered.

As has already been observed, there is nothing specifically about cloning in our catechism, nor is there anything in it about stem cell research or therapy. However, in Paragraph 2275, in relation to abortion, it says as follows: *'it is immoral to procure or to produce human embryos intended for exploitation as disposable biological material.'* This is taken from the *Donum Vitae* encyclical, from which most of the teachings of our church identified herein in relation to these issues have been gleaned. A secondary source of our church's teaching has been the writings of eminent clergy who are qualified in this area, such as Archbishop Fisher of Sydney, who has a doctorate in bioethics from Oxford University.

From the various sources, it is clear that our church considers the use of embryonic and foetal stem cells for medical research or medical therapy to be a serious sin against the fifth commandment because it involves the killing of the embryo or foetus to obtain the stem cells. The medical use of stem cells from aborted foetuses is also wrong, because the abortion, which made the stem cells available, is also a breach of the fifth commandment; it is immoral for anyone to benefit from such a sin.

Our church's teachings have been criticised by some medical researchers as being out of date and an impediment to progress and the advancement of human medical knowledge. The answer to this criticism is not just that our views are a matter of faith. Medical researchers are not above the secular laws, moral laws, or medical professional ethics, in particular the Hippocratic oath, which requires that medical practitioners do no harm to any person in their capacity as such. No one would seriously assert that the Hippocratic oath is out of date and an impediment to human progress.

The essence of the argument is a question of *'When does life as a human being begin?'* Our church, on the basis of some biblical support, has taught for the last 2,000 years that human life, having a soul, starts at the moment of conception and that the time between conception and birth is simply normal human development, just as the time between birth and death in old age is normal human development.

Many non-Catholics hold the view that human life begins at birth. There are even some ethicists, such as Professor Peter Singer, lately of Princeton University in the USA, who argue that an infant does not acquire the right to life until at least twenty-eight days after birth. He goes as far as to say, 'The grounds for not killing persons do not apply to newborn infants.' Some of Professor Singer's colleagues support this view. Professor Singer's views are discredited by the fact that most parents of a newborn infant would defend the life of their baby with lethal force if necessary.

We do not know when human life begins and when a soul is acquired, because God has not revealed this to us. We must trust and accept the teachings of our church, which pragmatically are in line with the wisdom that it is better to be safe than sorry.

5.1.9 Summary

- Murder, i.e. the intentional killing of another human being, is a serious breach of both divine and human law, subject to certain defences.
- Accidental killing of another person is not a breach of the fifth commandment of God, but it can still warrant divine recrimination if it involves reckless indifference to human life. The secular or civil laws treat negligent killing as a crime.
- Suicide is against the fifth commandment. It is no longer a crime under secular law because humanity has no way to punish it. Attempted suicide indicates mental disturbance and warrants and attracts medical help rather than punishment.
- Euthanasia is an intentional killing of another human being and is the same as murder, as regards the fifth commandment, even if it is only to the extent of enabling a person to commit suicide who does not otherwise have that capacity. The secular laws have historically regarded euthanasia as a crime, but this is changing in some places where it is called assisted suicide and, as such, is being decriminalised.
- Abortion is the deliberate killing of another human being and, as such, is a serious breach of the fifth commandment.

The essence of this conclusion is that human life begins at the moment of conception. The secular law regarded abortion as a criminal offence, but this has been eroded to the point where abortion has now been completely decriminalised.

- Human cloning is condemned by our church because the process of making a clone involves creating an embryo in a totally unnatural and artificial way for purposes unrelated to normal human reproduction. Human cloning has not yet been achieved, and research in this area will necessarily involve the killing of many embryos, which is against the fifth commandment because an embryo is a human being, regardless of whether it was brought into existence naturally or unnaturally or for what purpose it was generated. The secular law has banned human cloning research and experimentation in virtually every country on earth, but laws can change.

- Stem cell research and therapy is supported and encouraged by our church, provided the stem cells are adult stem cells, i.e. not sourced from embryos or foetuses. The production and cultivation of embryos for stem cell research or therapy is against the fifth commandment because obtaining stem cells from them necessarily involves killing them, which is killing a human being, because human life begins at conception.

5.1.10 Perspectives

5.1.10.1 The above summary of our church's teachings is not *rocket science*. It is straightforward and can be easily understood by every Catholic, except those that are severely mentally handicapped. There are many complex and convoluted arguments in the debate on the various issues which have raised these teachings of our church. Most of them have counterarguments which minimise their persuasive value, and some are peripheral and indecisive. For example, in relation to cloning, it is argued that it is potentially harmful to the health of women and degrading to be used as mere egg providers or as mere incubators of cloned embryos because science has not yet been able to create an artificial womb. This argument is valid but not decisive, because even if science can create an artificial womb, we would not withdraw our objection to cloning because of the substantive reasons outlined above, and this objection, based on the potential degradation of women, would become irrelevant.

5.1.10.2 The teachings of our church are catholic, i.e. they are the same for all Catholics in all countries. In addition, the basis of these teachings has been settled for many centuries. For example, in Paragraph 2271 of our *Catechism*, we are told that the church has condemned every procured abortion since the first century AD and that this teaching is unchangeable. This teaching is based on the premise that *'human life begins at conception'*. We also know that the dogmas of our church are teachings which are immutable or unchangeable. It is surprising, therefore, that the premise of *'human life begins at conception'* and the corollary premise that *'every human being has a right to life which is inalienable'* are not amongst the dogmas of our faith. We need finality on these premises because they will clarify our position not only on abortion but also in relation to cloning and stem cell research and therapy. Accordingly, it appears appropriate for the responsible clergy in our church to consider making these premises dogma. Perhaps some critics of our church will better understand our view if these premises can be identified as dogma. We can then evaluate the views of Prof. Singer and his supporters in the context of opposing views of some of the greatest moral thinkers in human history.

5.1.10.3 These teachings of our church are essentially prohibitions carrying the force of divine law. The secular laws related to these issues are entirely permissive—i.e. under secular law, we may do these things that are prohibited by divine law. Our obedience to divine law must take priority over obedience to secular law, especially as the secular law is merely permissive.

If a secular law required us to do something contrary to divine law, we would refuse to obey the secular law and suffer the secular consequences. Conversely, if divine law required us to do something contrary to secular law, we would have to obey the divine law and suffer the secular consequences, which could be serious. For example, in Islam, adherents are required to kill homosexuals. They do this even in countries where such a killing is a serious criminal offence, knowing that if they are apprehended and convicted of the crime, they will be severely punished. Fortunately, our faith does not require us to do anything contrary to secular law. Indeed, our faith requires us to recognise the authority of secular government and to *'give to Caesar is what is Caesar's and give to God what is God's'.*

5.1.10.4 Although the secular laws are permissive, it is still relevant for us to consider to what extent we should be proactive in voicing our objections to proposed laws which allow something that our church teaches is against God's law. In addition, we could also consider how proactive we could be in changing laws that already permit something that our church teaches is against God's law. Our reason for being proactive is that we may not wish to live in a society that allows something that we consider to be morally evil. While we may be in the minority, we do still have a right to be heard.

Another reason for being proactive is that there is some biblical authority which indicates that God is not infinitely tolerant. Examples of the biblical references are the destruction of Sodom and Gomorrah and God's anger at the Jews at various times. The wisdom that we can gain from this is that if we believe that God will become angry over the killing of many human embryos which have been thereby denied a chance for salvation, it would be unwise to be in the vicinity of those people who have become the focus of God's displeasure. We may even acquire some accountability for not voicing our objection to the passing of such laws in the first place or to tolerating their continued existence without protest.

5.2 Anti-Catholicism

5.2.1 The Issue

In modern times, most countries in the Western world have adopted generally effective anti-discrimination laws. Under these laws, it is illegal and punishable to discriminate against anyone on the grounds of their religion. Laws are not intended to deal with trivialities, and accordingly, the application of such laws are for practical purposes limited to the commercial aspects of the lives of the community members, such as job selection, workplace harmony and equality, access to services, et cetera. They also prohibit vilification of persons in the mass media, contrary to anti-discrimination principles.

These anti-discrimination laws are generally effective and may have a declaratory function in that they identify and specify the proper community standards in relation to dealing with members of a different race, gender, creed, disability, et cetera. Of course, no set of laws can ever be completely effective, because we cannot always know the real reason for a person's actions. Some biased or prejudiced people do discriminate, contrary to anti-discrimination laws, but the ostensible reasons for their actions appear to justify their actions, while their real reason remains hidden.

In such an environment, it is reasonable to question whether anti-Catholic bias or prejudice is a serious modern concern for Catholics.

To consider this question, we must firstly recognise that the anti-discrimination laws do not fully apply to our private or social lives. For example, refusal of membership of a social club on the basis of a person's religious beliefs may well be actionable at law, whereas private pejorative rhetoric, which may be felt as highly offensive, would not be actionable. In addition, we must also recognise that in modern times, the Internet and social media, such as Facebook,

Twitter, and electronic mail, provide extraordinarily abundant opportunity for the expression of anti-Catholic sentiments, opinions, and data. In most Western countries, there is freedom of speech. The Internet is international, and offences against anti-discrimination laws of one country cannot be effectively policed or prosecuted, especially since most of the worst offences are usually anonymous.

This work is written in English and is supported by research in the English language. The Internet is presented in many languages, with some facility to have the pages of such sites translated. But there is generally no such facility for social media and electronic mail. Accordingly, the extent of anti-Catholic action and attitudes in non-English-speaking countries that are primarily constituted by members of another faith, such as Islam, Judaism, Buddhism, or Hinduism, is beyond the scope of this work.

It would be naive to believe that human intolerance and hate can be eliminated by legislation. Perhaps these things are an integral part of human nature and can never be completely eliminated. And having free speech and the facility to act anonymously, it is inevitable that there will be—and in fact is—substantial anti-Catholic activity in the world today.

Accordingly, it is appropriate for us to consider who is anti-Catholic, what they are saying or doing, and how we should deal with this modern manifestation of anti-Catholicism.

5.2.2 Historical Insights

Significant action is generally taken to achieve a specific desired consequence. But sometimes such action has far-reaching, long-term, unanticipated, and even undesirable consequences. The significant events and actions in human history mostly have long-term effects and consequences, and it may aid our understanding of the causes of modern anti-Catholicism to consider some of the events in our history relevant to this issue.

Jesus himself was persecuted to the extent of being killed. Ostensibly, the reason for his execution was that he was a heretic to the Jewish faith, but there is the observation in the Gospels that the Jewish clerical leaders acted out of jealousy.

After the death of Jesus and the Pentecost, the apostles set about converting as many to Christianity as they could. The Jews opposed this, and they wanted to stamp out the heresy of Jesus. St Stephen was stoned to death, and many other converts were imprisoned. From this, we first see that what is important to some people is what one believes rather than whether one is a good and honest person.

Christianity grew until it became recognised as the religion of a minority. The Roman emperors then blamed the Christians for various political misfortunes and ignited popular hatred of Christians with false and pejorative propaganda, leading to the martyrdom of many Christians. From this, we see that governments and political leaders will seldom, if ever, accept responsibility for misfortunes, and they will blame the people who are their power base. They pick a minority group as a scapegoat and derogate them vehemently. That is still the way of politics today.

Christianity survived these persecutions and grew larger. In 311, the Roman emperor Galerius issued the Edict of Toleration, which officially ended the persecution of Christians. Galerius died that year, and in 312, Constantine and Maxentius fought a battle for the throne. Constantine won after a dream which predicted his win if he fought under a Christian emblem, which he did. Thereafter, as emperor, he favoured Christianity, brought his children up in this faith, and was himself baptised on his deathbed in 337. Effectively, he made Christianity the official religion of the empire and even convened the Council of Nicaea in 325.

The effect of Constantine's actions was to enable most of the empire to be converted to Christianity and for this faith to become catholic, i.e. universal, in the world of the empire, although moving the seat of the empire from Rome to Constantinople eventually created the Roman and Orthodox schism. Although the Roman Empire crumbled shortly thereafter, the presence of Catholicism as the major religion of the Western world persisted for over the next thousand years.

As the main religion of the Western world, the clergy of the church acquired substantial secular powers. They developed ecclesiastical courts and even became the secular rulers over several territories in Italy. In effect, the church became 'the establishment', which meant that a person could not be eligible for any prominent government position if he or she was not Catholic. No doubt this led to the conversion of many persons who were not true believers.

The most significant consequence of Constantine's conversion was the eventual fusion of church and state. This meant that church leaders, essentially the clergy, had either direct secular authority, the authority of ecclesiastical courts, or virtually compelling influence over non-clerical authorities. From even a superficial reading of history, we know that not all actions taken by the establishment are popular and acceptable to everyone. During the era of church and state unity, most of the actions of the establishment were seen as done in the name of, or with the support of, the church. Many such actions were done by true believers, acting in a way they believed to be morally correct, while some actions by non-believers were done for selfish purposes but ostensibly in the name of the church. The insight from this is that anti-establishment sentiment flowing from unpopular or unacceptable action by the establishment necessarily carried with it anti-church sentiment because of our human tendency to blame the organisation rather than the individual who takes unacceptable action in the name of the establishment.

About three hundred years after Constantine, Islam was founded by the prophet Muhammad. Eventually, the church perceived the spread of Islam as a threat and initiated and funded the Crusades to halt or suppress Islam. The church had no army of its own, so the popes recruited the Crusaders and enticed them with acquisition of the spoils of war. The Crusaders were essentially mercenaries and brigands, living in brutal times. They did many things which today would be regarded as atrocities. The insight here is that it would not be surprising if Muslims had strong anti-Catholic sentiments. However, this is not apparent in modern times because the theology of Islam regards Jesus as a great prophet while rejecting his divinity and because of the fact that Islam effectively won the Crusade wars.

Over the next 1,200 years after Constantine, the church acquired substantial wealth and power, and the further acquisition of more wealth and power became a priority especially amongst non-true believers, whose clerical lifestyle had become somewhat decadent. Naturally, abuses, corruption, and misconceptions about the function of the church arose, and these essentially precipitated the Reformation. The 'once were Catholic' reformers necessarily became anti-Catholic, because their condemnation of the Catholic Church abuses was severe enough to make them reject their former church, although some reforms were largely theological issues rather than corruption.

This condemnation of the Catholic Church occurred at the time of the discovery of the New World, when some of the reformers fled to the new lands. Later, some non-Catholic Christian denominations sent missionaries to distant parts of the world. Naturally, these missionaries took their condemnation of the Catholic Church with them. Of course, the Catholics also had missionaries, and the Spanish and Portuguese conquistadors were ruthless conquerors who converted many of their conquered people at the point of a sword. From this, we may understand the long-standing enmity of refugees from Catholic oppression and the resentment of people forced to abandon their cultural religious heritage.

The Reformation in England had the additional factor that the Reformation was initiated by Henry VIII for selfish political reasons, following which there was violent persecution of both Catholics and Protestants by Henry's daughters, Mary and Elizabeth. The conflict in Northern Ireland had complex causes but is another example of long-standing religious enmity perpetuated across successive generations not party to the original causes.

In modern times, with modern transport and communications, with immigration and refugees from troubled parts of the world, many countries have residents from a variety of racial origins and nationalities who have brought with them their culture and religion as well as their prejudices and enmities. Free speech is inherent in every truly democratic society. In this environment, with technology like the Internet, it is not surprising that there is more anti-Catholic sentiment expressed than ever in the past.

5.2.3 Modern Manifestations

5.2.3.1 Governments

As a result of abuses of power committed by Catholic officials, many governments passed laws prohibiting Catholics from occupying certain official government positions. The effect of such laws was the beginning of the process of separating church and state. In modern times, this process is effectively complete because today the Catholic Church has no official status in the governmental structure of any country. The current consequence of this is that Catholics who have the desire and ability to serve in the secular government of the country are being discriminated against. This has been overcome to a large extent. The USA has had a Catholic president, Australia has had a Catholic prime minister, and other countries have had leaders of various other religions. England has not yet changed its laws which disqualify Catholics from certain political positions.

Historically, the political motive for anti-Catholic action and attitudes was the assumption that a Catholic's loyalty to the Vatican would take precedence over loyalty to their national government and would lead to traitorous behaviour. In the two world wars of the twentieth century, Catholics fought and died for their country alongside soldiers of many other religions and atheists. This has been recognised and has largely abated the fear of Catholic disloyalty.

Anti-Catholicism was prolific, passionate, and violent in many countries, but most of these countries now have more or less effective anti-discrimination laws, which are becoming part of the culture of these countries. In most countries, most anti-Catholic laws have been repealed. However, there are still laws that discriminate against any religion, such as the laws relating to the funding of non-denominational schools. Such laws are not now purposefully anti-Catholic, although initially that was their function. Today such laws are simply aimed at governmental revenue-raising and reflect the unscrupulous policy of governments in relation to money.

In modern times, there is little anti-Catholic rhetoric in government deliberations in democratic countries. However, with the modern scourge of paedophilia, there has been an increase in anti-Catholic sentiment expressed in the governmental instrumentalities and media assigned to deal with this issue. Most of the sentiment has been directed at the Catholic clergy, although the facts are that this problem is much more widespread than that. Of modern concern is the criticism of senior Catholic clergy involved in the cover-up of paedophilia by priests. Such criticism is justified and cannot be excused or mitigated by the fact that the senior clergy were motivated by a desire to preserve the public confidence in the integrity of the Catholic clergy.

Most religions support government in that they teach and encourage a moral lifestyle which enables law and order, which is the first priority of governments. Civil disobedience is a legitimate precept of most religions, but only where there is a conflict between divine law and the secular law, which is extremely rare. Accordingly, there is very little government action, in modern times, to suppress or regulate religious activity, and from this, it follows that most democratic governments are not officially anti-Catholic, although some of the individual members of these governments may well have strong anti-Catholic views.

5.2.3.2 Other Religions

Other religions are the competition. It is a competition for souls. Each religion competes because each faith has a mandate from its god to convert the whole world to their one true faith. Catholicism has such a mandate, but it accepts the reality of free will and the consequent impossibility of converting everyone. The mandate is satisfied by telling everyone about Jesus. If they choose to reject his works and teachings, we must leave them alone and brush the dust of their town from our shoes as we leave. This enables us to be tolerant of other religions.

But Catholics were not always tolerant. The conquistadors converted pagans at the point of a sword. The Crusaders fought a religious war against Islam. Protestants and Catholics waged a civil war against each other, openly in Northern Ireland and more furtively in other places. Many wars throughout history have had religious enmity and animosities as a factor, but sometimes just as propaganda to either conceal or support the real cause of the war.

Religion-oriented conflicts in which people are killed produce animosities and hatred amongst the family and friends of those killed against the killers, which can last for many generations. Such hatred is mostly directed at the faith and church of the killers. Accordingly, it would not be surprising if Muslims held anti-Catholic sentiments arising from the Crusades. But in fact, Muslims are not generally anti-Catholic, and they tolerate the Christians because they regard Jesus as a great prophet in their own faith. And the Crusades happened more than six hundred years ago. On the other hand, the fighting in Northern Ireland only stopped a few years ago, and anti-Catholic sentiment amongst the Protestants in that region is very likely to persist for some time into the future.

In modern times, our church has moved towards ecumenism, while other Christian denominations have actually implemented church unification. There is now a dialogue between the church leaders of non-Catholic faiths with the leaders of our church. Our church has recognised that it was in need of reform at the time of the Reformation, and it has effectively completed a counter Reformation, although vigilance against new abuses and corruption is ongoing.

However, reunification of our church with the other Christian denominations is most unlikely, if not impossible, because Catholic theology is dogmatic, i.e. infallibly correct, and because it is most unlikely that the leaders and clergy of the non-Catholic denominations will accept subordination to the theology and authority of the Catholic Church. But the termination of anti-Catholic sentiment amongst other religions is clearly possible and has already been achieved to a certain extent.

5.2.3.3 Cults

Cults, as used here, is intended to mean '*an association of persons, identifiable by formal or informal membership protocols, which has as its primary function adherence to and promulgation of some political social or religious objectives*'. It is not intended that sports clubs, returned servicemen's clubs, chess clubs, and the like be included in this definition. The Catholic Church has cults within its structure, such as the Marian Cult and Opus Dei. Groups such as the neo-Nazis and the Ku Klux Klan in America are the type of group intended for inclusion in this definition. Many of these cults do not have anti-Catholicism as their primary objective, but if their objectives and methods are criticised by our church, they become anti-Catholic on the grounds that they can attack anyone who opposes them. Many cults are primarily anti-Catholic, such as the satanist and witchcraft cults that are present in several countries.

There are many cults which hold anti-Catholic sentiments and act on these sentiments. To identify all of them and consider their views and actions is beyond the scope of this work. The point for our consideration is that there are numerous cults that proliferate anti-Catholic sentiments. Our concern is with the degree of harm that such anti-Catholic action is doing by instilling anti-Catholic attitudes in people who are not currently anti-Catholic. Widespread anti-Catholic attitudes will lead to discrimination and hatred, which can only escalate into an undesirable social situation for Catholics.

The motives of certain cults for anti-Catholic action are diverse. Some are anti-Catholic because they have practices that our church regards as sinful and because the church has denounced the cult. Naturally, the cult has retaliated. Some cults still harbour resentment against our church for offences committed by our church in the distant past and are acting in revenge. Some cults or political lobbies that want some political reform that our church opposes, and they are acting to discredit our church in order to achieve their objective. Some cults are fledgling new religions whose theology or practices are contrary to Catholic doctrine, so they attack Catholicism to justify their views and attract adherents who may already hold anti-Catholic views. Some of these are even lapsed Catholics.

In modern times, most anti-Catholic action is manifested in communications, literature, mass media, and social media—in particular, on the Internet. Most of us Catholics know enough about our faith to not need to search the Internet for more information, and we have no reason to search for anti-Catholic sites. We are mostly unaware of the extent of anti-Catholic propaganda on the Internet. Unfortunately, the fact is that there is a vast amount of anti-Catholic material on the Internet. A detailed consideration of such sites is well beyond the scope of this work, but there is an informative and relatively short article on this issue by Robert P Lockwood on the Internet at https://www.catholicleague.org/anti-catholicism-on-the-internet/.

Most of the anti-Catholic websites do not present their views in a balanced dialogue on issues supported by logical argument and verifiable facts. Their presentation is mostly pejorative to the extent of being vitriolic, featuring profanity, nudity, obscenity, and licentiousness, as if these are the standards of a modern society. Essentially, they use the language of hate which soon becomes very obvious. Some of these sites masquerade as humorous sites. It is certainly legitimate to parody or satirise aspects of the Catholic religion which appear to be unacceptable or in need of reform. But the anti-Catholic sites that present criticism in humour are usually coarse, are not particularly funny, and harp on the same issues. It is not acceptable to be deceitful and offensive under the pretence that one is trying to be funny.

5.2.3.4 Individuals

The motives that some individuals have for expressing anti-Catholic sentiments are as diverse as cyberbullying, of which anti-Catholicism is an aspect. There may be disagreement with some actual or supposed Catholic doctrine. It may simply be for the excitement of doing mischief by young persons or simply a peer group activity.

What anti-Catholic individuals say is often based on an oversimplified understanding of Catholic teaching, obtained from children, which is uninformed about the true sophistication of Catholic theology. Their views on such a basis are essentially naive but may still have some persuasive value. Often, such views are expressed in pejorative language, which may be to express that the critic is passionate about what is being presented. But it may also simply be the language of hate.

Such sentiments are usually found on the social media resources of the Internet, such as Facebook and Twitter. There are also some panel discussion shows on television which ask viewers to comment via email during the discussion, and such comments are then shown as text on the screen. Sometimes such comments are absurd, but occasionally they are anti-Catholic.

5.2.3.5 Perspective

It is inevitable that an organisation such as the Catholic Church will have opponents and that not all opponents will be fair and reasonable. In all honesty, we must concede that our church has made some serious mistakes in the past which warrant opposition and criticism.

In modern times, most Western governments are largely atheistic and concerned with the secular aspects of their community. The inequalities that, in fact, discriminate against Catholics and other religions are generally for political purposes and are not primarily anti-religious. However, there are still some anti-Catholic laws and policies in non-Western countries that have not yet achieved the separation of church and state. So governmental anti-Catholicism is not a serious problem for us.

Some other religions have some anti-Catholic views, but they generally do not preach anti-Catholicism or encourage anti-Catholic action. The modern situation is that there is respectful dialogue amongst most religions. So this is also not a significant problem.

Anti-Catholic views proliferated by cults are of concern because they have the potential to influence or persuade many people to accept anti-Catholic sentiments. If enough people accept such views, they could become a political force which could result in legislation or policies which oppress Catholics. Legislation which allows something which is prohibited under Catholic doctrine, e.g. abortion, is something that we must tolerate, although we cannot take advantage of the secular legal freedom to do such a thing.

We know that hate is a stressful emotion which harms the person doing the hating more than it harms the person being hated. If the hate produces nothing more than anti-Catholic expressions in the language of hate, then our best option as Catholics is to feel sorry for the person hating us or our religion, and to regard what is said as uninformed opinions or ravings of the lunatic fringe.

5.2.3.6 Holier than Thou

The anti-Catholicism that is on the Internet is coarse, derogatory humour or hateful, vitriolic attacks usually based on lies or misconceptions. It is very much like the propaganda some governments inflict on their people to generate hate of the enemy in wartime. Unfortunately, many people believe this type of propaganda, which means that it has succeeded in proliferating hate.

It is normal for us human beings to deplore humour about us or our religion that has minimal humorous value and is basically intended to be offensive. Nor do we accept criticism of us or our beliefs based on misconceptions or lies. We feel hurt by such things especially if the attack is, to the best of our knowledge, unprovoked.

There is not a lot we can do about such attacks on our faith, and perhaps the best response is to follow the example of Jesus when he was falsely accused of capital offences before the Sanhedrin and Pilate.

However, most of us will be aware that there is also a substantial amount of anti-Semitic and anti-Islamic propaganda on the Internet. The purpose of raising that is to recognise that the Jews and Muslims feel just as hurt and dismayed at such offensive material as we do, and in most cases, it is also just coarse, unfunny humour or attacks based on misconceptions or lies. Certainly, some anti-Semitic material on the Internet by neo-Nazi cults are patently mere expressions of spite and hate, which from time to time have motivated hate crimes against the Jewish community.

Our faith requires that we love our neighbour as ourselves. The Jews and Muslims are certainly our neighbours. It is not the Jews and Muslims who generate or proliferate anti-Catholic materials on the Internet. Indeed, the Jews and Muslims are just as much, if not more so, the targets of such expressions of hate than we are.

What follows from this for us as Catholics is that we must have nothing to do with any Internet website and must simply delete any email communication that is apparently intended to be hateful and offensive to *any* religious or cultural community, without forwarding it to anyone. To do otherwise would make us like the hypocrites that Jesus scolded for not practising what they preached.

We should let our Muslim neighbours know that we will have no part in the proliferation of anti-Islamic material. That does not mean that we should ingratiate ourselves to our Muslim neighbours. There is much about their faith and culture that we find unacceptable, but we must recognise their right to reject the divinity of Jesus. They have done so, and they must take the consequences of that choice. In the meantime, treating them as we would wish them to treat us must begin with us.

5.3 Terrorism

5.3.1 Definition

To assess the extent to which we are concerned about terrorism, we must first have a clear understanding of what we are considering. The reason to clarify the concept is that there are currently some popular misconceptions about what terrorism is. The main misconception comes from the US president Bush's declaration of war on terror, which followed the 9/11 attack on the US Twin Towers. That attack was made by Islamic extremists and identifies terrorism as principally from this group. But terrorism, as more broadly understood, has existed for many years as a means of political opposition. This is still happening throughout the world, and it is this broader concept that is presented for consideration.

Definitions by various organisations and legislative definitions have proven to be inadequate. Accordingly, it appears necessary to take the more verbose approach and identify each of the elements that make up terrorism. What appears to make terrorism so difficult to define is perhaps that it is a pejorative term. This means that a person who commits a terrorist act is not praised by his or her compatriots as being a terrorist, but rather, he or she is praised and regarded as a freedom fighter, resistance fighter, hero, or selfless patriot. It is the victims who call the perpetrator a terrorist. It depends on your point of view.

5.3.1.1 What Constitutes an Act of Terror?

Essentially, an act of terror is a serious criminal offence in the jurisdiction where the offence is committed or against international criminal law. The act is mostly characterised by violence or the threat of violence, causing death, personal injury, or substantial property damage to one or more civilian persons who mostly have not personally aggrieved the person committing the crime. However, the terrorist act can be cyberterrorism, which is not directly violent, and the victims may be military, government agents, or officials such as police officers or diplomats.

5.3.1.2 Who Are Terrorists?

Terrorist attacks are mostly initiated by dissident groups or organisations who plan and then implement the attack. The planning is done by experts, and the implementation is done by either individuals or small groups or cells within the organisation. An attack can be initiated and implemented solely by one individual, but this is most unusual. The dissident groups may be political rebels, ethnic groups, or religious cults or factions. It has been suggested that even some governments can be considered terrorists. For example, Libya was considered to be a rogue state during the period in which Colonel Gaddafi supported and harboured terrorist groups. A point worth noting is that terrorists are not terrorists forever. There are cases of terrorists who have given up their cause and now lead law-abiding lives. Another example is the Taliban in Afghanistan. They were America's friends and allies in opposing the Soviet Union in northern Afghanistan but now are regarded as terrorists by Americans.

5.3.1.3 Terrorist Motives and Objectives

The motives of terrorists are a range of motives that is as broad as the range of normal human motives arising from hate, enmity, grievance, and other motives arousing violent response. The objectives of terrorism are as diverse as the strategic objectives in any violent conflict, in addition to the intention to create terror. Terror involves instilling in a population a fear or apprehension of further violent attacks. Obviously, there is no apprehension of what has already happened, only sadness. But what has happened shows the capacity and willingness of the terrorists to do such things. A comprehensive review of terrorist motives and objectives is beyond the scope of this work, but a few examples illustrating the above perceptions may assist our consideration.

In 1972, at the Munich Olympics, terrorists attacked the Jewish Olympians. Eleven Olympians were killed, as were most of the terrorists, but three terrorists survived and escaped. The Israeli Mossad hunted down the three survivors and assassinated two of them; the third died of natural causes. They also assassinated thirty-two other known anti-Israeli terrorists. The nature of this attack was clearly revenge, and the objective was to send a message to all anti-Israeli terrorists that any terrorist attack on Israel citizens would provoke a heavy response in kind.

On 10 July 1985, the French Secret Service sank the ship *Rainbow Warrior* in Auckland Harbour using explosives. One crew member of the vessel was killed. The attack was in response to the Greenpeace organisation's campaign against French nuclear testing in the South Pacific, with the objective being to incapacitate Greenpeace from further interference. The death of the crew member was probably not intended.

On 13 May 1981, Ali Agca shot and seriously wounded Pope John Paul II. The pope recovered. The assassin was a small-time criminal with connections to some terrorist groups. He appeared to be acting alone, but obviously he was resourced and later revealed that he had an accomplice who was supposed to explode a bomb to enable Agca to escape after shooting the pope. Agca appeared to have no motive, and it was thought that he was simply a delusional individual. He alleged that he had been commissioned by the Belgian Embassy to assassinate the pope. Later, documentary evidence suggests that the KGB had instructed the Belgian and East German secret services to do the assassination because Russia opposed the peace initiatives that the pope was promoting, which suggests that the motive for this attack was political, with the objective being to prevent further action by the pope.

On 11 September 2001, eleven terrorists hijacked three planes and flew two of them into the World Trade buildings in New

York City. The terrorists were all wealthy and well-educated young men who had undertaken a suicide mission. It was widely believed that Osama bin Laden was behind this attack, although there are some conspiracy theorists who disagree. Bin Laden was a strict Muslim from Saudi Arabia. He fought in the conflict in Afghanistan against the Russians, in which he was aided by the Americans. On return to Saudi Arabia, he regarded the presence of the Americans on holy ground as sacrilege, and he acted to oust the Americans. He wanted to free Mecca, Medina, and Jerusalem; to destroy Israel; and to start a worldwide jihad against the West. From this, it appears that the motive for this attack was essentially religious, which may explain why the eleven hijackers were willing to lay down their lives in this attack. However, history has shown that many have laid down their lives for non-religious causes. Bin Laden was assassinated by the American Special Forces on 1 May 2011 in Afghanistan.

There are other motives. For example, there have been aircraft hijackings and hostage-taking for the purpose of exchanging hostages for imprisoned freedom fighters or simply for ransom when the terrorists need money. These have occurred in civil wars in countries with unstable governments. There is also sabotage, which is often done by rebels and was widely used by resistance fighters in World War II, the objective being to weaken the enemy and exert political pressure.

5.3.1.4 Terrorist Methods

Terrorist attacks are rarely unplanned or opportunistic. In planning their attacks, terrorists have regard to their own resources and the capacity of their target to neutralise or defeat their attack. Of course, they want to achieve the objective of their attack, so they generally select what are called soft targets, i.e. targets that have no or little capacity to defend against their attack. Usually, this involves the terrorists, who are armed, attacking unarmed civilians. They rarely attack military targets, because the military is armed and trained to defend against attacks. Occasionally, suicide bombers do attack the military, sometimes in vehicles packed with explosives, but even then, military security usually prevents such attacks from having maximum effect.

Most terrorist attacks are comprehensively reported by the media in minute detail, such as in the Boston Marathon attack. There are suicide bombers in vehicles or pedestrians with explosives attached to their bodies, as in the Bali nightclub bombing. There are kidnappings for ransom, assassination of individuals from an opposition group, aircraft hijackings, and ambush skirmishes of opposition groups. A favourite form of many terrorists is the kidnap of a diplomat for money or to exert political pressure.

The form of terrorism that has become more common in recent times is the suicide bomber. Most of such attacks have been made by Islamic extremists. More recently, both women and young children have committed suicide in such attacks, although no religious leaders have done this. It seems that the courage to commit suicide for the Islamic faith comes from the Shia's heritage of martyrdom, which promises immediate entry into heaven for the suicide martyrs.

Our faith prohibits suicide, and we value all human life. But people laying down their lives for a cause should not surprise us. The Japanese kamikaze pilots in World War II did it, and most military groups have had suicide missions conducted by soldiers who volunteered, knowing the risk. We can probably expect to see more of this type of attack because it is almost impossible to defend against.

Naturally, terrorists want to maximise the effect of their attack. When instilling terror or exerting political pressure is a desired objective, the attack usually occurs in areas which cause maximum public disruption and where there will be substantial media coverage of their attack. The media aids the terrorists' terror objective by particularising the extent and savagery of the attack. But it is a two-edged sword, because such reporting is generally biased against the terrorists and, accordingly, increases contempt and opposition against the cause that the terrorists represent.

5.3.2 The Islamic Diaspora

5.3.2.1 Demographic

There are about 1.2 billion Muslims on our planet. About 800 million are the Sunni sect, and about 110 million are the Shia sect. The rest are in the 14 other Muslim sects. Of all Muslims, only about 260 million live in Arab countries, which is, of course, where Islam originated. Historically, the difference between Sunnis and Shias comes from the selection of the leader of Islam after its founder, Muhammad, died. The then homogenous Muslim community selected Abu Bakr as their leader. Ali, Muhammad's son-in-law, thought he should have been elected, and he created a schism in Islam which is now the Shia sect. The Shias developed their own strict theology and do not regard anyone who does not believe as they do as a true Muslim. They claim to be victims of Sunni oppression. Most of them live in Iran and other Arab countries in the region, such as Libya and Saudi Arabia.

There is real animosity between the Shias and the Sunni Muslims, and many Muslims have left their Arab homeland to escape the conflict. It is mainly the Sunnis who have emigrated and who have come to Western countries as refugees. The Sunnis are more moderate, and no doubt one consideration in their decision to migrate to Western countries is that they can obtain a better life in the Western countries, which offer more employment opportunities, greater income and social services, and access to quality-of-life-enhancing technology and appliances. The strict Shias do not want to be part of the decadent Western culture, so few of them emigrate. It is because of this emigration from Arab countries that most Westerners think that all Muslims are Arabs, but this is a misconception, because there are large numbers of Muslims in China, Pakistan, Indonesia, and Africa who are ethnically natives of their country.

5.3.2.2 Church and State

Islam has no prescription for the separation of church and state. In Christianity, we have Jesus saying, *'Give to Caesar is what is Caesar's and to God what is Gods.'* Constantine made Catholicism the official religion of the Roman Empire, which undoubtedly helped spread the faith. The feudal kings and princes all enforced Catholic morality until the Reformation and contact with other religions. Today our Western governments are fully secular, i.e. concerned principally with preserving peace and good order, although many of our laws have a moral basis.

Islam grew through the expansionist ambitions of the sultans and caliphs who had converted to Islam. Much of this expansion was by military conquest of neighbouring territories. Interestingly, the Islamic invaders offered an invitation to Islam before battle, and when that invitation was refused, the battle ensued. The spread of Islam in this way was remarkably successful. However, in modern times, there are many Muslims in non-Arab countries who owe their faith to evangelisation rather than conquest.

Because Islam does not legitimise secular law, the law in the Arab/ Muslim countries is essentially sharia law, which is derived from the Qur'an. In some non-Arab countries that have a significant Muslim population, some dissident Muslims agitate for the imposition of sharia law as the law of the land, replacing secular law. This is unacceptable to non-Muslims.

5.3.2.3 Jihad

A common misconception is that *jihad* means 'holy war' and that this is a war by all Muslims to convert all non-Muslims to Islam and is a war that will not end until there are no non-Muslims left. It may actually be understood by some radical extremist Muslims to have this meaning, but to most moderate Muslims, its meaning is quite different. The true meaning is that the evangelisation and conversion of non-Muslims to Islam is a desirable objective, which may be attained with the use of force if necessary. Of course, the process of evangelisation will not end until there is no one left to convert, but moderate Muslims are well aware that converting members of all other faiths to their faith is virtually impossible, and accordingly, the use of violence to enforce conversion cannot be justified. It is not a war; rather, it is a determination to spread the faith.

Catholicism does not have a spotless record in relation to this issue. The Gospel of Matthew, in Matthew 28:19, has Jesus saying, *'Make disciples of all nations.'* The Spanish conquistadors thereby converted the peoples they conquered at the point of a sword. The Gospels of Mark and Luke have Jesus instructing them to teach or evangelise all nations. In an earlier passage, Jesus sent the apostles out to evangelise (Mark 6:7–13), and if the people they addressed refused to accept their teachings, then the apostles were to leave that place and brush the dust of that place from their sandals, i.e. have nothing more to do with them. This reflects the modern Catholic approach to evangelisation, and the moderate Muslim approach is similar.

Accordingly, there is no need to fear a terrorist attack based on a desire to convert the target of their attack to Islam. Nor has it been recorded in any Islam-motivated terrorist attack, such as the 9/11 attack, that the terrorists offered an invitation to Islam before the attack.

5.3.3 Catholic Terrorist Targets

The attack on Pope John Paul II was either by a delusional individual or was politically motivated. It was not an attack on the principles of Catholicism. The conflict in Northern Ireland was also mainly political, with the involvement of some social issues. Clearly, this was not an attack on Catholic principles, because the principles of the Protestants are almost identical. What was involved was some residual anti-Catholicism left over from the Reformation, coupled with social issues, like competition for jobs.

In countries which have volatile political situations or civil war, there have been killings and kidnappings of Catholic religious persons such as nuns and aid workers, but these have mostly been criminal rather than terrorist attacks, although some have been held for ransom by rebel groups. Clearly, it is illogical to attack politically neutral persons who are there to help the people of the relevant country.

In modern times, there is very little terrorism from religious groups other than extremist Muslims. The leaders of most religions are in dialogue with the leaders of other religions, and the Christian denominations are moving towards ecumenism. Generally, the relationship between religions is amicable and based on mutual respect and tolerance. In countries where there is a separation of church and state, the various religions have no direct political power.

From the forgoing, it is clear that we need not be greatly concerned about terrorism aimed at us because of our faith. Even the Muslim extremists respect our faith, although they may want to convert us to Islam. So when Catholics are victims of terrorism, it is because they were simply in the wrong place at the wrong time and were seen by the terrorists simply as members of the community that is the target of their attack and not as Catholics.

5.3.4 Catholic Attitudes to Terrorism

As Catholics, we should support public condemnation of terrorism because it is criminal and against what we believe to be the laws of God. We can recognise that terrorism is a response to what the terrorists perceived to be a genuine grievance or cause but which we do not accept as a justification for criminality.

It has been argued that our response after a terrorist attack should be to carry on as normal, showing the terrorists that we are not afraid of them and that they have failed to terrorise us. The truth is that terrorist attacks do instil fear in us, because we recognise the capacity of the terrorists to do harm and we do not know where or when they will strike again. Pretending that we are unafraid is mere bravado, and both we and the terrorists know this. Our real response should be a determination to bring the terrorists involved to justice and to protect against similar attacks as far as possible. Such measures necessarily diminish some of our civil liberties and inconvenience us, but this is simply the price we must pay for security. For example, airport security has become much more stringent, but the number of aircraft hijackings has substantially decreased.

The war on terror is not just a piece of political rhetoric. It is a justification for the assassination of terrorists without bringing them to trial and judgement, as was done by the Mossad in retaliation to the Munich Olympic terrorists and by the Americans in retaliation to Osama bin Laden. Calling it a war allows the terrorists to be regarded as enemy soldiers who may be killed on sight. This is not a criticism or condemnation but merely an observation. It is probable that if bin Laden had been captured and held for trial, there would have been further terrorist attacks by al-Qaeda demanding his release. One observation that we can make about terrorism is that they must necessarily believe that the end justifies the means. This is not something with which we can agree, because our faith requires us to love one another and, accordingly, prohibits violence against one another for any reason.

It has been said that 'violence is the first resort of the unintelligent and the last resort of the intelligent'. Many terrorists are educated young men who may be intelligent but who are gung-ho about their cause and do not consider anything other than what they are taught. The use of children as suicide bombers is not justifiable by any intelligent standard. The planners behind most attacks do not participate in suicide attacks, which attributes intelligence to them but which may also indicate a lack of courage. There is little, if any, evidence that the leaders of terrorist groups are willing to participate in dialogue or peace talks.

Terrorism is inevitable in countries where the political system is unstable or volatile. We can minimise the risk to us personally by not going to such countries. Muslims are the primary target of Muslim extremist terrorists, and the statistics are that such terrorists have killed more Muslims than non-Muslims. However, some of their attacks are aimed at Western governments, particularly against America. Minimising the risk of such attacks is an ongoing process of increasing security measures based on experience. A potential significant risk, particularly in America, is if the extremist terrorists acquire nuclear weapons, because there is little doubt that they would use them. However, at present, the risk of death or injury in a terrorist attack is statistically much less than the same injuries being sustained in a motor vehicle accident.

5.4 Catholic Cults

5.4.1 The Issue

Most of what we hear about cults in mass media is negative. What we hear about is atrocities, imprisonments, financial tyranny, physical and mental abuses, et cetera. There are many cults within the Catholic religion. Public knowledge about cults would make us cautious and suspicious about having anything to do with any cult, especially since the structure, purpose, rules, and activities of most Catholic cults are not widely known amongst the Catholic laity.

The issue is whether our negative perception or disinterest in Catholic cults is the truth. Jesus said, *'I am the way, truth and life'* (John 14:6). Clearly, the truth is fundamental to our faith, and accordingly, an accurate perception of Catholic cults is important and worth considering. The sort of questions we should consider are as follows: how are they formed? What is their purpose and function? Are they legitimate? How is their membership recruited? What are the membership obligations in relation to confidentiality, financial support, termination of membership, activity commitments?

We know that some cults and sects are founded by charlatans and that not every Catholic will agree with or support the objectives of every Catholic cult. With this diversity in mind, it may be helpful to consider some criticisms of cults both from within and outside our church, bearing in mind also that there is still genuine anti-Catholic sentiment amongst some critics of our church. What we seek is to form a view on whether a Catholic cult is worthwhile or not.

5.4.2 Definition

It is important to distinguish between a cult and a sect. A cult is defined as *'devotion to a particular person or thing . . . by a body of professed adherents'* (*Shorter Oxford English Dictionary*, third edition). That is a very broad definition and would include the entire Catholic Church itself, but for our purposes, we can limit a cult to be a group within a religious denomination that is concerned solely with some devotional protocol and has no doctrine or theology divergent from its parent denomination.

A sect is defined as 'a body of persons who unite in holding certain views or beliefs differing from those of others who are accountable to be of the same religion' (*Shorter Oxford English Dictionary*, third edition). An example of this is the Lutheran denomination of Christianity, which started out as a sect, having different beliefs about the propriety and validity of the Catholic Church's teachings about indulgences, and subsequently evolved to be a separate denomination.

There are other groups, such as the Branch Davidians, that are usually called cults by the media but that do not fit under the definition we are considering. Unfortunately, it is usually such weird groups that do something that attracts the media's attention.

5.4.3 Cult Formation

Our faith has three main components: dogma, doctrine, and devotion. All these stem from the Old and New Testaments and have subsequently evolved to what our faith is today. A cult can be formed when some person, often a member of our clergy, has an idea relating to the devotional aspect of our faith that he thinks will assist the work of the church and will please God. That person then has the charisma and character to work to implement the idea through advocacy, example, and organising protocols for those who accept and wish to participate in the devotion.

The liturgical practices and commitments which our church requires of us are only minimally burdensome, amounting to little more than attending Mass on Sundays. What God requires of us is to lead our lives in accordance with the Ten Commandments and the teachings of Jesus, which are essentially to love God by keeping his commandments and to love our neighbour as ourselves, which is essentially the Golden Rule. None of this is very burdensome, and many Catholics who appreciate all that God has given us want to express their love of God by doing more than the bare minimum required of us. They want to go above and beyond the call of duty and, accordingly, are receptive to invitations to participate in the additional devotional activities proposed by a cult.

By comparison, the task assigned to the clergy of our church is almost impossibly burdensome. They have the task to evangelise every generation of every nation and to provide ongoing pastoral care to Catholics of every generation of every nation. There are currently over 1 billion Catholics on earth and not enough priests to service all Catholics to the optimally desirable extent. Obviously, there is much work to be done by our clergy in these tasks. The church relies on parents to assist in the task of generational evangelisation by requiring them to bring up their children in the Catholic faith, which is something most parents would do anyway out of love for their children if they are sincere practising Catholics.

In relation to pastoral care, the church recognises that many Catholics are willing to perform extra devotional work. Our church assists us by providing a resource that examines new cults and declares their legitimacy or otherwise. This it has done in cannons 294 to 329 of the canon law, in which it also identifies the clergy who can make such declarations.

5.4.4 Membership

The recruitment of membership of Catholic cults is mostly done by word of mouth, often at Sunday Mass, by a member of the cult speaking to the congregation, outlining the duties and benefits of membership. The duties are usually devotional works and sometimes some financial cost. The benefits may be to service a community need, and the cult may have funding and financial resources, although members' services are almost always voluntary and unpaid. Joining any such cult is voluntary and can usually be terminated at will, although the loss of a member by retirement may be lamented by other members, who may make their views known to the retiring member.

5.4.5 Illustrative Examples

5.4.5.1 The Society of St Vincent de Paul

Virtually no cults call themselves a cult, because the word *cult* has such negative overtones. This society is a cult founded by St Vincent de Paul. Jesus taught that we must love our neighbour. He gave us the parable of the good Samaritan. Essentially, this is the Golden Rule, whereby we deal with people who cross our path as we would like them to deal with us. Jesus also taught that charity was pleasing to God.

This society does charitable work. They receive donations from both Catholic and non-Catholic laity, which they distribute to the needy or present for sale to the public in a shop. The staff of the shop are all volunteers, and the profits from the shop are given to those needy who need money rather than other donated items.

Some of the volunteers provide visits to the sick or persons in nursing homes. They travel in their own vehicles at their own expense. Some use their trucks to collect donated furniture for distribution or sale. Some arrange temporary accommodation for the temporarily homeless, such as the victims of domestic violence.

The membership of this society is often older persons who are retired and have the time and resources to donate. As some older members die or retire, there may be a request for new members at a Sunday Mass, at which the work and conditions of membership are outlined.

This is a cult that implements the devotion of works of charity. It goes beyond the good Samaritan in that it is known to be a charitable organisation, and therefore, some of the needy approach it for help. In addition, some members seek out those reluctant or incapable of seeking help themselves. Naturally, such an organisation that only gives and takes nothing for staff or its members is not open to any significant criticism from anyone, although nothing is ever perfect and there are limits to what this society can do.

5.4.5.2 Opus Dei

This is an organised group of Catholics that is known as a personal prelature, which is the subject of canons 294 to 297 of the canon law. It can be regarded as a cult because it was instituted by a charismatic priest named Josemaría Escrivá in Madrid, Spain, in 1928 after he had a vision in which he saw what this cult could do. He called it Opus Dei, which means 'work of God', to make it clear that this cult was God's initiative and not his own.

The purpose and function of Opus Dei is to encourage its members to 'find God in daily life' and, accordingly, to live both their social and working life bearing in mind that God is the primary stakeholder in their activities, which in turn requires them to strive for excellence in their activities, which God may regard as holiness. A secondary aspect of such devotional activity is the evangelical effect of example. In 1939, Escrivá published a book called *The Way*, in which he identifies 999 maxims to assist laypeople in exercising appropriate spirituality in their daily lives.

The duty or commitment of members, in addition to constant mindfulness of God's interest in their daily lives, is set out in a list of daily, weekly, and annual devotional norms, which members are expected to perform once or more. For example, the daily norms include going to Mass, and the weekly norms include going to confession. There are only two annual norms, which are participating in a retreat for two or three weeks and going on a prayerful day pilgrimage in May, both of which are expected to be performed.

The cult also advocates mortification, which ranges from minor self-denial of some of life's luxuries to self-flagellation. The basis of this is to atone for the enormity of sin that the members may have committed and to comply with the teaching of Jesus that persons wanting to be his disciples should *'deny himself, take up his cross daily, and follow me'* (Luke 9:23).

In relation to self-flagellation, we should bear in mind that St Paul said *'Do you not know that your body is a temple of the Holy Spirit within you, whom you have from God, and that you are not your own? For you have been purchased at a price. Therefore glorify God in your body'* (1 Corinthians 6:19–20). Jesus suffered, but his pain was inflicted on him and was not self-inflicted. He accepted it because it was God's will, and he offered it in atonement for our sins. Self-flagellation is a form of masochism, which is a mental disorder. It disrespects the presence of the Holy Spirit in our bodies. With respect, those who practise self-flagellation as a Catholic devotion have simply got it wrong. However, it is not known how many members of Opus Dei actually practise self-flagellation. The expectation is that the percentage is no higher than the percentage of masochists in the entire human community. It is not a practice that is endorsed or encouraged by the managers of Opus Dei.

Members of Opus Dei currently number around ninety-five thousand. About 70% of these are called supernumeraries, which are ordinary lay Catholics living and working in secular society who observe the norms and contribute financially as their means permit. Other sections of membership are called numeraries, numerary assistants, associates, and the clergy of the Opus Dei prelature. The numeraries are celibate and essentially permanent staff of Opus Dei who are available for the tasks of the prelature. They comprise about 20% of total membership and live in centres run by Opus Dei, which are segregated by gender. Numerary assistants are essentially the domestic staff of Opus Dei centres and are part of the women's branch of Opus Dei. Associates are somewhere between supernumeraries and numeraries in lifestyle and availability to perform services for the prelature. The clergy of the Opus Dei are ordinary priests, many of whom were numeraries who undertook priesthood as their career path.

The demographic of Opus Dei is that about 60% are in Europe, and 35% are in the Americas. The rest are scattered across ninety countries, with establishment centres in sixty-nine countries. The numeraries and associates provide the training and education of new members and other Catholics. Opus Dei has recruitment resources and protocols. About 57% of members are female.

There has, of course, been criticism of Opus Dei from both within and outside the Catholic Church. On the other hand, there has been support of Opus Dei by several pontiffs, including Pius XII, John Paul II, Benedict XVI, and Pope Francis. A full consideration of all criticism is beyond the scope of this work, but a few are worth considering.

One criticism is that Opus Dei is cult-like in secretiveness. Jesus teaches that those who proclaim their good works have had their reward. The object of being a member is to obtain a reward after death in the next life. Accordingly, privacy is appropriate. There is no suggestion that there is concealment of negative activity, and all the information in this work about Opus Dei, and much more, is freely available to the public.

Another criticism is that its recruitment activities are sometimes aggressive. There is no evidence that anyone's will has been overborne to force them to become a member, so this criticism is merely a view of recruitment proprieties.

Another criticism is that the cult is elitist. The membership of Opus Dei includes many persons from low-profile occupations, so Opus Dei is certainly not elitist in this sense. However, it may be that members who observe the cult's norms diligently think that, therefore, they are 'holier than thou', the 'thou' being non-members. There is no indication in the teachings of Jesus that extra devotional activities will gain extra merit. His command was to 'love God with all your heart'. So if one has the capacity to love God with more devotion than our church's prescribed minimum, then that person should act in accordance with that capacity. Accordingly, elitism of this nature is unwarranted and should be discouraged.

Another criticism is that the management of the cult is misogynist. The fact that 57% of members are female and that membership is voluntary clearly indicates that this criticism is invalid.

Anecdotally, there are stories of members who have complained to their local bishop when their fellow Catholics do things that appear to have dubious official church support. Being a dobber or tattletale is not an admirable characteristic. On the other hand, if a member believes that there is a serious irregularity in the observance of Catholic morality or doctrinal adherence and believes that it is appropriate to report the irregularity to a proper authority, then the member must be true to himself and act accordingly. That is an admirable characteristic.

Overall, the criticisms are insufficient to discourage lay Catholics from considering joining this cult, although the official manifesto of this cult should make its views on self-flagellation and elitism clear.

5.4.5.3 The Order of St Charbel

William Kamm was a Catholic who started his religious career in the 1980s by arranging prayer meetings at the homes of Catholic friends and acquaintances. At these meetings, he claimed to have had visions or apparitions of Our Lady, Mary, the mother of Jesus, who called him 'the Little Pebble' and told him things in the nature of prophecies of doom. These he related to those present at the prayer meetings, and after some discussion, some prayers were said, asking God to avert the disaster.

Since those days, Kamm has founded the religious group known as the Order of St Charbel, named after the Maronite saint Charbel Makhlouf and which he claims is part of our Catholic Church.

In September 1989, Malcolm Broussard, a parish priest from Texas, was suspended for abandoning his priestly duties. In 2003, Broussard was consecrated as a bishop in Bavaria; however, this was not authorised by our church, and he was automatically excommunicated.

William Kamm was excommunicated from our church on 10 June 2003, and our church has officially declared that the Order of St Charbel is not a part of the Catholic Church but is a fringe Christian sect. Broussard ordained Kamm as a deacon of the sect in May 2004. Kamm has assembled a community of followers, who are accommodated in a compound near Nowra, which is a town about one hundred miles south of Sydney, Australia. With the financial support of his following, Kamm has become very wealthy.

In his manifesto pronouncements and prophecies, Kamm has made a number of amazing predictions, some of which are as follows:

- He will become a 'new Abraham', spawning a multitude of people.
- He will have eighty-four wives, twelve of which will be queens and the other seventy-two princesses.
- The world will be cleansed by a ball of fire.
- He will become the Catholic pope, taking the name Pope Peter II.

- Pope John Paul II would appoint him as a bishop and nominate him as his sole successor. When Pope John Paul II died in 2005, Kamm announced that 'heaven clearly changed its plans'.
- He will be the successor of Pope Benedict XVI.
- Pope John Paul II will rise from the dead and fight evil alongside Pope Benedict XVI.
- The rule of priestly celibacy does not apply to him.

On 14 October 2005, Kamm was sentenced to five years' imprisonment for a series of sexual assault on a fifteen-year-old girl, whom he claimed was one of his eighty-four wives living in the Nowra compound. In May 2007, Kamm was convicted of committing further sexual assault on another fifteen-year-old girl, after which he was sentenced to an aggregate term of fifteen years for the offences against both girls. He was granted parole on 14 November 2014 on certain conditions, which include not living near Nowra, being subjected to electronic monitoring, and not attending places where girls under seventeen normally reside. He still runs his website from Sydney and now goes by the name of William Costellia.

5.4.6 Conclusion

The word *cult* has been given negative overtones by the media and is possibly the reason for most devotional groups within our church not calling themselves a cult. However, cults have a legitimate place within our church to assist with the church's massive evangelical and pastoral responsibilities. So not only are these cults functionally beneficial, but they are also an opportunity for us, the laity, to love God to the full extent of our capacity.

In the examples considered, the Society of St Vincent de Paul is clearly a cult which is not only approved by our church but also laudable and free from any substantive criticism or objection.

Opus Dei is also a cult, because it is in complete conformity with our church's dogma and doctrine and has church approval of its devotional norms even though it is a personal prelature.

The Order of St Charbel claims to be a cult, but both the Maronite Church and our church have disowned it and regard it as a sect. It was included as an example here to illustrate the kind of information that could assist us in considering joining a sect. There are rogues and charlatans in our world who have some charisma and will exploit normal human gullibility for their own personal or financial gain.

The rationale appears to be that joining a Catholic cult is worthwhile and may be encouraged. But in considering joining, prudence requires a thorough check to ascertain whether the cult is approved by our church, exactly what is required by the cult, availability of exit from the cult, conditions of membership, and the credentials and reputation of the managers of the cult. It is also prudent to anticipate the evolution of a cult if one is involved in its formative stages and to reserve commitment in case the evolution turns out to be disappointing.

5.5 Modern Church–State Relationship

5.5.1 The Issue

The question that people who live in a democratic country must ask themselves when they vote in an election is 'What laws do we want to apply to the community in which we live?' This question becomes important because under the democratic party system, the competing parties offer different options of what they promise to make law, with the options sometimes being similar but with lower priorities and funding.

5.5.2 The Function of the State

The function of the government of a nation or state is to enforce the rule of law, without which there is anarchy and chaos, in which a government cannot function or survive. The areas that a government must address depend, to an extent, on the geographical location of the jurisdiction, the resources available to the government, and the demographic of its people. Typical portfolios are health, education, infrastructure, trade, commerce, foreign affairs, defence, treasury, housing, social services, et cetera. A government must make laws to enable its ministries to run in accordance with its political precepts and priorities.

For the orderly and peaceful interaction of its people, a government needs to have laws dealing with criminal conduct, commercial transactions, safe and efficient transport, succession, family and other relationships, conduct in public places, anti-racism and anti-discrimination, freedom of worship, international arrangements, et cetera.

The above list is not exhaustive, but hopefully, it indicates the scope and complexity of government concerns. While most governments already have a comprehensive body of laws, the ongoing task of government is to modify those laws by repeal, amendment, or replacement as the social, economic, and cultural development of its jurisdiction progresses, arising from a technological development, commercial and industrial innovation, natural disasters, variable demographic, et cetera.

5.5.3 The Function of the Church

The sole function of our church is to help us save our souls. We are individually responsible for our souls, and we will not attain heaven simply because we are members of the Catholic Church. Our church helps us in this endeavour principally with pastoral care, but before a person can receive pastoral care, that person must be a member of our church, which requires evangelisation and education from our church.

We have already considered the authenticity and authority of our church, and from the Gospels, it is clear that Jesus did not give the apostles the authority to make secular laws with which to rule our lives. In his teachings, Jesus made several references to secular law. Relevantly, in Matthew 21:21, he said, *'Then repay to Caesar what belongs to Caesar and to God what belongs to God.'* Here Jesus was talking about paying taxes, which is what all secular governments require in one form or another, while clarifying that God has no interest in money. It also clearly expresses the concept of the legitimacy and entitlement of secular government. Another instance appears in Matthew 5:25–26, where Jesus says, *'Settle with your opponent quickly while on the way to court with him. Otherwise your opponent will hand you over to the judge, and the judge will hand you over to the guard, and you will be thrown into prison. Amen, I say to you, you will not be released until you have paid the last penny.'* Here Jesus was teaching the wisdom of anger management, and again, his teaching presupposes a system and authority of secular law.

An underlying assumption in the teachings of Jesus is that there is no conflict between God's law or commands and the secular law, in that neither law will command us to do or not do what the other forbids or requires. This is normally the case, but in the past, some governments have attempted to neutralise the power or influence of the church by criminalising religious worship and observance. In the long term, none of these governments have been successful in permanently removing the Catholic faith from their territories.

Naturally, our church wants to coexist peacefully with secular governments. However, it has its task of evangelisation and pastoral care, and the question it must ask itself is 'What secular laws are most conducive to the discharge of our duties to our adherents? And if an actual or proposed secular law permits or requires something contrary to God's law, what must the church do about it?' This, then, is the issue for our church and our concern as Catholics.

5.5.4 Some Historical Insights

Amongst other things, the Old Testament of the Bible contains accounts of events against a background of secular governments, from the pharaohs of ancient Egypt to the Jewish kings, like David and Solomon. These led to the integrated religion controlled secular culture of Judaism after the Roman conquest of Israel, into which Jesus was born. Jesus formed a sect of Judaism because he claimed to be the messiah, which Orthodox Judaism rejected as heresy. Jesus did not challenge the secular laws, but he did discard some Jewish cultural norms, such as their dietary laws.

Catholicism, as founded by Jesus, grew and survived internal heresy, persecutions, and other adversities until the reign of the emperor Constantine, after which it became the accepted religion of the empire and led to the formation of the politically powerful Holy Roman Empire. As we have already seen, there were further heresies, schisms, and the division with what is now the Orthodox Church. Then there was a time when the Catholic clergy were the secular rulers of certain territories in Italy. And in the ages and places where the feudal system applied, the church had compelling influence over the kings and princes who ruled their feudal kingdoms.

Then came the Reformation, which arose from the abuse of political power, corruption, and theological arrogance that had arisen within the church. This topic has already been raised in this work and needs no further consideration here. In modern times, we have the phenomenon of globalisation, which results from technological advances in transport, communication, international legal bodies, and the spreading demographic of other religions. There has also been a significant decrease in the church's direct political power and influence, which has stimulated a substantial growth in atheism now that Catholicism is no longer a prerequisite for political, social, or financial advancement and, in some situations, may even be a disadvantage.

5.5.5 The Democratic Process

Those of us who live in a democratic country will be familiar with the democratic process, but for some others, a brief primer may be worthwhile. The fundamental concept of democracy is that it is *government of the people, by the people, for the people.*

In practice, there are people who want to do the work of government. Their motives for wanting this are diverse but may be altruistic. They may have a belief that they can do the job better than others, or it may be a desire to correct some perceived defect in the current situation or simply a desire for prestige and power. The selection of who is to govern is done by election, and those wanting to govern nominate themselves for election. The people vote in the election, the votes are counted, and under various systems of preferential values, the successful candidate is appointed. Most democratic systems operate under a party system, and most candidates belong to one such party. The benefit of this system is that it shows the direction in which that party proposes to take the nation during its term of office. The party that has the most elected representatives will have the majority in the parliament and, accordingly, can control the law-making process, with some exceptions and sometimes with coalition arrangements. The leader of the party that has the most elected persons is usually the nominal political head of the country, but some systems have a president who is separately elected.

The functions of government are usually implemented by a set of departments which have specific duties and responsibilities, are controlled by the elected person, and are staffed by permanent unelected employees.

The period for which a government is elected varies from system to system but is typically for several years. After, or towards the end of this period, there is another election in which those previously elected may and mostly do nominate for re-election. Typically, those seeking re-election campaign on the basis that they have done a good job while in office, whereas their competition argues the opposite and says that they, the opposition, can do better. Again, this is mostly presented against the background of the party system.

While in office, the governing party makes laws in the parliament at which all elected persons attend and vote. Mostly, the voting is in accordance with the elected person's party directives, but sometimes there is a conscience vote, in which each person votes in accordance with their personal beliefs. Sometimes there is a bipartisan vote because all elected persons agree that a particular law is necessary.

Within any party, there is usually competition for the leadership, especially if the leadership of the party is or is potentially the political head of the country. It seems inevitable that as long as a party has a leader, there will be others within the party who want the top job. History has shown us that the competition for such positions is not always entirely ethical, but human nature being what it is, this should not surprise us.

The forgoing outline of the democratic process is totally insufficient to do justice to the complexity and integrity of the political systems that do adhere to democracy, but it is sufficient to identify the political system which governs most Catholics living in the Western world. However, in most of these countries, Catholics are now a minority group, even where they are the largest religion.

5.5.6 Democratic Dissent

Sometimes governments make bad laws. Laws can be bad because they are made pursuant to some form of corruption, or they arise out of bad judgement or an error, although many errors only become apparent with the wisdom of hindsight. Sometimes the law is alleged to be a bad law by the political opponents of the government that made the law, while the correctness of the law may be a matter of opinion. In most societies, the law also has a declaratory function, which means that the laws specify the conduct that is acceptable or otherwise, according to that community's standards. Some laws are unenforceable because they are impractical or impossible to detect or prosecute breaches of such laws. Essentially, such laws are bad laws, even if they have a declaratory function, because any law that is not enforced brings the whole law into disrepute, which undermines the rule of law.

The question then arises as to what the members of the community can do about a proposed or existing law which they, as individuals, consider to be a bad law. In non-democratic countries, bad laws can lead to violent armed rebellion or even civil war. In democratic countries, the most common option is to exert political pressure on elected persons to not pass some proposed law or to change some existing law. This usually takes the form of lobbying, public protest gatherings, petitions, letters to the elected persons, and sometimes even public civil disobedience.

These forms of dissent are legitimate in a democratic society, so long as they do not include serious public disorder, such as a riot, personal violence, substantial property damage, or unacceptable disruption of normal legitimate conduct of personal and community affairs. We, as individuals, have the right to be heard by our elected representatives. Our church, as a legitimate organisation within our community, has the right to teach us the morality of our faith and inform us of whether actual or proposed laws accord with its teachings, although it does not have the authority to command us how to vote.

Governments and opposition parties do respond to such forms of political pressure because they need the support of the majority of the community in order to be elected or re-elected. If the issue or law is fundamental enough, the government may hold a referendum. If it is less fundamental, it may have a straw vote in the nature of a plebiscite. In relation to ordinary laws and policies, it may conduct surveys or simply consider the known views of dissenting groups.

5.5.7 The Church's Current Political Status

In our modern democratic society, our church has no direct political authority, nor does it have any direct authority in any non-democratic society except the Vatican. However, through the voting power of its adherents, i.e. us lay Catholics, it does have significant influence on the lawmaking process, depending on the size of the Catholic minority and the extent to which we are moved to proactivity by our church's commentary on some proposed or existing law. Essentially, the extent of the church's political influence is in our hands.

So why should we be politically proactive or vote a certain way? Perhaps considering the example of the abortion laws, which is an issue on which our church has lost, will illuminate the reasons for being proactive.

Our faith teaches us that we should love our neighbour as ourselves, our neighbour being identified as all mankind. In the abortion debate, we see the foetus or embryo as a real though incomplete person, with the same right to life as every born human being, because our church teaches that human life begins at conception. So it is out of love for the unborn that we speak on their behalf.

We also love the women who carry the unborn within them. We believe that an abortion is mortally offensive to God, and we do not wish them to incur the consequence of such a serious sin. Of course, we also love God, and we do not wish him to be offended by anyone, because we know that he loves all of us equally.

In addition to these religious reasons, we also have a say in the formation of the normal standards of our community. Naturally, we must be true to ourselves, and on some issues, this will require that we be proactive. There is some moral culpability in failure to affirm our true beliefs. Nor can we credibly complain about the degeneracy of moral standards if we have stood by and done nothing.

As already indicated, this is a debate that we Catholics have lost, and there appears to be negligible prospects of a reversal of the law. However, what we should bear in mind is that the law allows abortion on demand but does not compel it in any circumstances. The situation then is that a devout Catholic woman may not choose to have an abortion, whereas a non-Catholic woman, whose beliefs are otherwise, may. If the law required a woman to have an abortion in certain circumstances, which is a virtually unimaginable scenario, no doubt all Catholics in that government's territory would strongly object. There would be private civil disobedience, and that government's chances of re-election would be greatly reduced. This would come about because our church would undoubtedly strongly and very publicly oppose such a law. This then illuminates the current political status of our church in a democratic society.

5.6 Child Sexual Abuse

5.6.1 The Issue

The word *paedophilia* refers to sexual abuse of prepubescent children. The concern raised here for consideration is broader than paedophilia and is intended to include sexual abuse of children who have reached puberty and who are not yet mentally adult. While not specifically included, the issue raised here would apply equally to mentally handicapped persons of any age who have not obtained adult maturity and capacity.

This topic raises a number of questions, and our consideration may be best served by identifying some of the more critical issues and exploring possible answers. Much of the information that is presented here comes from the Royal Commission into Institutional Responses to Child Sexual Abuse.

5.6.2 Nature of the Offence

What type of conduct amounts to child sexual abuse? We do not need to go into specifics here. Suffice it to say that the conduct ranges from apparently innocuous touching of the child's genitals to rape as it is legally defined. The essential element is that the child formed the view that the perpetrator's conduct was inappropriate and a violation of the child's right to genital privacy and decorum.

5.6.3 Who Are the Offenders?

From the Royal Commission Final Report, in relation to claims made against the Catholic Church, 90% of perpetrators were male, and 10% were females. This was further subdivided into priests (30%), religious brothers (32%), religious sisters (5%), and laypersons (29%). The claims against other Christian denominations' clergy were roughly similar in percentage but not as numerous, because Catholicism is and was by far the largest Christian denomination.

Of course, there is child sexual abuse in other non-religious institutions and also by individuals not part of any institution. Court records disclose a significant number of sexual assault cases against children by family members or close friends of the family. Then there is an unknown number of such cases where no complaint was ever made, for a variety of reasons. However, the commission's statistics are an approximate guide. The commission considered about 4,029 allegations of child sexual abuse against religious institutions in private sessions, and our church informed the commission of 4,444 claims alleging child sexual abuse made between 1 January 1980 and 28 February 2015 pertaining to incidents occurring between 1950 and 2010. Clearly, most of the perpetrators of child sexual abuse committed more than one offence. Exactly how many more offences they committed cannot be known unless all victims complain and have their complaints substantiated, and this is patently unlikely. But from available numbers, it appears that about 7% of priests who ministered between 1950 and 2010 committed such acts, and on average, it was about 20% of the various orders of brothers who managed schools and residential institutions. We can only register dismay that there was so much child sexual abuse in Catholic institutions in Australia during that period, but it is illuminating that most of that conduct was not committed by our priests.

5.6.4 Who Are the Victims?

Who are the victims of child sexual abuse? Our concern is with child sexual abuse by priests and religious brothers within our church. The Royal Commission report documents data given by our church, which is as follows: the victims were obviously children. The average age of all claimants/victims when the sexual abuse began was 11.4 years old. Boys averaged 11.6 years old, and girls averaged 10.5 years old. Boys comprise 78% of claimants/ victims and girls the remaining 22%. Most of the sexual abuse occurred in the 1970s, with the average duration of the abuse lasting 2.4 years. The average delay between the commencement of the abuse and the making of a claim was 33 years. We have already noted that most of the perpetrators are adult males, and it is now clear that most of the victims were boys. This suggests that the perpetrators have homosexual preferences, but there is insufficient scientific and medical evidence available at this time to support that conclusion; also, the Royal Commission report formed the view that there is no link to homosexuality in these paedophiles.

5.6.5 Consequences

What are the consequences of child sexual abuse for the victims and their families? Again, focusing on child sexual abuse by Catholic clergy, we see from the Royal Commission report that, in many cases, the victims claimed to have lost their faith, no doubt due to disillusionment from seeing the representatives of Jesus doing shameful things to them. Some girl victims became pregnant and were then forced to have an abortion or to surrender the child for adoption or to marry. Many victims claimed that the abuse adversely affected their personality in relation to depression, self-respect, respect for authority, and other aspects, which led some to attempt suicide and others to claim that these personality changes made them less successful in their lives than they would have been had the abuse not occurred.

It is plausible that child sexual abuse can cause personality changes which make the victim less ambitious and competitive, leading to a less prosperous and successful life. Unfortunately, there is no way to prove that a victim of child sexual abuse would not have developed negative personality traits if the sexual abuse had not occurred. There are also cases of victims of child sexual abuse who have coped well with the abuse and have had highly successful and prosperous lives. However, most victims complain that the abuse has ruined their lives, while some have coped through faith, with the recognition that the perpetrators were acting contrary to our faith. There are also statistics of suicides proximate to clusters of child sexual abuse incidents in the same locality during the same period. It seems likely that such suicides were in consequence of child sexual abuse, but the evidence is insufficient to support this as a conclusion.

In addition to the consequences to the victims, the families of victims were also affected, especially when the child complained or revealed the abuse. Many parents did not believe their children, because of the highly respected status and reputation of the alleged perpetrator and because children do lie about such things for a variety of reasons. Families were torn apart, friendships ended, and in some cases, entire communities became divided.

5.6.6 Morality

Is paedophilia wrong? Clearly, paedophilia is against the criminal law of virtually every country, but it is not against any of the Ten Commandments of God. The *Catechism of the Catholic Church* has only one short paragraph dealing with paedophilia, which is as follows:

2389. Connected to incest is any sexual abuse perpetrated by adults on children or adolescents entrusted to their care. The event is compounded by the scandal or harm done to the physical and moral integrity of the young, who will remain scarred by it all their lives, and the violation of responsibility for their upbringing.

The *Catechism* was published in 1994, before the worldwide epidemic of child sexual abuse of the 1970s came to public notice, so the paucity of the Catholic catechism's teaching on this issue is understandable. Nor does the catechism deal with paedophilia by the clergy of the church, although the canon law is adequate to deal with it.

In these circumstances, we can look to the Gospel for guidance. In Matthew 18:5–7, Jesus says:

Anyone who welcomes one little child like this in my name welcomes me. But anyone who is the downfall of one of these little ones who have faith in me would be better drowned in the depths of the sea with a great millstone around his neck. Alas for the world that there should be such causes of falling! Causes of falling indeed there must be, but alas for anyone who provides them!

With the wisdom of hindsight, it is now clear to us that the downfall of the *little ones* includes the consequences of child sexual abuse, identified above. Referring to the little ones as those 'who have faith in me' suggests children who have been brought up as Catholics. The phrase 'causes of falling indeed there must be' may well mean that child sexual abuse is inevitable because totally selfish sexual lust is part of the human nature that God has instilled in man as something to overcome. Saying that it would be better for a person who causes such downfall of children to be drowned at sea is the second most severe condemnation by Jesus of sinful conduct in the New Testament, the most severe being the condemnation of blasphemy against the Holy Spirit, recorded in Mark 3:29 and Luke 12:10. From this, it is clear that Jesus taught that child sexual abuse and any other conduct that causes children to lose their faith is very seriously offensive to God.

5.6.7 Motives

Why do paedophiles do it? Currently, most of the medical profession and the wider community regard paedophilia as a mental disorder or mental illness. It has been suggested that the condition is genetic and therefore incurable and that the consequent behaviour is compulsive. Similarly, it has been argued that homosexuality is genetic, and while many people accept this as true, the medical evidence to support this conclusion is currently insufficient to enable the medical experts to regard this as a proven fact. Naturally, there has been far less research into paedophilia, and accordingly, the truth of the argument that paedophilia is genetic has little evidence to support it at this time.

Our church teaches that we have free will to choose between good and evil. From this, it follows that we will always have the strength to reject the evil option, although our culpability may be diminished by inordinate attachments. See the *Catechism of the Catholic Church*, paragraphs 1731 to 1738. What this means is that in relation to paedophilia, there is no such thing as a compulsion to commit child sexual assault, although a genetic predisposition to sexual attraction to children may diminish the culpability of the sin. Statistics suggest that there is a link between homosexuality and paedophilia, as it is mostly committed by adult males against boys, but this is inconclusive, because the statistics may merely reflect that the abuses occurred in all-boys schools, where all the teachers are males, or were done by priests to altar boys.

It has also been reported that paedophiles who have been apprehended express feelings of remorse, guilt, and shame, which suggests that there may be some level of inordinate attachment involved in their behaviour. On the other hand, most persons who have committed any criminal offence will express remorse and contrition when they expect to be convicted of the offence, in the hope of obtaining some leniency on sentencing.

5.6.8 Church Responses

How has our church dealt with complaints of child sexual assault by priests and other religious persons? The Royal Commission Final Report makes it clear that our church managed such complaints extremely poorly. The commissioners said that many people complained to the relevant religious institutions as soon as the child sexual abuse came to their notice. Most of the institutions dealt with such complaints in-house, keeping their investigations and other actions strictly confidential and not reporting the matter to the police, even though they must have known that the matter complained of was a criminal offence and that there was a legal duty to report the matter to the police.

Specifically, in relation to our church, the report said that our church's response to child sexual abuse was clearly aimed at avoiding public scandal, protecting the reputation of the church, and loyalty to priests alleged to have committed such acts. Often complainants were simply not believed and were treated as liars. Investigations were superficial compared to proper police investigations, and even where the bishops and committees handling these complaints formed the view that a priest had committed child sexual abuse, they dealt very leniently and ineffectively with that priest, if at all. In effect, the responsible bishops swept the matter under the rug, and it may well be that the church's response was a major factor in many Catholics' loss of faith in God and his church.

It is astonishing that the bishops involved in concealing paedophilia by priests did not consider whether Jesus would have done what they (the bishops) did or would have approved of their actions. As bishops, they certainly should have known that Jesus would certainly not have approved of concealment of paedophilia. Those bishops are accountable to Jesus, but it is not our place to make any sort of judgement of them. The reason for this negative assessment of their handling of such complaints becomes relevant to the issue of compensation to victims, which will be considered hereunder. The total ineffectiveness of the bishops' treatment of priests they believed to be guilty of paedophilia compounded the felony and led to many more cases of child sexual abuse than would have occurred had they taken effective action.

5.6.9 Compensation

What is the function of monetary compensation in child sexual abuse matters? In most legal systems, the law contains a principle called vicarious liability. Under this principle, the employer of a person who wrongly causes injury or damage to another person in the course of his or her employment is liable to compensate the person who suffered the injury or damage. Both the employer and employee may be sued, but often it is only the employer that is sued, because the employee has little or insufficient money for compensation. Priests and other Catholic religious are clearly in a master–servant relationship with our church and are subject to the directions of the relevant bishop. Also, priests have virtually no personal wealth. Accordingly, our church alone is sued under the principle of vicarious liability.

Our church has substantial financial assets and monetary resources, but essentially, all its wealth comes from donations from us, the laity, given to support the proper functions of our church. It is therefore somewhat vexatious for our church to be paying compensation to the victims of child sexual abuse when that conduct by the priest or brother or other religious is clearly contrary to the teachings of our church and could not conceivably be regarded as having been done in the course of his or her employment. Naturally, our sympathies lie with the victims of child sexual abuse, and no doubt most of us would approve ex gratia payments to these victims. Perhaps it is on this basis that our church has forgone the technical defence available here.

In relation to the cover-ups implemented by the bishops responsible for handling child sexual abuse complaints, the principle of vicarious liability clearly does apply. We accept that they acted in what they believed was the best interests of our church and that their action was undoubtedly in the course of their employment. But their action had no regard to their duty to protect potential future victims of paedophiles, and therefore, they failed to effectively prevent reoffending by those priests. Accordingly, these bishops can be regarded as negligent accessories before the fact of such subsequent child sexual abuse, and therefore, our church is vicariously liable.

Many victims of child sexual abuse have publicly stated that all they really want is a sincere official apology. Perhaps that is true for some, but a cynical person might wonder how many victims would have come forward if compensation were not available and if the only recourse was the criminal law sanctions against the perpetrators and their accessories. There is also the possibility that the facts of some alleged child sexual abuse cases have been embellished sufficiently to make the event compensable or simply embellished through the vagaries of human memory over lengthy periods.

5.6.10 Celibacy

Is the celibacy of priests and other religious a factor which increased the incidence of child sexual abuse by the Catholic clergy to a higher level than in the non-religious community? The Royal Commission stated, *'However, based on research, we conclude that there is an elevated risk of child sexual abuse where compulsorily celibate male clergy or religious have privileged access to children in certain types of Catholic institutions, including schools, residential institutions and parishes.'*

It is common knowledge that our human sex drive is our second most powerful instinct after our instinct of self-preservation. The permanent self-imposed suppression of our sex drives is clearly possible, because many priests have achieved this. However, it is unnatural and creates substantial psychological pressure or tension in the person attempting celibacy.

Anecdotally, some priests have publicly stated that celibacy is readily achievable and is not a factor in paedophilia. However, we do not know the strength of the sex drive in the men who become priests or their sexual preferences or what unobjectionable measures they take to relieve normal sexual pressures.

The Royal Commission report has made a number of recommendations to the Holy See, including some related to this issue. The commission's view regarding the increased incidence of paedophilia amongst celibate men is not an established proven fact and remains the view of a few based on some research.

Whether our church leaders implement any of these recommendations is a matter for them. It may be that the celibacy rule was initiated by St Paul, who was clearly right in saying that priests engaged in itinerant evangelical or missionary work in dangerous parts of the world should not be taking a wife and family with them. But that is not the case in modern priestly orders exclusively doing pastoral care. Furthermore, the marriage of priests in other Christian denominations have proven to be successful. For what it is worth, St Peter was married, because the Gospels record that Jesus cured Peter's mother-in-law.

Clerical celibacy is *not* a dogma of our faith, and our church clearly has the authority to nullify vows. Most of us members of our church laity have married and have experienced the true love of a spouse. In most cases, this has brought us closer to God. It is a joy that has not diminished the observance of our professional obligations, and there is no basis for suspecting that a married priest would put his duties to his family before his duties to God, even if conflict between these sets of duties were possible. It is puzzling why our church would deprive its priests of a sacrament that could bring them closer to God. If the marriage of priests reduces the incidence of paedophilia by Catholic priests or religious, that is certainly worth consideration by our church leaders.

5.6.11 Further Action

What should our church do to minimise paedophilia by Catholic clergy and to deal with victims in a true Christian manner? The Royal Commission recognised that most of the child sexual abuse incidents that it investigated occurred in the 1970s. In relation to these matters involving our church, it also noted that substantial changes had been made by the Australian Catholic Bishops Conference in the late 1980s and the Towards Healing and Melbourne Response initiatives in 1996, which substantially corrected the church practice of ineffective response to complaints of child sexual abuse.

While most of the allegations of child sexual abuse were historical, i.e. they occurred as much as forty years ago, the commission stated that paedophilia has been occurring since the earliest years of our church and that it continues to be a concern now and into the future. The findings of the Royal Commission and other investigations have been a major scandal, the core of which is the reprehensible conduct by bishops who allowed paedophile priests to commit further offences by not dealing effectively with these priests. Statistically, the number of paedophile priests is fairly small, but the number of their victims is alarmingly large. Many of these victims have lost their faith and others, including the families of victims and persons peripherally involved, have lost confidence and trust in our priests as a result of the scandal; they have therefore ceased coming to church and having anything to do with our priests, even if they still believe in God and Jesus. They have lost the assistance that pastoral care gives to us in saving our souls, and there will be an accounting for this. This has unfortunately occurred because the conduct of a few has tainted the reputation of many, because we cannot know who is a paedophile and who is not.

The Royal Commission made a number of recommendations specifically for the leaders of our church, in the light of their findings and the reforms already implemented. How our church leaders respond to these recommendations is a matter for them, and we should not be critical of our leaders if they do not adopt every recommendation, because the commission was focused on the interests of the victims of child sexual abuse and regarded Catholic theology, doctrine, and canon law as readily changeable to conform with their views on the necessities to minimise child sexual abuse.

What we can reasonably expect from our church leaders is a change in attitude towards child sexual abuse which reflects the vehemence with which Jesus condemned such action, while not just throwing to the wolves those priests who Jesus also loves, because they have given their lives of service to the church. Reporting child sexual abuse became compulsory for our church authorities in 2010, where the evidence is not obtained in a confession. Of course, where there is an admission or conviction for paedophilia, offending priests should be laicised to ensure that our church is not further scandalised, together with such other action as is considered appropriate to ensure that he does not offend further. Also, our church should ensure that the priest is offered whatever medication or aversion therapy may be available to cure or control the priest's paedophilia.

5.6.12 Confession

In relation to confession, the commission made two recommendations that are relevant for our consideration. The first of these, for our consideration, is that the civil law should be amended so that persons in religious ministry are required to report knowledge of child sexual abuse to child protection authorities and that information obtained from confession by a religious person, i.e. a priest or religious brother, is not exempted.

This recommendation appears to be based on a misconception of how the sacrament of penance works. The commission thought that a priest would try to resolve his guilt by confession. As Catholics, we know that absolution for our sins is conditional on being genuinely sorry that we offended God by our action or inaction, that we make a genuine resolution not to sin again, that we make reparation or restitution as far as possible where that is relevant, and that we perform the penance imposed by our confessor. What is said in confession has always been strictly confidential, and in most jurisdictions, the law has regarded anything said in confession as privileged from disclosure, in the same way that admissions to a legal representative are regarded as legal professional privilege.

Historically, our priests have always upheld the confidentiality of confession. Indeed, the procedure usually involves the identity of the penitent being concealed from the confessor by a screen or curtain. The confessor needs to be told the nature and frequency of the confessed sin, but not particulars, such as the name of the victim or where and when the sin was committed. The confessor only needs sufficient information to enable him to give appropriate advice about restitution and the avoidance of the occasion of sin if it appears to be a habitual offence, and to assess an appropriate penance.

Confession by a priest or religious brother is generally slightly different in that the penitent will be known to the confessor, and accordingly, the confessor will then know the identity of a priest who has confessed to committing child sexual abuse, but not the further particulars, such as the identity of the victim and where and when and exactly what happened. But what is known is probably sufficient to require reporting if the proposed law were enacted. If such a law were passed, a paedophile priest would most probably go to confession anonymously or not confess the sin at all, as he can still ask God for forgiveness directly. It is also unlikely that the confessor would report the matter in breach of his obligation to keep the contents of confession confidential. Furthermore, a prosecution of a confessor for failing to report such a confession would be rare, because no authorities would ever know what the penitent told his confessor unless the penitent himself revealed this, which seems unlikely. Accordingly, such a law would be a bad law because it would be unenforceable and would have no declaratory value to the Catholic Church. It would also be dangerous in the sense that it is the thin end of the wedge. What this means is that if the confidentiality of confession is diminished with this one exception it will eventually be diminished to require reporting of any criminal offence confessed by any penitent, which would lead to complete disuse of this sacrament by the Catholic laity.

The second recommendation of the commission was that the Australian Catholic Bishops Conference seek clarification from the Holy See as to whether a confessor should withhold absolution to a penitent confessing child sexual abuse until that penitent reported himself or herself to civil authorities. Again, this recommendation reveals misconception about how confession works, but the essence of the idea could be implemented by making the self-reporting a penance, the performance of which is required for absolution to become effective.

This idea has some merit, although the confessor has no power to enforce self-reporting by the penitent. The penitent may be so afraid of the consequences that he declines to do the penance, leaving some accountability in the confessor for imposing too harsh a penance. A negative consequence of this recommendation is that it is not framed as limited to confessions by priests and religious brothers, so it would apply to the whole Catholic community and, as a precedent, could eventually be extended to self-reporting of any criminal offence. Many sins are criminal offences. Self-reporting of criminal offences has long been considered by our church to be an inappropriate penance, because the function of confession is to reconcile with God for the offence to him, rather than as accountability to our community. Certainly, the power and authority to forgive or retain sins was given to our church and not to secular authorities. Our priests routinely forgive virtually all our sins and generously impose unburdensome penances to encourage us to use the sacrament to enable us to be at peace with God. Imposing unacceptable penances would undoubtedly lead to disuse of this sacrament to a significant extent. The power to retain sins is essential to enable our church to impose conditions on the grant of absolution.

5.6.13 Conclusion

One of the primary functions of our church is evangelisation of all generations in all places. This requires the evangelisation of youth. The Catholic education system and involvement of youth in parish activities are appropriate and legitimate means of implementing evangelisation. The scandal of paedophilia by priests and our religious brothers and sisters have substantially diminished the Catholic laity's trust in the integrity of our priests and bishops, and our clergy needs to regain that trust. We, the laity, should not be too critical of our clergy, because paedophilia by clergy has been happening throughout history and has not been previously dealt with by our church as a major problem. Our church's handling of the 1970s epidemic of paedophilia was poor and surprisingly out of step with true Christian principles. It was a learning experience, and our church has taken some appropriate steps to reform the future handling of this disgusting problem.

But more needs to be done. Our church must recognise that Jesus unequivocally condemned paedophilia as a serious offence to God. It must become proactive in eliminating paedophilia amongst priests and other religious orders; it must create and maintain an impartial, effective, and user-friendly complaints-handling system in relation to any type of complaint that it receives; and it must own some responsibility to help those priests or religious brothers or sisters who are afflicted with paedophilia with whatever support will help them overcome their inordinate attachment, while not allowing sympathy or loyalty to diminish our perception of the sinfulness of the paedophile's conduct.

5.7 The Tyranny of Numbers

5.7.1 World Population Growth

Currently, the population of the world is 7.6 billion people. Less than fifty years ago, in 1970, the population was 3.7 billion people. Some experts have estimated that our planet's food supply can only support up to 10 billion people and that by 2050, the population will be 9.8 billion people. In 1962, the population growth rate was 2.2% per annum, and now it is 1.1% per annum. So the growth rate is falling, but the actual numbers are dangerously high, having regard to our world's resources.

While the statistics are of concern in relation to several secular issues, the relevance to this work is how the population growth impacts our church's ability to implement its mission of evangelisation and pastoral care.

Even in the days of Jesus, 'the harvest was large and the laborers were few'. In 1970, we had enough priests to do missionary work in Third World countries and a parish priest for most urban parishes containing a few thousand Catholics in Western countries. Some rural parishes were territorially vast, but our priests managed; some parishes even had two or three priests.

Between 1970 and 2018, the world population doubled. The reason for this explosion in population numbers is essentially due to game-changing advances in medical technology. These advances happened as a result of advances in computer and electronic technology being applied to medical diagnosis, treatment, and research. Population is the measure of the number of people alive at any one time. Everyone born must eventually die, but if the birth rate is progressively increasing and the children's death rate is substantially diminished and the average life expectancy of adults has increased, the number of people alive at any one time will be increased. This is what medical advances have done for us, and although the dramatic increase due to the initial innovation of computer technology has tapered off, it is not over yet.

The issue for our church is this: the workload of priests has doubled in less than fifty years. The number of priests has not increased at the same rate over this period. What must the church do to continue to implement its mission of evangelisation and pastoral care effectively? There must be a way, because Jesus is divine and therefore would have known that this crisis was coming.

5.7.2 The Decline of Catholicism

There are currently over 1 billion Catholics in the world, which is probably more than there were at the peak of the Holy Roman Empire. As we have seen, when Constantine made Catholicism the official religion of the empire, it became necessary for people with ambition or desire for wealth and power to be Catholics. There can be little doubt that many people became Catholics to further such objectives and not because they were true believers. Since the clergy was essentially the most respected of professions, there were numerous cases of non-true believers becoming priests. History has shown this to be true from the plentiful accounts of priests who led unholy lives. In modern times, being a Catholic is more an obstacle to secular advancement than a necessity, so our church has declined in that people no longer become Catholics for such secular reasons. This is probably a good consequence.

The Reformation was another historical series of events that led to a decline of Catholicism. The number of Catholics was reduced by the number that chose to follow the various Reformist denominations. These were substantial numbers. For example, Henry VIII took most of England away from Catholicism. The number of Catholics was reduced by the number that chose to follow the Reformist denominations, both then and subsequently, as those denominations expanded in succeeding generations.

This was a substantial reduction in the number of Catholics, but it was inevitable, having regard to our church's need to reform, which it did in the Counter-Reformation.

With the invention of the printing press and the growth of literacy, the customary religious adherence became subject to intelligent discernment. This coupled with the Renaissance and the development of non-theological philosophies and the scientific method led to the legitimisation and growth of atheism. But for these developments, the large number of people who were affected by these developments would probably have been Catholics.

In addition to the losses identified above, our church had competition in evangelisation from other religions and was unable to access some sections of the world's population because they were already claimed by other religions as adherents. Catholicism is one of the big five religions. Another is Judaism, which had its diaspora to most nations, which has grown in number, and which has preserved its fundamental theology and identity, even amongst diverse racial groups. India is predominantly Hindu, which is a polytheistic religion. It is one of the big five because India has over a billion people. Buddhism is another large religion, although it is technically non-theistic. But it does teach morality, wisdom, and prayer. Asia and China are largely Buddhist, and again, the population of this region makes it one of the big five. The last of the big five is Islam. Currently, there are over 1 billion Muslims in the world. This religion originated in Mecca in about AD 600 and expanded throughout the Middle East. Our church tried to halt the expansion with the Crusades but failed. Now they have a substantial population in Europe and many other countries, and some countries like Indonesia are predominantly Muslim.

In addition to the big five, there are literally several hundred minor sects, religions, and cults, all of which have recruitment strategies which attract persons and thereby make them unreceptive to Catholic evangelisation messages.

Perhaps the most telling indicators of decline are the statistics from within our church. The statistics set out below are from the Australian government census in 1991 and 2016 and some internal church surveys. We expect that these statistics are typical of what is happening in many other countries, although the actual numbers will be slightly different.

In 1991, Catholics were 27.3% of the population, and in 2016, they were 22.6%. The actual number of Catholics actually increased by half a million, so the decline in percentage is explained by a national population growth with a higher proportion of non-Catholics than the 1991 local percentage. Naturally, this variation comes from immigration.

Currently, there are about 5.3 million Catholics in Australia. In 1996, the average Sunday mass attendance was 864,000, and the median age of attendees was fifty-two. In 2016, the average attendance was 623,400, and the median age was sixty-two. This means that of the 5.3 million Catholics, currently over 4.5 million are not practising. Also, we have an ageing population, and young people are not attracted to attending mass in a sustainable proportion.

The clergy numbers have also declined. In 1994, the number of diocesan priests was 2,189. In 2017, this number had fallen to 1,904, of which 491 were retired, leaving only about 1,400 for active ministry. In 1994, there were 8,314 religious sisters. In 2017, the number had fallen to 4,166. In 1994, the number of religious brothers was 1,338. In 2017, the number had fallen to 689. This huge decline in the number of religious brothers and sisters has led to a vast increase in the number of laypersons employed in the Catholic schools, health institutions, and aged care institutions that were formally staffed by religious brothers and sisters. The downside of this is that the religious education of the young and the quality of health and aged care is clearly more believable and more sincere when presented by a priest or a religious brother or sister than by a layperson. Accordingly, the effectiveness of the evangelisation of the young and the pastoral care of the ill and aged has declined.

In relation to the declining proportion of young people practising our faith, we can make the observation that our church liturgy is relatively uninspiring and boring, even after the changes to liturgy following Vatican II. Of course, our liturgy, especially the canon of the Mass, is good, holy, and meaningful, but young people seem to want something more exciting. Consequently, some charismatic sects have obtained a youthful following, as have some of the song-and-dance alternative religions. Young people eventually become middle-aged and then elderly. With maturity, they may come to see that most of these alternatives are all about separating them from their money rather than providing guidance to a happy hereafter. We can hope that with this realisation, some may return to our faith, but having already abandoned Catholicism, they may consider that it has nothing better to offer. So there can be no guarantee or expectation that they will re-embrace Catholicism.

We have already considered the loss of faith in a substantial number of Catholics caused by the paedophile scandal, but it warrants mention here as another factor involved in the decline of our faith.

5.7.3 Church Renewal and Vitality Initiatives

Our church leaders are well aware of all the above-mentioned trends and factors indicating a decline in Catholicism, even though the actual number of Catholics has increased. In response, they have implemented a number of initiatives intended to renew the appeal and vitality of our faith and to at least maintain, if not increase, the percentage of our church's market share of people who believe in God. A brief consideration of some of these initiatives may assist in giving our leaders some feedback on these initiatives, if the opportunity for that arises.

In relation to the paedophile scandal, we have already noted some of our church's initiatives. There are also the recent recommendations of the Australian Royal Commission, some of which are directed to the Holy See and will no doubt be properly considered, and appropriate action will be taken in due course. Our church leaders have made a formal apology to the victims of child sexual abuse, and the process of compensation is progressing. What is necessary now is to regain the trust lost by the sin of a few, and to this end, we need thorough publication of what action our church is taking to ensure that child sexual abuse is eliminated from all Catholic institutions as far as humanly possible. Beyond this, we need not further reconsider our church's initiatives in relation to this issue.

Another significant initiative of our church has been to modernise our liturgy, especially the Mass. The main changes have been for the priest to say Mass in the local language and to face the congregation. The singing of hymns has long been a part of the Mass and feast celebrations such as Christmas. However, the emotive and inspirational value of much singing in most Catholic churches leaves much to be desired in terms of quality and congregation participation. The chanting of the sacred words of the offertory distracts from the meaning of the words. Some of these initiatives were introduced to compete with the charismatics, but the necessity for this is not certain. We sing for joy and should remain mindful that the Mass commemorates, in essence, the death of Jesus. Whilst this has beneficial consequences for us, it is still a death, the need for which we should lament rather than cheer.

Our church teaches that it is a mortal sin to miss Mass on Sundays. We have already considered that the church does not have authority to create new sins. Put that way, this teaching is misleading. The real situation is that the third commandment of God requires us to *'keep holy of the sabbath day'*. The Jews have observed this commandment by abstaining from all work, resting, and praying at a synagogue on the day of the week they regard as their sabbath. Our church has had the Mass since its institution by Jesus, and in furtherance of its mission to help us save our souls and under the authority given to it by Jesus, it has declared that attendance at Sunday Mass is full discharge of our duty to *'keep holy of the sabbath day'*. This is far less burdensome than the Jewish perception of how to keep this commandment, but it is not the only way; the Jewish way must also be considered valid.

Apparently, many of the vast number of Catholics who do not attend Mass on Sundays do not regard their failure to attend Mass as sinful. The problem is that because every Sunday is a holiday, these Catholics who do not attend Mass regard the absence of the requirement to work on Sundays as sufficient discharge of their obligation under the third commandment. It is a matter for our church leaders to determine if that is correct, but if it is not, then there is scope here to ensure that the correct view is taught in schools and evangelisation activities and that there is an opportunity to run a campaign aimed at non-Mass-attending Catholics informing them of their duty under the third commandment and giving them the option of discharging this duty in the traditional Jewish way or the easy way of attending Sunday Mass.

Another initiative that our church has taken is more thorough screening of candidates for the priesthood. It is, of course, necessary that all Catholic priests teach the same dogma and doctrine. It happens that as novice priests study Catholic theology, they sometimes find themselves in disagreement with the church's doctrine flowing from that theology or even with the theology itself. So unless that novice is prepared to subjugate his views to the doctrine of the church, he should not be allowed to become a Catholic priest. If he were allowed to become a priest, then if he preached in accordance with his conscience, he would be preaching heresy or at least be inconsistent with the necessary catholicity of Catholic doctrine. Many young men have left the novitiate for this reason, but that does not mean that those who stayed cannot think for themselves. What this means is that they have the humility to teach the official version of Catholicism and not their personal theology. We also now know that there is scope for screening in relation to the paedophile issue.

Some years ago, it was thought that there might be a reunification with the Reformation denominations through the ecumenism initiative. Sadly, but not unexpectedly, this has not happened. It did succeed to an extent amongst the Reformation denominations, in that they formed the Uniting Church. However, Catholic dogma is too inflexible to allow Catholics to attend services where nonconforming and even heretical theology is taught or believed. Human nature is such that it is unreasonable to expect that the leaders of the Reformation denominations would surrender their theological differences from Catholicism and make themselves subservient to the authority of the Catholic leaders. Today ecumenism is little more than a mutually respectful dialogue between the Catholic Church leaders and the Reformation denominations leaders, which is as it should be. Of course, our church leaders also have mutually respectful dialogue with the leaders of the other major religions.

The evangelisation of youth is of primary importance to our modern church. Bringing young people back to Mass and participation in parish activities is the objective. Our church leaders are clearly focused on this, as is evident from their support of World Youth Day. Our church also has substantial institutional support for delinquents. But we do not see much of youth support activity at the parish level. Perhaps this is because of the paedophile scandal, which predicates that priests should not become too familiar with the youth of their parish. If this is the case, then clearly there is an opportunity here for us, the laity, to conduct some initiatives involving young people which appeal to their spirit of fun and adventure. We, the laity, remember what we wanted as youths, and it should not be beyond us to design appropriate activities using the church's facilities and connection, bearing in mind that the world has changed a bit with the arrival of modern technology.

Perhaps the most important initiative that has been implemented by our church is the embrace of modern communication technology, specifically the Internet. There is now a vast amount of information about the dogma, doctrine, devotion, and liturgy of the Catholic Church available on the Internet, and much of it can be found in the first pages of search engines like Google. Wikipedia also has much accurate information about Catholicism, its history, and its teachings, but it is not an official Catholic resource, though it remains valuable as a starting point and overview for further research, especially since it mostly provides references to its sources.

The wealth of information available on the Internet renders most parish programmes for the education of persons interested in becoming Catholics as redundant. However, a one-on-one session with a priest is generally much more efficient and informative, especially in relation to questions that have complex answers.

What is missing from the Internet is proactive use of this resource as a tool of evangelisation. For example, YouTube has many videos dealing with biblical prophecy, but few, if any, give the Catholic views on such issues. There is scope here for interesting action— for example, public domain movies of inspirational, exciting, or remarkable lives of saints could be uploaded to YouTube. In short, what our church has already done is brilliant, but there is room for more.

Missionary work is at the cutting edge of evangelisation. Originally, Catholic missionaries simply went to places where the people had no knowledge of Christianity and told them the essentials of our faith. People converted to Catholicism, and the missionaries then built churches, schools, and health facilities with the support of the converted community. In modern times, there are still many people who have no knowledge of Jesus, especially many children and the poor in Third World countries. The modern strategy of our church seems to be to send persons and resources to help the people intended to be evangelised with their quality of life in relation to food, water, health, education, et cetera. Much of the money funding such enterprises comes from direct donations by the laity. Having helped these people to a better life, they then teach them about our faith.

A cynic might see this process as bribing them to listen. But in reality, it is something quite different. The poor people of the world are increasing in number through normal population growth. Poor people tend to have more children than affluent people, so the percentage of poor people in the world is increasing, even though they have a higher infant and child mortality rate. The lives of the poor are hopelessly wretched, so telling them about Jesus is virtually meaningless. They first need to see that there can be more to life than their miserable existence, and then they need to acquire some hope to obtain such a better life. The missionaries who go there do so out of a genuine desire to help these poor people, because by going there, they put themselves at risk of crime, disease, and other misfortune, and they give up the luxuries of an affluent Western lifestyle. Giving the poor hope is truly loving your neighbour as yourself and is a highly commendable initiative of our church and its mission of evangelisation.

5.8 Our Church in the Future

5.8.1 The Promise of Jesus

The last sentence in the Gospel of Matthew 28:20 is Jesus saying to the apostles, *'And look, I am with you always; yes, to the end of time.'* We believe that if Jesus said that something will happen, then it is certain that it will happen. The unarguable inference from what Jesus said is that our church will last until the end of time—i.e. the end of the world. The certainty of this does not mean that we need do nothing to prevent the decline of our church. Those who perceive that the church and faith are in decline should do whatever they can to prevent or reverse further decline. If they do nothing, no doubt someone else will do what should be done, and the person who should have done it may be held accountable for his or her inaction.

5.8.2 The Evolution of Catholicism

In the earlier sections of this work, we considered some stages in the growth and development of our faith in some detail. We need not reconsider those issues here. Suffice it to limit our consideration to a gloss on church history, which starts with Jesus and the twelve apostles and continues for two thousand years to today where we have over 1 billion adherents and a massive church hierarchy. The point of this summary is that at no stage of our history has it been seriously alleged that the church has reached the apex of its evolution and achieved perfection in its tenets and procedures. That is as true today as it was in the past. What this means is that our dogma, doctrine, devotion, and liturgy will continue to evolve as technology and behaviour patterns change. The theory of evolution of animal species is often summarised as the theory of survival of the <u>fittest</u>. In fact, the real essence of this theory is survival of the <u>most adaptable</u>. Accordingly, it is our church's ability to adapt to the requirements of a changing environment and culture that will be its key to long-term survival and viability.

5.8.3 The Role of Theology

We, the Catholic laity, do not need a lot of theology. But we do need some. So what theology do we need? In other words, what theology is the necessary basis of our faith? To answer this question, we must first understand the role or function of theology.

The function of theology is to provide a rational explanation of supernatural beings and phenomena to the extent that such explanations are within human comprehension. The effect of a theological explanation is to provide a rational basis for belief in the reality of the existence of supernatural beings or phenomena which is sufficient to satisfy us that the supernatural being or phenomena is truly real and that our decisions and actions based on that satisfaction are justified.

The main problem with theology is that because it deals with subjects from the spiritual realm, there can be no evidence to support the theological proposition, which means that there cannot be any compelling proof of the theological proposition. Furthermore, whatever concepts our theologians have about the spiritual realm are subjective patterns of thought, and it is unlikely that there are words in any language that clearly and precisely illuminate such concepts. But words are all we have. There are no pictures of the spiritual realm. So theology is completely based on what is called analytic reasoning—i.e. based purely on logic or reason without evidence.

The justification for the above assertion that we, the laity, do not need a lot of theology is based on the teachings of Jesus. Jesus did not teach or preach theology. What he taught was identifying the human behaviour that is forbidden by God and the behaviour that is acceptable and pleasing to God and therefore conducive to eternal life. Jesus did not utter any theological argument to support the existence of God. He simply asserted the existence of God, his 'Father who is in heaven'. Nor did he need to do more, because he was mostly speaking to Jews, who already believed in the existence of God. Also, he simply asserted his own divinity and proved it by his miracles and teachings.

The danger of theology lies in the fact that all of it comes from the minds of men. We know from Jesus that men do not think as God does. Many theologians are very intelligent persons with superb capacity for analytic reasoning. It has happened in the past that some theologians have conceived some theological insights and were so convinced that they were right that they taught them as right beliefs. But sometimes they were so wrong that they were considered and declared to be heretical by our church leaders at the time. Several of our dogmas were specifically raised to counteract such heresies.

So what theology do we actually need to justify our choices to live the life that God wants us to live? What follows is a list of some basics, although some of us laity may need some more.

- Firstly, we need to know the arguments for and against the existence of God. From these, we can be satisfied that God exists. The proof of God's existence is not compelling, so neither are the atheists' proofs that God does not exist. The evidence that God does exist is more persuasive than the mere absence of God from physical manifestation on this planet and the flawed and incomplete arguments for spontaneous creation and evolution. This is the theme of Part 2 of this work.
- Secondly, we need to be satisfied that Jesus is divine—i.e. that he is both God and man. This is a difficult concept to understand. The evidence that Jesus actually lived as a man is overwhelming, although some have argued that the Gospels are a composite of a number of itinerant Jewish

566 • Peter Mazurek

rabbis of that time. That he was also divine is evidenced by his miracles and his teachings, and ultimately by his own words, admitting and claiming this aspect of his nature. This theology is the theme of Part 3 of this work.

- Thirdly, we need to believe that our Catholic Church is the one true church founded by Jesus and given the mission of evangelisation and pastoral care by Jesus. The evidence of the Gospels is sufficient to establish this historically. The branches of our church that became the Reformation denominations still have some merit, even though they have abandoned some of our fundamental theologies, such as transubstantiation. But prudence suggests that following the authorised line of succession of our clergy is a more reliable and authentic option. Nor do we need to study and reject the authenticity of other faiths if we are satisfied that our church is the one true church. This issue is dealt with in Part 4 of this work.

- Fourthly, we need to know the theology that underlies our creed, in particular the *'communion of saints, the forgiveness of sins, the resurrection of the body and life everlasting'*. These, and other related aspects of our faith, are not dealt with in this work, but they are dealt with in a clear and informative way in Part 1 of the *Catechism of the Catholic Church*.

Most of us laity will not need any more than these basics, but it can happen that a crisis of faith can involve a more esoteric theology. In such case, the best option to resolve the issue is to make an appointment to discuss the matter with a priest at length, because our priests are trained and authorised in the theology of our faith.

5.8.4 The Future of Evangelisation

'You have the poor with you always, but you will not always have me' (Matthew 26:11). With the percentage of poor people in the world increasing as the population increases, the need for missionaries

to the poor will continue to increase. This is a job for the Catholic clergy. Laypersons may be able to assist with the necessities of quality of life, but it is the clergy that should do the evangelisation. Nuns, such as Mother Teresa, have done remarkable missionary work in the past, but with the declining number of religious sisters, our church leaders must find a way to not only fill the gap but also to satisfy the increasing need.

Religious schools that have a daily religious class and catechists providing religious education to voluntary attendees in non-religious schools are legitimate ways of evangelising young people. But as has already been noted, the best persons to teach religion to the young are priests and religious brothers or sisters, because their lives evidence that they truly believe what they are teaching. Again, the declining number of priests and religious brothers and sisters raises the question for our church leaders of how to fill this gap and provide the best evangelisation for increasing numbers of young people. Letting the laity do this work can only be a transient solution.

5.8.5 The Future of Pastoral Care

The reduction in the number of priests has affected both evangelisation and pastoral care. In relation to pastoral care, we have seen a number of parishes become priestless. Mass on Sundays is said by visiting priests, and the parish council of the laity attends to the administrative needs of the parish. But there is no one there to provide the other sacraments, such as baptism, confirmation, penance, extreme unction, weddings, and funerals. Some such parishes have merged with neighbouring parishes, thereby doubling the workload of the neighbouring parish priest. Unless the number of priests can increase to previous levels and beyond that to provide for future needs, the situation is only going to become worse.

One solution that has been proposed to counteract the priest shortage is for our church to allow women to become priests— or more technically, priestesses. Throughout history, our church has consistently refused to allow women to become priests. The reason for this may be the opposition expressed by St Paul to women becoming teachers of religion. Other than this, our church's reasons for its stance are unclear and unconvincing. What is clear is that women are just as willing to devote their lives to the service of God as men, which is evidenced in history from the large number of women who have become celibate nuns. Nor can it be argued that women are inferior to men in terms of holiness or as teachers. In fact, in modern times, most schoolteachers are women, and there are many female saints.

It is not the purpose of this work to advocate allowing women to become priests. Our purpose is to let our church leaders know that a substantial number of the laity have no objection to allowing women to become priests. We note that forbidding women from becoming priests is _not_ a dogma of our faith. Accordingly, our church leaders can legitimately change church policy. Whether our church leaders do change this policy is a matter for them, but the need for this change is urgent and clearly necessary in the circumstances of diminishing priest numbers and the absence of any alternative strategy to restore and sustain necessary priest numbers.

The falling number of priests will eventually result in there being an insufficient number of priests to say Sunday Mass for the number of practising Catholics, which in turn will lead to many of them becoming non-practising. The obvious solution to this diminution of pastoral care is for our church leaders to adapt to this change by declaring that watching the Mass on television on Sundays is sufficient discharge of the duty under the third commandment of God. Of course, we cannot receive the Eucharist over television or put money on the collection plate! No doubt we should be urged to attend Mass in person whenever possible and perhaps be required to do so at least once a year. As a Sunday observance, such a ruling may well appeal to the non-practising Catholics and stimulate a revival of their faith. Also, masses broadcasted on TV can have their liturgy and homily more in accord with church doctrine and the music and singing of more emotive and inspirational quality.

5.8.6 The End of the World

Over the years, we have seen many prophets of doom. Many of these have been founders of some religious cult or sect. These founders usually claim to have some vision or supernatural insight which made it clear to them that the world was about to be destroyed. The message to potential followers was that they must participate in the cult's protocols if they wish to be personally saved or wish to help avert this disaster. The activity required is mostly prayer, following various rules and rituals, and providing financial support to the cult.

In our modern time, with the technology of the Internet, what we see is a vast amount of video prophecy about the end of the world or the identity of the Antichrist on YouTube. Many of these videos purport to prove their authenticity by reference to the correlation of their prophecies to those in the Bible. The profit for the producers of such videos lies in the reaction of the viewers to these videos. If a sufficient number of viewers electronically indicate that they like the video, the video producers receive money from advertising sponsors.

Generally, YouTube is a worthwhile resource. It contains many how-to videos which teach woodwork, metalwork, and many other skills and crafts. There are also videos about the prophecies and miracles of Fátima, some pornography, humorous cartoons, strange behaviour and events, history, inventions, and many other subjects that people find interesting.

Many of the prophecies of doom are poorly presented. Their arguments are mostly fragmented and unconvincing. Some are so far-fetched as to be humorous and amusing, such as accounts of the future by aliens and interdimensional time travellers. Most people regard such videos as entertainment rather than serious believable prophecies of coming events, but no doubt some people are taken in by such apparently serious presentations and click the Like icon on the computers, stimulating sequels and similar videos.

Jesus himself also made a prophecy of doom, which is recorded in Matthew 24:1–52. But Jesus did not ask for anything, nor did he require us to do anything to prepare for or avert this doom. Indeed, he predicted that a time would come when there would be many false prophets predicting his second coming. He warned against believing them. As for when this would come about, he said, *'But as for that day and hour, nobody knows it, neither the angels of heaven, nor the Son, no one but the Father alone.'* It is natural for us to want to know when some disaster is coming so that we can prepare for it or somehow avert it. But if God the Father has not revealed the time when the end will come even to Jesus, then clearly, he does not want us to know. Accordingly, we should regard any prophecy of doom as a reminder to all generations to always be ready to stand and be judged, having made our best efforts to ensure that the judgement of us personally is as we want it to be.

SOURCES

Hereunder is a list of books and Internet articles, with references, that were read or consulted and considered, and which underlie the information provided in this work. The list is arranged in sequence to accord with the sequence in which the topics are dealt with in this work. The book title, the author, the publisher, and the date of publication are identified, together with a comment containing a statement of the orientation of the work and a brief assessment of its value or function. The Internet references are provided; however, unfortunately, websites are removed from the Internet from time to time, so there is no guarantee that the references quoted will be available in the future.

Part 1.1
The source of this section of the work is essentially my knowledge and experience gained from a working life as a lawyer. The basis is that all legal jurisdictions seek to deliver justice. But you cannot deliver justice if you do not know the truth of the facts. Therefore, the best legal minds from many jurisdictions throughout the centuries have developed techniques of searching for the truth. These techniques have been encapsulated in this work because they are the best tools that we have available to discover the truth of matters, both factual and analytic, using logic, reason, and human experience. But the truth is not always easily known, and we can only be persuaded of what is the truth to varying degrees.

Accordingly, I considered it necessary to give some detailed consideration to the distinction between proof and evidence.

Part 1.2

This section of the work contains a number of personal insights and some original material. The section on the mechanism of Creation comes from the following work:

What on Earth Happened?   by Christopher Lloyd
Bloomsbury   2008
This is essentially a history of the world from the Big Bang to modern times. It is a reference work that is well-written, very readable, and well illustrated. It contains a number of useful charts, and the material it provides is mostly non-controversial, although it cannot be said that no other reputable historians disagree with anything in this book.

Parts 2.1 and 2.2

These sections contain the arguments for the existence of God. The books that support these arguments are as follows:

Why Us?   by James Le Fanu
Pantheon Books   2009
This book essentially argues that the complexity of the human body is not satisfactorily explained by the theory of evolution. It is cogently and intelligently written and is well worth reading by anyone who wishes to know the shortcomings of the theory of evolution.

Summa Theologiae   by Thomas Aquinas
Cambridge   edited by Brian Davies
University Press   2006   and Brian Leftow
This is the original work by St Thomas Aquinas, written around the thirteenth century, edited and brought up to date to make it readable in modern times. It is essentially a reference work, and the Five Ways of Aquinas are more succinctly considered in other works mentioned herein.

A Modern Introduction to Philosophy   edited by Edwards and Papp
Free Press   1968
This is essentially a reference work which contains philosophical articles by a number of the greatest philosophers through history. Many of the articles deal with the existence of God and also the arguments against the existence of God. Generally, the articles are well-written, but they do use some of the jargon and technical language of philosophy.

God Actually   by Roy Williams
ABC Books   2008
This book is an in-depth study of some of the arguments that have been raised against the existence of God by another former lawyer. It argues cogently for the use of reason and logic based on known facts and experience. It is very readable and thoroughly recommended as further reading on these issues. Its orientation is in support of the existence of God.

Part 2.3
The following works contain the arguments against the existence of God.

The God Delusion   by Richard Dawkins
Bantam Books   2006
Richard Dawkins is a very highly regarded biologist and outspoken proponent of atheism. This book by him is important, and his principal arguments are considered in depth in this work. His arguments are flawed, but the book is well-written and worth reading for a fuller understanding of the atheist view.

The Improbability of God edited by Michael Martin and Ricki Monnier
Prometheus Books   2006
This book is an anthology of thirty-two articles by highly regarded philosophers, scientists, and theologians. It deals with the cosmological arguments, the teleological arguments,

and the argument from the existence of evil as support of the argument against the existence of God. The articles are generally well-written but again contain jargon and theological technical language.

Parts 3.1 and 3.2

These parts of this work deal essentially with the extent to which the Bible, both the Old and New Testaments, may be regarded as historically accurate statements of fact. The books relevant to this issue are as follows:

The Oxford Companion edited by Bruce M. Metzger and Michael *to the Bible*   D. Oxford University Press
                          1993   Coogan

This is a reference work which is highly regarded and reliable, and it contains a vast amount of relevant information.

The Catholic Study Bible
Oxford University Press   2006
This also is a reference work which is highly regarded and reliable, and it contains a vast amount of relevant information.

The Bible as History   by Wernher Keller
Bantam Books   1982
This is an older book which deals comprehensively with the issue of whether or not the Bible can be considered a historical chronicle of events. It is well-written and worth reading from cover to cover.

Jesus and the Eyewitnesses   by Richard Bauckham
Eerdmans Publishing Co.   2006

This is a very well-written and well-researched book dealing with the authorship of the Gospels. It is a book that is intended to be read from cover to cover, and it underlies much of what is written in this work.

Who Wrote the New Testament   by Burton L. Mack
Harper Collins   1996
This is another book dealing with the authorship of the New Testament, and again it is intended to be read from cover to cover. It is worth reading as further reading on this topic.

Part 3.3
This section of this work considers the evidence of the divinity of Jesus. The books on which this information is based are as follows:

The New Jerusalem Bible
Doubleday   1990
This is the version of the Bible from which all the quotes in this work are taken. It is the currently approved version of the Bible for use by Catholics. To find some of the quotes used in this work, the concordance in the *Catholic Study Bible*, referred to above, was used. Also consulted was the *New American Bible*.

Evidence for Christianity   by Josh McDowell
Nelson   2006
This is essentially a reference work, but it contains a vast amount of information and a comprehensive consideration of the arguments in support of Christianity and the divinity of Jesus Christ. It is a valuable source for the information provided in this work.

The Complete Dead Sea Scrolls in English   by Geza Vermes
Penguin Books (Fiftieth Anniversary Edition) 2011
This is essentially a reference work and is intended for scholars and students of the Dead Sea Scrolls. It is included here as a source in order to compare and verify the conclusions drawn by Barbara Thiering in her work.

Jesus the Man   by Barbara Thiering
Corgi Books   1993
This is the book in which Barbara Thiering presents her theories and arguments against the divinity of Jesus. It is well-written and

is worth reading, but her explanation of the pesher technique is uninformative and unconvincing.

Part 4

This part of this work deals with the authenticity of the Catholic Church, its mission, its authority, its teachings, and some other minor issues. The books on which the material herein is based are as follows:

The Code of the Canon Law   by the Canon Law Society of Great
Britain and Ireland
HarperCollins   2005
This is a reference work intended to be in the nature of a handbook for priests. It is written in plain language and can be understood by laypersons. The function of canon law is considered in this work, and clearly any restrictions placed on priests by the canon law has a flow-on effect on the laity of the Catholic Church.

In the Name of God   by Michael Jordan
Sutton Publishing   2006
This book is a general reading work which deals with many of the crimes and atrocities that have been committed by religious persons in the belief that what they were doing was what God wanted them to do. It is an important book and worth reading because it is factually reasonably reliable, and it forces us to recognise that there have been many crimes committed by Catholics in the name of Jesus, although the work is not limited to the Catholic religion but deals with crimes committed by members of other faiths as well.

Fundamentals of Catholic Dogma   by Ludwig Ott
Tan   1974
This is the standard Catholic text on the dogmas of the Catholic Church. The book sets out the dogmas, each separately, and considers their sources and the arguments on which the decision to make the matter dogma is based. It is clearly a reference work,

and it deals with all dogmas, including some which are no longer relevant because they were created to counter heresies that are no longer current.

Enchiridion   by Heinrich Denzinger
Ignatius Press   2012
This is the standard Catholic reference work which contains most of the teachings of the Catholic Church, all the papal encyclicals, pronouncements by the magisterium, and other official bodies within our church hierarchy. It is clearly a reference work and not something that is intended to be read from cover to cover.

Church History in Plain Language   by Bruce Shelley
Word Publishing   1995
This book is an outline of the history of the Catholic Church written by a non-Catholic. It is a book that is intended to be read from cover to cover, although it is fairly voluminous. It is well-written and very readable. It was selected as a sourcebook to forestall any criticism that the historical facts mentioned in this work are a biased Catholic view of history.

A Concise History of the Catholic Church   by Thomas Bokenkotter
Doubleday   2005
This book is also an outline of the history of the Catholic Church. This book was written by a Catholic and is also intended to be read from cover to cover, although it too is fairly voluminous. It also is well-written and very readable. It covers essentially the same subject matter as the book by Bruce Shelley, referred to above, and does not display any Catholic bias, although it does not deal with the bad things done by Catholics as fully as the book by Bruce Shelley.

Catechism of the Catholic Church
St Paul's (Second Edition)   2009
This book is a reference work intended for the clergy of the Catholic Church. It is written in clear and plain language, and accordingly, it

577

has been taken up by the laity of the Catholic Church as the official source of the essential teachings of the Catholic Church.

Compendium of the Catechism of the Catholic Church
St Paul's   2013
This book was intended for the laity of the Catholic Church as a supplement or paraphrase of the *Catechism of the Catholic Church*. It deals with essentially the same issues as the *Catechism*, but it does so in question-and-answer format, though nowhere near the detail and sophistication of the *Catechism* itself. It is not a substitute for the catechism and is probably not worthwhile.

The 16 documents of Vatican II   compiled by Rev. J. L. Gonzalez
St Paul Edition
This book is a reference work which compiles the documents of Vatican II. It is of historical interest only, since events have, to an extent, overtaken many of these documents.

Part 5.1
The sources of this part are mainly from the *Catechism* and the *Enchiridion*, already referred to above, plus some Internet sources and the following book:

Stem Cells   by Norman M. Ford and Michael Herbert
St Paul   2003
This is a book which deals with the physiological aspects of stem cells and stem cell research. It is intended to introduce laypersons to the science of the issue. It does consider the ethics of the matter but is not primarily oriented as a Catholic work.

Reflections on Cloning
http://www.vatican.va/roman_curia/pontifical_academies/acdlife/doc...

Safeguarding Peace
http://www.vatican.va/archive/ENG0015/_P81.HTM

'Use of Embryonic Stem Cells'
http://www.catholicaustralia.com.au/links/stem-cells

'Abortion', *Congregation for the Doctrine of Faith*
http://www.vatican.va/roman_curia/congregations/cfaith/
documents/r...

Part 5.2
The sources for this section are as follows:

'Anti-Catholicism on the Internet' by Robert Lockwood
https://www.catholicleague.org/anti-catholicism-on-the-internet

'Anti-Catholicism'
https://en.wikipedia.org/wiki/Anti-Catholicism

Part 5.3
The sources for this section are as follows:

All about Terrorism	by Keith Suter
Bantam Books	2008

This is a general work providing substantial insights into the motivations and methods of terrorism. It is well-written and in plain language. It can be read from cover to cover. It is recommended to obtain greater insights into the nature of this issue.

Part 5.4
The sources for this section are as follows:

Opus Dei	by John L. Allen
Penguin	2006

This book is an in-depth study of Opus Dei and is recommended for anyone considering joining Opus Dei. Its orientation is objective.

The True Believers   by Peter Bowler
Methuen   1986

This book is an entertaining work which describes some of the strange things that some people conceive as being genuinely devotional. It does provide some insight into the psychology of cults, but its principal value is for entertainment.

'Opus Dei'
https://en.wikipedia.org/wiki/Opus_Dei

'William Kam'
https://en.wikipedia.org/wiki/William_Kam

'Cults in the Catholic Church' by J. Dunlap
https://www.catholic.com/magazine/print-edition/are-there-cults-in-the-catholic-church

Part 5.5
The sources for this section are as follows:

The Five Great Religions   by Edward Rice
Bantam   1977
This is a very readable short book which provides information about the theology, liturgy, and cultural aspects of the five major religions. It is well-written, in plain language, and recommended for anyone seeking further insight into the theology of the other major religions.

Comparative Religion   by A. C. Bouquet
Penguin   1962
This is also a short and very readable book which provides information about the theology, liturgy, and cultural aspects of many religions, focusing particularly on India and the East. It is not limited to the five major religions, so it has a slightly broader focus than that work. It is also well-written and recommended for further reading if a deeper insight into the theology of other religions is desired.

Part 5.6
The sources for this section are as follows:

The Gift of Confession by Father Michael de Stoop
Connor Court Publishing 2007
This is a book by a Catholic priest outlining the function and value of confession. It is included for the benefit of any reader who may not have a clear understanding of the Catholic theology underlying the process of confession, especially since the Royal Commission seemed to be of the view that the church's rules on the confidentiality of confession are something that can be easily changed.

Cardinal by Louise Milligan
Melbourne University Press 2017
This is a book by an investigative journalist targeting Cardinal George Pell as one of the senior church officials involved in the cover-up of child sexual abuse committed by Catholic clergy. It also details some vague and unpersuasive allegations of child sexual abuse committed by Cardinal Pell personally. The book is clearly biased, because the author spoke only to the alleged victims of child sexual abuse in circumstances where it was inappropriate for her to conduct searching cross-examination of the persons she was speaking to, and she may not be qualified to do such cross-examinations in any event.

Royal Commission into Institutional Responses to Child Sexual Abuse
https://www.childabuseroyalcommission.gov.au/religious-institutions

Part 5.7
The sources for this section are as follows:

World Population (2018– Population)
https://www.worldometers.info/world-population/#pastfuture

INDEX

A

a posteriori 7, 9
a priori 6
abortion 482-3
acolytes 402
Act of Supremacy 381
Act of Terror 508
Acts of the Apostles 456
adapt to this change 568
Agca, Ali 510
agnostics 84
agony of the moment 479
AIDS virus 226
Alexander V 371
Alfvén, Hannes Olof Gösta 70
Ali (Muhammad's son-in-law) 513
almah 284
almsgiving 393
Alzheimer's virus 227
Anabaptists 375-8
ancillary beliefs 97-8
angels and demons 110-11
Anglicanism 380
Annas 331
Anointed Prince 285
Anselm (saint) 126, 137
anthropic coincidences 202

anthropic principle 201-5, 207-8, 210, 212-17
anti-Catholic propaganda 504
anti-Catholic rhetoric 500
anti-Catholicism 494, 579
anti-church sentiment 497
anti-discrimination laws 188, 494-5, 500
anti-Islamic propaganda 507
anti-Semitic propaganda 507
Antichrist 569
apostolic Christianity 375
Aquinas, Thomas (saint) 126, 255, 572
Archbishop of Canterbury 381, 385
arguments 3-7, 10
Aristotle 126, 128
Arius 369
Artaxerxes 286
Arthur (Henry's deceased brother) 380
articles of faith 451-2
'Ask a Priest' 432
assassination of terrorists 517
assisted suicide 480
at the point of the sword 392
Augustine (saint) 126, 369
Australian Catholic Bishops Conference 547, 551

authority 406-7
authority by God 389
authority to bind and loose 412
authority to forgive sins 419
avatar 114-15

B

Bakr, Abu 513
Benedict XIII 371
Bernadette (saint) 169
best available evidence 250-1
Bethlehem 285
between humans 412
Big Bang 70-2
bin Laden, Osama 511
bind and loose marriages 414
bishops involved 544
black holes 142
Blaurock, George 376
bodies 40-2
Boleyn, Anne 381-2
Boniface IX 371
Book of Life 87
Boris (the king of Bulgaria) 370
Boston Marathon 512
Branch Davidians 520
Broussard, Malcolm 527
burden of proof 17
Byzantium 369

C

Caiaphas 331
caliphs 514
Calvin, John 378
canon law 417-19, 576
Capernaum 299
carefully consider 3-5
Carter, Brandon 202
*Catechism of the Catholic Church,
   The* 432, 434, 459-60
Catherine de' Medici (queen) 281

Catherine of Aragon 380, 382
Catholic cults 519
Catholic dogma 158
Catholic lay organisations 402
catholic oppression 499
Catholic terrorist targets 515
Catholicism
   decline of 554
   evolution of 563
causal determinism 86
causal link 131-2
celibacy 546
Celsus 278
centurion 314
change in attitude 549
charismatic sects 557
charitable work 522
charlatans 519
Charlemagne 384
Charles V (emperor) 373, 380-1
child sexual abuse 538, 581
   church response to 543
   consequences of 540, 542
Chlorus, Constantius 368
Christ 289
Christianity 336
church 357-9, 361-4
'Church and Money, The' 423
'Church and State' 514
church council
         pronouncements 457
church made errors 475
'Church Renewal and Vitality
         Initiatives' 557
church responses 543
church–state relationship 530
circumstantial evidence 25-7
civil liberties 517
Clement VII 370-1, 381
clergy 357-60
clergy numbers 556

cloned sheep 483
cloning 483, 578
coexist peacefully 532
Coloni, Michel 288
comfortable satisfaction 12
commissioned the apostles 362
common knowledge 18
communication 3
compelling proof 10
compensation 544-6
competition for souls 501
completely ridiculous anthropic
    principle 203
Comte de Montgomery 280
confession 189-90, 549-51
  confidentiality of 550, 581
conscience 164-6
conscious state 160
consciousness 41, 43
Constantine 368-9, 496, 498
contracts 412-13
corroboration 183
cosmological argument 138-9, 141
cosmology 73
Cost of Pastoral Care 424
Council of Chalcedon 369
Council of Nicaea 496
cover-ups 545
Cranmer 382
Creation 67-9
creation myth 69
creationism 204
cult is elitist 526
cult is misogynist 526
cults 502
cure of the paraplegic 324
cyanobacteria 78
cyberbullying 504
cyberterrorism 508

D

Darwinian evolution 205
David (king) 347
Dawkins, Richard 198, 400, 573
de facto pre-eminence 367-8
Dead Sea Scrolls 65, 343
declaratory function 416, 535
decree of Frequens 372
'Defence of the Seven
    Sacraments' 380
defences 479
delegation of authority 406
deliberate deception 173, 176
deliberate killing 478
democratic dissent 535
democratic process 533, 535
deoxyribonucleic acid 78
Descartes 137-8
design, elements of 152
determinism 86-8
devotional norms 523
Dickie, Robert 141
direct political authority 536
dissident groups 509
divine law 415-16, 418, 461
documentary evidence 27
dogma 97-100, 102
dogmas 435
dogmatic doctrines 431
Donation of Constantine 384
Donation of Pippin 384
donations 424-8, 545
Donum Vitae 476, 484-5
Drange, Theodore M. 199

E

earth 73-7
Ebola virus 226
eccentric beliefs 100-1
ecclesiastical courts 497
Eck, Johann 373

ecumenism 502, 560
Edict of Toleration 368, 496
Edward VI 382
efficient cause 129
electronic mail 495
Elizabeth I 382
the end justifies the means 517
end of the world 569
enforcement of morals 477
escape the conflict 513
Escrivá, Josemaría 523
essence equivalence 275
Essenes 344
establishment, the 383
eternal sin 421
ethics 164
eukaryotic cell 198
euthanasia 480-1
evangelisation, future of 566
evangelisation of children 400
evangelisation of youth 552, 560
evangelise 394
Everitt, Nicholas 197
evidence 18
evil human actions 228
evil natural laws 220
evolution 149-52
evolution of the mission 399
excommunication 384
Exodus, book of 167
exodus from Egypt 287
expert opinion evidence 140-1
extraordinary event 180
extrasensory perception 182
eyewitness accounts 260

F

faith 35
Farel, William 379
Fátima 169
fidelity issues 403

first clerics 365
first miracle 293
Fisher (archbishop) 489
five thousand men 303
Five Ways 126-7, 136, 138, 158, 162, 239, 572
forced baptism 392
forms of authority 406-7
forms of dissent 535
Forty-Two Articles 382
found a church 361-2
four Gospels 455
Frederick the Wise (duke) 373
free speech 499
free will 86-8, 543
freedom and responsibility 475
freedom fighter 508
French Secret Service 510
function of the church 531
function of the state 530
fundamental issue 153

G

Gaddafi (colonel) 509
Gaiseric (the king of the Vandals) 385
Galerius 368, 496
Gamow, George 71
Genesis, book of 65
genius 198
Gerasenes 301
ghosts 108-10, 112
gift of faith 124-5
give without charge 423
God Delusion, The 201, 573
God has to allow choices 231
God is not infinitely tolerant 493
Golden Rule, the 521-2
Goldilocks zone 206
Gospel origins 264
governance 135

governments 499-501
gradation 135
a great gale 304
Great Schism 370, 372
Grebel, Conrad 375
Greenpeace 510
Gregory the Great (pope) 384
Gregory XI (pope) 370
Gregory XII 371

H

Habakkuk 345
Hagia Sophia 383
Hall, George M. 154
Hasmoneans 344
hate 505-7
having a soul 489
he is not omnibenevolent 237
hearing of voices 181
heaven 115-17
hell 115-17
Henry II of France (king) 280
Henry VIII 380
hierarchical structure 366
Hindus 399
holier than thou 506
Holy Spirit 391-2
Holy Spirit guides 474
homicide 478
Homo erectus 81-3
Homo habilis 81-3
Homo sapiens 82-3
'How to Evangelise' 394
'How to Provide Pastoral Care' 397
Hoyle, Fred 70, 204
Hubble, Edwin Powell 71
huge decline in the number 556
human error 340
human freedom 85
human intelligence 162-3
human law 415, 466, 476

human life begins at
        conception 491-2, 537
Humanae Vitae 409
humans with God 412
Hume 148
Hutter, Jakob 376
Hutterian Brethren 400
hypocrites 507
hypostatic union 113

I

'I am' 331
'I am the Way' 318
Immanuel 284
Imperial Diet of Speyer 376
individuals 504
infallibility 452-5
infinite regression 129-30
Innocent III (pope) 385
inordinate attachments 543
Institutes of the Christian Religion 378
institution of the Eucharist 328
intelligent designer 147-9
intelligent life 79
interdict 384-5
Internet 494-5
intuition 91
invitation to Islam 514-15
Irenaeus 368
Is paedophilia wrong? 541

J

Jacobovici, Simcha 31-2, 317
Jairus's daughter 309
Jesus as a Nazarene 287
Jesus on the Cross 334
Jesus the Man 342
Jesus was a real person 276-8
Jesus wept 312
jihad 514
Job, book of 231

Johanson, Donald 80
John of England (king) 385
John Paul II 510
John Paul II (pope) 515
John the Baptist 322-3
John XXIII 371
John's question 320
Josephus, Flavius 277-8, 343
Judaism 399
Julius II (pope) 381
Justinian 369

K

kamikaze 512
Kamm, William 526-7
KGB 510
Khirbet 344
killing 473
Kittim 345
knowledge 35-9

L

lack of evidence 200
laicise the priest 412-13
laity 358-60
language of hate 504-6
languages 254-6
Lateran Treaty 384
laws 411-13, 415-17, 419
laws change 485
laws prohibiting Catholics 499
Lazarus 311-13
Le Fanu, James 154, 572
Lemaître, Georges 69
Leo (pope) 385
Leo X 373
life on earth 76
limbo 117, 191
Linus 367-8
Little Pebble, the 527
liturgy 399, 404

living organisms 160
Locke, John 160
Lombards 384
loose marriages 414
Lost Tomb of Jesus, The 66
Louis the Pious 384
love 88-90, 104-6
loyalty to the Vatican 500
Lucy (fossil) 80-1
Luther, Martin 372

M

Maccabee, Jonathan 344
Magdalene, Mary 311-12, 342
magisterium 452
magnetic field 74-6
Makhlouf, Charbel (saint) 527
Malone, John 154
Manz, Felix 375
Martha (sister of Lazarus) 311-12
Martin, Michael 197, 573
Martin V 372
Mary (daughter of Henry
        VIII) 381-2
mathematics 59, 61-2
matter of chance 195
matter of fact 239
Maxentius 368, 496
Maximus, Petronius 385
McHugh, Christopher 199
meaning of life 69
megaverse 208
Melanchthon, Philipp 374
memory 270
Mennonites 400
mere bravado 517
Messiah 283-4, 286, 290
methanogens 77-8
Mill, John Stuart 86
Miller, Stanley 76
miracle 290-1

miracles 290-2
mission authority 407
mission of the church 387
missionary work 562
modern medicine 473
modernise our liturgy 558
money-raising
    inappropriate aspects of 426
    ways of 425
monks 402
monotheistic 101
moral conduct 163, 166
morally wrong or bad 219
Mossad, the 510
Mother Nature 150-1
Muhammad 498, 513
Munich Olympics 510
Muslims 399, 513-14
my Son, the Beloved 322
mystical body of Jesus Christ 359

N

Nain 308
natural disaster 223
natural law 409, 411, 415-16, 418,
    462-5
natural moral law 461
natural things 225
nature of God 51, 436
nature of life 152
Neanderthals 82-3
neo-Nazi cults 507
New Jerusalem 116
New Testament, the 95, 253
Nicene Creed 91
ninety-five propositions 373
non-dogmatic doctrines 431
non-religious institutions 539
normal human motives 509
Northern Ireland 516
Nostradamus 280-3

not a kingdom of this world 332
number of religious brothers 556
nuns 402

O

official apology 545
omnibenevolent 217-19, 221-2
omnipotent 176
once were Catholic 498
ontologism 137
Opus Dei 523-6
    criticism of 525
Order of St Charbel 526-7
original records 291
ossuaries 31-5
Ottoman Turks 370
our solar system 69, 74

P

Pacific salmon 154-5
paedophilia 541-4
palaeographic analysis 345
Paley, William 148
papal encyclicals 457
paradigms of translation 255
paranormal manifestations 64
Pascal, Blaise 186
Pascal's wager 186
pastoral care 365-6, 390-3
    future of 567
Paul VI (pope) 409
pejorative 504-5
persecutions 366, 496
personality 42-3
pesher technique 345-8, 576
Peter's revelation 326
Pharisees 343-4
photosynthesis 78
physical substance 102-3
pi 106
Pilate 332-4

Pippin III 384
Pius X (pope) 124
placebo effect 184
plain meaning 408
Planck sphere 141
plasma theory 70-1
Plato 126
Pliny the Younger 278
political pressure 535-6
politically proactive 536
poltergeists 109
power of attorney 407
predictions about Jesus 252
priest shortage 568
primaeval atom 69-70
principle of credulity 183-4
principle of testimony 183-4
private miracle 179
private research 433
proactive 493
'Promise of Jesus, The' 563
proof 9-18
prophecies of doom 570
prophecy
  definition of 279
  function of 279, 283
psychosomatic illnesses 184
public condemnation of
    terrorism 516
public events 171
purgatory 117

Q

quality of life 481
quasars 71
Qumran 343-4, 346
Qur'an 514

R

radiocarbon dating 73
Rainbow Warrior 510

reasonable doubt 11
recruitment 521, 525
Rees, Martin 208
Reformation, the 372
relationship contracts 412
religious experiences 179
religious orders 401-2
religious schools 567
religious sisters 556
resistance fighter 508
resurrection of Jesus 314
reverence of icons 369
Ridley, Mark 207
right to life 482-3
rocket science 491
Rowe, William L. 223, 228
rule of law 530
Russell, Bertrand 10

S

sack of Rome in 455 385
Sadducees 343-4
safeguards 481
saints 169
Salmon, Wesley C. 197
Sanhedrin 329
scapegoat 496
Schleitheim Confession 376, 378
science 52-8, 60-1, 63-7
scientific method 63
scientifically inexplicable 184
scientists 58-9, 61-2, 65
screening of candidates 559
sect 519-20
separation of church and state 477
seven sacraments 397
severe condemnation by Jesus 542
Seymour, Jane 382
sharia law 477-8
Shia sect 513
should 3

Sigismund of Luxembourg 371
Simons, Menno 376
singularity 72, 139-44, 146
Sinnott-Armstrong, Walter 200
Smith, Quinton 220-2
social media 494-5
Society of St Vincent de Paul 522
soft targets 511
solar wind 74, 76
son of man 287-8, 324-6, 330
soul 40, 42
source of the donor stem cells 487
spiritual realm 104-8, 110-13, 115,
 117-18
St Joseph de Clairval Abbey 288
statistics 31-5
status of dogma 121, 474
Statute of Six Articles 381-2
Steinhardt, Paul J. 72
stellar evolution 202
stem cells 486, 578-9
 benefit of 486
 harvesting of 487-8
Stenger, Victor J. 195
Stephen (II or III) (pope) 384
Stephen (saint) 496
Stewart, James 49
stromatolites 78
strong anthropic principle
 (SAP) 203
subconscious 40-1
succession 365
suicide 480
suicide bomber 512
sultans 514
Sunday mass attendance 556
Sunni sect 513
supernatural design 158
supernatural powers 292
supernatural presence 181
survival instinct 149, 151-2

Susskind, Leonard 208
Swinburne, John 161
Swiss Brethren 400
syllogism 7

T

Taliban 509
Teacher of Righteousness 344-5
teachings of Jesus 317, 319
teachings of the church 121, 431
Telpiot 32, 35
Ten Commandments, the 455
terrorism 508-9, 512
terrorism is inevitable 518
testimony 261-2
Theia 74-6
theology
 danger of 565
 function of 564
 role of 564
theory of evolution 77-80
Thiering, Barbara 341-4, 575
Thirty-Nine Articles 382
thoughts and feelings 160-1
time 143-5
Tipler 202-3, 210
too harsh a penance 551
translation issues 255
translator's agenda 258
'true' church, the 361
truth 6-7, 9, 11-13, 337-8
 function of 260
Turok, Neil 72
two blind men 297-8
type of conduct 538

U

unanswered question 151
unclean spirit 299, 301
undiscovered laws 147
Urban VI 370-1

Urey , Harold (professor) 76
utopia 238

V

vacuum fluctuations 140, 145
Valance, Liberty 49
Valentinian 385
value of the Gospels 263
Vatican City 384
Vatican Council 121, 123
vestigial organs 197-8
virulent skin-disease 295
visions 180-2
Vladimir (the Grand Prince of
      Kiev) 370
void ab initio 414

W

walking on the sea 306
war on terror 508, 517
Wayists 364, 387
Wayne, John 49

weak anthropic principle
      (WAP) 203
wedding at Cana 293
What does *true* mean? 259
what God wants 199, 248
What is truth? 337
what Jesus said 319
Which denomination is the right
      one? 249
Who are the offenders? 538
Who are the victims? 539
Why do paedophiles do it? 542
why God allows such suffering 481
Wicked Priest 344-5
Widow's Son 308
Wise, Abegg, and Cook 345
withered hand 296
withhold absolution 551
world containing evil 218
world population growth 553
World Trade buildings 510

Z

Zwingli 379